POSTINDUSTRIAL EAST ASIAN CITIES

POSTINDUSTRIAL EAST ASIAN CITIES

Innovation for Growth

SHAHID YUSUF
KAORU NABESHIMA

A COPUBLICATION OF STANFORD ECONOMICS AND FINANCE,
AN IMPRINT OF STANFORD UNIVERSITY PRESS, AND THE WORLD BANK

1818 H Street NW
Washington DC 20433
Telephone: 202-473-1000
Internet: www.worldbank.org
E-mail: feedback@worldbank.org

1 2 3 4 09 08 07 06

A copublication of Stanford Economics and Finance, an imprint of Stanford University Press, and the World Bank.

Stanford University Press
1450 Page Mill Road
Palo Alto CA 94304

The World Bank
1818 H Sreet NW
Washington DC 20433

World Rights except North America
ISBN-10: 0-8213-5622-4
ISBN-13: 978-0-8213-5622-7
*e*ISBN-10: 0-8213-6649-1
*e*ISBN-13: 978-0-8213-6649-3
DOI: 10.1596/978-0-8213-5622-7

North America
ISBN-10 (soft cover): 0-8047-5673-2
ISBN-13 (soft cover) 978-0-8047-5673-0
ISBN-10 (hard cover): 0-8047-5672-4
ISBN-13 (hard cover): 978-0-8047-5672-3

Library of Congress Cataloging-in-Publication Data
Postindustrial East Asian cities : innovation for growth / Shahid Yusuf, Kaoru Nabeshima.
p. cm.
Includes bibliographical references and index.
ISBN-13: 978-0-8213-5622-7
ISBN-10: 0-8213-5622-4
ISBN-13: 978-0-8213-6649-3 (ebook)
ISBN-10: 0-8213-6649-1 (ebook)
1. Cities and towns—East Asia. 2. Service industries—East Asia. 3. East Asia—Economic policy. 4. East Asia—Economic conditions—21st century. 5. Technological innovations—Economic aspects—East Asia. I. Yusuf, Shahid, 1949– II. Nabeshima, Kaoru.

HT384.E18P67 2006
307.76095—dc22 2006050469

TABLE OF CONTENTS

Figures

Tables

PREFACE

This is the sixth volume in a series of publications emerging from a study cosponsored by the government of Japan and the World Bank to examine the future sources of economic growth in East Asia. The study was initiated in 1999 with the objective of identifying the most promising path to development in light of emerging global and regional changes.

The first volume, *Can East Asia Compete?*, was published in 2002. It provided a compact overview of the relevant strategic issues and future policy directions. *Innovative East Asia*, the second volume, was published in 2003 and analyzed each of the main issues and consequent policy choices, drawing comprehensively from recent empirical research and the findings of firm surveys conducted for the study. Its principal message was that sustained economic growth in East Asia will rest on the ability to retain the strengths of the past (stability, openness, investment, and human capital development); to overcome the sources of current weaknesses (in the financial, corporate, judicial, and social sectors); and to implement the changes required by the evolving economic environment, particularly with regard to technology development. The third volume, *Global Production Networking and Technological Change in East Asia*, published in 2004, was the first of two volumes of papers commissioned for the East Asia study. It presented detailed information, analysis, and case studies, showing that the economies in East Asia must adapt to the changing character of global production networks and nurture and develop their technological capabilities in order to sustain their growth prospects. The fourth volume, *Global Change and East Asian Policy Initiatives*, also published in 2004, included a separate set of papers that examined some of the key institutional weaknesses identified in *Innovative East Asia*. Contributors to this volume explored in depth topics ranging from regional issues arising from monetary and financial cooperation, trade, and harmonization to the national issues of public expenditure, corporate and public governance, the legal system, tertiary education, and finance. They also presented an array of policy options of value to East Asian economies. Some, if not all, of these issues are relevant to every country in East Asia. Both of the edited volumes complement *Innovative East Asia* and are addressed to researchers, students, and policy makers.

Although the first four volumes in this series presented a macroeconomic perspective, *Under New Ownership* focused on the microeconomics of business organization and state enterprise reform—issues that are of considerable importance for China. The main message of the book was that Chinese firms need to pursue strategies that will promote efficiency and innovation to compete in the global market. Much of the cross-country evidence to date suggests that state-owned firms are slow to adopt such strategies, and because these firms are generally subject to a different set of incentives than their private counterparts, their managers are less zealous in implementing those strategies. Chinese state-owned firms are not exceptions, and if thcy arc to compete in the global markets with other firms—especially the established large multinational firms—privatization is a necessary step to attaining international competitiveness.

As we have argued in the previous volumes in this series, future growth in East Asia will increasingly come from the strength of innovative activities instead of factor accumulation. Such innovative activities—especially in producer services and the creative industries—are concentrated in high-tech clusters in globally linked cities. This volume explores the growth prospects of six cities in East Asia: Bangkok, Beijing, Seoul, Shanghai, Singapore, and Tokyo. The development of such cities is influenced by ongoing structural changes and initiatives by governments and firms. A successful transition from export-oriented manufacturing to a service economy that is competitive and integrated with the global systems will involve a reshaping of the urban landscape so that providers of business services and the creative industries perceive it to be value-augmenting for their purposes and a basis for competitive advantage. This volume draws on a wide literature and on interviews of firms that were conducted for this study. It suggests how policies and institutions can induce and furnish an urban environment that supports innovative activities.

The financial backing of the government of Japan, through its Policy and Human Resources Development Fund, has provided vital support for this project, as have senior public officials who gave generously of their time. We are deeply grateful to Haruhiko Kuroda, Takashi Kihara, Naoko Ishii, Masahiro Kawai, Kiyoshi Kodera, Rintaro Tamaki,

Junichi Maruyama, and Takatoshi Ito. The staff of the World Bank's country offices facilitated our fieldwork in East Asia, and we greatly appreciate the assistance provided by Kirida Bhaopichitr (Bangkok), Jianqing Chen (Beijing), Shuichi Kiyanagi (Tokyo), and Peter Stevens (Singapore).

We owe special thanks to representatives of many firms whom we interviewed in the six cities. These individuals shared their insights and gave generously of their time despite their busy schedules. We extend our thanks also to Yee-Kyoung Kim, Kaoru Kimura, and Patharaporn Theeratham for conducting the interviews in Seoul, Tokyo, and Bangkok.

Five background papers commissioned for this book gave us the materials to build on. We thank Richard Child Hill, Kuniko Fujita, Yuen Ping Ho, Sock-Yong Phang, Annette Singh, Kim-Song Tan, Jici Wang, Poh Kam Wong, Weiping Wu, and Tong Xin.

At the World Bank, the Development Research Group provided a home for the study, and the East Asia and Pacific Region contributed consistent and unflagging support. We are especially indebted to Alan Winters, Paul Collier, Jemal-ud-din Kassum, and Homi Kharas for their encouragement and their faith in the value of the study.

The study team was ably supported by the research and production skills of Wei Ha, Jimena Luna, Jue Sun, and Tristan Suratos. We are grateful to them and also to M. Anjum Altaf, who contributed to the initial phase of this study.

Publications Professionals LLC did a fine and remarkably speedy job of editing, which we greatly appreciated. Production of the final manuscript was made possible by the unstinting support provided by Rebecca Sugui. Patricia Katayama and Cindy A. Fisher at the World Bank Office of the Publisher smoothly managed the operation from start to finish with a light yet firm touch, which ensured that neither the authors nor the logistics ever had a chance of faltering. We would not have pulled it off without them.

ABBREVIATIONS

3D	Three-dimensional
AI	Artificial intelligence
BMA	Bangkok metropolitan area
BMR	Bangkok metropolitan region
CAS	Chinese Academy of Science
CRT	Cathode ray tube
CMOS	Complementary metal-oxide semiconductor
DNA	Deoxyribonucleic acid
DVD	Digital versatile disc
EDB	Economic Development Board
ES	Embryonic stem
ETRI	Electronics and Telecommunications Research Institute
EVD	Enhanced versatile disc
FDI	Foreign direct investment
FEC	Foreign economic cooperation
G-8	Group of Eight
GDP	Gross domestic product
HD	High-definition
HDL	High-density lipoprotein
HDTV	High-definition television
IC	Integrated circuit
ICT	Information and communication technology
IMCB	Institute of Molecular and Cellular Biology
ISP	Internet service provider
IT	Information technology
IX	Internet exchange
KOCCA	Korean Culture and Content Agency

LCD	Liquid crystal display
MIT	Massachusetts Institute of Technology
MMORPG	Massively multiplayer online role-playing game
MNC	Multinational corporation
MRI	Magnetic resonance imaging
MUDI	Munich Urban Design International
NASA	National Aeronautics and Space Administration
NIH	National Institutes of Health
NTSC	National Television Standard Committee
NUS	National University of Singapore
OECD	Organisation for Economic Co-operation and Development
PAL	Phase alternating lines
PC	Personal computer
R&D	Research and development
rDNA	Recombinant deoxyribonucleic acid
RFID	Radio frequency identification
S&T	Science and technology
SMEs	Small and medium enterprises
TB	Tuberculosis
TD-SCDMA	Time Division–Synchronous Code Division Multiple Access
TEU	Twenty-foot equivalent unit
TIMSS-R	Third International Mathematics and Science Study–Repeat
UAV	Unmanned airborne vehicles
VCD	Video compact disc
WAPI	Wired Authentication and Privacy Infrastructure
ZGC	Zhongguancun High-Tech Zone

CHAPTER 1

EMERGING CITYSCAPES

The great cities of the world provide a foretaste of the economic future of societies. To paraphrase Shakespeare's immortal lines, cities are the stage where all the shaping forces come together, play their parts, and have their exits and entrances.[1] From observing a Seoul or a Shanghai or a Tokyo, one has a sense of where urban societies are headed, not in any linear fashion, but digressively, with many changes in direction and in the mix of policies and through much creative destruction. Most of humanity is leaving the fields and the farms for good. Most people during this century will find their joys, their sorrows, and their fortunes in cities. A growing minority of urbanites will be drawn by or pushed toward the megacities of the world, making many of those cities even larger than they currently are.[2] Indeed, the economic pull and cultural attractiveness of megacities could intensify—because of faster income and employment growth arising from agglomeration effects and the emergence of new industries;[3] because such cities tend to be the foci of innovation; because they usually take the lead in defining major public

1. On the winding history that has led from more than 11,000 years of urbanization to today's postindustrial cities, see Kotkin (2005).

2. Where megacities are poorly managed, deindustrialization, congestion, worsening pollution, poverty, crime, and increasing costs of living could act as a brake on growth, as is apparent in the case of Mumbai since the 1990s and Rio de Janeiro (Cullen and Levitt 1996). We fully recognize that the megacities will account for a minority of the urban population. The majority will be moving to and living in small and medium-size cities (Cohen 2004).

3. Agglomeration economies derive from the scale of production, industrial diversity, innovation spillovers, and deep labor markets. Agglomeration economies in the large cities appear to be particularly helpful to smaller firms with limited establishment-level technological capabilities. Such firms find it easier to adapt information technology, for example, in a dense urban environment with many services providers and the opportunities to learn from other firms that have

Table 1.1 Urbanization Rate in East Asia
(percent)

Year	China	Indonesia	Japan	Korea, Rep. of	Malaysia	Philippines	Thailand	Vietnam
1990	27.4	30.6	63.1	73.8	49.8	48.8	29.4	20.3
1995	31.4	35.5	64.6	78.2	55.6	54.0	30.3	22.2
2000	35.8	42.0	65.2	79.6	61.8	58.5	31.1	24.3
2004	39.6	46.7	65.6	80.5	64.4	61.8	32.2	26.2

Source: World Bank, World Development Indicators database.

Table 1.2 Urbanization Rate around the World, by Region
(percent)

Year	East Asia and the Pacific	Europe and Central Asia	Latin America and the Caribbean	Middle East and North Africa	South Asia	Sub-Saharan Africa	United States	World
1990	28.8	62.9	71.1	51.4	25.0	28.0	75.3	43.0
1995	32.6	63.2	73.2	53.2	26.2	31.1	77.3	44.9
2000	37.0	63.2	75.3	54.8	27.3	34.2	79.1	46.9
2004	40.2	63.6	77.0	55.9	28.3	36.7	80.4	48.6

Source: World Bank, World Development Indicators database.

policies; because they are the portals leading to the global market and are more open to trade, tourism, and the circulation of knowledge workers from overseas; and because they are more tightly linked to other global and regional cities (P. Taylor 2005; P. Taylor and others 2002).[4]

East Asia is where, arguably, the forces driving urbanization will be strongest, and economic growth centered on urban areas will continue to outpace the competition (see tables 1.1 and 1.2). By 2025, the United Nations projects that more than 50 percent of East Asia's population will be urban, as against 40 percent in 2000 (Yusuf and Nabeshima 2005).[5] Out

taken the lead in experimenting with new technology. As Forman, Goldfarb, and Greenstein (2005, 3) put it, "Firms act as if internal resources can substitute for the advantages of agglomeration." For a recent overview of agglomeration effects, see Rosenthal and Strange (2004).

4. Yue-man Yeung (2005) describes the emergence of the enormously dynamic network of cities composing the Pearl River Delta, China's export powerhouse, while Henry Wai-chung Yeung (2004) describes how the Chinese corporate and kinship networks that are rooted in Southeast Asian cities have infused investment, energy, and different forms of governance into those economies. The chapters in Lo and Yeung (1998) review how cities across the world are responding to openness and examine changes at the sectoral level.

5. In 2006, global urbanization reached the 50 percent mark.

Table 1.3 Megacities

2003			2015		
Rank	**City**	**Population (million)**	**Rank**	**City**	**Population (million)**
1	Tokyo, Japan	35.0	1	Tokyo, Japan	36.2
2	Mexico City, Mexico	18.7	2	Mumbai (Bombay), India	22.6
3	New York, United States	18.3	3	Delhi, India	20.9
4	São Paulo, Brazil	17.9	4	Mexico City, Mexico	20.6
5	Mumbai (Bombay), India	17.4	5	São Paulo, Brazil	20.0
6	Delhi, India	14.1	6	New York, United States	19.7
7	Calcutta, India	13.8	7	Dhaka, Bangladesh	17.9
8	Buenos Aires, Argentina	13.0	8	Jakarta, Indonesia	17.5
9	Shanghai, China	12.8	9	Lagos, Nigeria	17.0
10	Jakarta, Indonesia	12.3	10	Calcutta, India	16.8
11	Los Angeles, United States	12.0	11	Karachi, Pakistan	16.2
12	Dhaka, Bangladesh	11.6	12	Buenos Aires, Argentina	14.6
13	Osaka-Kobe, Japan	11.2	13	Cairo, Egypt	13.1
14	Rio de Janeiro, Brazil	11.2	14	Los Angeles, United States	12.9
15	Karachi, Pakistan	11.1	15	Shanghai, China	12.7
16	Beijing, China	10.8	16	Metro Manila, Philippines	12.6
17	Cairo, Egypt	10.8	17	Rio de Janeiro, Brazil	12.4
18	Moscow, Russian Federation	10.5	18	Osaka-Kobe, Japan	11.4
			19	Istanbul, Turkey	11.3
19	Metro Manila, Philippines	10.4	20	Beijing, China	11.1
20	Lagos, Nigeria	10.1	21	Moscow, Russian Federation	10.9
			22	Paris, France	10.0

Source: United Nations, World Urbanization Prospects: The 2003 Revision database.
Note: For the purposes, of this table, megacities are those with a population of 10 million or more.

of a total of 20 megacities in 2003, 6 were in East Asia.[6] These megacities are projected to expand through the next two decades (see table 1.3), and they will be joined by numerous other large cities, each with populations in the many millions. However, if the megacities are going to lead this field, they will require some specific capabilities. They will need a diverse mix of industrial engines with the requisite power to propel these large and complex economies. They will need to mobilize fully the local and national reservoirs of human skills, energy, and creativity and, by virtue of their perceived potential, raise capital internally and supplement this internal capital with investment from external sources. It is almost inconceivable

6. A *megacity* has a population of 10 million or more. The concentration of people within a single megacity is apparent through much of East Asia.

that a megacity that is isolated from the global system could flourish for long. Hence, openness and integration with the global economy will be near the top of the urban policy menu.

As more and more industry migrates to East Asia, the region's cities will determine the tempo of economic activity in this emerging industrial heartland of a globalizing economy. The past and current competitiveness of East Asian industry has derived from the quick assimilation of production techniques, hard and soft, and a profound readiness to learn. These aptitudes have been reinforced more recently by an equally remarkable ability to introduce incremental innovations in shop-floor processes and logistics that have progressively improved quality, delivery times, and speed of response to market demands. In high-value products such as electronic components, East Asians have also reduced failure rates (Puga and Trefler 2005). Future competitiveness that will help bring per capita incomes closer to those of the industrial countries now requires a higher level of innovativeness in several different spheres, extending from products to the organization of firms. In this area, the major cities must take the lead, because all the elements of the innovation system are located in key urban centers. These cities are the harbingers of emerging urban economic dynamics. And because of the salience of these cities, their influence will be felt around the world.[7]

In this volume, we examine industrial change in six East Asian cities.[8] Each is a prime mover within its country, is at the leading edge of policy and structural changes, and is the epicenter of innovation. In each of our six selected cities, we examine one or two key components of the economic engine—industries that provide a reliable metric of the cities' prospects. To take the pulse of the energy and creativity of the cities, we will analyze the development of these industries, their innovativeness and global links, and their potential for generating well-paid jobs.

7. Hospers (2003, 147–48) divides creative cities into four groups. The birthplaces of innovation are the "technological innovative cities, in the past places such as Detroit and more recently San Francisco and Cambridge, United Kingdom. Those places where a rich culture coexists with vibrant intellectual activity are the cultural-intellectual cities symbolized by Paris and Vienna in times past and Boston and Toulouse in the present. Cultural technological cities such as Toronto, Los Angeles, and Austin combine these two forces to advance technology and promote particular strands of culture. Then finally there are technological-organizational cities, such as Paris, London, and Antwerp, Belgium, that have found in the design of buildings and in transport systems original solutions to problems stemming from large scale urban life."

8. Five of these cities are national capitals and are the largest (or, in the case of Beijing, among the three largest) cities in their respective countries. Shanghai, the only exception, is the leading industrial, financial, and commercial center in mainland China.

Throughout the past nearly five decades, there has been a strongly dirigiste flavor to development in East Asia.[9] Governments have directed development and managed markets. In several instances, the public sector spearheaded development and is now only gradually relinquishing its leading role. However, throughout the region, governments continue working closely with the private sector, as is strikingly apparent in the major cities. Thus, the shape of urban industrialization to come is closely intermeshed with industrial policies and with policies toward globalization.

TOWARD A POSTINDUSTRIAL URBAN WORLD

In the early 19th century, as technological opportunities and market widened, a wave of industrialization gripped the leading cities of Western Europe and accelerated the transfer of rural workers to urban areas. Between 1800 and 1913, the urban population increased by a factor of seven.[10] Employment in manufacturing rose from 6 million to 38 million, while close to 35 million people found jobs in the services sector (Bairoch 1988, 269). What are now viewed as the traditional manufacturing industries, such as textiles, iron and steel, and machine building, remained at the core of the urban economy for an extended length of time. It was not until nearly a century and a half later that these cities began crossing a threshold into what is frequently described as the postindustrial age.

Industrialization came much later to most of East Asia. Japan and a few parts of China were exceptions.[11] The rise of modern industry in most major East Asian urban centers began in earnest as recently as the 1960s. But whereas European cities followed a long, slow trajectory into industrial maturity, their East Asian cousins, after a brief adolescence and what

9. This topic is a contentious one, with much sniping across the ideological boundaries that separate the dirigiste camp from the territory staked out by the free marketers. See Yusuf (2001) for a review of a substantial fraction of the literature and Amsden (1989), Amsden and Chu (2003), Campos and Root (1996), Kohli (2004), Stiglitz and Yusuf (2001), Tabellini (2005), and Wade (1990) for more in-depth discussions.

10. The industrial revolution was the outcome of a cluster of inventions and their commercialization in a small number of Western European countries and the United States during 1760 to 1830. Among the inventions, the Arkwright water frame, the Hargreaves spinning jenny, and the Crompton mule were among the most revolutionary (McCloskey 1985; Mokyr 1990).

11. Japan began industrializing toward the end of the 19th century, starting with textiles but then moving quickly into iron and steel, engineering industries, and shipbuilding. Chinese industrialization was concentrated in a few coastal cities, chiefly Shanghai and the Japanese-controlled Manchurian region to the northeast (see Yusuf 2005). On the early industrialization of China, see Rawski (1989), and on Japan, see Howe (1996) and Morris-Suzuki (1994).

amounts to a mere brush with maturity, are also having to adapt to rapid changes in the industrial composition of their economies. The geographic product cycle—the *clockspeed*[12]—which was once measured in decades, is now measured in years. A decade can now embrace several product cycles in an industry such as electronics—less so in the engineering, air transport, and chemicals industries.

On the wings of globalization and technological change, the postindustrial age has arrived in the middle-income urban centers of East Asia.[13] From Tokyo to Bangkok, the high tide of traditional industrialism is gradually ebbing, as first manufacturing and then some services are being enticed by lower costs to other locations, some in nearby edge cities, some in the deep hinterland, and some in the developing economies elsewhere in Asia. Many of the industries that remain in the major cities are shedding low-skill jobs and becoming more capital intensive.

However, activities that register the highest rate of increase in employment are disproportionately concentrated in the large urban centers. In the United States, for example, between 1992 and 2002, the largest increase in employment was in professional and business services, followed by education and health services, information services, and leisure and hospitality services (Bureau of Labor Statistics 2004). This trend is expected to continue until 2014, with education services leading the pack (Saunders 2005). Typically, these jobs gravitated toward the major metropolitan areas. Similar trends have surfaced in East Asia, although the degree of concentration is significantly greater in Japan, where Tokyo accounts for close to one-half of all jobs in information, research, and advertising services. Even higher levels of concentration are apparent in Seoul and in Taipei.

With the increase in professional and information services, the geography of work in the metropolitan area is also changing. Close to 15 percent of the U.S. workers did a part of their primary job from home for a portion of the week, invariably with the aid of a computer and a phone.[14] Four-fifths of those working from home held managerial, professional, and sales jobs (Bureau of Labor Statistics 2002, 2005). This pattern is less prevalent in East Asia, but easier, more user-friendly electronic communication, coupled with the desire to cut down on long commutes from

12. The notion of an industrial and product clockspeed that reflects the intensity and velocity of change is discussed by Fine (1998).

13. Daniel Bell noted in *The Cultural Contradictions of Capitalism* that industrial societies, which had long emphasized goods production, would soon have to adjust to a world in which services dominated economic activities (Bell 1976, 147–48).

14. This trend toward working at home goes hand in hand with the increase in part-time work.

distant suburban homes, could very likely lead rapidly to polycentric urban forms that are more efficient, albeit spatially more dispersed. For employers, this trend can be advantageous on two counts: (a) smaller investment in downtown office space and (b) greater number of hours worked by employees, who spend less time stuck in traffic.[15]

Together with the widening use of information and communication technology (ICT) and the restructuring of tasks to maximize the benefits, these trends lead to the emergence of the new industries—and in some cases industrial clusters—that are redefining the allocation of space in cities. They are also leading to a spatial consolidation of business services in the leading cities throughout the world.

No major city in East Asia is prepared for the departure of manufacturing industry, which still is largely the basis of urban prosperity. Although soothing voices are heard forecasting a seamless transition to a new urban services economy even more dynamic than the industrial economy that it would be displacing, cities that are confronting an industrial upheaval far earlier than they anticipated are in for a sea change in the structure of the metropolitan economy and the entire fabric of the urban society.

Postindustrialism has many dimensions, each deserving close analysis. Within our urban frame of reference, we have singled out the economic dimension. Social, political, and other facets are equally important, but to encompass them adequately would take us far afield and would dilute our selected focus. Our point of departure is the central attribute of postindustrialism: the relative diminution of manufacturing and the shift in the composition of the manufacturing activities that remain. It is this shift—not the cessation of manufacturing altogether—that initiates a fission of change that touches every grain of the urban system. Services of all kinds gradually take over as the principal producers and employers. Most manufacturing plants and their blue-collar workers are pushed to the margins of the urban landscape, and in their place come businesses that supply producer services of all kinds, myriad retailers, and so-called creative industries.[16] The life of the postindustrial city and its inhabitants revolves mainly around the production, purchase, and consumption of services. Manufactured products remain ubiquitous. Most services require manufactured inputs, such as computers, medical imaging, musical equipment, and telecommunication equipment, and a significant volume of skill- and

15. *Still Stuck in Traffic* is the title of Downs's (2004) illuminating dissection of a worsening problem in many cities.

16. *Creative industries* are generally ones whose products or services are covered by intellectual property laws.

capital-intensive manufacturing continues to flourish in the city, often adjacent to centers of research. Nevertheless, the bulk of the urban gross domestic product (GDP) originates in the services sector. In fact, up to one half of the value added in the average manufacturing firm generally comes from in-house or contracted services—is directly or indirectly created by the inputs of services, whether in-house or purchased from knowledge-intensive service providers or the creative industries. Something as ordinary and inexpensive as a pair of jeans is now transformed by the alchemy of designers, marketing experts, public relations specialists, publishers, and others into a fashion statement. A hefty dose of creative design, advertising, and efficient logistics can make an ordinary article of clothing into a high-fashion commodity commanding a global market.

In the typical postindustrial city, manufacturing now accounts for a small fraction of the gross product and employment. Even as employment is scaled back, hours worked in manufacturing are becoming more flexible, because employers avoid hiring new workers and absorb business fluctuations by varying time on the job (Glosser and Golden 2005). We will argue later that even this remaining manufacturing activity is vital to the city's economic health, but the retreat of industry as a producer and employer is seemingly unstoppable. The implications are far reaching, especially for cities with growing and relatively youthful populations. The turn toward postindustrialism can be traced to the changing shape of consumer demands as incomes rise, to differential gains in productivity among industries, to technological developments, to the declining relative prices of manufacturing, to forces that affect urban land use and land pricing, and to the extraordinary proliferation of global value chains that are part and parcel of industrial globalism. The wide diffusion of manufacturing capabilities and the organizational capacity to integrate suppliers from distant places into a seamless production network is a remarkable innovation that is profoundly influencing industrial geography within and among countries.

What does the postindustrial future hold for these cities? Which industries will serve as the new economic axes and sustain income growth? What is the mix of skills, technologies, and institutions that will sustain growth momentum? What are the implications of globalization? And will the state and its industrial and urban policies serve as the principal driver, or will market processes become the main determinants? Plausible answers that are grounded in the most informed empirical research in several branches of economics, together with numerous interviews in the cities concerned, provide the warp and weft for later chapters. In this chapter, we first need to unroll the postindustrial canvas that we will be working on and sketch the picture with broad strokes. In the next chapter, we will paint in some of the details and introduce the reader to the cities that will populate our chosen urban landscape.

DEMAND ELASTICITIES

One of the most resilient stylized facts in economics is the high-income elasticity of demand for services. When incomes are low, households spend a high proportion of their earnings on food, housing, and clothing. As incomes rise, accompanied by an increase in the opportunities for leisure, the purchase of basic necessities gives way to larger expenditures on manufactured goods and services of all sorts (see figure 1.1). This trend persists as people move into higher income brackets. It is a pattern of

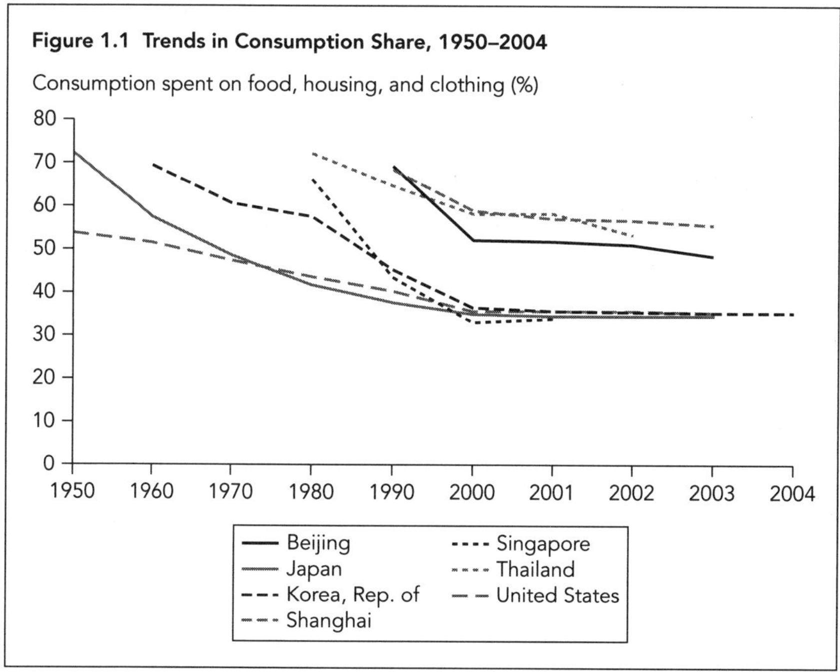

Figure 1.1 Trends in Consumption Share, 1950–2004

Sources: China: *China Urban Residents Household Income and Expenditure Investigation Materials*, various issues, and *China Price and Urban Residents Household Income and Expenditure Investigation Statistical Yearbook*, various issues. Japan: Statistical Survey Department, Statistics Bureau, Ministry of Internal Affairs and Communications. Singapore: National Statistical Office 2002. Thailand: National Statistical Office various years. United States: Bureau of Labor Statistics various years.

Note: The Republic of Korea starts from 1963 instead of 1960; data for Singapore in 1980 are from 1978, and data from 1990 are from 1991; data for Thailand in 1980 are from 1981.

spending that is being replicated around the world. From figure 1.1, we can see how household spending in the United States went through an upheaval over a 50-year period. In 1950, one-third of total expenditure was on food, followed by expenditures on housing and clothing. These three essential items absorbed more than half of total household consumption. By 2003, the share of these items had dwindled down to 30 percent, with the share of food in the household budget dropping from 30 to 15 percent and of clothing from 12 to 5 percent. During the past five decades, the expenditure on medical services, personal business (mostly expenditures associated with financial services), recreation, education, religion, and welfare (including day-care services) has been on an upward trend, while the expenditure on household furnishings and transportation has been relatively stable. Spending on medical services has risen most steeply.

This pattern was approximately replicated by Japanese households during 1950 to 2003, although Japanese consumers still spend one-fifth of their income on food. However, the consumption shares of food and clothing in total consumption are declining over time, and those of education, medical services, and recreation are on the rise. The Republic of Korea is fast approaching the consumption patterns of the United States and Japan. Although spending on basic necessities remains high, the consumption pattern of China is likely to resemble that of other countries as income increases.[17] The signs of such convergence are already visible among the affluent younger generations of Chinese consumers, most of whom have a college education. The spending patterns of these consumers are similar to patterns seen in industrial countries ("Golden Boys" 2004).[18] By and large, average household incomes in the leading East Asian cities are higher than in the rest of the country. They have also tended to rise more rapidly, and this steep increase in incomes within a little more than two decades, combined with economic openness, has dramatically transformed the structure of the urban economy.

17. An income of US$5,000 is considered to be the point where discretionary spending takes off. In 2004, 17 percent of urban households in China had an income above US$5,000, and this proportion is expected to rise to 90 percent by 2014 ("Young Consumers" 2005). Chinese consumers are also gaining similar protections seen in other countries through three laws strengthening consumer rights: the Consumer Protection Law, the Law against Unfair Trade, and the Advertising Law (Davis 2005).

18. Increasingly, the celebration of Christmas and other occasions as gift exchange opportunities is becoming popular among young, affluent Chinese, leading to a further shift in consumption patterns relative to previous generations ("Ho, Ho, Hao" 2003).

PRODUCTIVITY GROWTH, INDUSTRIAL COMPOSITION, AND INCOME DISTRIBUTION

Until recently, labor productivity and growth in manufacturing far exceeded labor productivity and growth in services. As a result, demand for manufactured products can be met with a progressively smaller workforce. Less than 10 percent of total U.S. employment in 2004 was in manufacturing industries ("Industrial Metamorphosis" 2005). The figure was 14 percent in the United Kingdom and 18 percent in Japan, though still over one-fifth in Germany and Italy. The growth of average nonfarm labor productivity in the United States between 1973 and 1995 was 1.3 percent, while that of services industries was 1 percent or less. Only after 1995 did the productivity growth of the services industries and of the overall economy reach parity (Triplett and Bosworth 2003).

In the past, the lagging productivity of the services industries relative to that of manufacturing was ascribed to lower capital intensity, a slower pace of technological and organizational innovation, and less exposure to competition, especially from international sources. Those factors are changing with the adoption of ICT. Such technologies are beginning to impinge strongly on the productivity of the financial, wholesale, retail, and logistics industries. In the United States, these services industries, which are among the heaviest users of ICT, were able to improve their productivity dramatically since 1995 (Triplett and Bosworth 2003).[19]

Services have benefited from a surge in innovation in areas such as financial trading, inventory management, and e-commerce.[20] By one estimate, two-thirds of the productivity growth in the United States since 1995 was mainly the result of organizational and other innovations in services industries such as retailing that use information technology, and Wal-Mart was a major driving force (McKinsey Global Institute 2001). Other estimates give greater weight to productivity gains in the ICT-intensive manufacturing industries (chapter 3; see also Indjikian and Siegel 2005; OECD 2004a). ICT has rendered many previously nontradable services tradable and is helping to further unify not just national but also global labor markets (Freeman 2005). It has paved the way for the offshoring of numerous activities, such as engineering, design, and software development, bringing skilled professionals in developing countries such

19. Seoul's traffic system uses a standardized smart card for fares, greatly contributing to the convenience of commuters who need to use multiple modes of transportation ("Smart Way" 2005).

20. In Korea, 68 percent of stocks are traded online, and 12 percent of retail shopping is conducted over the Internet (Shameen 2004).

as China and India into direct competition with their counterparts in the advanced economies.[21]

In parallel, since the 1990s, more and more businesses are pursuing vertical disintegration. When opportunity permits, firms are choosing to externalize activities and are opting for a flatter organizational structure, with fewer layers and less overhead. ICT is facilitating the management of such dispersed production and is a driving force behind the global value chains referred to above (Yusuf, Altaf, and Nabeshima 2004). This process enables a firm to prune its staff and to focus on the core activities in which it has the greatest comparative advantage and from which it can reap the highest returns.[22] Other activities are distributed among specialized providers. As Bryson, Daniels, and Warf observe (2004, 79), "The firm is no longer a unitary organization but a network of organizations in which external economies of scale have replaced the internal economies of scale associated with the Fordist systems of mass production."

Such vertical disintegration is leading to a finer social and economic division that promotes flexible production technologies and is affecting the location of industries in higher-cost urban areas. The advances in ICT and the virtual agglomeration of services permit companies to work with providers that are spread across the national economy and beyond, often in many different time zones. Firms engaged in producing software or supplying Web services, for example, can sustain round-the-clock operations by distributing their production activities among several centers, such as Bangalore, Tel Aviv, Zurich, and San Francisco. Soon this list could include many other medium-size cities in Asia and throughout the world.

The global networking facilitated by ICT favors larger companies that can more easily tap—often at lower cost—production and research skills from around the world[23] and can generally command the resources to finance long-term research and development (R&D) and sustain an international brand name. Small and medium-size enterprises rely far more on local resources, and theirs is frequently a local and in-house expertise. Such local knowledge can be an asset in promoting a product or service or in developing a new product. Thus, a local partner is often necessary for a foreign firm seeking to enter the Chinese market, though the preference

21. This trend is quantified in "Does IT Improve Performance" (2005).

22. See also Roberts (2004, chapter 5) on the changing organization of the multinational corporation.

23. Carlsson (2006) and Foray (2006) have emphasized the globalization of research and the relative advantages that multinational corporations have in sourcing research expertise from around the world and using the most talented research teams.

is for a medium-size or large firm. Small size is a handicap when it comes to reducing unit costs, selling to an international clientele, or building the capacity to innovate within the firm[24] or through outsourcing, because transaction costs and information asymmetries make it more difficult for the firm to link up with universities or research institutes. There are signs of increasing concentrations in several industries—including retailing, accounting, telephony, and electronics—that could lead to a more bimodal industrial distribution.[25]

The major East Asian cities are acquiring strongly dualistic characteristics with expanding islands of highly competitive manufacturing industries, coexisting with swaths of industry populated by firms of often suboptimal size and by sheltered inefficient services providers. The larger Asian companies have been slow to adopt a flatter organizational structure and to pursue vertical disintegration. The ICT-led productivity revolution that is sweeping through the industrial countries is beginning, but it is still in the early stages. For instance, labor productivity in Korea's retail sector is only 32 percent of the U.S. level (Baily 1998). Much of the lagging productivity stems from the fact that 99 percent of retail stores in Korea in 1998 were single-unit stores, not belonging to any chains. By contrast, 80 percent of stores in the United States are department stores, specialty chain stores, and discounters (Baily 1998).[26]

The definite trend already very visible in manufacturing is toward capital intensity, automation, computerization, rising skill coefficients, and outsourcing. Services providers in East Asia were able to resist the pressures because of low labor costs and limited competition, but in the megacities, change is stirring rapidly. Two of the leading services industries, retailing and finance, are both being transformed by advances in computerization, digitization, automation, logistics, and communications that were introduced by companies such as Wal-Mart,[27] Carrefours,

24. Most small firms do not introduce more than a single new product or service.

25. An analysis of innovativity in seven European countries based on firm-level information on innovative products confirms that larger firms are more innovative on a continuous basis—with the help of R&D—and that process and product innovation can go hand in hand. Germany was identified in this study as the country with the largest share of innovative firms (Mohnen, Mairesse, and Dagenais 2006).

26. Even the productivity of a small number of department and specialty stores in Korea is only 60 percent of similar types of stores in the United States (Baily 1998).

27. Solow (2001) makes the point that the surge in productivity between 1995 and 2000 was the result of management innovations made possible by advances in ICT, with Wal-Mart being the prime example ("Wal-Mart Effect" 2002). The effect of Wal-Mart is also spreading around the world, with imitators springing up in Asia. In India, for example, a half-dozen Wal-Mart–style chains have emerged, such as Big Bazaar, Westside, Shoppers Stop, and Spencers ("Here Comes" 2005).

GE Capital, and Citicorp. These industries are substantially reducing the number of workers required while raising the productivity of the ones who remain, are transferring jobs to other low-wage locations, and are slowly ratcheting up the cognitive content and skill intensity of the work that remains.[28]

These developments are spilling over into neighboring subsectors, such as health, which is likely to undergo its own revolution through the interaction of biotechnology, pharmaceuticals, information technology (IT), engineering, materials and electronic technologies. In addition to improving the quality of health care, such developments will drastically reduce hospital stay while increasing the roles of telecare and telemedicine and will begin to trim administrative costs, especially those arising from billing, recordkeeping, and sharing of patient records. In the United States, these costs account for 31 cents of every dollar spent on medical care ("Digital Hospital" 2005; "No-Computer Virus" 2005; "Smoother Operation" 2005).

What will these developments do to the industrial economy of the East Asian city? Labor-intensive light manufacturing will exit the megacities. This exit does not mean that manufacturing is on its way out, but that the viable manufacturing industries will be capital-, skill-, and technology-intensive ones. One offshoot will be a diminution in the number of highly paid blue-collar jobs. If those jobs are replaced by more productive ones in new creative industries and services, and if the number of new jobs rises strongly, the future for the postindustrial city is bright.[29]

But the "if" is a troublesome reminder of uncertainty. An early glimpse of what might be in store for other cities that are slow to diversify their industrial base as traditional industries fade is provided by Hong Kong (China) which has experienced a sharp dip in the share of manufacturing in GDP from 25 percent in 1985 to 7 percent in 2003. Consequently, despite of the growth of services, income distribution in Hong Kong (China) has deteriorated steadily since the early 1970s, with the cumulative share of the bottom 60 percent of households falling and the top 10 percent enjoying a substantial increase (Zhao, Chan, and Sit 2003).[30] Chiu and Lui

28. Gordon (2004b) attributes much of the productivity surge in the United States to ICT-using industries such as retailing and financial services.

29. In the U.S. context, it has often been noted that several cities have, after an interval, exploited the space created by the exodus of industry to launch urban development schemes, which attract high-income households, as in SoHo in New York and LoDo in Denver (Siegel 2002).

30. See also Sassen (2001, 2002) on factors contributing to increasing inequality in other major cities.

Table 1.4 Employment Elasticity of Output in China

	1981–85	1986–90	1991–95	1996–2000	1998–2003
Primary employment	0.094	1.083	−0.404	0.190	0.204
Secondary employment	0.477	0.438	0.095	0.002	−0.041
Manufacturing employment	0.218	0.186	0.007	−0.583	−0.361
Tertiary employment	0.400	0.636	0.598	0.218	0.270

Sources: Primary, secondary, and tertiary employment data are derived from the employment section of various issues of *A Statistical Survey of China*. Manufacturing employment data are derived from tables on the number of staff and workers in industry in various issues of the *China Statistical Yearbook* (National Bureau of Statistics of China various years), except for 1981 data, which are calculated from the employment section of the *China Statistical Yearbook*.

(2004, 1875) trace the "widening income disparity in Hong Kong to the structural changes brought about by its transformation towards a global city. De-industrialization and the rise of [services] supporting these changes all contributed to the worsening income inequality."

The risk of growth that is not jobless but that generates relatively few new jobs and heavily favors the highly skilled is present throughout East Asia, even in China (Friedmann 2005, 127).[31] The disquieting trends in employment elasticities for China are evident from table 1.4. Since 1998–2003, the employment elasticity for manufacturing has been negative. It is also negative, but less so, for secondary industry as a whole. Most striking is the sharp decline in the jobs being created by the tertiary sector per unit of growth. The elasticity, which was a healthy 0.636 during 1986 to 1990 had dropped to 0.270 in 1998 to 2003 (World Bank 2005). For the postindustrial East Asian cities—and for that matter any major city in the industrial world—the need to refresh and expand the industrial base is urgent and increasing. Technology, globalization, and the increasingly footloose behavior of industries and of multinational corporations have made it imperative for cities to anticipate continuums of change. In those circumstances, it is becoming hazardous to assume that market forces will smoothly orchestrate structural changes across the competing urban centers and, on balance, engineer positive-sum outcomes. The more plausible

31. The widening difference between contracted and actually used foreign direct investment signifies the lack of a pool of skilled workers needed by foreign producers; over 80 percent of some high-tech products are produced by foreign-invested enterprises ("China: Labour Market" 2004). One consequence is that the wages of these hotly sought after jobs in multinational corporations are rising 6 to 10 percent a year when the overall inflation rate is only 2 percent. However, even with attractive pay and benefits, the turnover rates of Chinese professionals are about 11 percent ("China's People Problem" 2005).

inference is that the economic integration and fluidity of movement introduced by globalization have made it more urgent for metropolitan centers to be closely tracking industrial changes, scrutinizing the actions of their competitors, and planning their own moves well in advance. Postindustrial cities now need their strategies.

TECHNOLOGY AT THE ROOT

The swelling demand for services and the growth of industrial productivity has many causes, and this chapter is not the place to elaborate on those causes. What we want to emphasize is (a) that the key determinant of both trends is technology and (b) that technology can bring jobs to urban areas as well as take them elsewhere. Advances in technology—especially in IT—have enormously expanded the menu of services that are available to us and have created entirely new wants. Some of those wants now border on necessities. Many new services—for instance, in the field of communications and in the realm of entertainment—are tightly interlaced with manufactured products such as the now ubiquitous mobile phones, so that urbanites consume "bundled" goods and services. The purveyors of those bundles, such as NTT DoCoMo in Japan or Apple, are finding that the profits accrue more from the innovative services component than from the equally innovative hardware.[32] For example, 36 percent of Japanese users of the Internet through mobile phones accessed for-fee contents. The most commonly purchased items were ring tones (84 percent), images for wallpaper (43 percent), music (22 percent), and games (20 percent). Each transaction typically cost less than ¥500, with yearly spending per user averaging ¥2,658 (Ministry of Public Management, Home Affairs Posts, and Telecommunications 2003).[33] Even in the United States, where mobile phones are used more sparingly for purposes other than as phones, 63 percent of mobile phone users ages between 18 and 27 now send text messages using their mobile phones ("Study: 'Texting'" 2005).[34] China's more than 416 million mobile phone users already sent 132 billion text messages in

32. Nearly 44 million mobile phones were sold in Japan in 2004. ("Japanese Mobile Phone" 2005).

33. Although trailing in popularity behind ring tones and music downloads, reading books on cell phones is catching on in China, Japan, and Korea ("Mobile Page Turner" 2005).

34. The use of "texting" is highly correlated with age. Only 31 percent of mobile phone users between 28 and 39 years old send any text messages, and those over 60 years old rarely send any ("Study: 'Texting'" 2005).

the first four months of 2006 (Zhao 2006). The race is intensifying, not only to introduce innovations in hardware but also to multiply the range of services offered by tapping latent wants or creating entirely new ones.

Starting with the industrial revolution in the United Kingdom more than two centuries ago, the story of industry is inextricable from that of technology. Technology has continually introduced new products through epochal innovations such as the steam engine, electricity, the internal combustion engine, synthetic fibers, the integrated circuit, robotics, and the Internet, each of which brought huge waves of change in industrial processes extending over decades. The full effects of the integrated circuit and the Internet have yet to be felt, and those of biotechnology are still over the horizon; however, the early experience with the diffusion of ICT is that it is accelerating the pace of creative destruction (Chun and others 2004).

Three types of process innovations are particularly relevant for our story. First are those that have displaced human labor by harnessing other sources of energy—mainly hydrocarbon-based energy. Water, electricity, and the internal combustion engine fall into this category. Second are the innovations that have substituted capital equipment and primitive forms of artificial intelligence for human operators. Such innovations range from forklifts to various kinds of industrial robots,[35] to computerized monitoring equipment, to diagnostic programs, to speech recognition software. Third, and most recently, are the enormous gains in logistics and communication technology that are enabling companies to change the geography of manufacturing by exploiting the diminution of distance to substitute cheaper labor in the hinterland of the country or in other nations for higher-paid urban workers. Those technological steps have also resulted in an increase in the ratio of skilled workers in the total industrial labor force, although this increase is by no means a steady or uniform trend. Some of the most advanced process technologies in the consumer electronics and auto industries continue to employ large numbers of semi-skilled or unskilled workers, who perform narrowly defined, repetitive, and specialized tasks on vast assembly lines. But on balance, process technologies are becoming more human capital intensive.

Manufacturing firms are coming to recognize and capitalize on the complementarities among manufactured products and services. Leading firms such as IBM continue to produce mainframe computers and integrated circuits (31 percent of IBM's turnover is from hardware), but now

35. Japan is the leading user of industrial robots, with an installed base of 348,734 units (UNECE 2004).

the bulk of their profits are derived from IT, software, and related management services ("Business's Digital Black Cloud" 2005). General Electric, a leading producer of locomotives, now markets haulage services to railway companies rather than selling its engines. Some companies, such as Sun Microsystems and Nike, do not directly engage in production at all but focus on design, R&D, system integration, marketing, and after-sales support. Ford and General Motors are active in financial services and insurance, businesses that dovetail with their mainstream operations. Sony, Samsung, and Nokia are all seeking to enlarge the entertainment market and the services that they provide through their hardware. Hardware can be quickly commodified, but entertainment offers a larger stream of rents. Schindler, one of the leading producers of elevators, anticipates that by the end of the decade only 10 percent of its workforce will be in manufacturing; the rest will be providing services. In the automobile business, design is increasingly critical. The role of BMW's much expanded design team has been frequently noted. "Rather than engineers being fully responsible for the design of cars, designers, market researchers, and marketing experts are instructing engineers in what they should design" (Bryson, Daniels, and Warf 2004, 57). In a buyers' market with low entry barriers, "[m]aybe the most important producer services directly involved in product innovation are design companies. . . . The use of design had improved products and service quality, improved image, and increased turnover and profitability" (Bryson, Daniels, and Warf 2004, 68).[36]

The activities that have displaced manufacturing in the central areas of the city are labor- and often skill-intensive. Their productivity and innovativeness depends on the exchange of ideas and tacit knowledge, often through face-to-face contact, which is facilitated by clustering in the central areas of a city, as observed by Leamer and Storper (2001). Producer services—for instance, financial and legal ones—fall into this category, as do the creative industries such as publishing, multimedia, design, and entertainment. Silicon Alley arose from such a grouping of business

36. Whether it is apparel or flat panel televisions or cell phones or cars, the hotly contested global marketplace is making design a key to competitiveness. Successful firms such as BMW are able to strike a balance between art and commerce that leaves them profitable but also distinguishes them as a premium brand in the eyes of consumers by virtue of a unique style that shines through every finely crafted product (Bangle 2001, 47). Not only does the design help raise the sales of the product, it also helps recruit promising workers. BMW is ranked as the top choice of employer by U.S. undergraduates. Apple, which has been missing from this list for a long time, made it back to the top 15 employers after the introduction of the iPod ("In Search of the Ideal Employer" 2005).

services in New York City (Indergaard 2004), and the future of robotics development in Tokyo depends on a network of researchers and producers clustered in two contiguous prefectures.

Indergaard (2004, 5) observes,

> Silicon Alley was the latest round in the long struggle to reinvent New York as a postindustrial city—a process that elite property interests began to promote while factories still dominated Lower Manhattan. In fact, large-scale deindustrialization of Lower Manhattan over the last four decades was not only the result of changes within industrial sectors, but also the product of commercial redevelopment (and related rises in real estate prices) that dislodged manufacturers. Consequently, New York, like many cities, has become increasingly dependent on cultural industries and producer services that produce or manipulate symbols.

Indergaard (2004, 8) continues,

> The commercial idea behind Silicon Alley was that the core problem (and opportunity) for Internet business was not developing technology per se, but creating and distributing new modes of expression that use Internet technology. The Internet economy was said to be a new media and communications business where the main avenue for creating value was developing creative business applications.

The germinating of these clusters and their physical embedding in Lower Manhattan was the work of venture capitalists, a few major corporations, and key real estate developers. According to Indergaard (2004, 7), "These early industry-builders focused on creating spaces—social as well as physical—wherein connections could be woven between the web pioneers and various business interests." He describes the venture capitalists as "architects of change who brought together the new media entrepreneurs and Manhattan monied classes" (60).

Meanwhile, the real estate developers saw in Silicon Alley a means of filling "empty office buildings in the Financial District, where vacancy rates exceeded 20 percent in the early 1990s. . . . This strategy was all the more attractive when the new media was becoming identified as the first new industry to form in the city in half a century. Their provision of subsidized wired space in fourteen buildings played a major role in causing some seven hundred tech firms to settle Downtown (Indergaard 2004, 7). Moreover, the "cultural mobilization of new media districts complemented the financial mobilization. The districts not only produced visions of epic forces, but also artifacts attesting to the material reality of a new kind of firm: loft workplaces, a distinctive social scene, and employees with quirky looks and attitudes" (Indergaard 2004, 59).

As the Silicon Alley experience illustrates, suppliers of producer services rely heavily on the expertise and reputations of professionals. From law firms, investment banks, and venture capitalists to providers of accounting, consulting, publishing, multimedia, and advertising services, all depend on the knowledge, skills, contacts, and standing of their staffs. Hence, in an urban economy dominated by services, highly skilled professionals—especially ones that have accumulated a measure of reputational capital—are coming to play an increasingly decisive role. This so-called creative class is becoming the hinge of the new urban economy (Florida 2002). Such professionals are among the more mobile—both geographically and occupationally—and also the more demanding consumers of urban services and amenities. A high proportion of "creative workers" are concentrated in the large metropolitan areas that are rich in amenities and that provide access to housing and social services that are of good quality and are attractively priced.[37] The most vibrant cities tend to attract these creative workers not just from the surrounding countries, but from around the world (see figure 1.2).[38] Where a concentration of skilled workers can be sustained and augmented from local world-class universities, cities can experience economic resilience and virtuous industrial spirals. The skill-driven recovery of Boston's economy described by Glaeser (2005a) is one example. People with higher education are more likely to start up a new company and, on balance, will hire more skilled workers, thereby strengthening the human capital resource base of the urban area (Colombo, Delmastro, and Grilli 2004).

Jane Jacobs saw early how diversity was the motor of great American cities. She described how the mixing of talents and the upward spiral can continue indefinitely. In the Jacobs schema, economies derive from the way in which "people with specialties can further dynamic improvements if they jostle together with people of other specialties within a company. Or companies with specialties jostle together with other companies within a versatile city. But when a whole city specializes and trades with other specialized cities, then that locked-in pattern of static efficiency is a recipe for stasis and long term decline" (Ellerman 2005, 64–65).

37. Terry Nichols Clark (2004) lists a number of "natural" and "constructed" amenities that contribute to the attractiveness of a city. The former includes water area, temperate summer, and topographic variation. The latter includes operas, research libraries, and coffee bars.

38. The mosaic index measures the diversity of the immigrant population. Using this metric, East Asian cities do not fare well, highlighting the fact that most of the foreign population comes from only a handful of countries.

Figure 1.2 Mosaic Index

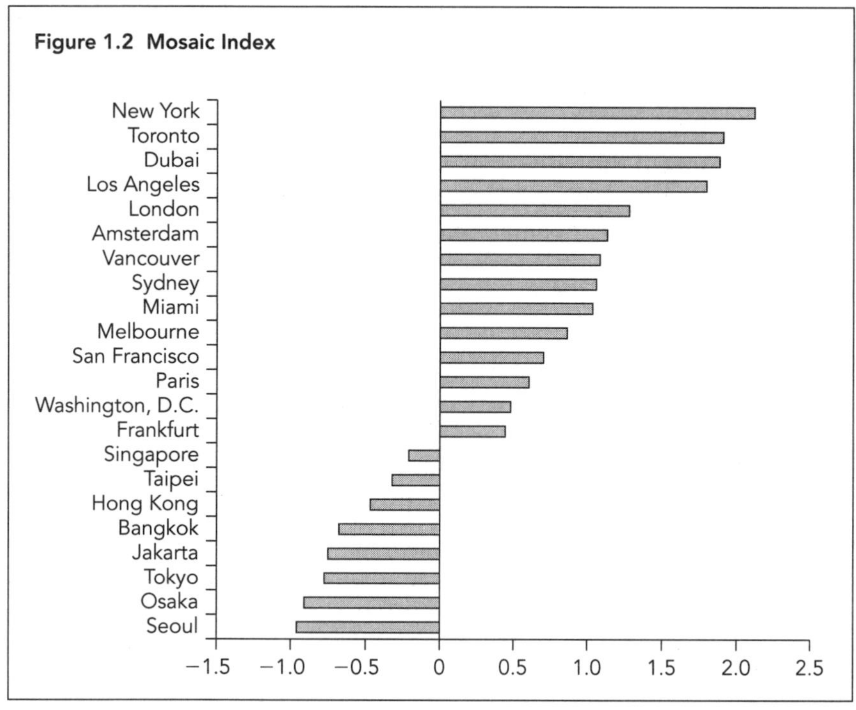

Source: Benton-Short, Price, and Friedman 2004.
Note: The mosaic index measures the diversity of the immigrant population. The larger the number, the more diverse the immigrant population is.

Patterns of land use guided by land prices in urban areas are reinforcing the push exerted by technologies on industries. All cities are subject to rent gradients, with prices declining with distance from city centers, which encompass the choicest pieces of real estate and are the focus of activities commanding the highest prices.[39] A hundred years ago, the leading cities in the West were thickly populated with manufacturing industry, and the remnants of this once strong army can still be found in Shanghai, Beijing, Bangkok, and Seoul. But rising urban land prices, competition from other uses for valuable downtown real estate, and new zoning regulations that were introduced by municipal authorities to capitalize on higher potential land values and to improve the physical environment in the downtown

39. This pattern can be made worse by deliberate policy actions. For instance, only 0.2 percent of available land in Korea is designated as a commercial zone, forcing a concentration of population in Seoul (Baily 1998).

areas have combined to push industries that do not depend on the central city location to the suburbs and beyond. The preferred one-floor layout for modern factories, which requires more space, and the importance of efficient logistics for just-in-time delivery and distribution of products also are pulling industry to places where land is plentiful and where multimodal transport services are readily available. As infrastructure improves, options are multiplying—and they span the globe.

The displacement and migration of manufacturing industries, the spreading of services, and the emergence of activities rooted in new technologies and wants occurred at a leisurely pace throughout much of the first 70 years of the 20th century. But this pace turned into a gallop starting in the 1980s. ICT—in particular the Internet—and the associated globalization have had a big hand in this acceleration. In a matter of years, major cities in the higher-income countries completed their transition to postindustrialism, and newly industrializing countries that are still several decades behind the industrial leaders are finding this model difficult to resist. We believe that the accelerating trend toward postindustrial urban societies in East Asia has derived additional impetus from two developments that compound the influence of technological change: (a) the dissolving of trade barriers and (b) decentralizing tendencies that are shifting the weight of policy-making responsibility to urban centers, thereby giving them more autonomy to chart their development paths.

CITIES IN THE GLOBAL MARKETPLACE

Globalization is creating an international environment that is integrating at many levels, primarily through the major cities.[40] It is forcing urban economies to seek efficiency gains and to recognize that industrial geography is fluid and changeable, because many technologies are codified and diffusing quickly and the labor market no longer stops at the boundaries of a region or a nation. Cities are also having to move gingerly toward environments that promote innovativeness through openness to talented people and to fresh ideas. There is no tested formula, although Florida (2002) has put forward an intriguing recipe that highlights the importance of teaching and research institutions, of diversity, of recreational and cultural

40. The latest round of integration, which accelerated in the 1980s, parallels an earlier round that occurred roughly three decades before World War I. The ongoing globalization is proceeding much further, and the effect on urban areas is greater (Nayyar 2006; A. Taylor 2006).

amenities, of urban infrastructure and services, and of location.[41] These are plausible building blocks that attempt to identify the DNA of the New Yorks, San Franciscos, Austins, Bostons, and Seattles of the world. The fastest-growing cities in the United States have other attributes as well—good and affordable housing, high-quality schooling, health and other urban services, low crime, and first-rate IT and transport facilities, along with low levels of environmental pollution.[42] Globalization has served to highlight, if not actually give rise to, a pecking order of world cities, regional cities, and lower-tier cities that are distinguished by a number of characteristics. It has stirred an arms race among East Asian cities that see a higher-order status—and a brand name—as the means of attracting the next generation of industries to ensure continuing prosperity.

The partial unraveling of the centralized state has led to other developments: greater reliance on market signals, but also a deconcentration of administrative and fiscal authority (World Bank 1999). The responsibility for making policy is becoming multilevel in China as much as in the United States. Increasingly, it is the city mayor who joins forces with central and often provincial governments and makes policy to cope with externalities and missing markets, to provide public goods, to promote industrial change, and to boost employment. Some megacities have acquired more latitude to manage their affairs, but they and the central government also confront the need to take developmental initiatives with longer-run implications. The successful ones are gaining better access to additional resources from foreign direct investment, fiscal effort, bond financing, and private participation, to finance local development.[43] At the same time, they are having to worry about their standing in the global financial marketplace.

41. One such city is Austin, Texas, which offers an equable climate, numerous outdoor activities, universities, and the cultural amenities sought by creative workers ("Why Everyone Loves Austin" 2005).

42. In a recent survey, Minneapolis was identified as the leader among principal postindustrial high-technology urban centers in the United States, with reference to a number of indicators ranging from the number of technology-intensive companies, to intelligent transport solutions, to Energy Star buildings ("Technopolis Found" 2005).

43. In China, fiscal decentralization is occurring grudgingly and haphazardly, with the result that resource assignments are frequently insufficient to cover the newly inherited expenditures and that subnational governments struggle to balance their books, often using extrabudgetary sources. Chinese cities are faced with fiscal adjustment to align long-term expenditure responsibilities with revenues (Dabla-Norris 2004; World Bank 2002). The vast array of policy instruments mobilized by state governments in the United States to attract or retain industry are described and analyzed by Jenkins, Leicht, and Wendt (2006).

Thus, the factors leading to globalization and the associated flows of trade and of resources have spurred a parallel "localization" (World Bank 1999). Willy-nilly, leading East Asian cities are entering the uncertain seas of postindustrialism with few reliable charts to navigate by. Many subnational governments are having to build the administrative capacity, the financial management skills, and the institutions of governance to efficiently manage the transition. However, they are learning quickly, helped by a tradition of industrial policy making. For them, the demands of the new world of postindustrialization call for an adaptation of policy making to deal with new global exigencies and for implementation at metropolitan levels and with respect to a changed mix of industrial activities.

THE SHAPE OF THINGS TO COME?

It is rash to make confident predictions, because social upheavals, unforeseen technological developments, and regional or global political crises, as have happened too frequently in the 20th century, can stall or reverse trends or can send the postindustrial world down unanticipated tangents.[44] However, barring such events, the postindustrial metropolis in East Asia—or for that matter anywhere in the world—will be drawing its economic lifeblood from a blend of activities in which manufacturing will retain a key role, though admittedly a minor one in terms of sheer scale. Other activities are on track to enlarge their roles, including services of all kinds, which are constantly adjusting to the changing demographics and work rhythms of cities. Very likely, these services will be exposed to the full force of technological advance, and some of the most venerable and labor-intensive ones, such as health, education, retail, and logistics, will experience substantial gains in productivity, thereby freeing workers for other jobs, assuming that such jobs materialize. The implications for urban labor markets, in particular, are immense. The postindustrial labor market in East Asia's megacities will need to contend with pressures from two directions.

First, in most of these cities, the workforce will be growing—through natural increase, lengthening life expectancies, further entry of women into the labor force, and in-migration. The influx of workers from elsewhere, especially of the skilled and entrepreneurial ones, will be an

44. Four plausible technological cum social scenarios for the global society are sketched by Glen and Gordon (2004).

important source of energy and creativity.[45] Two or three decades from now, such demographic change will taper as a consequence of much reduced fertility in recent years, but that is already a longtime horizon. In Japan, the male population began declining in 2004,[46] and China's population, which reached 1.3 billion in 2005, will soon begin to stabilize, though the urban share of the population will continue to grow in China and in much of East Asia.

Second, these cities will be fully exposed to the economic pressures arising from national and global integration. Labor-displacing and increasingly skill-intensive technologies will eat away at most routine, clerical, and repetitive jobs with limited cognitive content. Broad swaths of blue- and white-collar jobs are certain to be nudged to extinction by IT. No doubt new ones will spring up in their place. Technologies that destroy some jobs can create others, but often these jobs are very different and require other skills not readily acquired by laid-off, middle-age workers. For instance, no one knows how the millions of retail workers released by the labor-displacing "Wal-Mart effect" will be absorbed. East Asia may continue to benefit from the export of work from higher-income countries, but it is difficult to be sure.

Very likely, leisure time will grow. The number of hours worked has declined in Japan and Korea following a trend that surfaced in the industrial countries some time ago. The tilting relationship between work and recreation can be illustrated by a few statistics from selected countries. For an urban worker in the United States, the average workweek stretched to more than 70 hours in 1830. By 2002, it was down to 41 hours—the norm in many Organisation for Economic Co-operation and Development countries by 1970—while weekly earnings had risen by a factor of nine. Similarly, the average housewife, who would put in four hours per day of housework in 1929, now will do less than two hours (Greenwood and Vandenbroucke 2005). The average American male engaged in 61 hours of market and nonmarket work each week in 1965. The average woman spent 54 hours working. By 2003, men worked eight hours fewer per week, and women six hours fewer, resulting in an increase in leisure time of 11 to

45. Hall (2000) associates the creativity of cities such as London with their openness to young migrants from all over the world. It is also worth noting that the economic development of Shanghai over a hundred years, starting in the mid-19th century, is directly attributable to the influx of entrepreneurial migrants.

46. Japan is not alone. Europe's demographic circumstances are very similar, and Korea is fast approaching this stage (Lowe-Lee 2003; "Population Ageing" 2005).

13 percent (Aguiar and Hurst 2006).[47] A similar downward trend has been evident across the world. Hours worked have fallen by 11 percent since 1991 in Japan, by 10 percent in France, and by 5 percent in Korea ("Real Reasons" 2005). Rising incomes and fewer hours of work have led to a parallel rise in expenditures on recreation, from 3 percent of personal consumption in the United States in 1900 to 8.5 percent in 2001 (Greenwood and Vandenbroucke 2005). In many industrial countries, the share of part-time workers is increasing. In Japan, more than 25 percent of workers are part-time workers ("Part-Time Workers" 2005). More leisure time allows people to acquire and pursue many new interests, which induce the growth of existing urban industries and spawn entirely new ones as well.[48]

Perhaps the most striking increase in leisure time is occurring in the transition economies—in particular, China. The average urban resident had just 2 hours and 21 minutes of leisure per day in 1980. Ten years later, leisure time had doubled, but more importantly, leisure time was now under the control of the individual and not the work unit (*danwei*). A significant share of this time was initially spent watching television; however, Friedmann (2005, 79–80) observes that the Chinese urbanite is learning fast. There are now "thousands of hobby associations from stamp collecting to breeding fish . . . and crickets. Millions of readers eagerly snap up the skyrocketing number of publications. And wave after wave of new enthusiasms [have] swept across China, such as qigong fever, tourism

---

47. This conventional view has been challenged by Ramey and Francis (2006), who maintain that per capita leisure time in the United States was unchanged between 1900 and 2000—it was 6,657 hours per year a century ago and is 6,634 hours in the early 21st century. They compute leisure time by subtracting market work, schoolwork, commuting to work, and housework. They include personal care time in leisure and view the time spent sleeping as a matter of choice. The increase in schoolwork is the variable that biases their results downward.

48. One corollary to the rising productivity of tertiary industries is the spread of self-service activities, which eat into the leisure time of consumers. Activities ranging from retailing to travel are transferring more and more of the work to the consumer, whether this work is checking out and bagging groceries or searching for deals and making travel arrangements. Some of this transfer of responsibilities to the consumer and the household that is being expedited by ICT and the Internet is leading to better informed consumers and buyers of insurance, medical care, autos, and financial instruments. Information is flowing more freely than ever before, and the consumer and investor (potentially, at least) has the upper hand. But without a doubt, the division of labor between service providers and users is shifting, and in the process, many urban jobs are likely to vanish. Down the road, this change has implications for the health sector throughout East Asia, as the population ages. Unless international migration augments the supply of health workers or technological advances reduce the need for nursing and other services, caregiving by family members—mainly women—will make large claims on time (Huws 2003).

fever, keeping fit fever, and dressmaking fever, as people [have] indulged their new freedom." With more time, money, and household space, Chinese households can also indulge their long-suppressed urge to shop. In the cramped, Spartan, and frugal living conditions of the early 1980s, per capita living space was a bare 8 square meters; by 2005, it had risen to 25 square meters (Wang 2003, National Bureau of Statistics of China 2005).

Be that as it may, the most vital concerns for postindustrial East Asian cities are the industries to sustain their hitherto headlong income growth, the nature of the jobs that such industries may provide, and the kinds of skills that workers will require. Urban training institutions and job machines backed by ICT that improve the level of skills and the efficiency of the labor market by matching workers with appropriate job openings would help ensure rising living standards and social stability (Freeman 2002; Lindsay 2005). Job machines—even high-tech ones—that generate meager employment could be the start of widening inequalities and the immiserization of the majority.[49] The resilient and dynamic city is more likely to be a city richly supplied with skills (Glaeser and Saiz 2003).

In his study describing a century of change in a midsize American city, Douglas Rae (2003, 7) observes,

> Capitalism drives growth by remorselessly refusing to preserve the past. . . . No place—city, suburb, hamlet, or farmstead—is secure against the emergence of a new economic geography that drains vital populations and investments in the space of a few decades. In seeking ever fresh forms of production, ever larger markets, ever higher returns on investment, capitalism routinely destroys older technologies, older plants—and in so doing, profoundly transforms the communities that have formed around them.

Rae goes on to describe how New Haven, Connecticut, an important American city in the 1920s, has spiraled into decrepitude and seemingly irremediable urban blight because it failed to replace industrial activities that faded away.

While analyzing what is in store for East Asia's major cities, we intend to emphasize the creative rather than the destructive side of industrial change. Whether East Asian cities are able to nurture a generation of

49. Growing inequality of incomes in China, in Japan, and even in Hong Kong (China) is a source of growing concern, because such inequality will undermine not just welfare but also social and political stability.

industries that interlace high-tech manufacturing with knowledge-intensive services will determine how these cities fare. Industries such as biotechnology, IT, multimedia, robotics, and fashion are among the promising candidates that we examine in the book. This new phase of industrialization leads into uncharted territory. The challenge for the megacities is to augment and realize their dynamic comparative advantages. By doing so, they will generate growth, vitally needed jobs, and momentum for the entire economy.

CHAPTER 2

MEGACITY PROFILES

Outside of Japan, only a small handful of cities are—or will shortly be—entering the postindustrial stage. The small number of these cities, however, belies their importance. Ten years ago, naming a single one would have been difficult. In the early 1990s, as noted in chapter 1, East Asian development was still focused on building manufacturing capability in a few strategically located urban areas. Now, some light manufacturing and resource-based industries are beginning to leave the major cities, and the economic spotlight is turning toward more advanced manufacturing and, in particular, toward services. Because the transition is in its early phase, postindustrial cities in East Asia constitute a hierarchy. At the apex stands Tokyo, in certain respects an atypical postindustrial metropolis, followed by Singapore, Bangkok, Seoul, Beijing, and Shanghai. These cities are the dramatis personae of our story, and hence, each needs to be introduced and its inclusion in the postindustrial hierarchy explained.

TOKYO

Tokyo clearly leads this field. It is a world city more populous than New York and London, the only true comparators, and larger in economic scale. Also, Tokyo, with a gross domestic product (GDP) equal to almost one-fifth of Japan's total national product, is the locus for Japan's vast banking industry and deep capital markets, though it lacks the global heft of New York and London in equity and foreign exchange trading.[1] Unlike London and New York, however, Tokyo offers a more powerful

1. Tokyo's specialization is principally in the trading of bonds.

lens for viewing the evolution and prospects of postindustrial cities in East Asia. The recent trajectory of those cities resembles that of Tokyo in the 1970s and 1980s, which has retained a sizable manufacturing sector in the outlying prefectures even as services have increased their share of the urban production in the core areas.

Tokyo's origins lie in a castle town called Edo, established by the Uesugi family in the mid-15th century. During the 17th century, Tokugawa Ieyasu completed the unification of Japan begun by Oda Nobunaga and Toyotomi Hideyoshi and made Edo the seat of his shogunate, although Kyoto—where the emperor lived—remained the capital. Under the long-running Tokugawa dynasty, Japan's political as well as the economic center of gravity shifted toward Edo. At the start of the Meiji era in 1868, the new emperor formally moved the capital to Edo and renamed it Tokyo, or Eastern Capital. Tokyo was transformed into Japan's leading industrial city.

Despite the massive destruction wreaked by air raids during World War II, Tokyo recovered within a decade because enough of its human capital and social infrastructure survived and, amazingly, the industrial geography of Japan remained unchanged, a phenomenon that has been recently documented by Davis and Weinstein (2002).[2] Interestingly, the urban geography of Tokyo also did not change much. The city of Edo was divided into two parts: the Yamanote, or high city, which spread out across the Kanto plateau, contained the homes of the *daimyo* and an assortment of temples, while the nearby and much more crowded Shitamachi, or low city, was where the commoners lived. The streets of Edo formed an interlocking maze around Edo castle, which made it difficult for invaders to find their way to the city center. The twisted tangle of streets and alleys was re-created when Tokyo was reconstructed in the 1940s and 1950s. The streets still curved and meandered, and they lacked names and a logical system of numbering to identify homes (Richie 1992, 55).

By the late 1950s, a broad base of manufacturing industries had reemerged that asserted Japan's position in the international trading system and accounted for more than one-third of the GDP of the Tokyo

2. Similarly, when plague struck London in 1665 to 1666, nearly a quarter to a third of the population was struck down. But despite extraordinary rates of mortality, urban craft and manufacturing industries continued to function even as the ranks of workers and businesspeople were gravely thinned out. When the plague was over, recovery was rapid (see Moote and Moote 2004). Likewise, the 9/11 attack on New York did not lead to the initially feared exit of firms, although some have dispersed their operations so as to minimize the disruption that any future attacks could cause ("After the Fall" 2005).

metropolitan area, which embraced some five contiguous prefectures surrounding Tokyo. The share of industry peaked in the early 1970s and since then has been on the decline under the pressure of forces described in chapter 1. This slide accelerated from the latter half of the 1980s, when the appreciation of the yen that resulted from the Plaza Accord among the Group of Eight (G-8) countries and skyrocketing real estate prices in the Tokyo area led to a progressive transfer of manufacturing plants to other parts of Japan and to Southeast Asia.[3]

Nearly 20 years later, the population of Tokyo continues expanding, mainly by absorbing migrants from other parts of Japan. This population growth is contributing to the economic growth of the urban region, as is the accumulation of human capital. Tokyo's economy also gains from the increasing scale of the metropolitan market, the synergy among the multiple nodes of a polycentric urban structure, and the advantages bestowed by industrial diversity.[4] Tokyo has all the lineaments of the postindustrial city that is distinctively East Asian and arguably serves as a reliable guide to what other cities in the region could experience. Manufacturing industry in the central districts of Tokyo now produces just 10 percent of GDP, compared with over 20 percent in the early 1990s, whereas services account for over three-fourths and utilities for the balance. In the greater Tokyo area, the share of manufacturing was 13 percent in 2002. These broad aggregates are but a small numerical tip of a complex, many-layered iceberg with a fascinating past. Japan's economic performance continues to depend on a small number of highly competitive automotive, engineering, metallurgical, and electronics subsectors. The extraordinary productivity and innovativeness of those industries have more than counterbalanced the weaker performance of other subsectors, and for the foreseeable future, export-led manufacturing will remain Japan's principal sectoral source of growth. This fact draws attention to Tokyo's role in Japan's industrial system, highlighting the interaction between city and industry and pointing to one of the principal vulnerabilities of the Japanese economy. The competitiveness of Japan's leading manufacturing

3. The grouping of some Japanese firms into *keiretsu* may have accelerated the pace at which industry transferred out because suppliers tended to follow the lead firms abroad (see, for instance, Blonigen, Ellis, and Fausten 2005).

4. On market size and productivity, see Davis and Weinstein (2001). They estimate that the productivity gains can be as much as 3.5 percent from a doubling in area. On the scope for synergy in polycentric urban regions, see Meijers (2005). The advantages of diversity were empirically demonstrated by Glaeser and others (1992) and since then has also been shown by other researchers. See Rosenthal and Strange (2004) for a review of this literature.

industries, which are largely centered on Tokyo, underpins Japan's economic prowess; were the efficiency and innovativeness of those industries to falter, Japan would be plunged into severe difficulties.

This industrial system consists of five complementary components. First and foremost are the leading multinational corporations (MNCs) themselves, their own production facilities, those of their main suppliers, their headquarters, and their research labs.[5] Tokyo has a commanding lead over other cities in terms of the concentration of large firms. More than a third are located in Tokyo, compared with a little over one-tenth in Osaka, the second-largest concentration (Bureau of Industrial and Labor Affairs 2005).

A multitude of subcontractors and smaller businesses is the supporting cast—the second component. Some are linked closely to one or a few MNCs; others sell directly to consumers and households in the urban marketplace. The longstanding competitiveness of the leading Japanese firms derives in no small part from their relations with subcontractors that work closely with the industrial corporations to research, design, and produce components (Smitka 1991). These groupings of firms, called *keiretsu*, are widely seen as a cornerstone of Japan's industrial strength. Tokyo's suburban ward of Ota-ku,[6] for example, is home to 6,000 manufacturing firms specializing in machinery and metal working. These firms serve as subcontractors to larger firms (Fujita and Hill 2005). Orders that individual contractors cannot fill are farmed out to neighboring firms. This strategy has resulted in a cross-hatching of vertical (from the larger firms) and horizontal (among subcontractors themselves) subcontracting arrangements. Many of the small factories in Ota-ku were established by entrepreneurs during the 1960s when the Japanese economy was taking off. Of all the new start-ups between 1960 and 1985, 90 percent were in the machine tools sector. Ota-ku is the only place in Japan where the entire process of making an industrial machine can be done in one area. Many of these establishments specialize in few processes in which they excel,

5. Also, Tokyo is where the majority of foreign firms prefer to locate. About 60 percent of the offices of foreign firms are in the Tokyo area (Bureau of Industrial and Labor Affairs 2005).

6. Ota-ku is a rather small ward, with a land area of only 54 square kilometers, about one-fortieth of Tokyo's total area. During the Edo period, the area specialized in agricultural products and fishing supplies. Only in the 1920s and 1930s did manufacturing industry start to take root in Ota-ku. This development can be traced to the expansion of manufacturing activities outward from other areas in Tokyo and Yokohama and the rapid increase in military procurement. Although much of Ota-ku was destroyed during the Allied bombing of Tokyo, the factories were rebuilt during the special procurement for the Korean War and with the reclamation of Tokyo Bay to isolate often-polluting factories from the residential districts (Whittaker 1997).

although they do take orders that may be outside of their expertise to broaden their capabilities and to supplement their own line of business (Whittaker 1997).

The urban labor market is a third building block. Tokyo's market is vast and richly supplied with skills, which makes it hugely attractive for business firms, especially in the high-tech and creative industries. This market in turn is fed from the natural growth of the population and by immigrants from other parts of Japan plus a small number from abroad. The skills the workers bring with them depend on a host of teaching institutions and training received on the job.[7] Many of Japan's leading public and private universities are located in Tokyo, and aside from their critical role in educating the workforce, these institutions are a source of innovation and technology transfer through their research, their consulting, and the informal contacts between faculties and business entities (Jiang and Harayama 2005; F. Kodama and Suzuki 2005; T. Kodama 2005).[8] As Japanese industry becomes more capital and technology intensive, the quality and variety of skills available through the urban labor market are becoming an important determinant of how industrial capability evolves, how reliably it supports industrial competitiveness across a spectrum of activities, and how economically resilient the Tokyo region remains.[9]

The fourth component comprises the several levels of government—central, prefectural, and municipal—whose regulatory hand grasps, or at least grazes, most major and many minor elements of the urban economy. No doubt the regulatory hand is less obtrusive than in the past, but the reach of government regulation remains pervasive and the influence of policy and of institutions is palpable at the macro level and often extends all the way to the most micro passageways of business.[10] Government policy strongly influences both urban development and industrial change in the Tokyo region.

The fifth and final component is the buying public itself. The front rank of consumers of the products and services produced by Tokyo's

7. In Japan, with its long tradition of tenured employment for the core labor force of the larger firms, the main source of firm-specific skills is on-the-job training and formal training by the firm, which expects to retain most of its workers.

8. University-industry linkages are discussed in more detail by Jiang and Harayama (2005) and F. Kodama and Suzuki (2005).

9. Glaeser (2005a) attributes the recovery of Boston's economy in the 1980s and the performance since then to the supply of skills from local universities and the stock of skilled workers in the area.

10. The regulatory guiding hand has acquired a lighter touch since the late 1980s, but the Japanese state still extensively governs the market and guides economic activity (see Carlile and Tilton 2005; Lincoln 2001).

businesses are well-to-do and discriminating buyers with a keen eye for novelty, quality, and design. Even firms that market their products globally and perhaps sell the bulk of what they manufacture abroad still find that a product's reception in the domestic market can be a good indicator of wider success. Moreover, the 28 million–strong consumers in the Tokyo metropolitan area not only provide a highly lucrative market but also are a source of valuable customer feedback that enables companies to modify, improve, or simply weed out new product offerings. In addition, these consumers lend the impetus for customizing of products that is opening not only new opportunities for mass customization but also incentives for cultivating niche tastes that can prove far more financially rewarding if pursued through effective e-marketing. By putting these five elements together, we can view the dynamics of the Tokyo economy and see where postindustrialism is leading.

Having a foothold of some kind in Tokyo is advantageous for business firms, especially the larger ones. This factor explains why so many corporations have located their headquarters in Tokyo and why they continue trickling in from other major cities, such as Osaka and Kyoto. Firms might want to place their headquarters in Tokyo for many reasons. Tokyo is the principal metropolitan market and clearly the trendsetter for the rest of the country. Frequent formal as well as informal contacts with the central government's regulatory agencies are viewed as desirable and beneficial by both the business community and officialdom. Proximity to public agencies reduces transaction costs. Tokyo is also at a crossroads for the global economy. For firms that are thinking strategically and looking beyond the confines of the Japanese market, Tokyo is the appropriate international gateway.

Although company head offices have gravitated to Tokyo to be near key government agencies and knowledge-intensive business services, as well as to benefit from the readier availability of qualified personnel, their presence contributes to the knowledge intensity of the urban economy. The modern MNC is a highly complex organism that places heavy demands on the head office to gather, process, and disseminate information with reference to an overall strategy. In fulfilling all those functions, head offices are a major force in the urban system that feed off information streaming in from local and international sources while injecting high-value information of their own into the system. They also have the budgets and authority to sustain numerous well-paid jobs.[11]

11. See Jakobsen and Onsager's (2005) analysis of the head offices of Norwegian companies.

As more and more firms locate their headquarters in Tokyo, the pressure on others to join them has intensified. It is not just a matter of image. Proximity facilitates face-to-face communication, both casual and formal, as well as decision making. Socializing after hours and a regular round of golf with a business partner or competitor cement business and personal relationships. To a greater degree than in the West, the restaurant and the golf course are an integral part of the space in which business is consummated. Furthermore, the agglomeration of headquarters draws in its wake numerous other service providers, creating clusters that deliver gains in efficiency for the users and positive spillovers for the participating firms. Firms providing marketing, advertising, and legal and accounting services all have tended to colocate with the major MNCs.

Tokyo's water trade (*mizushobai*) is rightly famous. This subculture of entertainment emerged in the 18th century, when Edo, as Tokyo was then called, was Japan's military capital and home to thousands of samurai and their retainers.[12] Kabuki theater flourished, as did other common and exotic forms of revelry (Screech 1999). The water trade covers a vast archipelago of bars, eateries, cabarets, and clubs in Shinjuku, Shibuya, and Roppongi—ranging from the tiny to the cavernous—and in its recesses are multiple echoes from the past. "In the bustle and color of a few water trade quarters in Tokyo," writes Morley (1985, 189), "one could still for a brief moment enjoy the illusion of standing on a street in Edo." Through its multiple surfaces and enduring underlying codes, the water trade has enabled a vital current of Tokyo's life to maintain "constancy despite change, permanence despite vicissitudes of individual fate" (Morley 1985, 190). For all these reasons, Tokyo continues to exert a pull on companies despite the higher congestion and overhead costs of locating there.

Agglomeration of corporate research facilities has paralleled the coalescence of headquarters. The presence in the Tokyo metropolitan area of many of Japan's leading universities and research institutes has only reinforced the incentives for companies that depend on innovation to remain competitive.[13] The Tokyo area has a comparative advantage in research that feeds into the export of services as well as of technology-intensive

12. The concentration of daimyo and their retainers in Edo was mandated from 1622 onward under the *sankinkotai* (alternate attendance system). This system required the daimyo to keep their families in Edo as hostages and to come to Edo in alternate years to pay homage to the shogun (Jansen 2000). On the Edo of the 17th and 18th centuries, see Nouët (1990).

13. Seventeen percent of universities (both public and private) are located in Tokyo, as are one-fourth of undergraduate students, 26 percent of graduate students, and 27 percent of faculties (MEXT 2004).

goods.[14] With research, the gains from proximity to leading institutes and universities are, if anything, greater. Institutes and universities are a source of talent and, in many instances, serve as the crucibles within which important basic research is conducted. Moreover, highly skilled knowledge workers are drawn to the open, cosmopolitan, and culturally rich environment that Tokyo provides—the same environment that is conducive to making informal contacts and transacting business. For these reasons, many of Japan's technology-intensive companies have preferred to keep some of their leading research facilities in the metropolitan area, and they have been joined by other companies in search of deep labor markets for scientific and engineering skills. Although much of the applied research with commercial potential is conducted in corporate research labs, universities are the training grounds for researchers and are active on the frontiers of key research fields. Furthermore, university professors provide consulting services and serve as the nodes for informal research networks, mentoring the work of their former students, coauthoring papers with corporate researchers, and serving as gatekeepers for the filtering and circulation of knowledge (F. Kodama and Suzuki 2005).

It is becoming evident that, even though the Internet has dramatically telescoped distance, the latest scientific knowledge has an important tacit dimension. It diffuses slowly and then mainly through word of mouth among members of close-knit and highly specialized communities of knowledge workers who are in frequent contact with one another through conferences and informal meetings.[15]

Other advantages accrue from concentrating research activities in the Tokyo area. They derive from the multifaceted nature of the most significant technological advances. Whether it is in automobiles, consumer electronics, medical devices and implants, or food processing, innovation more often than not entails a coordinated step forward straddling several

14. See Kiyota (2005) on the research context of Japan's trade in services.

15. A number of studies have explicitly looked at the distance that knowledge travels through different channels. A study by James Adams (2002) finds that knowledge transfers from universities tend to be concentrated within 200 miles. However, the distance of technology transfer seems to be affected by both the quality of university research and the size and sophistication of research and development activities of firms. The larger and more sophisticated research and development facilities tend to cooperate with universities farther away, and they are willing to tap universities even though these institutions might be located 900 miles away or more on average. A study in the Netherlands shows a much shorter distance of 40 kilometers for technology transfer from universities (van der Panne 2005), and for Poland, a study shows only 25 kilometers for the knowledge spillovers from foreign direct investment (Halpern and Murakozy 2005). When technology diffusion is viewed as a global phenomenon, the half-life distance is about 1,200 kilometers (Keller 2002).

disciplines. Electronics and software are embedded in many automobile components and, in fact, account for close to one-third of the value of a sedan. Among the most profitable technological advances are navigation systems, in which Japanese companies have a lead.[16] Implants such as heart pacemakers and insulin pumps combine the expertise of medical specialists with that of engineers and scientists working on materials and electronics. Being able to tap such diverse fields of scientific knowledge and production experience, which no single corporation or research center can easily marshal, is a great advantage. In the Tokyo metropolitan area, locating the technical skills to fulfill myriad requirements is relatively easy, as is finding firms that are able to design, produce prototypes, and manufacture an extraordinarily wide variety of components and complete products. The environment is ideal for routinized innovation because so many more new ideas can be realized in a tangible form, tinkered with, tested, refined, and then marketed to Tokyo's affluent consumers and dynamic firms.

As a marketplace, Tokyo has distinctive attributes that distinguish it from other Japanese cities. First are the sheer size and the average level of household income. On both counts, Tokyo definitely holds the edge, and year by year since the 1970s, the margin in Tokyo's favor has widened. Second, Tokyo has for more than a century "combined East and West, past and present" with style and verve, which has sharpened the sophistication of consumers (Richie 1992, 68).

Beyond that, Tokyo's consumers are unusually willing to push the boundaries of fashion, to expand the range of wants by seizing on a product, and to initiate the buzz that starts a trend or launches a new fad. For clothing, accessories, and electronic consumer products, Tokyo is the mecca for shoppers looking for the latest fashions and technologies and, by the same token, for producers waiting to try out their latest offering. Harajuku, Shibuya, and Aoyama are where Tokyo's young and well-heeled consumers congregate, sample the newest fashions in clothing and accessories, and pass judgment. For instance, Shibuya station, where six different train lines meet, caters to 2.2 million passengers per day and has more than 900 retail stores within the train station itself, with close to 600 restaurants and bars just outside the train station (Fujita and Hill 2005).[17]

16. The demand for car navigation systems in Japan is high, especially in Tokyo because the city contains many winding and curved roads without any logical naming system. It is quite different from cities in the United States or Beijing that are laid out the form of a grid.

17. Most of Tokyo's 23 districts blossomed around these major rail and metro stations. By generating traffic, the intersection of several lines triggered retail, commercial, and residential development. Shinjuku station is the busiest station in Japan with 3.5 million people using the station every day (http://www.city.shinjuku.tokyo.jp/about/about_tokei.html).

Ten percent of all electronics sales and a rising volume of sales of video games and software in Japan occur in Akihabara, which has come to be known as "Electric Town."[18] The strength of this district lies in its wide product offerings, ranging from the newest finished product to the smallest parts imaginable, such as transistors and even vacuum tubes (Fujita and Hill 2005). Until 1995, more than 50 percent of all personal computers sold in Japan were through Akihabara. This sprawling electronics bazaar is where a vast array of products and components jostle for attention and where the pioneering shoppers—the ones who are willing to experiment with new products and to pay premium prices—play a decisive role. Producers need these intensively competitive and demanding markets that give them rapid and valuable feedback. Akihabara, for example, is a vital part of the innovation system for electronic products, such as digital cameras and now video games, which are the lifeblood of the Japanese electronics industry.

The success of many innovations can be traced to the interaction between producers and customers that leads to the refinement of a product or substantial modification to suit latent or engendered wants. The so-called antennae markets of Tokyo provide firms with intelligence on which products are likely to succeed and what modifications could further improve the prospects of a commodity or a service. Japanese culture, the fads propagated by Japanese teenagers congregating along Takeshita Street in Harajuku and Omote-Sando Avenue in Aoyama,[19] and the choices of electronics aficionados now have a global appeal, so Tokyo is an important site for the initial "soft launch" and the debugging of a product. By colocating headquarters, research, production, and marketing in the Tokyo area, a company can stimulate innovation and accelerate the commercialization of the more promising products that emerge from the research labs. If an item commands a broad following in Tokyo, it can be aimed at other markets.

The prolonged stagnation of the Japanese economy during the 1990s—the lost decade—has led to a hollowing out of industry and has raised questions about Tokyo's future. Can this complex system be sustained as other cities, particularly in China, broaden their appeal; as the Chinese economy pulls abreast of and overtakes Japan's; as more and more Japanese companies shift their production to other parts of East Asia; and as the

18. Akihabara is also becoming a "ghetto for geeks." The *otaku*, or nerds, have begun congregating there in even larger numbers looking for role-playing games, Japanese animation, and *manga* comics ("In Tokyo" 2005).

19. Harajuku became associated with avant-garde fashion following the 1964 Olympics in Tokyo.

composition of Tokyo's population tilts toward older age groups? The answer depends on the dynamism of certain established industries, such as robotics and animation, which are sensing opportunities but must move quickly to grasp them. Little doubt exists that Tokyo must be prepared for a long spell of creative destruction. Continuing global dominance by Tokyo's existing industries requires combining innovativeness with continuous refining of manufacturing capability in core areas, inspired design, and the honing of marketing skills. Firms such as Sony, Canon, Matsushita, Fanuc, and others are struggling to find a viable mix of those ingredients and the lean organizational form to support it. Not all of the current stable of industries will survive; to fill the gaps left by the ones that exit, existing business will need to expand, and new industries will need to arise. They will define Tokyo's economic future.

SINGAPORE

In the 14th century, the kingdom of Majaphit occupied the island of Temasek and renamed it Singapore (from the Malaysian terms for lion city). This island remained a vassal of the kingdom of Malacca until early in the 16th century, after which it dwindled into a meeting place for pirates and other human flotsam or *orang laut* (sea people) (Rowe 2005). Sir Stamford Raffles, the former governor of Java and Sumatra, ended and reversed Singapore's downslide when he seized on its strategic importance to establish a British trading station in January 1819. He anticipated that the station's location would have a high payoff. Raffles was right. By 1869, the opening of the Suez Canal dramatically compressed the duration of voyages to Europe while the spread of tin mining and the plantation-based production of rubber in Singapore's immediate hinterland led to the rapid growth of trade in those two staples. As traffic through Singapore's port expanded, it pulled in other entrepôt trade from around the region, and the island became a magnet to immigrants, mainly from China but also from India. According to a European observer, Singapore in 1879 had the "air of a Chinese town with a foreign settlement" (Huff 1994, 25). A half-century later, Singapore was home to the largest concentration of overseas Chinese. Their energy and commercial skills multiplied Singapore's network of trading links with other parts of the region and consolidated its role as Southeast Asia's leading entrepôt.

When the British withdrew from their colonial possessions in the Malayan peninsula in 1959, they placed Singapore, which had already been separated from Malaya in 1946, on the road to its present status by incorporating it as the self-governing state of Singapore. Four years later, on September 16, 1963, the city-state became part of the Federation of Malaysia, following prolonged behind-the-scenes negotiations involving Tunku Abdul Rahman, the Malaysian premier; the British colonial office, which had earlier formulated a "grand design" for the region; Lee Kuan Yew, the young leader of the fledgling state; and the leaders of Sarawak, North Borneo, and Brunei Darussalam (K. Lee 2000). This marriage soon dissolved; however, it and the political currents buffeting Singapore's relations with Malaysia exerted a significant formative influence on the political economy of the city.

Today, Singapore, in its own tropical air-conditioned way, is as neat and orderly as Tokyo. The city-state self-consciously pursues creative destruction with the government at the forefront of the process, but unlike Tokyo, Singapore has fewer industrial options, and creative dynamism is an objective that has remained tantalizingly beyond the reach of its technocratic policies. Still, Singapore's brief economic history is little short of spectacular, and unlike other cities in East Asia, the city-state is planning carefully for the postindustrial future. In just 40 years, Singapore has emerged as one of the world's most affluent countries, with a per capita GDP of US$25,000. By comparison, when the island-state separated from the Federation of Malaysia in 1965, average incomes were a meager US$2,675 (constant 2000 U.S. dollars), and with an adult literacy rate of about 50 percent, the newly independent nation appeared to have few prospects (C. Chang 1976). Perceiving the enormity of the challenge, Lee Kuan Yew initially despaired, but then under his leadership, the People's Action Party moved quickly to improve the human resources and exploit the locational advantages of Singapore. By dint of inventive and forward-looking economic policies and a single-minded commitment to economic progress, the Singapore government invested heavily in education, devised schemes to maximize the level of individual savings by expanding the Central Provident Fund,[20] modernized transport and urban infrastructure, offered attractive fiscal incentives, and made an all-out bid to attract foreign direct investment (FDI) that would create jobs and transfer technology. Faced with few competitors in the early 1970s, Singapore found that its recipe succeeded beyond all expectations. Political stability and the government's commitment to export-led growth based on manufacturing industry brought in foreign companies seeking production platforms in

20. Those schemes required compulsory monthly contributions by each employee and employer (S. Lee 1976).

Southeast Asia. Singapore's tax benefits, increasingly efficient port facilities, and location in the Straits of Malacca further compounded the advantages of what became a literate, disciplined, English-speaking workforce.[21]

By efficiently implementing education and training policies that augmented the supply of skills, by carefully carpentering the institutions of a market economy, by investing strategically in logistics infrastructure—the software as well as the hardware—to keep pace with emerging technologies, and by implementing a multitude of actions aimed at improving the business climate, Singapore's economic managers induced real GDP to grow by an average rate of 8 percent between 1970 and 1990. By then, Singapore's economic credentials, prosperity, and reputation as a leading business center in East Asia were firmly established. Moreover, starting in the latter half of the 1980s, Singapore had begun leveraging its expanding base of skills—local and imported—to diversify into products and services in which the domestic value added was higher, by implementing measures to raise labor costs and by aggressively seeking FDI in high-tech industry. Manufacture of fashion garments displaced that of cheaper textiles, and the research, design, manufacture, and testing of parts for hard disk drives (of which Singapore was the world's largest producer in 2005) as well as of audio components began edging out the assembly of televisions and small consumer electronic products (McKendrick, Doner, and Haggard 2000). Singapore-based builders began specializing in oil rigs, of which the island-state is now the largest producer, and petroleum refining expanded, pushing Singapore to third place in the international lineup ("Singapore: Reform Needed" 2005). Singapore also began developing a market for financial and other producer services, following in the footsteps of Hong Kong (China). Such diversification, directed by the government's industrial and technology policies, has allowed Singapore to maintain its growth momentum through the early years of the 21st century, with only a brief hiatus in the immediate aftermath of the East Asian crisis of 1997–98. Nearly 40 years after its precarious beginnings, Singapore has an urban economic system that is among the most competitive in the Southeast Asian region.

21. The port facility was inherited from the colonial era, when Singapore served as the hub of the regional entrepôt trade and was a major base for the British fleet. The British defense umbrella was finally withdrawn in 1971. Today, the port of Singapore is considered one of the most efficient, if not the most efficient, and it is subject to lowest political risk in the Southeast Asian region (Tsai and Su 2005).

Singapore is not a megacity or a world city,[22] but it is certainly one of the leading global cities. Singapore has a fraction of the population of a Jakarta or a Bangkok or a Shanghai, but its GDP greatly exceeds those of the first two and still is ahead of Shanghai's. Singapore illustrates how an industrial strategy pursued single-mindedly by a strong state with an honest and skillful bureaucracy can achieve remarkable results when complemented by economic openness and an unusually dynamic regional environment. As manufacturing industry begins fleeing Singapore, however, the limits of the earlier strategy are becoming more evident, as are the constraints on Singapore's future growth.

Singapore's locational advantages are being whittled down by four changes, although it was the world's second busiest container port in 2005 after Hong Kong (China), with a throughput of 23 million 20-foot equivalent units (TEUs) ("How Hong Kong Stays King" 2006). First, competing ports and airports have emerged in nearby Malaysia that are almost equal in efficiency and that offer lower prices. Tanjung Pelepas, just a hundred miles to the north, quotes loading and unloading rates for containers that are two-thirds of those charged by Singapore's port authority.[23] Second, dramatic improvements in the efficiency of container ports and airports, some of them spearheaded by Singapore, have reduced the share of logistics cost in the prices of final goods; hence further reductions in handling and facilitation charges confer less advantage. Third, East Asia's economic center of gravity has shifted northward, partly because of China's ascendance and partly because Singapore is deriving less of a boost from the two largest economies in the neighborhood and facing sterner competition from Malaysia. Indonesia has lost some of its economic luster and is growing more slowly. The economy of the Philippines, while continuing to drift forward, has never been—and shows no signs of becoming—a driving force in the region. Thus, Singapore's immediate hinterland is less supportive to the development of the city-state than it used to be in terms of demand for services and manufactures. Down the road, India could become a thriving market, but by the same token, as we discuss in chapter 4, Indian industries and cities will also compete against Singapore.

---

22. Singapore is highly connected to other cities and is positioned as a regional command center with sufficient financial service presence (P. Taylor and others 2002).

23. For instance, two leading shipping firms, Evergreen and Maersk, have shifted their operations to the port of Tanjung Pelepas from Singapore, a move that worried the Singaporean authorities, who were concerned about Singapore's future as a leading port city (Tan and Phang 2005).

Fourth and finally, tight management of the economy and society succeeded all too well in curbing population growth and any vestiges of unruly social behavior and provided stable employment for the majority of workers. The price of this success is a nearly static and aging population that is notoriously risk averse. Singapore needs entrepreneurs with a nose for innovative products and the knack for thriving in the global marketplace. Singapore needs researchers who will challenge "normal" science and associate Singapore's name with creative products. Instead, it has a superabundance of able technocrats with lofty ambitions and disciplined managers who, in a civilized environment, have achieved remarkable results.

State-of-the-art services and urban infrastructure have served Singapore well. Combined with an efficient regulatory environment and low taxes, they have been a big draw for businesses seeking an attractive urban locale for their regional headquarters. Tourists, mainly from nearby Asian countries, are enticed by Singapore's orderliness, but only for a brief stay—60 percent stay for two days or less. By maintaining standards of services and continuously modernizing the infrastructure, Singapore could hold onto the headquarters business and the tourist trade.[24] Yet other cities are catching up fast, offering health and education services of nearly equivalent quality at lower prices and a relatively crime-free environment, all of which attract corporate headquarters. Cities such as Bangkok and Shanghai also provide a far more vibrant urban milieu, a business culture that encourages greater initiative, and a bustling economic hinterland.

Singapore's openness to trade is increasingly being matched by its competitors as multilateral and regional free trade agreements dismantle barriers in Asia. Other cities have made less progress, however, in paring transaction costs for businesses. In this respect, Singapore retains a lead, which it is attempting to widen by introducing procedures that make it easier to harness user-friendly e-government. In fact, the quality of governance remains one of Singapore's most enduring attractions, which, for many foreign corporations, partially offsets the higher cost of operating in the city-state.

Singapore's own leaders and many observers believe that Singapore's future depends on the quality and innovativeness of the workforce. All of the factors noted previously will contribute, even though Singapore no longer enjoys a commanding lead in transport infrastructure or in the

24. With the legalization of gambling casinos, Singapore hopes to enlarge its clientele of visitors and induce them to stay longer.

degree of openness or with respect to the social environment. India is overtaking Singapore in certain services and Internet sales; even Creative Technology, Singapore's own world-renowned producer of sound cards, is moving production to China. Human capital, however, is what will tip the scale in favor of continuing robust economic performance. Although much of its workforce is likely to be homegrown, Singapore probably cannot avoid becoming more reliant on foreign talent. This human capital will drive technological change and productivity in new industries such as biotechnology. Because of Singapore's size and the nature of its hinterland, the future of the city-state rests with industries that do not depend on scale economies to be profitable and on niche activities that leverage technology and design. Unlike Tokyo, Singapore does not have the springboard of an innovation system anchored in world-class corporations or a many-faceted manufacturing capability. Singapore has cultivated efficiency to good effect; now it must complement that efficiency with innovativeness that results in sustained commercial success.

BANGKOK

Where Singapore is compact, gleaming, and meticulously regulated, Bangkok, a thousand miles to the north, is sprawling, congested, untidy, and more laissez-faire. Bangkok's modern face began to emerge only in the latter part of the 20th century. It was a village in the 16th century, which was designated the capital in 1782.[25] Late in the 19th century, Bangkok was a small administrative and trading center crisscrossed by canals.[26] Sampans and ox carts were the principal modes of conveyance. Although Bangkok was a cosmopolitan city with a large Chinese and Southeast Asian population and significant commercial links with other parts of East Asia (Askew 2002), expatriates compared it unfavorably to Singapore as well as Hong Kong and Shanghai in China.

By the middle of the 20th century, Bangkok's population was in the region of 1 million, but topographically the city had changed little from the compact, horizontal, luxuriantly tropical place of 50 years earlier, with the canal system and floating markets still largely intact. Since then, motorization and the associated construction of roads have erased this feature of

25. The name Bangkok denotes the water hamlet of the wild plum tree (Askew 2002).

26. The ubiquitous canals, which owe their existence to state and local initiative, assisted commerce, irrigation, and transport of troops for defense (Askew 2002).

the city and have permitted the emergence of a sprawling suburbanized structure that urban planners anticipated in the 1960s and sought to minimize. More recently, elevated expressways have tightened the grip of the automobile, worsened air pollution, and further subtracted from the remaining charm of the downtown areas—even though only 6 to 7 percent of the Bangkok metropolitan area (BMA) is devoted to roads and parking and a costly mass transit system is now in operation.[27] A few small lush islands from the past remain, but the green and graceful city in old pictures is no more. As Van Beek (1999, 120) observes, "The city skyline has changed dramatically, with sacred spires dwarfed by secular towers of commerce. Look east from the Golden Mount across the rooftops of the old city and see a jagged mountain range of skyscrapers, a transformation reflecting a philosophical shift in values."

Ever since export-oriented industrialization commenced in the mid-1980s, the BMA, aside from being Thailand's administrative center, has become the nation's economic heartland. Bangkok's somewhat chaotic growth over the past three decades amply reflects the dramatic industrialization of the Thai economy and the relatively localized ambit of industrial change in Thailand. Close to a third of Thailand's GDP is produced in the BMA and to a large extent consumed by Thailand's affluent middle class, which has congregated in the city. Much of the FDI that has flowed into the automotive sector (particularly in the Eastern Seaboard Industrial Estate) (D. Webster 2004) and electronic firms (in Ayutthaya) to produce components is concentrated in the corridor extending from Bangkok to the Eastern Seaboard.

But change is in the air. Efforts by the government to disperse industry, coupled with congestion in the BMA, are inducing firms to move to the fringes of the Bangkok metropolitan region (BMR) and beyond. However, the advantages of industrial agglomeration are such that firms often choose to remain and many that relocate do not go far. Bangkok also gains from the abundance of social and cultural amenities that have accumulated over the years and reinforced the city's distinctiveness. No other urban center in Thailand comes close, and the gap is not narrowing. In line with trends elsewhere in East Asia, where the major cities are the principal destinations of foreign investment, Bangkok's amenities, as well

27. The BMA is nested within the much larger Bangkok metro region (with an area of 1,569 square kilometers), which consists of the BMA and five adjacent provinces: Nakon Pathom, Nonthaburi, Pathum Thani, Samut Prakarn, and Samut Sakhon (Overseas Economic Cooperation Fund 1996; D. Webster 2004).

as its cultural openness and excellent air transport links with the rest of the world,[28] have attracted FDI to the BMR together with more than 800,000 expatriate workers. These flows contribute to the clustering of industrial activity because suppliers of components and services follow the foreign investors (as, for example, in the case of the Japanese auto industry), creating a snowball effect that then pulls in other investment—private as well as public—in infrastructure and supporting services.[29]

The BMR has a high concentration of manufacturing industry; in the periurban areas of the BMA, 63 percent of the gross product is derived from manufacturing.[30] Much of it is medium- or low-technology industry. In the higher-tech, export industries, the domestic value added is typically low. For instance, Bangkok has not challenged Singapore in the research, prototyping, and testing of hard drives, and it is facing tough competition from China in the production and assembly of the latest generation of electronic products. If future prosperity depends on adding greater value in manufacturing and services, Bangkok's innovation system is clearly not yet in a position to deliver results.

The BMA's longer-term industrial prospects are much less clear if manufacturing activities relocate to the neighboring provinces. Moreover, the limited evidence available suggests that the economic space created by their departure may not be filled on a sufficient scale by high–value adding producer services as has happened in some other megacities in East Asia. For example, the financial, accounting, and legal services providers are expanding to meet the needs of local industry, but Bangkok is a long way from becoming a regional provider of business services and will face severe competition from Singapore and Hong Kong (China), which also have a head start in enhancing the English-language skills of the workforce and in attracting multinational service providers. However, Bangkok does compete with Singapore and Hong Kong (China) in the aviation, media, and advertising industries that have flocked to Bangkok and account for much of the growth of the commercial sector's considerable success in this area (Muller 2005). Although tertiary-level education and technical institutions have multiplied, the level and quality of skills imparted still lag.

28. By 2005, Bangkok was the principal air transport hub in Southeast Asia, having edged out Singapore.

29. See Takayasu and Mori (2004) on Japanese FDI in the Thai auto industry and the pattern of such contracting.

30. For the BMR as a whole, manufacturing accounted for 27 percent of GDP in 1990 (Overseas Economic Cooperation Fund 1996).

Economic change in Bangkok might follow a different path with the formation of a number of industrial and services clusters catering to multiple, relatively narrow niches of several regional or global markets, the so-called long-tail markets (Anderson 2006). Among the industries that could buttress Bangkok's future economic performance, four deserve special attention, because together they could differentiate the city from others in the region and keep alive its economic momentum.

Production of natural fiber-based luxury garments is a traditional industry that could grow on a substantial scale. The beginnings of such an industry already exist, grounded in Thai silk weaving, but a luxury goods industry requires, aside from the quality of materials, distinctive designs and branding. Developing local design capacity is a necessary first step. Initially design could be outsourced, but for the luxury garments and accessories industries to take root in Bangkok, the skills need to be deepened. Local designers need to work closely with craftspeople and weavers to produce items with a strong global or regional appeal. A fruitful interplay of locally sourced materials, local skills, and design could be the basis for Thai luxury brands that are able to command premium prices in international markets. The Jim Thompson brand, with its chain of stores, although American owned, is a step toward creating a niche for Thai materials and garments, but Thompson has yet to acquire significant name recognition much beyond Thailand and its immediate neighbors, unlike the French and Italian brands. The opportunity is now at hand for Thai producers to create and market products with a broad appeal that endures. The international luxury brands are already putting their bets on the name-brand-conscious shoppers, who are multiplying in East Asia. Like Milan in Italy, Bangkok could aim at becoming a center of that industry and the focus of intersecting clusters that produce materials as well as some specialized manufacturing equipment in close coordination with designers and a global marketing industry.

Jewelry is a related industry that is centered on Bangkok. It has a long history and origins in the mining of gemstones in Thailand as well as some of the neighboring countries.[31] Over time, Thailand has acquired skills in the heat treating of gemstones; sorting, cutting, and marketing of stones; metal fabrication; and design that is unique to the region. As with the jewelry business in other cities, such as New York, Antwerp, Tel Aviv, and Mumbai, jewelry firms are family owned; the business depends on the

31. Earlier, the Bangkok jewelry business was dominated by ethnic groups from the Indian subcontinent, but ownership is now more diversified (Askew 2002).

bonds of trust among a close-knit group of participants, and most firms are clustered in a couple of neighborhoods in the metropolitan area. The jewelry business thrives in Thailand, but Thai styles and brand names are barely known in the region and have made no impression at all on Western markets despite substantial exports and the massive number of visitors who have been exposed to the offerings of the industry. The weakness, as with the garments, might well be in the design, which caters to the local market but has not caught global attention. Unlike H. Stern from Brazil, no Thai firm has attempted either to design for a rich international clientele or to market its jewelry in the Fifth Avenues of the world's major cities. Thai design is not yet associated with exclusivity for which people might pay premium prices. Yet both garments and jewelry have the potential to move upscale and to serve as the foundations of a luxury goods sector such as that which, for example, buttresses the prosperity of Paris (Scott 2000b).

Tourism is an industry that, with the right policies, has a bright future. It is not so much an urban cluster as a set of complementary services that cover parts of the city. Between 1990 and 2004, the number of international visitors to Bangkok rose from 3.5 million to 7 million. The importance of this industry, which is a large employer and supports 94 registered hotels, could increase. Although transport and hotel services producers are at the forefront of beneficiaries, many other providers, such as restaurants and myriad retail establishments, benefit from tourist spending. A significant slice of Bangkok's GDP, perhaps as much as 5 percent, is likely to derive from these interlocking activities. Currently, however, the average visitor spends fewer than two days in Bangkok, even when the average length of stay in Thailand is eight days. Much depends on investments that enhance the attractions of Bangkok for the long-staying, the high-spending tourist or convention participant or the "medical" tourist.[32] The quality and efficiency of the hotel infrastructure is only a part of the investment. For example, the Banyan Tree chain is one example of an indigenous upscale hotel business emphasizing the luxurious spa experience that is spreading throughout East Asia. Developing neighborhoods or nearby sites for tourists to visit will be equally important, as will be the quality of the urban environment.

32. Bangkok was able to take advantage of the higher cost of medical services in Singapore and offer such procedures as heart bypass operations, cosmetic surgery, and chemotherapy at significantly lower rates ("Glow in the Dark" 2005; Tan and Phang 2005). For instance, one-third of patients at Bumrungrad Hospital are foreigners, contributing 42 percent of the revenues ("Foreign Patients" 2005).

If one Thai product has won widespread acclaim, it is the cuisine. Because Thai migrants diffused less widely than Chinese, or even Japanese, the cuisine is not as well known, but it has a secure foothold in Western countries and in developing regions as well. Not surprisingly, therefore, the Thai food-processing industry is the fourth candidate on our list of subsectors with long-term potential in the Bangkok metropolitan economy. Thailand is already a significant exporter of rice, fruit, meat, feed, and processed foods. CP, one of the leading firms in the country, started out in the foodstuffs sector and thereafter diversified. CP and other Thai firms are integrated into global agribusiness networks, and the export of processed and semiprocessed foodstuffs earns US$10 billion annually (USDA 2003).[33] Processed foodstuff is a growth industry with stable prospects. It is research and marketing intensive, and it promises significant local value added in both manufacturing and services. Moreover, food processing and agro industries are relatively labor intensive and hospitable to a mix of firms, especially small firms.[34] These industries have a limited footprint, but they can be the basis for expansion, particularly through investment in research, marketing, equipment, and skills. Bangkok is not the place where a food-processing cluster could be revived; instead it is where the upstream work on research, marketing, product development, and testing can be concentrated. The proliferation of schools and programs that offer locals and foreigners training in Thai cuisine is one initiative that could accelerate the globalization of Thai food products and possibly become the basis of Bangkok-based international restaurant chains. French chefs such as Robuchon and Ducasse have begun establishing global chains. Thai chefs could follow this lead by offering the more varied (fusion offerings) and upscale dining experiences already being tested in restaurants in the trendy parts of Bangkok ("They Came" 2006).

In the rush to build electronics and auto industries and create financial hubs, one often forgets that the growth possibilities in some traditional industries are far from exhausted. Those industries support numerous backward and forward links and can catalyze technological development

33. Thailand is not only the largest food exporter in Southeast Asia but also a major global food exporter. Thailand is the largest exporter of frozen shrimp, canned pineapples, and pineapple juice and concentrates; the second-largest exporter of seafood; and one of the top 10 exporters of frozen chicken (USDA 2003).

34. Thailand has more than 10,000 firms in the food-processing industry, and 80 percent of them are small firms (USDA 2005).

in a number of areas. The luxury goods sector, composed of jewelry and fashion garments, which we examine in chapter 7, has the potential of becoming a leading sector for the BMA economy.

SEOUL

Seoul's strategic location within the transport network of the Korean peninsula has been long recognized. In 1394, the unifying Yi dynasty selected the spot on the Han River as their *seoul*, which is the Korean term for capital city.[35] From then onward, under a succession of rulers, Seoul has remained the leading urban center for the peninsula as a whole, through the early 1940s and since 1945 for the Republic of Korea.

The Korean War, which ended in an uneasy armistice in July 1953, left Seoul in ruins.[36] Virtually the entire physical infrastructure, housing, and commercial real estate had to be reconstructed from scratch—not to mention the industry that has since provided the economic basis for recovery. The Republic of Korea is a charter member of the group of four East Asian Tigers, whose economic achievements since the mid-1960s are the stuff of legend and fill some of the most hopeful chapters in the recent annals of development economics. The Korean "miracle," now entering its fifth decade, can be described with little exaggeration as a miracle that occurred in and around Seoul. Korea's industrialization that transitioned in the latter part of the 1960s and early 1970s into rapid, export-led growth commenced mainly in the capital region. Between 1986 and 1993, the economy of the capital region grew at an average rate of 10.6 percent, whereas national GDP grew by 9.1 percent per year. Thus, the lion's share of Korea's industrial capacity remains concentrated in an area within a 50-mile radius of downtown Seoul.

Despite concerted efforts by successive Korean governments to disperse industry and the population for strategic reasons and in the interest of broader regional development, about one-fifth of the population—nearly 10.5 million people—resides in Seoul city, which also still generates more than one-fifth of the GDP.[37] The capital region housed 22.5 million

35. Another name for Seoul is Hanseong, which denotes a fortified city on the Han River.

36. Close to one-third of all buildings in Seoul were destroyed (Kwon and Kim 2001).

37. For instance, the Korean government implemented the Industrial Placement and Factory Construction Act in 1977 and the Seoul Metropolitan Readjustment Plan in 1984 to discourage new establishments that could intensify the concentration of population in the Seoul area (Shin and Byeon 2001).

people in 2003 and produced almost one-half of the national product (OECD 2005). More important, many of Korea's future growth industries are in Seoul city or its immediate vicinity. Korea's electronics, information technology (IT), multimedia, telecommunications, and embryonic biotechnology industries are all in the capital region, as are the design and development centers for the auto industry. The bulk of Korea's business services have agglomerated in Seoul, not the least because it is Korea's only global city, with a concentration of corporate headquarters, universities, and research facilities. Almost 80 percent of employment is in services, and 87 percent of all businesses are in the services sector (OECD 2005). In 2002, 52 percent of the IT-related firms, the majority of firms in the digital-content subsector, and 41 percent of finance and insurance services were located in Seoul (OECD 2005; Shin and Byeon 2001). And in Inchon, adjacent to Seoul, is Korea's budding free economic zone, which is seeking to become the transport hub for the northeast Asian region.[38]

As household incomes have risen, Seoul's consumer economy has begun resembling that of Tokyo, with a similarly demanding clientele seeking innovative products of high quality. In fact, Seoul is emerging as another Tokyo (Seoul Development Institute and Nomura Research Institute 2003) and as a potential test market for new products of MNCs, in particular high-end technology-based products. One indication of this development is the average shelf life of mobile phone models in Korea, which is approximately 18 months. Yongsan, the largest electronic and electric goods distribution district in Korea, is beginning to resemble Akihabara in Tokyo. Many electronics stores run their online shopping malls in Yongsan, where rapid and valuable feedback on product innovation is listed on a real-time basis. This online interaction between producers and customers, which is becoming a key to the success of many innovations, is unique to Korea because of the high penetration rate of broadband connections. Seoul has one of the nation's highest online shopping rates, with one in five Internet-connected households regularly shopping online. Customer reviews of products are critical and reflect the customers growing expertise. This online feedback from consumers provides firms with information for upgrading and modifying their products.

The Myeongdong district, which attracts 1.5 million to 2 million visitors per day and up to 2.5 million during weekends, is where females in

38. Inside the free economic zone, a new city—Songdo—is being constructed to provide a venue for the corporate headquarters of firms using Inchon's transport facilities.

their teens and 20s congregate. Despite high rents, many fashion houses have their outlets in this area because such outlets serve as antennae to track consumer tastes. Adjacent to Myeongdong are some of the largest upscale department stores, with shops selling luxury-brand goods. A traditional inexpensive market is located in the Namdaemun district.

Locational advantages and a highly dirigiste government industrial policy generated the centripetal forces that induced the clustering of industry in the Seoul region. With the business sector taking its cues from the state and being forcefully motivated by government financial, fiscal, and trade-related incentives, proximity to the center of power inevitably became an advantage. A culture that assigned importance to personal relations and face-to-face contact also encouraged firms to relocate at least their headquarters, if not their production facilities, in Seoul to be close to government agencies, which often micromanaged the development process in the private sphere as much as in the public sphere (Amsden 1989).

When the Korean export phenomenon began gathering momentum, buyers flocked to the country. They came mainly to Seoul because Seoul was Korea's portal to the international economy. Production facilities close to Seoul were easier for foreigners to visit and easier to export from.[39] No doubt the huge Korean and U.S. military presence in and around Seoul provided a much-needed sense of security in a country that maintained a tenuous armed peace with its belligerent neighbor to the north. A side benefit of the militarization of Seoul was that it generated demand for supplies and for services. Defense spending pumped money into Seoul's economy, which was good for business—not to mention the growth of an extensive services economy.

By the end of the 1980s, Seoul had evolved into a leading city with a large and competitive manufacturing sector that generated not only much of the growth but also a broad-based, albeit inefficient, services sector composed in the main of small-scale businesses. Since then, rising wages and overhead costs have combined with the government's regional and environmental policies to bring about an exodus of manufacturing from Seoul city. Some of this industry has dispersed into the fringe metropolitan suburbs, some has moved to other provincial cities, and a small but growing share has now begun moving abroad. Korean FDI is flowing to China, to Southeast Asia, and into the building of automotive plants and

39. Even as recently as 2001, Seoul accounted for nearly 19 percent of total exports, which was down to 13.5 percent in 2004 (OECD 2005).

factories producing electronics in the United States and the countries of the European Union. Because nature—as well as the state—abhors a vacuum, the economic space vacated by manufacturing is being colonized by services drawn by market forces powerfully abetted by policy initiatives of the state. Among them, IT-related, digital content, multimedia, and financial services are the expanding the fastest. They are being actively promoted by the government, which has made Seoul into one of Asia's most wired cities to stimulate demand for IT services.[40] Koreans can use their mobile phones to pay for everything from coffee at cafés and snacks at convenience stores to large purchases at department stores, either in person or online. The Korean version of m-commerce refers to financial transactions taking place on- and offline, via mobile terminals. More than 470,000 locations nationwide will accept m-payments. Users can also use their mobile phones to pay for public transit. They simply scan their mobile phone over the receiver, and the money is debited. In addition, with mobile online banking, users can transfer money through mobile settlement banks in near real-time transactions.

The objective of the government and leading *chaebol* (that is, conglomerates), such as Samsung, LG, and SK, is to strengthen Korea's leadership in electronic components, design technology, and new IT-supported services. Financial services are another objective, and logistics a third. These latter two services are fairly typical sectoral aspirations of major cities in East Asia. However, the question for Seoul, as for as other cities in the region, remains whether sufficient demand will materialize to absorb the potential capacity and whether Seoul's IT-, finance-, and logistics-related activities will fill the gaps left by the retreat of manufacturing.

A number of considerations need to be balanced here. On the positive side is the size and continuing diversity of Seoul's urban economy. Somewhat like Tokyo, Seoul retains the higher-tech ends of the manufacturing sector—in particular, the electronics, multimedia, and telecommunications industries—and it is cultivating the biotech sector. The city is rich in skills, with by far the most dynamic labor market in Korea supplied by the

40. Although Korea is the most wired country in the world, it is also investing heavily in wireless technologies. Telecommunications carriers worldwide have deployed wireless hotspots at popular public venues where laptop users can surf the Internet at high speed. Korean firms are investing in this infrastructure, with K T's NESpot alone offering service at more than 23,000 locations nationwide by the end of 2004. Some 375,000 Koreans subscribe to the service as a US$10 add-on to their wired Internet or mobile phone subscription.

country's leading educational institutions. And virtually all the Korean *chaebol* operate from Seoul. Thus, the advantages of agglomeration are highly concentrated in the Seoul region. Moreover, Korea's status as a major trading economy generates a substantial ready-made demand for logistics services.

Offsetting those apparent advantages is the relative inefficiency of the service sectors in Korea, which have been sheltered not just from international competition but also from FDI. As a result, most services—from banking to wholesaling—are not globally or even regionally competitive. In many instances the operating scale of firms is well below optimal. Some of the leading providers of financial business and IT services are affiliated with the *chaebol*. Although such affiliation provides access to an internal market for capital and skills and can serve as a buffer against unforeseen shocks, the diversified *chaebol* are rarely able to provide their many activities with the strategic focus and the managerial inputs so vital for growth in productivity, innovativeness, and—through those—competitiveness in overseas markets.

By remaining wary of FDI and foreign control over local industry, be it manufacturing, finance, or retailing, Korean industrial firms, banks, accounting firms, wholesalers, and other services providers have also neglected an important channel for the transfer of technology and skills and have limited domestic market competition from this source. Since 1997, however, FDI has begun flowing into the services sector, with Seoul attracting 60 percent of the total (OECD 2005).

Among Beijing, Shanghai, and Tokyo, limited space exists for a fourth mega urban economy offering a similar range of tradable and now increasingly footloose services without the cushion of a large domestic market (OECD 2005, 58). Seoul is not as dependent as Singapore on exports for survival, but more than 70 percent of Seoul's exports are drawn from just the subsectors of electronics (31 percent), textiles (23 percent), and machinery (17 percent). A Seoul that relied mainly on services would need to be as export oriented as it was in the past, and although electronics remains a profitable export, most services do not make the grade as yet. A few promising points of light exist, such as movies and online games, which we discuss in chapter 6, but these industries need to grow and to multiply.

Recognizing that a postindustrial Seoul must explore a broader set of options and that multimedia deserves special attention, the government launched an urban industrial strategy equal in scope to those of Beijing, Shanghai, and Singapore. Three projects are especially noteworthy and have considerable potential: Guro Digital Valley, Digital Media City, and the development of the video games and moviemaking industries. These projects are all part of a scheme to introduce new clusters to the Seoul urban region.

Guro Digital Valley is a new name for the Guro Export Industrial Complex, which in the 1960s and 1970s was the industrial center of Seoul that manufactured electronic components and assembled electric appliances. Since its launch in 1997, Guro Digital Valley is facilitating start-up companies with venture capital. An estimated 3,100 firms employing close to 50,000 workers were housed in the industrial complex in 2005, many specializing in IT and design-related activities. The government plans to further develop the complex into a home for various Internet and software-related start-ups in tandem with Teheran Valley (Gangnam venture town) in southern Seoul.

The Digital Media City project, started in the late 1990s under former mayor Goh Kun, is attempting to make Seoul the high-tech industry's axis. Digital Media City seeks to carefully interweave broadband technologies to spark innovations that could give rise to clusters of high-tech companies. It occupies 570,000 square meters in the 6.6 million square meters of Sang-am Millennium Town.

The *chaebol*, however, are not pursuing complementary strategies that will give a definitive direction to Seoul's development. Although several producers of electronics, such as LG and Samsung, are currently among the world leaders, they are moving some of their production out of the Seoul area to lower-cost sites. More production is sure to follow. The base of high-tech manufacturing in the Seoul region is not sufficiently broad for this process to continue for long without the city's fortunes being affected. Tokyo can derive substantial mileage from a matrix of high-tech industry, research and development (R&D) headquarters' activities, and hundreds of efficient suppliers of state-of-the-art components. Seoul lacks depth and technological expertise in the components industry, a legacy of the *chaebol* tendency to favor vertical integration over subcontracting. Whether in electronics or automobiles, Korea is no match for Japan at the upper end of the technological spectrum or at the lower labor-intensive end for China.

Despite the Korean government's aspiration to be an R&D hub in Asia, Seoul Development Institute and Nomura Research Institute reported that only a very few foreign firms among the top 100 global companies had established an R&D center in Seoul by 2004 (Seoul Development Institute and Nomura Research Institute 2003): Hewlett-Packard, IBM, Intel,

Microsoft, and Siemens.[41] Microsoft's research center in Korea is developing technologies for wireless devices in Seoul, with plans of investing up to US$30 million over the next three years.

Moreover, spinoff companies, whether from universities or the large *chaebols* and MNCs, that can bring a steady flow of new technologies into the Seoul economy are relatively few, although they are heavily concentrated in Seoul. In particular, along with the government policies supporting new "venture firms," 73 percent of all venture firms are concentrated in the Seoul metropolitan area, and 47 percent are located inside Seoul.[42] By districts, the Gangnam area (the southeast part of Seoul) accommodates 57 percent, whereas the southwest part containing Guro Digital Valley houses 21 percent. The Gangnam area offers a state-of-the-art communications infrastructure, has access to convenient transportation networks, and has begun attracting corporate headquarters, which are the major customers.

How many of these new firms will introduce technologies that can command an international market, as distinct from local niche markets, will have an important bearing on Seoul's prospects. The economic future of the urban region will hinge on, for instance, the multimedia firms that are aggressively competing in the national market and establish a firm foothold overseas.

BEIJING

Kublai Khan made Beijing the capital of the Yuan dynasty in the latter half of the 13th century. The city was named Dadu, and the Mongol rulers imposed a spatial orientation and a grid layout with the emperor's palace at the center. Beijing evolved under the Ming and Qing dynasties through the 19th century and then under the short-lived Nationalist regime in the

41. Intel's R&D center in Korea focuses on advanced wireless communications technology, high-quality media coding, and next-generation platforms for content distribution and consumption. Intel has also signed a memorandum of understanding with the Electronics and Telecommunications Research Institute (ETRI). Intel and ETRI have agreed to jointly develop new technologies related to multistream media distribution over home networks, home automation, and next-generation home servers (http://www.intel.com/pressroom/archive/releases/20040308corp.htm). Whether this venture actually links with and reinforces technological advances in Korean high-tech manufacturing is an open question.

42. Much of the venture capital flows into mezzanine-level financing because the Korean venture capital industry is reluctant to support start-ups and is not yet mature enough to provide the necessary coaching, contacts, and managerial assistance (Sohn and Kenney 2005).

first half of the 20th century. In 1948, after a brief siege, the Nationalist general Fu Zuoyi surrendered the city to the People's Liberation Army. Hutchings (2001, 44) writes that "Beijing, its grandeur much faded but its imperial form still essentially intact despite the ravages of revolution, occupation and modernization, quietly received its new ruler."

Regrettably, perhaps, plans devised in the 1940s and in the beginning of the 1950s to keep the graceful old walled city with its many temples[43] intact and to build a new city to the west were shelved. Thus, first the walls and gates of Beijing were removed by the road builders. More slowly, many of the old buildings came down. And now most of the *hutongs* are being erased to make way for another clump of "drab and utilitarian" multistory blocks, definitely more functional but bereft of the cultural trappings that dignified Imperial Beijing (S. Chang 1998). The city that has arisen bears no resemblance to the Imperial Beijing, whose dimensions and texture and flavor can be glimpsed in old, sepia-tinted photographs.

Until well into the 1980s, Beijing remained largely an administrative center with a sizable industrial base. Shougang Steel was the biggest single industrial enterprise. In addition, enterprises produced machinery, textiles and petrochemicals, and food and beverages. The government was the main employer, and the government was responsible for much of the economic activity.

The pulse of change began to quicken from the mid-1990s as China's reform moved into a higher gear, and with the reform came an increasing flow of domestic and foreign investment into consumer electronics and IT. The Ninth Five-Year Plan initiated the privatization of smaller state-owned enterprises and acknowledged the key role of the private sector. It also committed China to actively developing technology-intensive industries by leveraging the domestic innovation system and increased spending on R&D. The former has injected new vigor into industrial change. The latter has provided a new focus for this change.

Beijing will host the Olympic Games in 2008. In preparation for this event, which has become a rite of passage for East Asian cities, Beijing's already rapid urban development is being accelerated further. The growth of housing stock and commercial real estate is expanding at a feverish clip, as is the transportation infrastructure to lessen the congestion caused by an estimated 2.6 million autos (in 2005), projected to reach 3.6 million in 2008 (Wang 2006). An ambitious tree-planting program in Beijing and in Hebei

43. Susan Naquin (2005) provides the most detailed account of the temples of Imperial Beijing and of the vanished urban ambience.

is attempting to partially efface the brown and dusty image of the city and control the sandstorms that sweep across it, and a determined effort is being made to contain pollution by upgrading the stock of cars, which is growing at double-digit rates, and by relocating some factories and regulating others.[44]

Beijing's development now has three sectoral drivers. First and foremost are the services associated with governments, both central and municipal. Second are the producer and other commercial services that have proliferated as Beijing has grown larger and more prosperous and has embraced the market economy. Although China currently has no intention of grooming Beijing to become a financial center, being the capital has given Beijing prominence in the Chinese economy and has attracted foreign banks. As a consequence, Beijing now vies with Shanghai as the preferred location for providers of legal, accounting, advertising, marketing, and consulting services.

Fifteen years ago, Beijing had nothing resembling a central business district; now clusters of glass towers are appearing in parts of the city where business firms have begun congregating, and some of the biggest names in the international architectural design industry, such as Rem Koolhaas, Jacques Herzog, and Will Alsop, are engaged in creating the skyline for Beijing's emerging commercial sector.

Creative industries in areas such as electronics, software, video games, biotechnology, and nanotechnology are a third, newly acquired driver. Recognizing that it has less hope of competing in its traditional, mainstay textile and food-processing industries, Beijing has rightly aimed at the higher-technology end of the spectrum that can draw on the strongest base of universities in China. In making a bid to become the high-tech industrial capital of China, Beijing has also begun attracting FDI in research centers. Firms such as Microsoft, Siemens, and Cisco are eager to establish a foothold in China's budding innovation system and to employ the

44. Currently, the Chinese emission standards are equivalent to the European standards in 1994. Much of Beijing's pollution comes from automobiles. For instance, 92 percent of carbon monoxide, 94 percent of hydrocarbons, and 68 percent of sulfur oxides are traceable to auto emissions. Reducing pollution from auto emissions requires improving the quality of fuel, because part of the reason for the high emissions is the high content of sulfur in Chinese gasoline compared with gasoline used in developed countries ("China to Quench" 2005; Gallagher 2006). Tougher fuel efficiency requirements are expected to be introduced in 2007, partly in preparation for the Olympics in 2008 ("China to Quench" 2005). In addition, use of alternative energy sources is being actively pursued. Currently, 3 million square meters of buildings in Beijing have adopted geothermal energy technology, and this number is expected to rise to about 20 million square meters by 2010. By adopting this technology, Beijing should be able to cut carbon dioxide emissions by 280,000 tons and sulfur dioxide emissions by 2,640 tons ("Beijing Digs Deep" 2005).

talent that is available in the Beijing area at a fraction of the cost in their home countries. Among the industries being groomed, electronics—with its short product cycles and relatively quick payback—is more likely to generate the gains in production and employment Beijing is seeking. This industry is the topic of chapter 9.

Starting with Zhongguancun Science Park in the Haidian district adjacent to Beijing University, the central government has now designated areas across the metropolitan region for high-tech industry in the hope that start-ups, FDI, and spinoffs from the major universities and firms will give rise to several interlinked and dynamic clusters. In support of this strategy, the central government is offering generous tax incentives, risk capital, space for firms to set up production and research facilities, and a business-friendly regulatory environment. For Chinese researchers overseas, whom the government would like to lure back, a package of inducements includes housing, lab facilities, research funding, and seed capital for start-ups. The government is also becoming aware that an attractive physical and cultural environment, good housing, and school and medical facilities are necessary conditions for the development of high-tech industry. The latter three present less of a challenge and are easier to provide. Where Beijing lags and may continue to lag is with respect to the environment—physical and cultural. The cultural ambience is immeasurably improved over what it was a decade ago. But the physical environment, especially air pollution, is proving recalcitrant. Even if industrial pollution is curbed, the rising tide of cars threatens to undo the gains.

Beijing's strategy resembles that of Singapore on an even larger scale. In both cities, the government has a dominant role, and development is being orchestrated in detail by the state, with lavish expenditure on improving the physical infrastructure and increasing the supply of skills. Both cities are pinning their hopes on high-end producer services and creative industries to serve as leading sectors, with the government sector providing a stable base of demand. In Beijing as much as in Singapore, there is a keen realization that a footloose army of knowledge workers will determine the success of a strategy that is technology driven and requires an open environment conducive to creative destruction. In both countries, governments are struggling to craft environments that will challenge and hold the creative class (see Florida 2005). Some evidence indicates that the incentives are working, with Beijing and Singapore benefiting from "brain gain." Not just nationals but also foreigners have gravitated to these cities and have augmented the skilled workforce. Meanwhile, MNCs have invested in R&D facilities, thereby adding to the capacity to innovate.

Nevertheless, neither Singapore nor Beijing has yet been able to come to terms with the need for openness, for a competitive market environment in which not just the entry but also the exit of firms is subject to few constraints, and for an entrepreneurial culture with a healthy appetite for risk taking as well as a tolerance for the failure of many start-ups. The openness to ideas and with it the legal protections afforded to the right of free speech that is intrinsic to a creative society remain an issue. Entry of firms is subject to few hurdles in Beijing and fewer still in Singapore. Exit is another matter. Firms that are state owned or supported have a penchant for lingering on with the help of the banking system long after they plunge into the red. Beijing is acquiring a reputation for entrepreneurship and risk taking, but such behavior remains exceptional in Singapore despite much government effort; neither society has embraced the inevitability of failure by the majority of new businesses or has erased the stigma associated with failure, although Beijing, on balance, provides a more forgiving environment. Shanghai is akin to Beijing in this respect.

SHANGHAI

Each of the five cities we have traversed has a claim to eminence, but all eyes are on Shanghai. For the other cities, Shanghai is the one to watch and to compete against. In the early decades of the 20th century, long before the term *global city* was coined, Shanghai already enjoyed that reputation. A fishing village in the 10th century and a county seat from the 11th, Shanghai's fortunes rose steadily once it became an important node of the trading network radiating out from the port city of Ningbo.[45] By the mid-19th century, Shanghai had surpassed Canton to become China's foremost trading city. Following the Treaty of Nanking in 1842 that ended the Opium War, Shanghai became the leading treaty port, acquiring within a few decades the largest foreign community in East Asia. An unusually variegated cosmopolitanism and openness produced a memorable cultural exuberance, perhaps more exotic than that sweeping Weimar Berlin in the 1920s, while the development of modern industry, mushrooming foreign trade, and trafficking in drugs made the city wealthier but also stoked social turbulence. Shanghai's fame, verging on notoriety, through the early

45. Shanghai's early history and development through the mid-19th century is described by Johnson (1995).

1930s was well deserved.[46] The city was the urban icon of the Far East, and it is this iconic status that the new Shanghai is seeking to regain after a long, monochrome interregnum during which the city was isolated from the international community and subsisted only as one of China's several industrial engines.

The revival began in the early 1990s; it was spearheaded by an ambitious plan to widen Shanghai's economic focus by radically expanding the scale of Shanghai's business and commercial activities and by developing a 523-square-kilometer area in Pudong on the other side of the Huangpu River.[47] This strategy goes hand in hand with a many-pronged effort to redirect resources into higher-technology industries and producer services and to recapture the urban glamour of the old Shanghai through an architectural makeover that is attempting to erase four decades of acquired drabness.

Determined leaders with capital who are subject to relatively few institutional checks can move mountains. In a little more than 10 years, visually, Shanghai has changed out of almost all recognition and in the process has acquired a skyline rivaling New York's—and one as distinctive. More than 3,000 buildings taller than 18 stories have been constructed since the mid-1990s. Moreover, an attempt is being made to redevelop the grandeur of the majestic buildings lining the Bund and some of the old villas, such as the Hangshan Moller Villa, now a boutique hotel. Near the old French concession, American architect Benjamin Wood had attempted to recapture Shanghai's past through a development called Xintiandi (New Heaven and Earth). In this cluster of mid-19th century, three-story Shikumen townhouses, lining alleyways are scores of boutiques, cafés, and nightclubs "created so that people in China can experience the same finely wrought balance of theme park and shopping mall that increasingly passes for upscale urban life in the United States" ("Shanghai Surprise" 2005).

46. The period literature describes Shanghai variously as the "pearl of the East" and the "Paris of the East." It depicts a nascent industrial and commercial society composed of urban communities from across China and the world for which Shanghai offered a scarce freedom and diverse opportunities if they were willing to accept the squalor, the risks, and the predatory gangs, such as the famous Green Gang. On this colorful period, see Lu (1999), Martin (1996), Sergeant (1991), and Wakeman (1995).

47. The idea of developing Pudong germinated through the research done by the Shanghai Academy of Social Sciences in 1983 to 1985 under the leadership of Wang Daohan, who was then the mayor. The project was formally proposed to the central government in 1986, and the ideas were discussed in numerous conferences during 1986 to 1988. Finally, in 1990, a consensus was reached, and the Pudong scheme was approved on April 18, beginning the renaissance of Shanghai. See also Yatsko (2001).

The change is not only skin deep. The physical infrastructure of the city in the form of bridges, tunnels, ring roads, and underground metro network, as well as water and sewerage systems, is expanding in step, causing the city to sink by 2 centimeters per year (Yusuf and Wu 2002). Shanghai Hongqiao International Airport is now complemented by a second, much larger international airport in Pudong that is linked to the downtown area by a state-of-the-art Maglev rail line. Similarly, the capacity of Waigaoqiao port will be augmented by a vast new 50-berth offshore port taking shape on Yongshan islands in Hangzhou Bay. This port will be connected to the Nanhui district in Shanghai by a recently completed 27-kilometer-long bridge, which constitutes the first phase of this Y 10 billion project ("China: Leading City Needs" 2005).[48]

Cultural software is also evolving, cautiously at first and now exuberantly, to fill the huge physical shell that is being created. The cultural revival is seeking a uniqueness that can win back the global renown Shanghai once enjoyed, this time as one of the world's leading postindustrial cities.

Under the planned economic system, Shanghai evolved into a closed, industrial city that was home to virtually every kind of manufacturing activity. The great challenge for the emerging Shanghai is to carve out and expand those industrial segments that are likely to be viable over the long term and to divest itself of activities that would be a drag on the metropolitan economy. To the activities salvaged from the inherited economic base must be added emerging technology-intensive industries and business services that will contribute to the prosperity of a postindustrial future.

Shanghai resembles Tokyo in the 1960s in that its industrial capability is very deep. Much like Tokyo, Shanghai derives productivity gains from agglomeration economies, and the rapid development of the city's hinterland is giving rise to demand for business and logistics services that Shanghai is increasingly well positioned to supply. By 2005, Shanghai's population, including more than 4 million migrants, already exceeded 19 million. In fact, the true scale of what is now a multicentric metropolitan region is much larger. This metropolitan region extends as a continuous belt from Ningbo and Hangzhou in Zhejiang, through Shanghai, all the way to Nanjing in Jiangsu, encompassing Wuxi and Suzhou along the way. It is an

48. Yangshan port will take the pressure off Shanghai port, which in 2005 will handle 17.5 million TEUs and 400 million tons of cargo. Yangshan, which began operation in late 2005, has the stable 15-meter depth the Shanghai port lacks and would be able to handle 20 million TEUs by 2020 when all 52 berths have been completed ("You Must Expand!" 2005).

urban region with a total population of 55 million. If the hinterland is assumed instead to be the Yangtze Delta area within a day's drive from Shanghai, then the population is in excess of 100 million and far exceeds that of the hinterlands of Tokyo, Seoul, and Bangkok (Leman 2002).

Recently Shanghai celebrated, with considerable satisfaction, the 15th anniversary of the Pudong project. By all accounts, Shanghai is clawing its way back to near the top of the global hierarchy of cities, and for the other major centers in East Asia, it is the metropolitan region to be reckoned with. Will this headlong rush forward continue, and is the direction reasonably well defined? In the absence of a rigorous study, casual empiricism suggests that Shanghai's growth is driven in large part by state-directed capital investment, particularly in infrastructure and real estate, but also in manufacturing and some of the service industries. The huge outlay of capital is helping to realize a vision conceived by planners in the 1980s and continuously annotated since. The plan calls for an architecturally imposing city that embraces five distinct functions: those of a manufacturing base, a financial center, a focus for cultural activities, a center for research and high-tech development, and a logistics hub for the region as well as China's principal link with other global cities. Each of those functions has been conceived and integrated into the overall plan by splicing the key attributes of successful cities around the world. Thus, Shanghai is busily investing in six pillar industries—transportation,[49] steel, biotechnology, pharmaceuticals, electronics, and chemicals[50]—because recent experience suggests that these industries have registered a robust performance. By the same token, Shanghai is shuttering or relocating to the hinterland textiles and other light industries, which are no longer competitive.

Whether this metropolitan industrial policy is coordinated with similar industrial policies being pursued elsewhere in China or informed by parallel industrial experiences from around the region is not apparent. The policy assumes that the Shanghai region has or can acquire a comparative advantage in all these industries, but few grounds exist for comfortably believing that the selected assortment of promising industries, ranging from medium to high technology, will provide the durable industrial foundation

49. Shanghai Automotive Industry Corporation, through its joint ventures with Volkswagen and General Motors, is the largest producer of automobiles in China. When the Chanxing shipyard has been completed, it will be the largest in the world, with a capacity of 12 million tons.

50. A major new industrial park is taking shape at Caohejing in western Shanghai. A 900,000-ton ethylene plant will begin production in 2005. BASF opened the world's largest polytetramethylene ether glycol plant in March 2005 and is building a second facility to produce this material, which is used for elastic spandex ("Manufacturing on the Move?" 2005).

that Shanghai is seeking a decade and more into the future. In fact, transportation, steel, and chemicals, at least, would seem out of place in the postindustrial stage of urban development. And the other subsectors will have to struggle hard to remain profitable. From a forward-looking perspective, Shanghai's industrial policy looks questionable.

The realism of the ambition to become a major financial center is also open to question. Commercial real estate, which Shanghai has thrown up in abundance, is only a small part of what it takes for a city to join the ranks of the world's leading financial powerhouses. Much more important is the level of industrial maturity, the volume and quality of professional skills, the extent to which those attributes are buttressed by tested regulatory institutions, the experience of the participants, and the emergence of durable traditions that provide the glue of trust.[51] In recent years, Shanghai's stock market has performed poorly because corporate governance is weak, disclosure is inadequate, and malpractices remain rife—all pointing to the inadequacy of monitoring institutions and organizations that enforce rules.[52]

Shanghai's location will also affect market demand for financial services, because competition exists from other existing or emerging financial centers in the vicinity. Hong Kong (China), Singapore, and Tokyo are three cities with a large presence of globally linked financial firms (P. Taylor 2005).[53] These three cities are already in the position to challenge London and New York. Moreover, questions exist regarding the global supply of financial services. Is an impending glut possible? Is consolidation in fewer key locations a possibility given developments in IT?

---

51. Most of the brokerage firms in Shanghai (about 130) are said to be insolvent ("Marginalised Market" 2005). The firms have been slow to accumulate the necessary skills and technology because, so far, market forces and institutions have exerted a minimal influence on the working of the stock market. To develop those capabilities, the firms may need to find foreign partners and be allowed to invest in foreign shares ("Marginalised Market" 2005). Life insurers do not earn much return either. They are required to invest mainly in Chinese banks and government bonds with at most 15 percent of investment in equities, and they are barred from investing in foreign equities ("Off with a Bang" 2003).

52. The nontradable shares account for two-thirds of the US$400 billion market value of firms listed in Shanghai and Shenzhen stock exchange. Lack of much activity in the equity market is preventing other financial developments, such as derivatives and corporate bond trading ("Hangover Cure" 2005). On May 1, 2005, China's Securities Regulatory Commission issued guidelines to convert the nontradable shares. The conversion must be approved, and anyone purchasing the stocks will not be able to sell for one year ("Hangover Cure" 2005). The pilot scheme covered 46 firms, and following its initial success, the conversion process has now been extended to cover all 1,300 firms, although the actual conversion process is likely to take a long time to ensure price stability ("China: Share Sale" 2005).

53. Hong Kong (China) and Singapore both have a large number of insurance providers, although only firms in Hong Kong (China) are globally connected significantly (P. Taylor 2005).

These considerations and questions raise doubts over the plan to build an East Asian Wall Street in Pudong, as distinct from a regional financial center that serves the considerable requirements of the Yangtze Valley Basin, with a population of 600 million that produces two-thirds of China's GDP. Even this more limited objective could take time because of the condition of China's banks and the limited progress with reforming and privatizing the state sector. Furthermore, the regulatory infrastructure that is vital to the functioning of financial markets is in its infancy with much tempering of the rules ahead, not to mention a profound strengthening of the legal system to implement the rules (Perkins 2004). Other issues exist as well. With a well-established financial market in Tokyo and in Hong Kong (China) and smaller markets also in Seoul and in Taipei, can East Asia accommodate another market in Shanghai? If so, how large could it grow and what would be the nature of its specialization, with Tokyo already well entrenched in the bond market? More narrowly, from Shanghai's standpoint, how much of a boost would it provide to metropolitan GDP over the longer term, especially when the long-run trend for the employment in New York's financial sector is downward, reflecting the consolidation of firms ("After the Fall" 2005)?[54]

From official statements, the objective of acquiring a piece of the global financial business is one element of the larger objective of delivering two-thirds more of GDP from services within the next decade. This target is derived from historical averages. Major cities in industrial countries depend on services for much of their income; therefore, Shanghai's economy is being made more services intensive, with financial services in the forefront, followed by other producers and commercial services. Is this model the best for Shanghai, and should Shanghai forcefully pursue a rapid planned transition of the economy?

The unsettling aspect of this monumental urban project is that an industrial policy and a policy to dramatically increase the weight of the services sector in Shanghai's economy are being attempted alongside two other expensive and ambitious schemes: (a) to combine in one city the cultural vigor of a London with the creative industries that flourish in San Francisco and (b) to construct a multimodal transportation network spanning the Yangtze Delta area with Shanghai as its apex—a project bigger than Rotterdam and Antwerp combined.

54. Employment in the financial sector typically is highly cyclical. In New York, the financial sector added 34,000 new jobs during the boom years of 1995 to 2000, but quickly lost all of those newly created jobs after the crash of stock market ("After the Fall" 2005).

Table 2.1 Gross Investment in Shanghai
(US$ billion)

Year	Investment
1990	4.7
1991	4.9
1992	6.5
1993	11.3
1994	13.0
1995	19.2
1996	23.5
1997	23.9
1998	23.7
1999	22.4
2000	22.6
2001	24.1
2002	26.4
2003	29.6
2004	36.9
Total	**292.7**

Sources: National Bureau of Statistics of China 2005; Shanghai Municipal Statistical Bureau 2004.

No precise figure measures the magnitude of the investment that has been poured into these several projects. The cumulative gross investment since 1990 is equal to about US$300 billion (see table 2.1), and the tangible evidence of this spending is everywhere: in the new auto factories in Anting; in the chemical plants in Shihua town; in new financial skyscrapers; in the recently expanded ports; in the cultural centers and the several science parks, such as the 25-square-kilometer Zhanjiang, where a new breed of high-tech electronic firms—including SMIC, Hongli Semiconductor, and Tailong Semiconductor—are building their operations; and in the science parks of Jiaotong and Fudan universities.

Whether the skills, the software, and the institutions can be quickly assembled to derive the economic payoff that will make this great Shanghai experiment into a self-sustaining process that leads to a global city is much less obvious. Just as no precedent exists for Singapore's attempt to implant a biotech industry through brute financial force, so, too, one searches in vain for any past example of a city that moved purposefully to accomplish six complex objectives and to fuse them into an organic, smoothly functioning whole. New York, for example, has achieved the rank of a world city, but in many senses that rank is a hollow achievement. The city has gradually lost its base of manufacturing industry.[55] It is no longer an important logistics hub. New York is the leading financial center and is richly endowed with producer services; arguably its creative industries are among the most dynamic in the world. The city can be proud of its universities and hospitals, and the cultural infrastructure draws millions of tourists. Yet New York teeters on the edge of financial crisis. Its physical infrastructure and public services are no more than adequate, given the level of income, and the city confronts income inequality and a level of relative poverty that would be considered intolerable in Shanghai today (Glaeser 2005c).

Ambition, drive, focus, and financing can produce dramatic results—if overextension can be avoided. The ambition and drive of Shanghai's authorities to make Shanghai into a world city are very much in evidence. But the breadth of the ambition suggests a blurring of focus. Shanghai has demonstrated a comparative advantage in manufacturing industries, in transportation logistics, and, more recently, in construction and engineering services. The three together provide an integrated basis for a thriving urban industrial economy. How they can coexist with a dominant cluster of producer services, a growing creative industry, and a variegated industry supplying cultural products and services is impossible to ascertain. No other city besides possibly Tokyo embraces the range of activities Shanghai is tackling simultaneously, and in Tokyo's case, the city followed a certain progression, a gaining of experience, and a process of industrial adjustment during which some industries exited only to be replaced by others. A lot of creative destruction of a broadly positive nature was in evidence, which depended on Japan's manufacturing capability and an innovation system centered in Tokyo. Those changes were also influenced by international circumstances, which allowed space for a more gradual transition.

Shanghai's planned approach is of a very different cut from Tokyo's. A complex whole made up of many parts is being assembled all at once with little thought to sequencing or market forces or comparative advantage. Not much attention is being given to changing world supply and technological circumstances, which makes it much harder to gauge the longer-term viability of manufacturing industries now being expanded in Shanghai. The demand for these industries might well be forthcoming to

55. New York once had the largest urban manufacturing sector in the United States, with close to 1 million workers in the 1960s, mainly in the garment and printing industries ("After the Fall" 2005).

the extent being assumed. By the same token, it may materialize only in part. Many other competitors are jockeying for the same choice markets—and not only the cities included in this volume. Are autos and banking the industries that will sustain Shanghai's prosperity? Is construction? We are particularly struck by the scale, links, and technological reach of the construction industry and explore some of its potential in chapter 8. Undoubtedly, policy makers and investors must make bets, but with a careful assessment of potential and a weighing of the odds. In the pell-mell rush to develop, these niceties might not be given their due.

CONCLUSION

Tokyo, Singapore, Bangkok, Seoul, Beijing, and Shanghai are among the six most important global cities in East Asia. They are on the threshold of a postindustrial era. Each city is marked by its own unique industrial history, which has imparted a mix of capabilities. How those capabilities are mobilized will determine whether the next chapter on the life of these cities is one about economic achievement of a high order or of a middling kind, or whether it is a paean to decline. Much depends on the industries on which the mantle of leadership comes to rest. It is difficult to predict which industries will take up the challenge and actually deliver. However, we have nominated some contenders with plausible credentials, and in later chapters we will assess those credentials.

CHAPTER 3

DISAPPEARING MANUFACTURING

Postindustrial cities cannot dispense with industry if they are to continue as successful economies. But it is the message of this book that they will need a change of horses—and in fact more powerful horses—because the next leg of development is steeper. This change does not mean that all labor-intensive manufacturing activities are disbarred—after all, fashion garments can certainly thrive under postindustrialism. It means only that skill- and technology-intensive industries are more likely to sustain competitiveness in an urban milieu in which wage costs are high and rising, skilled workers are relatively abundant, and the infrastructure for design and technology development either has already taken root or can be brought into existence through policy actions.

Each city in our sample benefits from—but must improve on—six attributes, which we will describe and compare across the cities in this chapter:

1. Size, which gives rise to agglomeration economies
2. Broad industrial base, which can serve as the foundation for postindustrial development
3. Large and skilled workforce, which effectively fuels industrial change
4. Urban innovation system composed of universities and research institutes, which can lead or support industrial evolution and competitiveness
5. Urban information technology (IT) infrastructure, which can undergird industrial advance by enhancing productivity and spurring technological improvement in industries ranging from retailing to logistics
6. Urban amenities such as public services, green spaces, and low levels of pollution, which contribute to the livability of a city

These attributes, individually or taken together, are not sufficient conditions for rapid economic growth in a postindustrial environment; however, they are the hallmarks of successful postindustrial cities. We should also note at this point that the available indicators offer at best a coarse-grained picture of the attributes that count. Nevertheless, we believe that they usefully underscore urban preparedness for a transition to postindustrialism and give a sense for the range of potential options available to our selected East Asian cities.

POPULATION

The optimal city size has eluded researchers, if we assume that an optimal condition is defined in economic terms with respect to economic growth and factor productivities and also with respect to costs arising from congestion and the demand for space. Small, ill-managed cities can be inefficient and unlivable, as can large ones. But if a city achieves a broadly satisfactory level of management—which includes fiscal and financial management and the adequate provision of services—and of governance, it is not easy to define an upper limit of population when there are no binding constraints imposed by the availability of land and water. Some research on China suggests that labor productivity is maximized in cities with populations in the region of 5 million (Henderson 2004a, 2004b). But evidence also points to constant and even increasing returns to scale. In principle, if one were to believe these findings, then there is no apparent upper bound on performance as long as services can be efficiently provided and congestion costs are kept in check, possibly through efficient traffic planning and a polycentric urban structure.

The concentration of people within a single city is apparent through much of East Asia. "The population of [the greater] Tokyo . . . has risen from 15.6 percent of Japan's population to 25.2 percent, Taipei from 13.3 percent to 27.7 percent of Taiwan's population, and Seoul from 8.4 percent to 22.0 percent" (Rowe 2005, 25). All six of the East Asian cities in our sample are large or very large by global standards. Even Singapore, the smallest city, has a population of 4.2 million, which is higher than that of Ireland. Beijing, Shanghai, and Tokyo each have a population exceeding 10 million (see table 3.1). One must remember that in the case of Tokyo and Bangkok, the table refers to the core districts only and not to the metro area, which is far more populous. If scale and agglomeration economies are important, then the bigger cities clearly give firms an edge. By being able to serve an urban market of 10 million customers, the size of a small country, companies can reap the benefits of scale economies and can minimize the costs of transportation and marketing. Except for Singapore, the sample cities offer markets of between 10 million and 20 million people if the relevant boundaries of the city are taken to be the metropolitan area.

Table 3.1 City Population and Share of National Population, 2003

Attribute	Bangkok	Beijing	Seoul	Shanghai	Singapore	Tokyo
Size (thousands of people)	5,885	14,560	10,277	13,418	4,185	12,310
Share of national population (%)	9.33	1.13	21.45	1.04	100	9.65

Sources: Bangkok: Bangkok Metropolitan Administration various years. Beijing: Beijing Municipal Statistics Bureau. Seoul: Seoul Metropolitan Government 2004. Shanghai: Shanghai Municipal Statistical Bureau 2004. Singapore: Singapore Department of Statistics (http://www.singstat.gov.sg/). Tokyo: Ministry of Internal Affairs and Communications, Statistics Bureau (http://www.stat.go.jp/english/).

Again, if size matters, then future trends favor Beijing and Shanghai. Both cities have been growing steadily, mainly because of immigration, with urban fertility being exceedingly low. Moreover, given the relatively low level of urbanization in China (42 percent in 2004), the attractiveness of those cities for migrants, and the cities' small share of the national population (at about 1 percent as against more than 9 percent for Tokyo and Bangkok), each city could add 10 million or more people within the next two decades. Aside from scale economies, the advantage of such influx is that it would dampen the aging of the workforce and provide those cities with a supply of relatively youthful, entrepreneurial migrants who would bring energy and ideas and stimulate consumption (Bloom and Williamson 1997).

As figure 3.1 shows, the demographic profile is most favorable for Bangkok, Beijing, and Shanghai, with the largest cohorts being in the 15–19 through 45–49 age groups. In the other cities, the 1990s witnessed an increase in the weight of older cohorts. Seoul, Singapore, and Tokyo will still expand, but more slowly because their rural hinterlands have been largely depleted (see table 3.2). Bangkok could attract rural migrants, but they might go to the distant suburbs and the Eastern Seaboard. Nevertheless, the Bangkok metro region is far from having exhausted its growth potential. The projection for future immigration also does not suggest that those cities will grow rapidly through this channel. The United Nations forecasts that net migration to Singapore will drop to zero by 2030, after an average intake of 50,000 people per year in 2000 to 2005 ("South-East Asia: Population Ageing" 2004). Similarly, the projection for Thailand is that immigration is expected to decline to 4,000 per year between 2025 and 2050, down from 6,000 per year between 2000 and 2025 ("South-East Asia: Population Ageing" 2004).[1]

1. Thailand had 900,000 foreign workers in 2002, although the country exported 193,000 skilled workers in 2001 ("South-East Asia: Population Ageing" 2004).

Figure 3.1 Population Age Pyramid for Cities

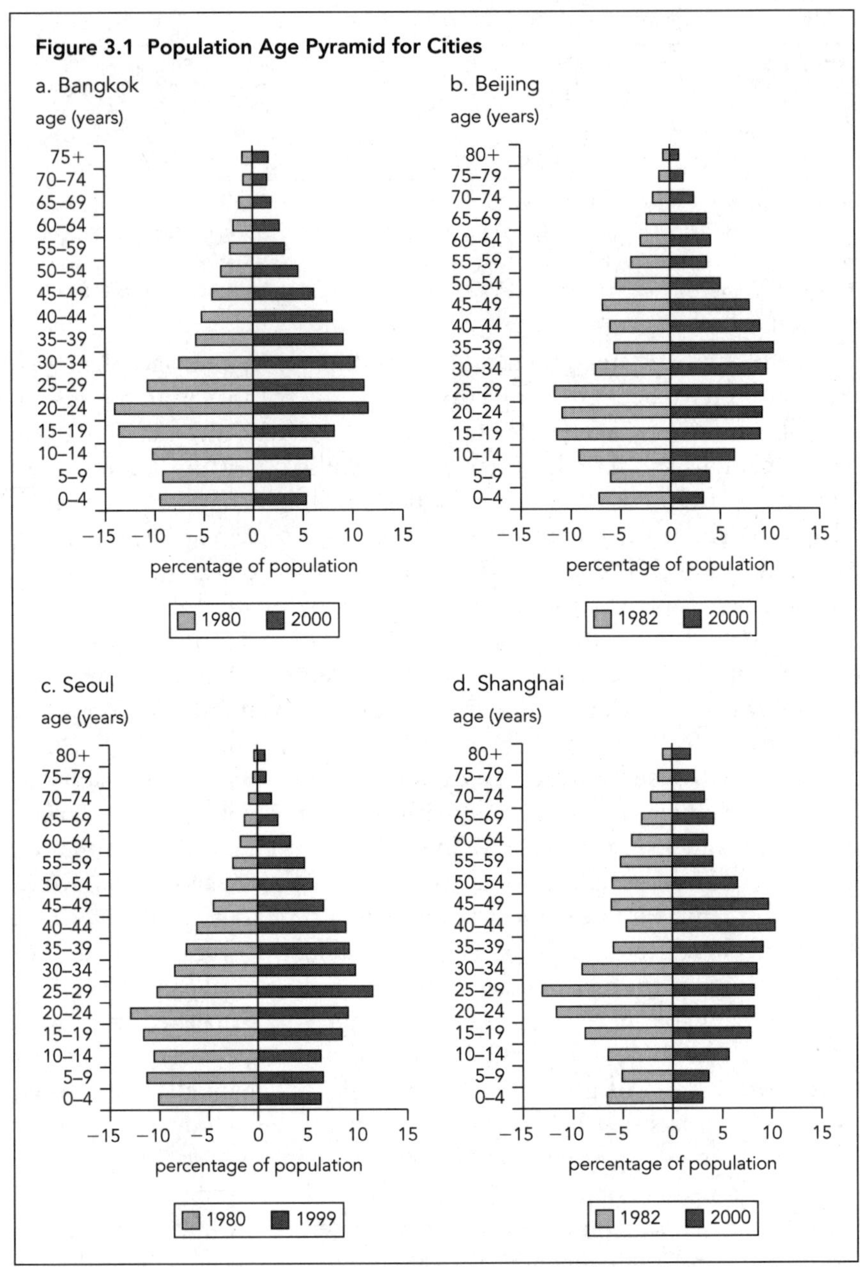

Figure 3.1 ***(Continued)***

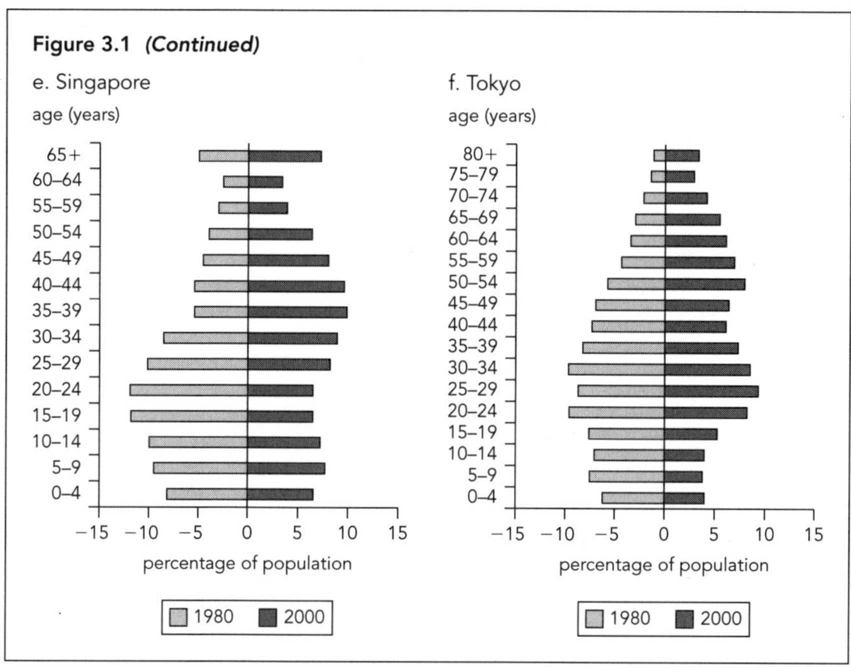

Source: Bangkok: Bangkok Metropolitan Administration various years. Beijing: Beijing Municipal Statistics Bureau 2004. Seoul: Seoul Metropolitan Government 2004. Shanghai: Shanghai Municipal Statistical Bureau 2004. Singapore: Singapore Department of Statistics 1980, 2000. Tokyo: Statistics Bureau of Japan 1980, 2000.

In addition, lower fertility rates and lengthening life expectancy in these countries will affect the growth of these cities. All five countries now have fertility rates that are below replacement levels. Meanwhile, with improvements in health, people can expect to live longer. A person born in Asia in 1900 would expect to live on average until the age of 28. By 2001, life expectancy in Asia had risen to 67 years (Riley 2005). Life expectancy is substantially higher in East Asia and is still inching upward. Japan has the highest life expectancy in the world for women (85.3 years) and the third highest for men (78.4 years). By 2025, the life expectancy for women and men in Japan is expected to reach 89.4 years and 83.9 years, respectively ("Japan: Population Trends" 2005). The average life expectancy in the Republic of Korea in 2000 was 75.9 years, and it is expected to increase to 81.5 years in 2030 ("Preparing for a Mature Society" 2004).

Reflecting the national trends, the populations in these cities are also graying (see figure 3.1). The median age of a Japanese citizen is 43.1 years old. One in five Japanese is over the age of 65, and some 5 percent are over

Table 3.2 Net Migration (Foreign and Domestic) to Six Cities in East Asia, 1980–2003

City	Type of migration	1980	1985	1990	1995	2000	2003
Bangkok	Foreign	—	—	—	—	—	—
	Domestic	499,700	427,500	519,900	415,800	443,000	—
Beijing	Foreign	—	—	—	—	—	—
	Domestic	52,000	0	37,944	63,000	89,000	141,100
Seoul	Foreign	—	—	—	5,826	6,199	—
	Domestic	—	—	—	−321,898	−81,122	—
Shanghai	Foreign	—	—	—	—	—	—
	Domestic	76,700	53,000	14,600	62,700	111,900	111,900
Singapore	Foreign	76,600	−35,100	27,900	51,300	25,500	−45,100
Tokyo	Foreign	1,926	7,328	29,526[a]	−4,628	19,506	11,068
	Domestic	−92,482	4,851	−50,441	−33,692	53,245	64,859

Sources: Bangkok: Bangkok Metropolitan Administration various years (figures from Registration Record, Bureau of Registration Administration, Ministry of Interior). Beijing: Beijing Municipal Statistics Bureau various years. Seoul: Seoul Metropolitan Government 2004. Shanghai: Shanghai Municipal Statistical Bureau various years. Singapore: Singapore Department of Statistics (http://www.singstat.gov.sg/keystats/hist/population.html). Tokyo: Tokyo Metropolitan Government various years.

Note: — = Not available. Data for Bangkok are the gross flow of migrants. Data for Seoul in 2000 are from 1999. In Seoul and Tokyo, data for net foreign migration was calculated from the difference in the number of registered foreign residents. Domestic data for Shanghai are based on the number of people who changed *Hukou* (household registration) permanently. Data for Singapore are the changes in nonresident population, and the data in 1980 are from 1981. Data for Tokyo in 1990 are from 1991.

the age of 80 ("Japan: Population Trends" 2005). In 2000, 7.2 percent of the population in Korea was over 65 years old. This figure will have climbed to 14.4 percent by 2019, and to 23.1 percent by 2026 ("South Korea: Ageing" 2005). The proportion of the economically active population (15 to 64 years old) is expected to peak in the late 2010s and then start to decline. China will begin to catch up by 2027, when 14 percent of its population will be 65 years or older ("China: Demographic Trends" 2004). Japan moved from having one of the youngest populations among the Organisation for Economic Co-operation and Development (OECD) countries to one of the oldest in 15 years ("Japan: Population Trends" 2005). The United Kingdom took 80 years to change from an adult to an aged society; China will do so in 20-plus years ("China: Demographic Trends" 2004).

The effect of such aging on the growth of the gross domestic product (GDP) will be a reduction in GDP growth rates of about 0.25 to 0.75 percent in Japan and Europe ("Preparing for a Mature Society" 2004). Similar effects can be expected in the other East Asian cities.

INDUSTRIAL BASE

Although population is one crucial indicator of urban scale, urban GDP is one of equal significance in this regard. As East Asian countries have industrialized, an ever larger share of the GDP is generated by urban-based secondary and tertiary industries. Because the productivity per worker in these sectors far exceeds productivity in agriculture, the percentage of GDP derived from urban activities is well in excess of the share of the population. For instance, although only 42 percent of China's population is classified as urban, 88 percent of the GDP is generated through nonfarm activities, the bulk of which are located in urban areas. Given the magnitude of urban factor productivity, it is not surprising, therefore, that all six cities are prominent contributors to the national product. Bangkok tops the list with a 36 percent share in 2000, which reflects the high degree of urban and industrial concentration in Thailand (see table 3.3). Seoul, with a quarter of the national product, is a close second. Both of those cities have benefited from virtuous spirals resulting from the agglomeration and clustering of industries and, in particular, the high concentration of manufacturing activities that are closely linked with the growth of productivity, a phenomenon that is known as *Verdoorn's Law*.[2] The notable difference between Bangkok and Seoul is that Bangkok's share of GDP peaked in

Table 3.3 Cities' Share of National GDP, 1985–2003
(percentage)

City	1985	1990	1995	2000	2003
Bangkok	35.94	40.5	39.08	36.31	—
Beijing	2.1	2.7	2.4	2.8	3.1
Seoul	24.9	25.3	24.9	24.0	24.1
Shanghai	5.2	4.1	4.2	5.1	5.3
Singapore	100	100	100	100	100
Tokyo	—	17.6	16.1	16.6	16.8

Sources: Bangkok: Bangkok Metropolitan Administration various years. Beijing: Beijing Municipal Statistics Bureau 2004. Seoul: Korea National Statistical Office (http://www.nso.go.kr/eng/). Shanghai: Shanghai Municipal Statistical Bureau 2004. Singapore: Singapore Department of Statistics (http://www.singstat.gov.sg/). Tokyo: Tokyo Metropolitan Government, Bureau of General Affairs (http://www.toukei.metro.tokyo.jp/).

Note: — = Not available.

2. Verdoorn's Law states that the manufacturing sector is subject to substantial increasing returns to scale; hence, the growth of productivity in manufacturing is an endogenous result of the growth of output. For more discussion on Verdoorn's Law, see McCombie, Pugno, and Soro (2002).

Table 3.4 Sectoral Composition of City GDP in Six Cities, 1980–2003
(percentage)

City	Sector	1980	1985	1990	1995	2000	2003
Bangkok	Primary	1	1	1	1	1	—
	Secondary	54	48	51	50	55	—
	Tertiary	46	52	48	49	44	—
Beijing	Primary	4	7	9	6	4	3
	Secondary	69	62	52	44	38	36
	Tertiary	27	31	39	50	58	62
Seoul	Primary	—	1	1	0	0	0
	Secondary	—	21	20	19	14	14
	Tertiary	—	78	79	81	85	86
Shanghai	Primary	3	4	4	3	2	1
	Secondary	76	70	64	57	48	50
	Tertiary	21	26	32	40	51	48
Singapore	Primary	2	1	—	0	0	—
	Secondary	36	34	—	33	34	—
	Tertiary	62	65	—	67	66	—
Tokyo	Primary	1	—	0	0	0	0
	Secondary	34	—	24	21	18	17
	Tertiary	66	—	76	79	82	83

Sources: Bangkok: Bangkok Metropolitan Administration various years. Beijing: Beijing Municipal Statistics Bureau various years. Seoul: Seoul Metropolitan Government 2004. Shanghai: Shanghai Municipal Statistical Bureau 2004. Singapore: Singapore Department of Statistics (http://www.singstat.gov.sg/). Tokyo: Tokyo Metropolitan Government, Bureau of General Affairs (http://www.toukei.metro.tokyo.jp/).

Note: — = Not available. Data for Tokyo are from 2002.

1990 and since then has been declining as industry moves out of the Bangkok metro area and is not replaced by services with higher value added per capita. Seoul, on the other hand, appears to have successfully maintained its share of GDP in the face of substantial migration of manufacturing industries and changes in the sectoral composition of economic activities (see table 3.4).[3]

Tokyo's share of GDP is commensurate with its rank in Japan's urban hierarchy and its percentage of GDP has been approximately stable since 1990. In China, the country's size and its policy of restricting migration to the urban areas, which is only now being dismantled, have prevented the emergence of many large cities. Nevertheless, Beijing and Shanghai have quickly moved into the ranks of the world's most populous cities, even

3. The growth of cities in the United States is tied to the composition of industries in cities. Cities with many new industries that tend to rely on skilled workers grow much faster. The existence of those industries in a city is influenced by the local availability of skilled workers (Simon 2005).

Table 3.5 Per Capita City GDP and Per Capita National GDP, 2003
(U.S. dollars)

City	Per capita city GDP	Per capita national GDP
Bangkok	7,845	2,021
Beijing	3,040	1,099
Seoul	14,297	12,693
Shanghai	5,628	1,099
Singapore	22,605	22,605
Tokyo	62,232	31,181

Sources: Bangkok: Bangkok Metropolitan Administration various years. Beijing: Beijing Municipal Statistics Bureau 2004. Seoul: Korea National Statistical Office (http://www.nso.go.kr./eng/). Shanghai: Shanghai Municipal Statistical Bureau 2004. Singapore: Singapore Department of Statistics (http://www.singstat.gov.sg/). Tokyo: Tokyo Metropolitan Government, Bureau of General Affairs (http://www.toukei.metro.tokyo.jp/).

Note: Data for Bangkok are from 2000. Data for Tokyo are from 2002.

Table 3.6 City GDP, 2003
(US$ billion)

City	Bangkok	Beijing	Seoul	Shanghai	Singapore	Tokyo
GDP	44.56	44.26	146.90	75.52	94.61	764.17

Sources: Bangkok: Bangkok Metropolitan Administration various years. Beijing: Beijing Municipal Statistics Bureau 2004. Seoul: Korea National Statistical Office (http://www.nso.go.kr./eng/). Shanghai: Shanghai Municipal Statistical Bureau 2004. Singapore: Singapore Department of Statistics (http://www.singstat.gov.sg/). Tokyo: Tokyo Metropolitan Government, Bureau of General Affairs (http://www.toukei.metro.tokyo.jp/).

Note: Data for Bangkok are from 2000. Data for Tokyo are from 2002.

though each accounts for only a little over 1 percent of the nation's population. High urban productivity, attributable in large part to the concentration of manufacturing industry in Shanghai, accounts for that city's 6 percent share of GDP, whereas Beijing's much smaller share reflects the greater intensity of services activities associated with the central government.

Tokyo and Singapore are the two leaders with respect to per capita GDP (see table 3.5). However, the total GDP of the Tokyo metropolis in 2002 was more than twice the combined total of the five others (see table 3.6). Seoul ranks second for total GDP, almost twice the level of Shanghai in fourth place. However, at the rate Shanghai is growing—10 percent annual growth of GDP since the mid-1900s—it will very likely pull ahead of Singapore within this decade to become the city with the third largest GDP in East Asia.[4] Likewise, though Bangkok and Beijing

4. Shanghai accounted for 8 percent of national industrial output in 2003.

were roughly comparable in size in 2003, Beijing's growth rate during the five years preceding 2003 was almost twice that of Bangkok. By 2010, if not earlier, it will become the fifth ranked urban economy within this group. Already, Beijing and Bangkok are almost half the size of the economy of Pakistan, and their GDP is substantially larger than that of most African countries.

The key to the rapid growth experienced by the six urban centers between 1980 and 1990—growth that was sustained by all but Tokyo through 2000—is the interaction among industrial structure, size, and outward orientation. The focus on the manufacturing sector promoted the absorption of technology from domestic and foreign sources and raised factor productivity. The size of the cities gave rise to the agglomeration economies and made it easier for producers, who initially relied on the domestic market, to achieve scale economies. Openness to trade further widened the market, ensured demand, intensified competitive pressures on firms, and in at least four of the six cases—Seoul and Tokyo are the exceptions—pulled in foreign direct investment.

Typically, urban areas are richly provided with services, and the six cities are no exceptions. However, manufacturing loomed large in the 1980s, accounting for between 30 and 40 percent of the GDP even in Tokyo, which was at a mature stage of industrialization. The share of manufacturing peaked in the first half of the 1990s and stabilized in Shanghai and Beijing at 50 and 36 percent, respectively, while declining gradually in the other cities, to be replaced by services.[5] The share of services saw tremendous growth in Beijing, increasing from 27 to 62 percent in just over 20 years. Beijing's broad economic structure is quite similar to that of Singapore, where the services sector also accounts for about two-thirds of the city economy. Tokyo is by far the most services-intensive city, with 83 percent of its economic activities stemming from that sector in 2002. During that time period, we can see the forces of change at work, with the footprint of manufacturing shrinking because of the migration of industry, the reduction in the relative prices of manufactured products, and the falling coefficient of employment for manufacturing industry as a whole.

In the most recent period for which data are available—through 2004—the absolute value of manufacturing is still rising in all but Tokyo. The pace has slowed in Bangkok, Seoul, and Singapore as the sectoral emphasis of development has begun shifting. In Beijing and Shanghai, however,

5. The apparent decline in the share of manufacturing has been exacerbated by the fall in the relative prices of manufactured goods. Thus, the share of GDP belies the actual change in the volume and scale of manufacturing activities.

there is no evidence of a letup as the government, while switching some attention to higher-tech industries, continues to invest in manufacturing to stave off a hollowing out of industry.

A comparison between Tokyo and Shanghai can help highlight the subsectoral characteristics of the transition from manufacturing as the leading sector during the industrial phase of development to services in the postindustrial stage. Thus, the mix of industry can change even in the manufacturing-led phase, as is happening in Shanghai. Even though manufacturing accounted for about half of Shanghai's GDP in 2004, the city's composition was shifting rapidly toward more capital and skill-intensive production activities.

Starting in the early 1990s, Tokyo's GDP growth slowed, and the slowdown persisted into the next decade. Although decomposing the various causes of the slowdown is empirically quite difficult, we can see that a good part of the slowdown was the consequence of macroeconomic factors that affected the entire Japanese economy and inevitably impinged on Tokyo. However, structural changes associated with postindustrialism are also slowing the tempo of economic activity. The shrinking role of manufacturing has reduced the impetus to productivity and to overall growth that the sector can impart. Many of the services that drive the urban economy and that could offset the smaller contribution of manufacturing productivity are technologically sluggish and have shown meager gains in productivity. Together, these developments have acted as a brake on growth (Nordhaus 2006).

Two scenarios, among many, are most plausible. In one, the Tokyo economy continues to shed manufacturing jobs, and more industry relocates to areas where wages and overhead costs are lower. There is, in addition, a continuing trickle of services being outsourced and a persistent technological stagnation in much of the services sector. This scenario is a recipe for medium-term stagnation and long-run decline.

A second, more positive scenario can also be read into the industrial statistics. In that view, the share of manufacturing activities stays broadly constant or even increases somewhat because of the innovativeness of the electronics, IT and robotics, materials, and transport industries. Manufacturing productivity rises steadily, and spillovers benefit other activities. Side by side, there is an upsurge in productivity growth in key services, such as retail, wholesale, finance, logistics, health, education, and construction, with back-office services where the value added is modest being sent offshore. With the spread of IT into services, the scope of productivity improvements is substantial, as evidenced by a wealth of empirical findings from OECD countries. IT, computers, and digitization can trigger a productivity spiral, inducing the rational redesign of procedures and processes, a delayering of organizations, and an efficient and timely use of great volumes of market information.[6]

In this scenario, the increasing share of telecommunications, financial, and nonfinancial services, as well as other business services, is a positive development. If such services link with and reinforce technological advances in manufacturing, growth in Tokyo could rise to the levels attained in the early 1990s, if not the late 1980s.

Shanghai is in a position to sustain a much higher rate of growth than Tokyo. Past trends suggest that an industrial structure that is weighted toward manufacturing will be pushed further and faster by productivity and technological changes. However, IT and innovations in processes as well as in the organization of firms have opened the door to a postindustrial renaissance in the growth of services. Furthermore, the bias in manufacturing toward capital and skill intensity, miniaturization of certain types of products, greater reliance on multidisciplinary technologies for product development, and shorter product cycles can breathe new life into high-technology urban manufacturing activities. A postindustrial Tokyo with broad research and manufacturing capabilities is well suited for this role. Shanghai could be, too, possibly a decade from now.

HUMAN CAPITAL

Without capital, cities cannot build factories, housing, or infrastructure. But without suitable human resources, cities cannot be productive and innovative or, to put it in different terms, competitive and prosperous. As cities move toward a postindustrial stage, the reliance on human resources only increases[7] because most of the infrastructure is in place and capital is not generally the binding constraint on growth—it can be raised locally or borrowed from elsewhere. But the quality of the human capital can be pivotal. As Glaeser (2005b, 596) states, "Skilled people are the key to urban success." An empirical analysis of industrial skill intensity in U.S. cities comes to the plausible conclusion that cities beginning from a position of human capital abundance are more likely to gain in terms of skills, because in such cities more of the new starts will be by entrepreneurs who

6. When IT is merely grafted onto an existing system with processes designed for the preelectronic era, the full benefits from computerization and the Internet are difficult to realize, and gains in reducing transaction costs are modest (Rose 2004).

7. See Glaeser and Mare (2001) and Glaeser and Saiz (2003).

have high levels of education, who will be technologically more advanced, and who will employ a higher proportion of skilled workers. Thus, "to whosoever hath, to him shall be given and he shall have more abundance."[8] And we have the makings of a virtuous spiral that would augment agglomeration economies by deepening the pool of skills (Berry and Glaeser 2005). The literature repeatedly underscores three characteristics. One is youthful dynamism and entrepreneurial risk taking. They are the source of energy, new starts, productivity in the workplace, and high savings that are transformed into complementary physical capital. A second is the level of skill and how rapidly the composition of skills can be varied in response to market demands. A third is creativity, which is associated with skills and level of education, but whereas skills are correlated with productivity and efficiency, creativity is linked to innovation.

Clearly, a global city needs a blend of all three characteristics—however, cities that are closer to the postindustrial end of the spectrum are more dependent on the innovativeness of the workforce. At that point in the life cycle, prosperity hinges on better ideas and products rather than on production skills. We hasten to add that the two are not by any means mutually exclusive. Highly trained people are also the ones more likely to be innovative. By the same token, the younger age cohorts are on average more brimful of ideas. The distinction we would like to draw from the various possible blends is that the postindustrial city is less reliant on the skilled and semiskilled blue-collar production workers, because many assembly line jobs, whether in manufacturing or in services such as back-office services, have moved away.[9] The greatest added value comes, therefore, from knowledge workers or, as Florida (2002, 2005) describes them, members of a "creative class." Knowledge workers are not the only sources of ideas that generate commercial outcomes or other urban spillover effects, but they have emerged as a major source—especially in the leading cities.

The creativity of knowledge workers is loosely correlated with the workers' level of education, with the heterogeneity and size of the community of such workers, and with the openness of the urban culture to new ideas and their circulation. However, the creativity of urban communities is an inexact science, with plenty of plausible hypotheses but none that has

8. Matthew 13:12 (King James Version).

9. The manufacturing assembly lines may have gone, but their legacy lingers. After the representatives of Wipro, one of India's leading IT firms, visited the Toyota subsidiary in Bangalore to learn about the Toyota Production System, they adopted some of the lessons learned such as the rearranging of office space to resemble an assembly line. This rearrangement increased the labor productivity by more than 40 percent ("Taking a Page" 2005).

been rigorously proven.[10] Similarly, the factors responsible for translating urban creativity into consistent commercial advances are fairly hard to pin down, although three types of nuclei are regularly linked to the commercial success of innovations. These three are large universities with a strong emphasis on research, major corporations that are technology oriented, and venture capitalists and other providers of business services that serve as handmaidens to the creative industries. However, for the nuclei to fulfill their role, there is the need for entrepreneurs who can cause clusters of firms to congeal by raising capital from local and external sources and by helping build the institutions that add to the stickiness of certain urban locations for industrial clusters (Feldman, Francis, and Bercovitz 2005; Markusen 1996). The attractions of the industrial cluster are augmented by the endogenous tendency toward self-perpetuation if not growth. One of the ways self-perpetuation can occur is through the training of new entrepreneurs by existing firms. Having acquired skills and insider knowledge, these budding entrepreneurs can go on to set up their own firms, sometimes with the help of contacts in the venture capital industry or with the backing of their previous employers. As Guiso and Schivardi (2005) note, learning by doing is a key to becoming an entrepreneur. The large, open cities are more likely to harbor and attract people who have an accumulation of diverse experience, which is noted as being a hallmark of entrepreneurs (Lazear 2002). The significance of openness is equally important at the level of the firm, although the two are surely interrelated. Research in Europe appears to demonstrate that firms adopting more open technology strategies tend to be closer to technology frontiers because they are more likely to interact with university-based researchers and overseas universities (Laursen and Salter 2004; Monjon and Waelbroeck 2003)

Of course, open cities with most of the ingredients present can still fail to be both innovative and prosperous in economic terms because the policy environment is unfavorable. And there is no doubt that high transaction costs and adverse macroeconomic circumstances can undermine urban dynamism—although in the East Asian context, regulatory

10. Creativity is a delicate plant not readily planned into existence. Mommaas (2004, 52) remarks that the "famous creative quarters such as 1900s Montmartre, 1960 Rive Gauche, and 1970s Sotto were never planned as such. Instead they developed more or less spontaneously out of favorable conditions only identified retrospectively, conditions which were, in many ways related to their status as marginal spaces. Also many of them had a rather transient character. Their cultural success triggered social, economic, and institutional processes which struck at the roots of their very success as alternative spaces of creativity and innovation." The story of Silicon Alley in New York is a recent instance of the waxing and then the partial waning of a creative cluster.

impediments, limited protection of intellectual property, and weak legal regimes have not generally proven to be serious obstacles to industrial development. Still, all these issues are of minor or diminishing importance in our six cities, which brings the focus back to the nature of the human resources that those cities command or will command.

Broadly in line with expectations, the vast majority of school-age children have been receiving at least primary education in all six cities going back to 1980. Predictably, the percentage is highest in Tokyo and somewhat lower in Bangkok. However, by the 1990s, the scores were virtually identical across the cities. Predictably also, the numbers receiving college education were low everywhere in the early 1980s, although Japan at 40 percent was respectable by the standards of the day. Those percentages began climbing steeply in the 1990s and are higher in Beijing, Seoul, Shanghai, and Singapore.[11] They show that the majority of workers in these cities have basic and even secondary schooling, and a significant proportion have received higher level training. These figures, of course, do not include recent migrants, but their numbers as a share of the total urban population are large only in a few major cities such as Beijing and Shanghai. Even the Beijing metro area hardly registers much net in-migration, and the small trickle of migration to the three other cities includes numbers of workers with secondary or more education and industrial skills.

Of equal importance is the level and composition of skills. In this regard, five of the cities are richly endowed in at least industrial skills that have accumulated and deepened over several decades. By all accounts, Tokyo's labor market is highly efficient and provides employers with a wide spectrum of manufacturing and services sectors. Seoul and Singapore are strong in some areas of manufacturing and producer services. The strengths of Beijing and Shanghai are concentrated more in manufacturing; however, both cities are rapidly deepening their labor markets for services.[12] Bangkok trails the other cities with respect to level and

11. In China, there were 3.4 million university graduates in 2005, and the number was expected to be 4.1 million in 2006 (Ministry of Education 2005, 2006).

12. Every year, 300,000 or so engineers graduate from China's universities ("China's Challenge" 2005). From 30,000 in 1980, the number of scientists and graduates with technical qualifications climbed to 1.3 million by 2004 ("Long March" 2005). Chinese universities produced more than 200,000 graduates in computer and information systems in 2004 ("We've Got the Solid Grounding" 2005). There is no shortage of software engineers in China. More than half of the 1,800 researchers who work for Lucent Technologies in China are software engineers. However, most Chinese software firms still lack much of the capital, management, and marketing skills to compete against established international software firms ("Open Source" 2005).

diversity of skills because of its narrower base of production activities and its weaker infrastructure for training.

To a remarkable extent, the labor markets of Bangkok and Singapore are being bolstered by the inflows of expatriate workers. That openness is closely associated with economic growth and creativity, as has been widely noted by, among others, Florida (2005) and Hall (1998) in the context of cities. Measuring openness is tricky; however, there is some consensus around the share of the urban population that is foreign born. Urban diversity, as measured by the number of foreign-born workers in a U.S. city, has been shown by Ottaviano and Peri (2004) to enhance the overall productivity of U.S.-born workers and income accruing through rents. Florida (2005) reports on some of the estimates, in particular the mosaic index by Benton-Short and Associates (see chapter 1 and Benton-Short, Price, and Friedman 2004). The mosaic index shows that cities such as New York, Toronto, and Dubai are in the lead (figure 1.2). In fact, 8 of the top 20 cities are in North America, and all but 6 of the remaining ones are in Europe. This situation might change with the entry of some East Asian cities. A very high percentage of researchers in Singapore are expatriates, and Bangkok relies on expatriates for mid- and high-end technical skills across many industries. Seoul and Tokyo have far smaller communities of expatriates, most falling into the managerial and technical categories. In Beijing and Shanghai, the number of expatriates with technical and managerial skills is growing fast, with a swelling inflow from around East Asia, Europe, and the United States.

More than 90,000 foreigners worked in Beijing in 2004. The presence of so many foreign workers adds an extra dimension to the labor markets in each of the cities, but those workers are probably contributing most to local innovation in Bangkok and Singapore for two reasons. First, the numbers are much larger in absolute terms and as a proportion of the skilled urban workforce. Second, many of those workers, particularly in Singapore, are engaged in local research or are affiliated with local institutions and businesses. Hence, their direct contribution to urban creative industries and to other activities is greater. In the other cities, many expatriates work for foreign companies in managerial or technical positions, with the majority in a small group of producer services. Because of language barriers, their interaction with locals and their effect on the local economy is necessarily smaller. This situation may change in Beijing and Shanghai as more and more foreign-owned research facilities spring up and local English-language skills improve, but so far, the big benefits to labor markets in the leading Chinese cities derive from the reflux of Chinese nationals who had settled abroad.

Although the labor markets of Seoul and Tokyo are richly supplied with a wide mix of skills, for a whole host of reasons having to do with culture, language, and opportunities for foreigners, these cities have not induced the circulation of knowledge workers from abroad that would contribute significantly to diversity. If heterogeneity of outlooks, frames of reference, ideas, and lifestyles are vital to a many-faceted and enduring creativity, then for all their current strengths, these cities risk falling behind in the race to become innovative.

URBAN INNOVATION SYSTEM

The labor market—in particular the market for skilled and technical workers—is central to the urban innovation system, but there are other parts to the apparatus of creativity as well. One of those parts comprises research institutes and universities that conduct research and development (R&D). Several of the cities are richly endowed with such institutions. Table 3.7 shows that while Tokyo leads the field in terms of the number of universities. However, the Chinese cities marshal large numbers of research entities. Shanghai is a host to 839 research institutes, and there are 267 in Beijing (National Bureau of Statistics of China 2001).[13] In recent years, the Singapore government has been promoting R&D activities and, as a consequence, the number of research institutes in the city has increased from 21 in 1990 to 37 in 2000. Firms that engage in R&D are a

Table 3.7 Number of Universities in East Asian Cities, 1990–2003

City	1990	1995	2000	2003
Bangkok	—	78	80	—
Beijing	67	65	59	46
Seoul	34	35	39	38
Shanghai	50	45	37	57
Singapore	5	6	6	—
Tokyo	105	107	113	116

Sources: Bangkok: *Report on Educational Statistics* various years. Beijing: National Bureau of Statistics of China 2001. Seoul: Seoul Metropolitan Government 2004. Shanghai: National Bureau of Statistics of China 2001. Tokyo: Ministry of Education, Culture, Sports, and Science 2004.

Note: — = Not available.

13. The number of research institutes in these two cities is in decline following the restructuring of public research institutes.

Table 3.8 Number of Patents Granted in the United States, by Economy of Origin, 1964–2004

Economy	1995	2000	2001	2002	2003	2004	1964–2004
Japan	21,764	31,295	33,224	34,858	35,516	35,350	591,683
Taiwan (China)	1,620	4,667	5,371	5,431	5,298	5,938	46,684
Korea, Rep. of	1,161	3,314	3,538	3,786	3,944	4,428	33,865
Hong Kong (China)	86	179	237	233	276	311	2,565
Singapore	53	218	296	410	427	449	2,547
China	62	119	195	289	297	404	2,115
Malaysia	7	42	39	55	50	80	436
Philippines	4	2	12	14	22	21	266
Thailand	8	15	24	44	25	18	223
Indonesia	4	6	4	7	9	4	155
Vietnam	0	0	0	0	0	1	12

Source: U.S. Patent and Trademark Office (http://www.uspto.gov/web/offices/ac/ido/oeip/taf/cst_utl.htm).

second component to the apparatus of creativity. In most countries, they conduct two-thirds or more of all the research and inevitably lead the commercialization of findings. Data on the number of firms doing research at the municipal level are lacking, as are statistics on corporate R&D at the local level. Table 3.8 presents national statistics on patents applied for by a number of East Asian economies and granted in the United States and should more or less faithfully convey the situation in cities.

How well the innovation system performs is measured indirectly by indicators such as productivity growth at the national or sectoral levels and the competitiveness of exports. More directly, the performance is reflected in the output of patents, new products, and scientific articles. Those outputs are all inexact metrics, especially new products, the characteristics of which are fairly subjective. Moreover, most patents and scientific articles do not have commercial outcomes or significant technological spillovers, and the element of discovery in patents and what a patent represents in terms of scientific investment varies widely among industries such as pharmaceuticals and electronics. Nonetheless, those indicators, alongside the data on skilled and scientific workers, help to construct a picture of innovative capacity, and the statistics on patents and scientific publications are a crude measure of innovative output. They are complemented by actual macroeconomic outcomes. Those economies that have high ratios of skilled workers and R&D personnel in the total labor force, that invest at least 2 percent of GDP in R&D, and that generate the largest number of patents are also among the economies that register a steady increase in total factor productivity and have sustained industrial competitiveness in key areas.[14] Japan clearly leads the pack with more than 35,000 patents granted in 2004, while Taiwan (China) and Korea received close to 6,000 patents and 4,500 patents, respectively. Patents granted to residents of Singapore and China in 2004 were still low in number: 449 and 404, respectively. The recent surge in patenting by Korea and Taiwan (China) reflects technological prowess in export-oriented manufacturing sectors and is responsible for the remarkable market penetration by firms such as Samsung, LG Electronics, TSMC, Hon Hai Precision, Asustek, Mitac, and Quanta.[15]

In the lineup of cities, Tokyo is the heavyweight by a wide margin, irrespective of which indicator is selected. Whether it is the number of universities or the number of patents, Tokyo stands apart from the other cities, which is not surprising given Japan's lead over the other countries and its unusually prolific innovation system. Although Tokyo is home to 14 percent of national universities and 19 percent of private universities (overall, 17 percent of universities), it accounts for close to one-fourth of undergraduate students, 26 percent of graduate students, and 27 percent of faculties in Japan (MEXT 2004).[16] In terms of patents, almost one-half of all the patent applications filed by Japanese residents are from Tokyo (175,234 applications from Tokyo out of 362,711 total applications), which is why two-thirds of all Japanese attorneys are in Tokyo.[17]

Reflecting the concentration of universities and other higher education institutions in Tokyo, university start-ups are also concentrated in Tokyo. It has 26 percent of such ventures, while Osaka, with the second largest concentration, has about 7 percent (Bureau of Industrial and Labor Affairs 2005).

14. A paper by Ciccone and Papaioannou (2005) shows that countries with an abundance of human capital adopted more skill-intensive industries and grew more rapidly in the 1980s and 1990s.

15. In 1980, only eight patents were granted to the residents of Korea. This number has steadily increased to more than 4,000 patents in 2004. Most Korean patents are granted for electronics and computer-related technology. These sectors accounted for 63 percent of patents in 1998. In addition, much of the patenting activities are by major *chaebols* such as Samsung, LG Electronics, and Hyundai (Hu and Jaffe 2003).

16. Only one-third of undergraduates who study in Tokyo graduated from high schools in Tokyo. The remaining students come from other prefectures.

17. There are close to 3,500 patent attorneys in Tokyo, accounting for 63 percent of all patent attorneys in Japan (Japan Patent Office 2004).

For almost two decades, Japan has invested nearly 3 percent of GDP in R&D to promote technology absorption and innovation. This high level of investment is apparent in the numbers on Tokyo, which stands at the apex of the innovation system. Among the other five highlighted cities, there is strong evidence of intensive efforts at technological catch-up, with the exception of Bangkok, which is lagging behind in the technology race. In China, Korea, and Singapore, rising expenditures on R&D and skills development are funneling resources into the innovation systems of their leading cities, whether into public universities and research institutes or into private research entities.

The top universities in East and South Asia, ranked mainly by their research output, are dominated by universities in Japan (see table 3.9).[18] Some of them are also included among the top 100 in a worldwide ranking. They are followed by the top universities from Singapore, Korea, Taiwan (China), China, and Hong Kong (China). Notably missing from the list are universities from other Southeast Asian economies, which are not even listed in the top 500 for the world as ranked by Shanghai Jiaotong University.

Tokyo hosts three of the top-ranking Japanese universities: Tokyo University, Tokyo Institute of Technology, and Keio University. Beijing has two of the top Chinese universities: Tsinghua University and Beijing University. Similarly, Korea's premier universities are located in Seoul.

In these East Asian cities, public spending on the innovation system is both complementing and drawing in private investment. The biggest gains are apparent in Beijing and Shanghai, which, starting from a low base, are ratcheting up expenditures on R&D, the training of science and technology workers, and patenting. Both cities have been assisted by the inflow of qualified Chinese researchers trained abroad and by government policies that have induced foreign companies to plow resources into R&D facilities. The quality of the research skills and the value of the patents now being generated might still not be up to the standards of industrial countries; however, with continuing investment and learning, the quality should improve. Finland, for instance, went from being a technological backwater in the late 1960s to becoming, through government investment in the innovation system and complementary corporate effort, one of Europe's technological leaders in IT and biotechnology. Finland increased its number of universities from 3 in 1967 to 20 in 2001 and built up clusters

18. All the top-ranked Japanese universities are national universities, except for Keio, which is a private university.

Table 3.9 Top Universities in East and South Asia, 2005

East and South Asia Rank	Institution	World Rank	Economy	National Rank
1	Tokyo University	20	Japan	1
2	Kyoto University	22	Japan	2
3	Osaka University	62	Japan	3
4	Tohoku University	73	Japan	4
5	Tokyo Institute of Technology	93	Japan	5
6–11	Hokkaido University	101–52	Japan	6–9
6–11	Kyushu University	101–52	Japan	6–9
6–11	Nagoya University	101–52	Japan	6–9
6–11	National University of Singapore	101–52	Singapore	1
6–11	Seoul National University	101–52	Korea	1
6–11	Tsukuba University	101–52	Japan	6–9
12–22	National Taiwan University	153–202	Taiwan (China)	1
12–22	Tsinghua University	153–202	China	1
12–22	Chinese University Hong Kong	203–300	Hong Kong (China)	1–3
12–22	Hiroshima University	203–300	Japan	10–13
12–22	Hong Kong University of Science and Technology	203–300	Hong Kong (China)	1–3
12–22	Keio University	203–300	Japan	10–13
12–22	Kobe University	203–300	Japan	10–13
12–22	Okayama University	203–300	Japan	10–13
12–22	Beijing University	203–300	China	2
12–22	University Hong Kong	203–300	Hong Kong (China)	1–3
12–22	Yonsei University	203–300	Korea	2
23–47	Indian Institute of Science	301–400	India	1

Source: Adapted from Institute of Higher Education, Shanghai Jiaotong University (http://ed.sjtu.edu.cn/rank/2005/ARWU2005_TopAsia.htm).

Note: Spanned rankings mean that a tie exists or that the rankings were determined only as a span.

of high-tech companies in the Helsinki-Espoo-Vanta-Tampere region, in Oulu, and in Turku (Castells and Ince 2003).

In the absence of tried recipes, building an innovation system that buttresses commercial prosperity must inevitably remain a gamble. Investing in high-level skills is seemingly an absolute necessity for postindustrial cities. This investment needs to be supplemented by spending on research, which harnesses those skills. The share of R&D in Beijing is 6 percent, while that of Shanghai and Singapore is only 2 percent each, although in both cities the absolute expenditure on R&D has been growing much faster with the overall rise in city GDP (National Bureau of Statistics of China 2001). Whether the outlay of human capital and R&D results in an adequate payoff depends both on the strategic choices with respect to the areas of research, incentives, and institutional mechanisms that lead to the exploitation of promising innovations and on a big dose of luck. In later chapters, we describe some of the industries that appear at this juncture to deserve the attention of researchers, recognizing that in attempting to identify technology winners, one will inevitably make mistakes. Yet there are no options. The game must be played and expensive bets be placed. Inevitably, only a few wagers will prove to have been right, but as every venture capitalist and every business firm knows, the pain of failure is part of the game.

INFORMATION AND COMMUNICATION TECHNOLOGY INFRASTRUCTURE

No discussion of the innovation system can now be complete without a careful glance at the physical IT infrastructure. Innovation was always dependent on access to information and the filtering of the information to isolate the required building blocks of knowledge. The volume of information has exploded, and the urban innovation system must be able to tap into the vast and expanding stock of knowledge generated, local as well as global.[19] Effective research is inseparable from the traffic in scientific information among knowledge workers, and such exchanges depend on an infrastructure comprising computers and telecom equipment. Such an infrastructure is the vascular network of an IT system.

Initial tentativeness over whether IT contributes to economic performance has mostly dissipated as evidence accumulates showing that investment in IT explains some of the increase in total factor productivity. IT investment typically accounted for between 0.3 and 0.8 percentage points

19. Numerous studies have examined the effect of the growing stock of knowledge on innovation. Because knowledge generation is a cumulative process, as the existing stock of knowledge increases, it becomes harder to master the existing stock in order to add to that supply. One consequence is that it now takes longer to gain a Ph.D. Furthermore, the age at which significant discoveries are made is now eight years later than at the beginning of the 20th century (Jones 2005a, 2005b). Thus, innovation may be harder to come by. In fact, starting from the 15th century, the rate of innovation peaked in the mid-19th century and has been slowly declining since (Huebner 2005).

Table 3.10 Contribution of IT Investment in GDP Per Capita Growth, 1990–2000 *(percentage points)*

Country	1990–95	1996–2000
Japan	0.1–0.2	0.4–0.5
Korea	1.4	1.2
United States	0.4–0.5	0.9–1.0

Source: Adapted from OECD 2004b.

of growth in GDP from1990 to2000, although the contributions were much higher in certain subperiods (see table 3.10) (OECD 2004b).[20] Moreover, the part explained by IT is expanding, especially within the megacity context, not to mention the new markets created by the emergence of IT and the wide adoption of broadband connections. Graham and Marvin (2000, 72, 77) observe that "most IT applications are largely metropolitan phenomena . . . and telemediated flows operate to sustain very local relations [and] teleworking." As a consequence, the importance attached to computers skills, the development and application of software, and the continuous upgrading of the telecommunications infrastructure to keep in step with new technologies has taken on extreme importance. The experience in European and U.S. cities, which is now being replicated in East Asia, shows that a well-developed communications network is critical in attracting high-technology investment.[21]

A postindustrial city dependent on knowledge-based industries for economic survival must give due attention to the progressive deepening of IT skills in the workforce and complement those skills with a modern telecommunications system. Anything less risks being left out of the knowledge and production network.

20. The contribution of information and communication technology (ICT) to economic growth can be broken down into contributions from ICT-producing sectors and ICT-using sectors. With the rapid increase in the quality of ICT products, the production sector has contributed significantly to growth. In the United States, the labor productivity growth of the ICT-producing industry between 1990 and 2001 was 8.7 percent. The ICT-using sectors (mainly retail, wholesale, and financial services) also grew rapidly at 4.7 percent during the same period. The difference in growth in the latter sectors set the United States and Europe on different growth trajectories, although Gordon (2004b) attributes this divergence to other institutional factors in Europe. Also, the physical investment in IT needs to be complemented by training in IT and by organizational changes and improved management so as to fully use IT ("Does IT Improve" 2005; Indjikian and Siegel 2005).

21. Harwit (2005) describes the development of the IT infrastructure in Shanghai and discusses the conditions that could promote future advances.

Realizing this need, governments in Seoul and Singapore have pushed computerization and have invested heavily in telecom facilities.[22] To a lesser degree, the other cities are also attempting to increase the leverage derived from a state-of-the-art telecom network. A few indicators can highlight the level of IT development that has occurred and the incredible rapidity with which the new technology has moved to the forefront of urban priorities.

The number of computers as a ratio of the urban population tells one part of the story. Seoul and Singapore are pinning some of their hopes on the spread of computer literacy, with the other cities following but progress being slowest in Bangkok. Other critical indicators are the number of telephone land lines, although this figure is less important than the number of cellular phone users. Mobile telephony has overtaken its land-bound cousin and appears to be the wave of the future.[23] Access to high-speed data lines is an index of speed, convenience, and volume of information that can be distributed and opens up new venues for media distribution and shopping as fiber-optics and other broadband connections become more widespread.[24] China has surpassed Japan with 34 million broadband lines installed, second only to the United States in 2005 (Reardon 2005).[25] Although a large number, it represents only 3 percent of the Chinese households, and there is scope for much more expansion. In both Beijing and Shanghai, one-third of the population (about 4 million) used the Internet regularly at the end of 2004. In Korea, broadband penetration reaches 75 percent of households (Economist Intelligence Unit 2005). In all the cities, money is being poured into ever more capacious pipes for transporting information, including wireless connections.

In terms of physical infrastructure, access, and pricing, Seoul and Singapore are in the lead. The rate at which facilities are being created coupled with advances in technology suggests that the physical telecommunications infrastructure will not be a significant constraint on

22. Korea is typically regarded as the most wired country in the world, with 78 percent of households connected through broadband connections. Some factors, such as the concentration of urban residents in high-rises, facilitated the rollout of broadband connections, and price regulations have contributed to the affordability of such connections (Shameen 2004). In addition, Korea also has 35 percent of all wireless hot spots in East Asia (Shameen 2004).

23. Shanghai had more than 11 million cellular phone users in 2004 (Harwit 2005).

24. In Korea, 12 percent of shopping takes place online (Economist Intelligence Unit 2005).

25. The number of subscribers in China is now close to 40 million (Economist Intelligence Unit 2006). The number of broadband installations in Japan in 2003 was 17.2 million (Economist Intelligence Unit 2005). It was 12 million in Korea (Shameen 2004). In contrast, less than 5 percent of Thais in 2003 had Internet access, and there were only 200,000 broadband lines (Shameen 2004).

Table 3.11 E-Readiness Ranking, 2004 and 2005

Economy	2004	2005
Hong Kong (China)	9	6
Singapore	7	11
Korea, Rep. of	14	18
Japan	25	21
Taiwan (China)	20	22
Malaysia	33	35
Thailand	43	44
Philippines	49	51
China	52	54
Indonesia	59	60
Vietnam	62	61

Source: Economist Intelligence Unit 2005.

the productivity of the innovation system in any of the six cities. The constraints will arise from the capability of the researchers and firms to create usable knowledge from the virtually limitless volume of information that has suddenly been brought within reach of anyone with a personal computer and an Internet connection.

Although infrastructure investment is an important first step, taking advantage of the availability of such infrastructure depends on the business and regulatory environment and the existence of supporting industries. Table 3.11 shows the e-readiness ranking of East Asian economies based on a composite index of various factors. The ranking did not change dramatically between 2004 and 2005, although Hong Kong (China) and Singapore swapped the top places. Japan saw its ranking move up by four places, mainly through an improvement in network security, while Korea's ranking declined by four places because of weaker network security and a lack of entrepreneurship (Economist Intelligence Unit 2005).

Among cities in Japan, Tokyo has the highest density of broadband connections with 38 percent of households subscribing to such a service. (The national average is 27 percent; see table 3.12 for further details about connections in Japan.) Losing patience with the slow rollout of affordable broadband connections by the incumbent local telephone and cable companies, many municipalities in the United States are now investing in broadband infrastructure and offering it to residents, a direction cities in Asian countries might also take. Philadelphia, Pennsylvania, is planning to cover 135 square miles with wireless connections (one megabyte per second synchronous) with the Internet service provider EarthLink for US$20 per subscriber.[26] San Francisco, California, is considering similar

Table 3.12 Number and Types of Internet Connections in Japan, 1999–2002

Fiscal year	Digital subscriber line	Fiber-to-the-home[a]	Cable television service net	Cellular phone terminal[b]	Dial-up[c]
1999	211	—	216,000	7,499,000	11,940,000
2000	70,655	—	784,000	34,567,000	17,280,000
2001	2,378,795	26,400	1,456,000	51,925,000	20,230,000
2002	7,023,039	305,387	2,069,000	62,460,000	20,480,000

Source: Data from Telecommunication Bureau, Ministry of Internal Affairs and Communications.

Note: — = Not available.

a. The number of fiber-to-the-home services provided to general households.

b. The sum of the users of i-mode service provided by cellular phone enterprises, with service by Ezweb (including former Ezaccess) and by J-Sky.

c. This computation is based on an index that is 100 in the number of subscribers (approximately 10,594,000 persons) to 15 large providers as of the end of March 1999 (1,059.4 × year-end index/100).

Table 3.13 Comparison of Broadband Prices, 2004
(US$ per 100 kilobytes per second)

Economy	Price
Japan	0.06
Korea, Rep. of	0.24
Sweden	0.24
Taiwan (China)	0.44
Hong Kong (China)	0.85
Canada	1.14
Belgium	1.46
Singapore	1.55
United States	1.77
China	1.89
Germany	2.77
Switzerland	3.25
Italy	3.29
Netherlands	3.77
France	4.12
United Kingdom	6.18

Source: International Telecommunication Union 2004.

services ("Philadelphia to Be City" 2005). Even for this service, the cost of broadband access for consumers is US$2 per 100 kilobytes per second in Philadelphia, 33 times the price in Japan and 8 times the price in Korea (see table 3.13).

26. Verizon offers asymmetric digital subscriber line services with 768 kilobytes per second download and 128 kilobytes per second upload speed for US$14.95 ("Philadelphia to Be City" 2005).

ATTRACTIVE URBAN AMENITIES

There remains one mundane yet vital piece of the postindustrial urban story. Cities that are attempting to increase the share in urban GDP of skill-intensive creative industries will need a particular ambiance. They will require an environment that suits a workforce heavily weighted toward individuals with tertiary education who are mostly in the upper income deciles and are geographically mobile. Members of this creative class, as Florida (2002) has categorized them, are seeking an assortment of urban attributes. The quality and cost of housing, health services, and schooling and the incidence of crime make up one set of concerns, which are uppermost for any group of workers and not just the technically qualified.[27] However, for knowledge workers, Florida maintains that the recreational amenities, the cleanliness of the environment, and the state of the physical infrastructure (transportation and telecommunications, for example) also loom large.

Finding quantitative indicators of those attributes for the East Asian cities is a tall order. A small scattering of statistics and impressions must suffice. The cost-of-living index, which gives most weight to housing, is steep for several of the selected cities. Bangkok is at the lower end of the spectrum. At the opposite end is Tokyo, which is the most expensive city in the world ("Cost of Living Index" 2005).[28] Seoul predictably is second from the top, followed closely by Singapore and Shanghai, where housing costs have been rising sharply. Bangkok's relative price advantage has made it a favorite for expatriates living in East Asia. Many maintain a permanent apartment in Bangkok and use it as a base for business ventures in China and other parts of East Asia. Housing and other services are cheaper in Bangkok, and the city's bustle and exuberance (*joie de vivre*) is a big draw for itinerant knowledge workers. Bangkok's openness to foreigners and its diversity also gives it an edge over the other cities in this important respect.[29]

27. The decline in the crime rate significantly enhanced New York's "livability." In 1990, there were 2,290 murders in the city. By 2004, the number had dropped to 566 ("Town of the Talk" 2005).

28. Living in Tokyo is more than 40 percent more expensive than living in New York, while the cost in Bangkok is 40 percent lower than in New York ("Cost of Living Index" 2005).

29. Bangalore, the center of India's foray into the global software industry, seems to be moving toward clamping down on entertainment venues, which gives zest to Bangalore's night life. For instance, the dance floor of Taika, a Thai-themed restaurant and bar in Bangalore, used to be packed with more than 500 people, many of them engineers, consultants, and call-center employees in Bangalore. However, following the passage of the Licensing and Controlling of Public Entertainment Order in July 2005, the dance floor has been empty. The law itself does not ban dancing, but it introduces stricter safety, building, and lighting requirements such that none of the 60 applicants so far have been granted a license ("Often Footloose" 2005).

Table 3.14 Mathematics Scores from TIMSS-R, 1999

Economy	Math score	Math rank	Higher than international average?
Singapore	604	1	Yes
Korea, Rep. of	587	2	Yes
Taiwan (China)	585	3	Yes
Hong Kong (China)	582	4	Yes
Japan	579	5	Yes
Malaysia	519	16	Yes
United States	502	19	Yes
Thailand	469	27	No
Indonesia	403	34	No
Philippines	345	36	No

Source: Nabeshima 2003.

Note: Thirty-eight countries participated in the TIMSS-R. The international average score was 487.

Table 3.15 Science Scores from TIMSS-R, 1999

Economy	Science score	Science rank	Higher than international average?
Taiwan (China)	569	1	Yes
Singapore	568	2	Yes
Japan	550	4	Yes
Korea, Rep. of	549	5	Yes
Hong Kong (China)	530	15	Yes
United States	515	18	Yes
Malaysia	492	22	Yes
Thailand	482	24	No
Indonesia	435	32	No
Philippines	345	36	No

Source: Nabeshima 2003.

Note: Thirty-eight countries participated in the TIMSS-R. The international average score was 488.

The quality of schooling is captured by the Third International Mathematics and Science Study–Repeat (TIMSS-R) scores, which place Japan, Korea, and Singapore near the top with Thailand trailing in 27th place in math and 24th in science behind the United States (see tables 3.14 and 3.15). East Asian schools emphasize rote learning and strict class discipline. Students receive a thorough grounding in mathematics and the sciences on which new ideas can be built. But creativity is not a strong point of the East Asian countries.

Singapore and now Bangkok have begun offering world-class medical services and have become major destinations for medical tourism. Health care services in Beijing, Seoul, Shanghai, and Tokyo are also of a high

Figure 3.2 Health Expenditure as Share of GDP, 2003

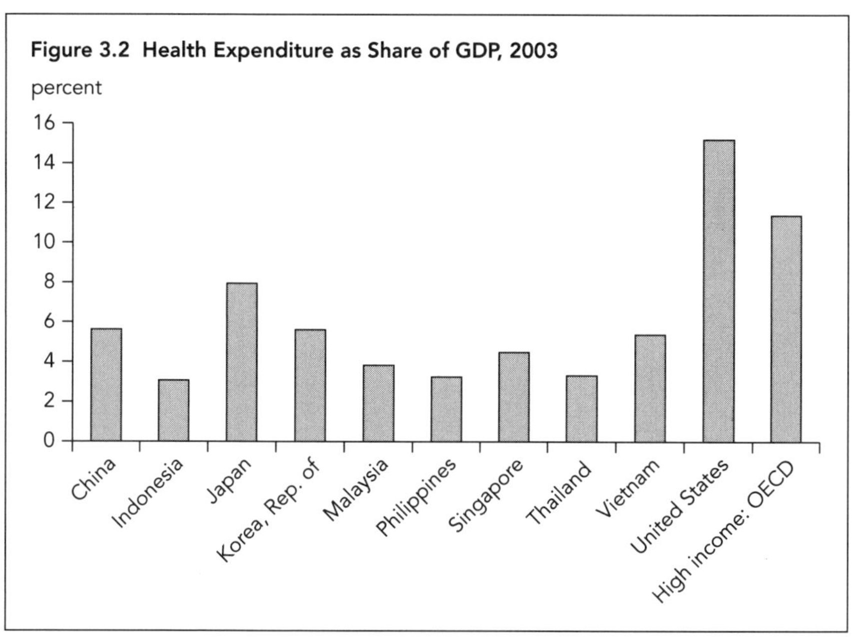

Source: World Bank, World Development Indicators database.

order. Moreover, costs are moderate relative to Europe and the United States if the aggregate outlay as a percentage of GDP is an approximate guide (see figure 3.2).

Rates of urban crime in East Asian cities are toward the lower end of the international spectrum, although in several cities the incidence of crime has risen as those cities have grown in size. Size and the influx of migrants are correlated with crime, which might explain the increase in property crime in Beijing and Shanghai over the past decade (Messner, Liu, and Karstedt 2005). Nonetheless, these cities are safe by the standards of global megacities. Table 3.16 provides a ranking based on what are usually conservative official statistics, showing Beijing as the city with the lowest crime rate and Seoul as the one with the highest.[30]

Among other environmental indicators, air pollution is one on which good standardized data are available. Air quality, both in Beijing and in Shanghai, is extremely poor, even though the municipal governments are making determined efforts to achieve acceptable standards. With the volume of vehicular traffic rising inexorably, air quality is unlikely to improve

30. Data for Bangkok are not available.

Table 3.16 Number of Crimes per 100,000 Population, 2000 and 2003

City	2000	2003
Bangkok	1,908	—
Beijing	748	618
Seoul	3,974	—
Shanghai	794	779
Singapore	807	799
Tokyo	2,415	2,421

Sources: Bangkok: Royal Thai Police. Beijing: Beijing Municipal Statistics Bureau 2004. Seoul: Yusuf and Nabeshima 2005. Shanghai: Shanghai Municipal Statistical Bureau 2004. Singapore: Singapore Department of Statistics (http://www.spf.gov.sg/statistics/stat_index.htm). Tokyo: Tokyo Metropolitan Government various years.

Note: — = Not available.

over the medium term. The other cities have managed to check—or, in the case of Tokyo, reverse—the deterioration in air quality, but standards are in the moderate range even in Singapore, in part because of smoke from fires in nearby Sumatra that are used to clear the land under the remaining forest cover for oil palm cultivation.

All six cities now have world-class shopping and dining facilities. Beijing and Shanghai, both of which only a decade ago were drab industrial cities with no charm and little to offer by way of culture, have improved dramatically. Bangkok and Tokyo, each in its own way, hold the pole positions. For recreation and culture, the Chinese cities are catching up fast, although their parks, green spaces and outdoor recreation, climate, and congestion are and probably will remain problem areas. Bangkok, Seoul, and Singapore have dedicated urban parkland, but these areas cannot count as major attractions.

In sum, each of the cities is a star in the national context. Even by international standards, they merit high scores on all counts except air quality and traffic congestion. For the international knowledge worker, the issues might be ones of openness and the familiarity of the locals with English. Most Singaporeans are bilingual in English and Mandarin or a native tongue; Bangkok is more open and freewheeling. The other four cities are less user friendly to foreigners.

INVESTING IN GROWTH, ATTRACTING TALENT

As the transition to postindustrialism gathers momentum, city governments and national governments are coming to recognize that different strategies are needed. Although capital and infrastructure will continue to contribute to economic growth, blends favoring venture capital and infrastructure for recreational amenities deserve more emphasis. Furthermore, as the hold of manufacturing on the six cities weakens further, talent- and creativity-feeding services and high-tech industries are emerging as the drivers of growth in the leading cities. Those services and industries are linked to the quality of the innovation system and its openness. And the openness attracts talent depending on the quality of the urban experience that is offered.

CHAPTER 4

DECIPHERING THE DNA OF THE BIOTECHNOLOGY INDUSTRY

Since about the early 1950s, the field of medicine has been transformed by revolutions, first in the field of bioengineering and more recently in biogenetics. The bioengineering revolution introduced new imaging equipment, such as magnetic resonance imaging (MRI) and ultrasound, into everyday use; made a wide range of medical implants, from valves to pacemakers, available for patients; and brought devices such as the heart-lung machine and apparatus for hemodialysis into hospitals and clinics. This revolution is being renewed by advances in biogenetics, which promise new and more potent drugs and replacement parts that exactly mimic the enzymes and organs of the human body (Citron and Nerem 2004).

With so much excitement in the air, the lure of the health products and services industries for a postindustrial city can be almost irresistible. It is widely assumed that, as incomes rise, so too will the demand for health care—and possibly much more than is proportional—as people seek to improve the quality of what are increasingly longer life spans (Murphy and Topel 2005).[1] Among the Organisation for Economic Co-operation and Development (OECD) countries, the United States spends the most on health care—more than 16 percent of its gross domestic product (GDP) in 2005.[2] The Asia region, by comparison, spends only 6 percent of its GDP

1. Murphy and Topel (2005) argue that longevity has yielded enormous gains, which they estimate to equal US$1.2 million per person during the 20th century. According to them, a 1 percent fall in cancer mortality would be worth US$500 billion.

2. In spite of this vast expenditure, 45 million lack medical insurance and 52 million are being supported by a limping Medicaid program (P. Webster 2006). At current rates of growth, U.S. spending on health care is projected to reach close to 19 percent of GDP by 2014. Two factors

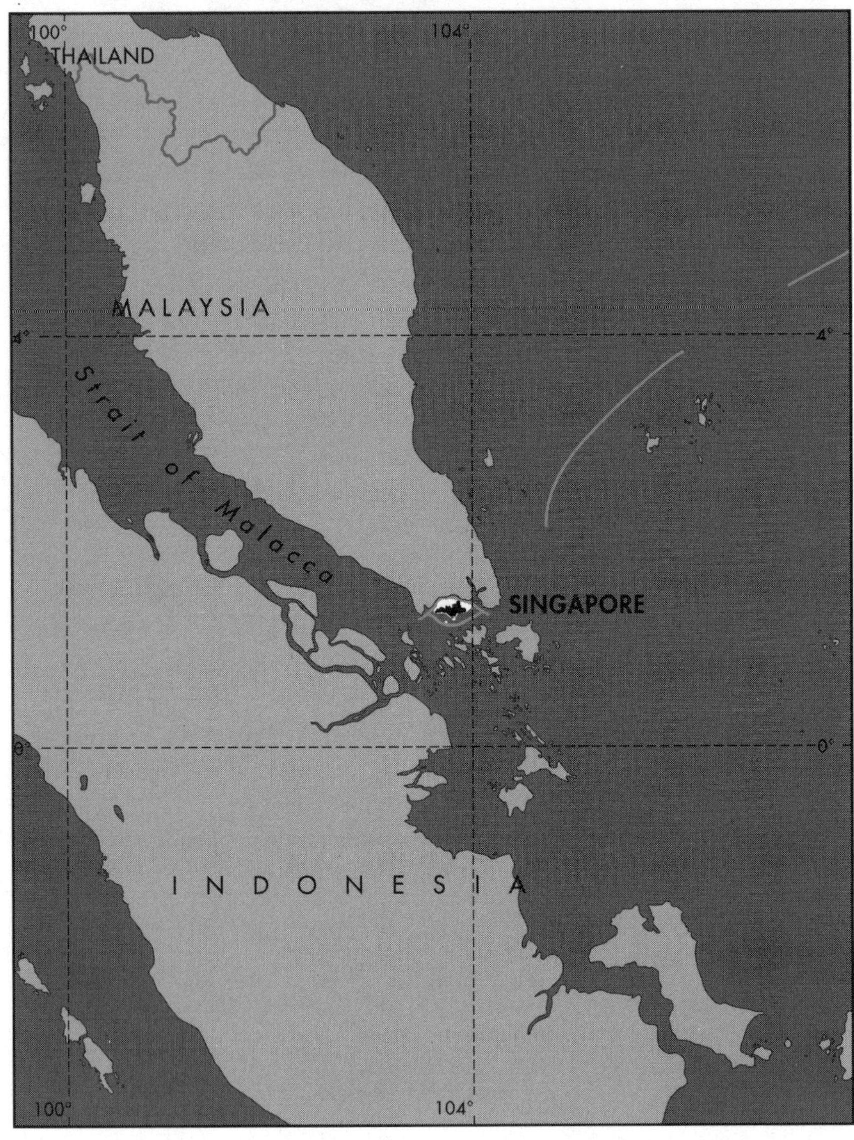
IBRD 34931
JULY 2006
CITY OF SINGAPORE, SINGAPORE
CAPITAL (SINGAPORE) URBAN EXTENT
0 100 200 Kilometers
100°
104°
THAILAND
MALAYSIA
4°
Strait of Malacca
SINGAPORE
0°
INDONESIA

on average, with Indonesia allocating 3.2 percent and India and China each allotting close to 6 percent ("One Sick Patient" 2005). If we look ahead, the trend is most definitely going to be upward ("Health Spending" 2003). Nowhere are these tendencies more striking than in the major cities, where incomes are also higher on average and where sedentary lifestyles are making more people susceptible to chronic ailments. Modern medicine frequently cannot cure these maladies of advancing age, but it is ameliorating them, which allows those with access to the latest drugs and medical technologies to enjoy a much healthier older age.[3] The availability of new medications and procedures has been made possible by a readiness on the part of individuals—and the wealthier societies—to cover the cost of ever more sophisticated health care. That readiness has contributed to the high and consistent profitability of the pharmaceutical industry worldwide during the past two decades.

With the number of people in the upper age groups expected to rise sharply in the coming decades and with the deciphering of the human genome having potentially multiplied the avenues for attacking diseases and partially negating the process of aging, the biomedical industry is a natural candidate for a postindustrial metropolis looking for a growth engine. Biotechnology affects many other industrial fields, such as medicine, informatics,[4] materials science, agriculture, and engineering, and these intersections can magnify the gains. For instance, the rising demand for health care means that there is an expanding market for new biogenetic drugs, for bioengineered implants or replacement body parts, and for bioinformatics that make possible the computerized processing of data on deoxyribonucleic acid (DNA) sequences. The marriage of data-processing

are responsible for this increase, which to a greater or lesser extent will also exert an upward pressure on the currently much lower rates of spending in other countries. The first is the increasing prevalence of lifestyle conditions and age-related chronic conditions, combined with the lowering of thresholds for medical intervention (for example, for blood pressure and cholesterol). The second is the advent of new and often costly treatments (Heffler and others 2005; Reinhardt, Hussey, and Anderson 2004; Thorpe 2005). Whether a rationing of such treatments might need to be enforced in even the wealthiest countries is a question being debated, and if it comes to pass, there will be feedback effects on the level and direction of research and development.

3. For the contribution of new medications toward extending life expectancies in the United States and for a cost-benefit analysis of their advances, see Lichtenberg (2002, 2004) and Lichtenberg and Virabhak (2002).

4. Developments in information technology that facilitate electronic keeping of medical records, online health education, and some level of patient-doctor interaction have the potential of saving an immense amount of resources—up to US$165 billion annually in the United States according to one estimate.

capacity with much more penetrating medical diagnostics promises to improve the prediction of disease in later life and to prompt early remedial action to prevent chronic diseases that are expensive to treat ("Prognosis of Healthy Profits" 2006). Transgenic technologies are revolutionizing crop production, the nutritive content of food crops, and food processing. And organic light-emitting diodes for flat screen televisions and organic diodes for lasers are among the fruitful outcomes of the marriage of biology and electronics. This technology can enormously increase the efficiency with which energy is converted into light.[5] Biotechnology may not be as subject to scale economies as some of the more traditional industries, nor does it benefit from the network economies that have boosted the sales of Internet- and telecommunications-related products; however, it could provide fertile ground for many more niche products, making it especially attractive to firms in countries where local or regional markets are smaller.

BIOTECHNOLOGY RISING

The recent, relatively short history of the biotechnology industry, mainly in the United States, encourages metropolitan scale economies to aspire toward a homegrown biotech sector that can compete in the global marketplace. To understand why Singapore is willing to place large bets on cultivating a world-class biotechnology industry, a process that could take a decade or more, we need to familiarize ourselves with the recipe that policy makers are reading. This recipe is an unusual one in that it places an advanced science-based industry potentially within the reach of a small, late-starting economy that lacks both a long tradition of academic research in organic chemistry and indigenous corporate research and development (R&D) and marketing capabilities in the field of pharmaceuticals.

The essentials of biotechnology are taught in leading schools throughout the world, but biotechnology as a viable industry has taken root in only a handful of urban economies richly endowed with universities and research centers. The leading contenders among those economies are Boston, Massachusetts; San Diego and San Francisco, California; the

5. Standard incandescent bulbs convert only 10 percent of the energy supplied into light. Fluorescent bulbs convert 70 percent. Organic light-emitting diodes could convert even more ("Organic LEDs" 2005).

Washington, D.C., area; and the Research Triangle in North Carolina. Smaller clusters have sprung up in Finland, France, India, Switzerland, and the United Kingdom.[6] Nevertheless, it is the U.S. experience that entices late-starting economies.

Progress in biotechnology and its several affiliated subdisciplines, more so than advances in other fields such as electronics and engineering, is closely linked to basic scientific research. The roots of biotechnology lie in university labs. In fact, the production of chemicals is the earliest science-based industry, and owes its origins to the research done in German universities in the late 19th century.[7] This research made Germany the world's leading producer of chemical products, and the findings that emerged from university and corporate labs through the early decades of the 20th century kept Germany at the forefront of innovation in the field of chemicals.[8] It was the fruitfulness of research conducted in the U.S. universities in the 1920s that prompted pharmaceutical companies to invest in their own laboratories and to enter into collaboration with universities.[9] Over time, this relationship has deepened and become more complementary; universities, generally with substantial financial backing from the state, concentrate on the vital basic research, and companies devote more of their energies to the downstream work of isolating promising molecules and engage in their development and marketing for targeted maladies. Where medical biotechnology has traveled from the lab and entered the commercial arena, it is by virtue of the mediating role played by senior scientists. The icon of the biotechnology sector—Genentech—was founded by a scientist at the University of California–Berkeley, who made

6. Two interesting and relevant examples of budding clusters are in Turku, Finland, and in Pune, India. In the case of Turku, the emergence of a cluster is based not only on investment in research in the university sector but also on the prior existence in the area of pharmaceutical, materials, and food-processing industries (Srinivas and Viljamaa 2003). The cluster in Pune depends on the existence of the National Chemical Laboratory (Basant and Chandra 2005).

7. Felix Hoffman's synthesizing of acetylsalicylic acid in the laboratories of the German dye maker Bayer was arguably the event that gave rise to the pharmaceutical industry (Santos 2003). The dyestuffs industry was located adjacent to the silk and textile industries in France and Germany, which is why some of the early discoveries were in cities such as Basel, Switzerland, which lies on the crossroads of France and Germany (Pisano 2002).

8. Germany also emerged as a leader in the pharmaceutical industry. However, during the past decade, Germany's fragmented pharmaceutical industry, with its many medium-size firms, is facing difficulties competing with the giant multinational corporations that dominate the business ("Too Little, Too Late" 2006).

9. Mowery (1990) traces the spread of corporate research to the U.S. government's antitrust policies that encouraged firms to seek profitable avenues for diversification.

recombinant DNA a reality, and his venture capitalist partner.[10] This pattern has persisted. All too frequently the gems of the biotech world are being discovered in the university labs, and because the invariably time-consuming process of commercialization often calls for continuing scientific inputs, academic researchers are generally the ones who give birth to biotech firms, frequently in conjunction with a financial sponsor.

In other words, a local biotech industry or a major research institute such as the Scripps and Salk Institutes in San Diego and the National Institutes of Health (NIH) in Washington, D.C.,[11] is inseparable from a leading research university with a focus on the life sciences, such as the University of California–San Diego, the University of San Francisco, and Johns Hopkins University. As just one example, the Maryland suburbs of Washington, D.C., and Baltimore have 2 major universities and 26 other institutions offering a basic degree in bioscience or more (Feldman and Francis 2003). The industry tends to be localized because uncodified knowledge at the scientific frontier diffuses slowly and mainly through face-to-face exchanges. The entry and clustering of firms is relatively more important in the biotech subsector because growth is more dependent on the inflow of new firms and less on the growth of existing ones. Moreover, small biotech firms are more reliant on other firms, on universities, and on a support infrastructure (Niosi and Banik 2005; Van der Voort and De Jong 2004; Zhang and Patel 2005).

Although the leading university is one part of the picture, the success of such a university in triggering the development of a biotech cluster rests in no small part on the presence of star scientists with an entrepreneurial bent, whose labs are the loci of significant discoveries, who attract talented researchers and funding, and whose reputations are supported by a long list of frequently cited articles. When it comes to commercialization of scientific findings and the financing of nascent start-ups, reputation and the record of publications clearly count in finding backers and winning credibility in the marketplace (Niosi and Banik 2005; Smilor and others 2005; Zhang and Patel 2005).

Because star scientists need an environment that is conducive to research and its commercialization, a third element must be added to the

10. Before the discovery of recombinant DNA (rDNA), it was not possible to manufacture proteins or large molecule-based compounds in quantity. Hence, most drugs were based on organic compounds and the assembly of simple small molecules, with the exceptions being a small number of antibiotics. However, rDNA and advances in monoclonal antibodies and combinatorial chemistry have greatly widened the scope for drug development (Pisano 2002).

11. See Biotechnology Information Institute (1994).

recipe, again from a reading of the U.S. experience. Prolonged and costly research on biotechnology cannot be supported from the resources of a university alone, or even from the lavish support of foundations in the United States. It needs government backing on an extensive scale, and the National Science Foundation and NIH have funded 75 percent of the basic research in the life sciences, paving the way for a succession of path-breaking discoveries.[12] In addition, the life sciences also receive funding from the Department of Defense, Department of Agriculture, Department of Health and Human Services, Food and Drug Administration, and National Institute of Standards and Technology (Feldman and Francis 2003). Nearly three-fourths of all papers cited in industrial patent documents were financed by the U.S. federal government (Narin, Hamilton, and Olivastro 1997). But the government has done much more than simply provide the grants that have fueled decades of fundamental research. To spur industrial activity, it has encouraged universities to license and patent federally funded research through a series of legislative initiatives, among which the Stevenson-Wydler and the Bayh-Dole Acts of 1980 were the landmark steps. In turn, universities have encouraged staff members to be innovative and enterprising by helping them to license and patent their findings, by encouraging consulting, by setting up university-owned businesses, by embarking on a variety of collaborative arrangements with researchers in private institutes and throughout the world, and by being flexible in assigning teaching obligations—and generous with granting leave as well—so that faculty can pursue research projects.

Capping all of this government support and institutional incentives is the system for protecting intellectual property. In a field such as biotechnology, where many years, if not decades, separate the discovery at the scientific bench from a commercial product, affordably priced and credibly enforced patent protection is essential for translating scientific discoveries into innovations, some of which might ultimately lead to viable products and even to blockbuster drugs.

The story of biotechnology in the United States would be incomplete without reference to five other crucial handmaidens. First, and foremost, is risk capital. Drug discovery is expensive, and it takes a long and painstaking search through molecule libraries to identify candidate molecules and to go from discovery to regulatory approval (Santos 2003). In the United States, only 5 out of 250 compounds graduate from clinical to human trial

12. The public funding that became available in large amounts after the 1970s in the United States imparted a strong impetus to biotech developments (Pisano 2002).

phases (Danzon, Nicholson, and Pereira 2005). The estimates of the cost of developing new drugs in the United States can be as much as US$1 billion (in 2000 dollars) (C. Adams and Brantner 2004; DiMasi, Hansen, and Grabowski 2003).[13] A biotech start-up with a promising idea must find patient capital for the teething years, when the start-up is burning cash. Financing comes from government bodies such as the Small Business Innovation Research program or state-level agencies and venture capitalists that see the need to support firms from inception, possibly through the mezzanine stage. Undergirding these sources are public institutions that have made the venture capital industry—including angel investors—in its many manifestations a vast and dynamic force in the United States—a force, moreover, that is inextricably associated with technological advances in information technology, electronics, and biotechnology.

Second, large corporations—in particular pharmaceutical giants—play a role that is somewhat complementary to that of venture capitalists in the United States. Aside from spending vast sums on R&D themselves, the big pharmaceutical companies have more often than not taken a biotech product to fruition using their immense development and marketing capabilities. In the process, by buying up small biotech companies, they have richly rewarded the scientist entrepreneurs and their initial financiers by providing one of two essential keys to the incentive system, the other being the initial public offering on the financial market.[14]

Third, budding biotech companies need financing, but they also need space for their laboratories and initial-batch production facilities.[15] These facilities can often be of a specialized nature not readily available through the commercial sector. In the key biotech centers in the United States, the problem has been tackled by way of incubators, mostly set up by universities or state governments and by the creation of science parks, which include the requisite specialized facilities. Science parks may be set up either by universities or by municipalities, with or without the participation

13. However, there are large variations among drugs for different symptoms and among different firms. For instance, the average cost of new drugs for HIV/AIDS is US$479 million, while that for rheumatoid arthritis is US$936 million. Some firms spend only US$500 million or so on development of a new drug, while other firms may spend upward of US$2 billion (C. Adams and Brantner 2004). Serious questions have been raised by Light and Warburton (2005) as to how these costs are calculated, including the opportunity cost of capital committed.

14. The big pharmaceutical firms are key players, if not in exploration, then in the exploitation of new findings (Cooke 2005; Santos 2003).

15. In fact, the supply of new biotechnology-engineered medicines has been constrained by shortages of highly specialized production capacity ("Demand Far Outstrips Supply" 2002).

of private developers. Such arrangements have enabled biotech firms, both start-ups and more mature firms, to find the accommodation that matches their requirements at each stage of their development.[16]

Fourth, biotech firms that are taking aim at the medical marketplace must fine-tune and test their products. They require real-time feedback from the users and ultimate recipients of their products and need clues to guide the development of a piece of equipment or a drug delivery system or to direct the targeting of a molecule. Such feedback is facilitated by the proximity of a network of hospitals—preferably teaching hospitals such as those in San Francisco and Boston—that are geared to conduct research experimentation and are staffed with professionals motivated to push the boundaries of medical science. Biotech companies can emerge and even flourish in a variety of environments. However, the nature of their business is such that an adjacent, strong hospital complex is a great asset, and all the notable biotech clusters in the United States—for example, the one in Washington, D.C., metropolitan area—benefit from the presence of a hospital network that is supportive of medical innovation.

Fifth, biotech firms rely on an array of other research and professional service providers, including suppliers of reagents and test kits, lawyers, headhunters, management consultants, marketing specialists, and many others.[17] The collective efforts of these varied professionals are critical to the occasional success of the exotic offerings of the biotechnology industry. Typically, these elite professionals seek an environment that suits their tastes and is congruent with their incomes and lifestyles. Hence, the geography of the biotech industry in the United States is determined not just by the presence of world-class research universities and hospital centers but also by where certain kinds of professional elites, angel investors, venture capitalists, and the biotech entrepreneurs themselves want to live. Invariably, they prefer metropolitan areas in some of the choicest locations—ones that are richly endowed with recreational amenities; high-quality housing, schooling, and public services; and relatively mild weather. There are many world-class universities in the United States that have failed to attract biotech clusters or any industrial clusters. Sometimes these clusters form elsewhere because of a university philosophy that deliberately eschews commercial involvement and focuses exclusively on academic

16. See Walcott (1999) on the role of developers and the transport network in the development of the biotechnology industry around Atlanta, Georgia.

17. In fact, services companies catering to the needs of the NIH and local hospitals provided a springboard for the development of the biotech industry in the Washington, D.C., metropolitan area (Feldman and Francis 2003).

achievements, as in the case of Johns Hopkins University in Baltimore, Maryland (Feldman and Martin 2004). More often, as in the case of Yale University, the University of Pennsylvania, and Carnegie Mellon University, it is because the urban surroundings and mix of amenities simply do not attract the assortment of talented people who are the makings of a dynamic biotech industry (O'Mara 2005). New Haven, Connecticut, was once a thriving and attractive city—the 16th-ranked industrial city in the United States as recently as 1950. Today, it is an impoverished and blighted urban area that can derive no energy or commercial boost from the presence of the second-ranked university in the United States (Rae 2003). Similarly, the lack of space for industry and the concentration of low-income households in the immediate neighborhood have prevented the University of Pennsylvania from catalyzing a cluster of high-tech firms in its Philadelphia locale.

Broadly, this summary shows how the biotechnology industry simmered into existence in the United States. In just 25 years, the industry has advanced from Genentech in 1979 to 1,500 firms, including some very large ones such as Biogen Idec, Amgen, and Chiron. The industry now employs 187,500 people and has a turnover of US$46 billion. It attracted US$4.9 billion in venture capital in 2004, and it generates more than 7,000 patents annually.[18] Biotechnology is a hive of activity in the United States. The institutions—and individuals—that are plowing billions of dollars into the industry clearly believe that its long-run prospects are exceptionally bright. But the dark and open secret is that most biotech firms make no profit; they burn through investors' cash in pursuit of wonder drugs and exotic medical implants, but so far their commercial success is meager.

BIO-SINGAPORE

Singapore has swallowed the promise and is systematically implementing the U.S. model on a scale appropriate for its size.[19] In its efforts to diversify industry and move up the technology ladder, the government views

18. Biotechnology Industry Organization, "Biotechnology Industry Facts," (http://www.bio.org/speeches/pubs/er/statistics.asp).

19. A study of technological prowess and innovativity in eight OECD countries shows that the smaller ones, such as Belgium and the Netherlands, are in the lead and that biotech is a fertile source of innovations (OECD 2006). Ireland, with a population comparable to Singapore's 3.9 million, is also pursuing a pharmaceuticals cum biotech cluster ("Dublin Thinks" 2003), as is Finland in the vicinity of Turku.

biotechnology as the industrial driver with the best job and export prospects, given Singapore's resource base, the emerging demands for health care in the Southeast Asian region, and the industry's continuing, possibly growing need for innovating smaller players.

Having built tertiary-level teaching institutions for nearly three decades, Singapore now has the capacity to train researchers and expose them to basic research in the university environment. There is now a pool of local talent, and plans are being implemented to make it grow. The National University of Singapore has embraced the model of an entrepreneurial university (à la the Massachusetts Institute of Technology) and has introduced courses to instill the entrepreneurial spirit in its graduates (Etzkowitz 2002; Wong 2006a). Moreover, public health and hospital facilities are well equipped and efficiently staffed. The hospital infrastructure, whether or not it is affiliated with universities, is a source of demand for products, offers arenas for testing new therapies, and makes it possible for researchers to practice medicine part time, giving them valuable practical knowledge. The Singapore government has begun investing in state-of-the-art laboratory facilities and bidding for experienced foreign researchers, including star scientists. The city-state has established a strong production base for pharmaceuticals. It has set up incubators to supply the space and some of the patient risk capital to help new firms to make a start, and the government is offering large foreign firms attractive fiscal incentives in the hope that they could become the source of spinoffs and the axes for a cluster. Singapore's robust legal system and efficient courts underpin rules protecting intellectual property rights that are among the best designed and most effectively enforced in Asia.

Last but not least, in Southeast and South Asia, the market for blockbuster medications is on the rise as the ailments of affluence, such as cancer, heart disease, and obesity ("Of Mice and Men" 2003), become more widespread. At the same time, there are also many substantial niche markets for drugs and vaccines to treat conditions specific to the region, including a number of infectious diseases endemic to tropical regions. This niche could be profitable for Singapore because only 1 percent of the 1,400 new drugs approved for commercial purposes during 1975 to 1999 were for tropical diseases, which afflict the vast majority of the world's population and kill millions each year. In large part, that lack of tropical disease–oriented drugs is because the major companies see little profit and many risks from investing in medications for people with limited buying power (Farlow 2005; Kremer 2000). Their reluctance to enter those thin markets opens the door for smaller companies that are less encumbered with overhead and high expectations regarding profits and that have the staying power and can mobilize the talent. These are not trifling conditions, but they also challenge companies to evolve technologies and seek breakthroughs ("Exotic Pursuits" 2003).

Among the age-old infectious diseases against which an effective and long-lasting vaccine has yet to be developed, three—from a number of candidates, including the lethal diseases caused by the Ebola and the Marburg viruses—are uppermost: tuberculosis (TB), malaria, and influenza ("Diseases Remain" 2005; "Knockout Malaria Vaccine" 2005). They present challenges for researchers in Southeast Asia, with the avian flu emerging as a peculiarly deadly threat in 2005 and 2006 ("Vietnam's War" 2005). However, more than researchers face challenges because the financing of the development and the pricing and purchasing of the vaccines for widespread use all pose difficult hurdles for firms, insurers, and governments (see Coleman and others 2005; Hinman 2005; Kremer 2000; Pauly 2005). Novartis has set up a research facility in Singapore focusing on dengue fever and multidrug-resistant TB.[20] These smaller markets offer opportunities for new start-ups from a Singaporean cluster.

Are the chances for newcomers to the biomedical and pharmaceutical industry improving, or are the odds against commercial success lengthening? Certainly the declining number of first- or second-in-class drugs, the proliferation of copycat drugs, the limited offerings of the leading biomedical companies, and the human and financial toll inflicted by blockbuster drugs, such as Vioxx, that have caused complications, raise concerns.[21] Moreover, the purportedly rising costs of development and testing of new drugs and the increasing resistance to the rising retail costs of drugs all argue against Singapore's industrial strategy.

Still, there is another side to the picture, which is appreciably brighter. There are three reasons for viewing the glass as being half full. First is the persistent evidence that small start-ups, many by university-based researchers, are a major conduit for discoveries in the medical field. Those start-ups frequently must join forces with the giants to test and market their findings, but they are the sources of the products. Second, recent findings raise questions about the claims made that bringing a drug to the market can take 12 years or more and can cost between US$800 million and US$1.5 billion. Light and Warburton (2005) estimate that once capital costs are readjusted and the initial contribution of academic

20. GlaxoSmithKline also initiated research into malaria and TB in Spain in 2001 ("Exotic Pursuits" 2003; "Game Is On" 2004).

21. See, for instance, "These Pills" (2003) on AstraZeneca's drug Nexium, which is similar to its earlier antiulcer drug, Prilosec.

researchers is factored in, the true cost could be closer to US$220 million, which, if correct, would suggest that entry barriers are much lower. In this context, a third factor, which is the promising research on biomarkers, should expedite the screening of molecules for their therapeutic properties and reduce search costs. Customizing drugs for smaller target groups with specific genetic characteristics will further reduce the outlay on tests ("Biotech, Finally" 2005; "Drugs Get Smart" 2005; "Prescription for Change" 2005).[22]

Based on international experience and Singapore's own track record with the electronics industry, the case for targeting the biotech industry is, in principle, a good one. The government is carefully assembling the individual ingredients with fairly lavish upfront expenditures. What are the chances that the effort will succeed, and can biotechnology fulfill the needs of the island-state for a reliable engine of growth and employment? To answer that, we first need to review what has been achieved to date and then examine the odds that the government and industry must overcome.

Scaling the Heights of Biotech

The manufacturing of pharmaceuticals in Singapore was initiated by Glaxo which, in 1982, established an operation to produce the active ingredient for Zantac. A few other investments followed, which prepared the ground for the Institute of Molecular and Cellular Biology (IMCB), founded in 1987 (Finegold, Wong, and Cheah 2004), and for the Bioprocessing Technology Center Incubator Unit some 10 years later ("Of Mice and Men" 2003).

Since then, the biomedical and pharmaceutical industry has emerged as the fourth pillar of the Singapore economy, along with electronics, chemicals, and engineering, with output from that industry amounting to S$12 billion and value added was S$7 billion in 2003 (see table 4.1) ("Singapore's Man" 2004).[23] The target for 2015 is set at US$15 billion ("Irresistible Force" 2005). In 2004, biomedical manufacturing, including pharmaceuticals and medical technology, accounted for 2.6 percent of employment, 9.1 percent of output, and 21.3 percent of the value added in total manufacturing (see table 4.2). This industry is a capital-intensive

22. The use of genomic markers being developed by the science of pharmacogenomics to determine drug response will, if successful, significantly cut costs (Vernon and Hughen 2005).

23. Much of the manufacturing of these drugs is done by the major pharmaceutical companies such as Pfizer, Merck, Eli Lilly, and GlaxoSmithKline ("Singapore: Pharma Industry" 2004).

Table 4.1 Output and Value Added of the Singapore Biomedical Industry, 1997–2004
(S$ million)

Year	Manufacturing output	Value added
1997	2,600	1,900
1998	4,000	2,700
1999	6,300	2,500
2000	6,400	3,800
2001	6,800	3,700
2002	9,700	5,800
2003	11,300	6,900
2004	12,180	—

Source: Parayil 2005.

Note: — = not available. Manufacturing output for 2004 is an estimate.

Table 4.2 Biomedical Manufacturing in Singapore, 2004

Sector or subsector	Employment		Output		Value added	
	Number	Percentage	S$ million	Percentage	S$ million	Percentage
Biomedical manufacturing sector	9,225	2.6	17,199	9.1	10,072	21.3
Pharmaceutical subsector	3,851	1.1	15,167	8.0	8,980	19.0
Medical technology subsector	5,374	1.5	2,033	1.1	1,092	2.3

Source: Ministry of Trade and Industry (Singapore) 2004.

Note: Share of total manufacturing.

one, with average capital per worker of close to S$1 million in 2003 and with average output per firm of S$255 million, both significantly higher than the average for all manufacturing in Singapore (Wong 2005).

The government's strategy is to create an entire value chain in Singapore rather than to focus on just one aspect of the biotech complex. If it succeeds, far more of the value adding and employment benefits can be internalized. Among the subcomponents of the biotech sector that Singapore's Economic Development Board (EDB) wants to develop are biotechnology, pharmaceuticals, medical devices,[24] health care services,

24. The opportunities for small but significant advances in implantable devices are legion. Thus, the effectiveness of cardiac pacemakers has been steadily enhanced by the introduction of dual chamber devices and rate response algorithms and by improvements in the implantability of sensors for optimal response (Trohman, Kim, and Pinski 2004). However, the problem with

Table 4.3 Biomedical Public Research Institutes in Singapore, December 2002

Institute	Year established	Size of staff	Number of publications	Number of patents filed
Institute of Molecular and Cell Biology	1987	380	987	206
Bioprocess Internship Programme	1990	126	67	3
Genome Institute of Singapore	2000	112	4	3
Bioinformatics Institute	2001	40	0	0
Institute of Bioengineering and Nanotechnology	2002	53	2	9

Source: Parayil 2005.

and bioinformatics (Parayil 2005). The strategy is being put through its paces on some land set aside for this purpose near the National University of Singapore and its medical facilities.

Biopolis

An investment of US$286 million has resulted in a complex of seven connected buildings called Biopolis[25] that houses five public institutes specializing in fields such as informatics, bioengineering, and cell biology (see table 4.3). Biopolis sits on 18.5 hectares within a much larger development, which is called One North Science Park covers more than 200 hectares ("Game Is On" 2004; Tan and Phang 2005).[26] Underneath

Guidant's pacemakers also points to the risks of these devices and the associated liability costs. Cochlear implants and various kinds of "electronic pills," implantable pumps, and electrodes are also coming into wider use ("Eat Your Own" 2003; "Listen" 2005). Some companies specializing in imaging, such as Olympus and Canon, are teaming up with biotech firms to devise techniques for cancer detection ("Cangen Finds Niche" 2005).

25. The building of One North Science Park is modeled after Silicon Valley (Koh and Wong 2005). Singapore is quick off the mark to build the physical infrastructure for new clusters in the hope that the businesses that will populate those clusters will materialize, whether from abroad or from within the local economy. Two other recent examples are the S$667 million Esplanade Theatres on the Bay, which were constructed in 2002 to "put Singapore on the map for arts and cultural tourism" (Yeoh 2005, 949). The other complex is Suntec City, a S$2 billion project to build a services and entertainment complex housed in five office towers, a mall, and an exhibition center. Whether the high value adding activities can be attracted and made to put down roots is debatable, but the physical environment has been created with careful attention to detail.

26. The Singapore government plans to invest S$15 billion to develop One North as the R&D center for scientists and researchers in three industries: biomedical science, information technology, and media (Tan and Phang 2005).

the complex lies a vivarium, which houses a quarter-million mice for research purposes ("Of Mice and Men" 2003). The vivarium opened in October 2003. Unlike many other science parks, Biopolis is designed to provide a place where biomedical researchers can "work, live, play, and learn," complete with offices, condominiums, and shopping and entertainment facilities (Parayil 2005). Recognizing that biomedical researchers need to be in close contact with their peers around the world, the designers of the complex equipped it with the latest telecommunications facilities, thus permitting fast Internet connection with other main research centers. Hence, Singapore-based researchers have the computing power they need to analyze molecules and models and to explore genetic combinations using grid computing ("Of Mice and Men" 2003). By 2005, a fraction of the complex was occupied with a small sprinkling of restaurants and shops. The planners envisage an eventual community of 2,000 researchers in the seven buildings (Tan and Phang 2005).

In an effort to replicate their successful strategy of attracting global electronics firms to Singapore, EDB is pulling all the stops to draw the pharmaceutical and biomedical giants to Singapore and to make Biopolis the leading biotech center of Southeast Asia. Through EDB's efforts, foreign direct investment in biomedical science in 2001 reached US$483 million, a growth of 6 percent compared with the previous year ("Can Money Turn" 2005). The companies that have invested in production capacity or research include S*Bio, Merlion, and Lilly Systems Biology, among others. S*Bio is a joint venture between Chiron and EDB to develop products for cancer and for infectious diseases that are endemic in Asia (Wong, Ho, and Singh 2005). Merlion was originally a joint venture with Glaxo and EDB that was spun off as an independent entity following the merger of Glaxo Wellcome with SmithKlineBeecham to form GlaxoSmithKline. It inherited a vast library of more than 450,000 natural compounds, which can be mined to identify natural compounds for new drugs. By leveraging this collection, Merlion has entered into collaboration with firms such as Merck, British Biotech, and NovImmune (Wong, Ho, and Singh 2005). Schering-Plough has invested close to S$1 billon in Singapore, as has GlaxoSmithKlein, and Pfizer has plowed S$600 million into a facility to produce active pharmaceutical ingredients (Parayil 2005). Lilly Systems Biology, a wholly owned subsidiary of Eli Lilly, has an R&D center staffed by 50 scientists to explore computational tools for drug discovery. Similarly, the Novartis Institute for Tropical Diseases has 60 researchers working on treatments for infectious diseases common in the region. And a Japanese pharmaceutical company, Chugai Pharmaceutical, has initiated a small venture called PharmaLogical Research with

Table 4.4 Three Phases of Clinical Trials

Phase	Description
I	Based on a small number of volunteers (healthy or sometimes with specific diseases) to test for safe dosages, absorption, distribution, metabolic effects, excretion, and toxicity.
II	Based on patients with conditions for which the proposed drug is to test the preliminary efficacy of the drug and its safety. Typically, this phase involves hundreds of patients.
III	Based on a large number of patients to establish efficacy and to test for side effects. Typically, this phase involves thousands of patients.

Source: DiMasi, Hansen, and Grabowski 2003.

Note: In the case of the United States, a phase I clinical trial is often conducted outside of the country.

10 researchers ("Can Money Turn" 2005; Wong, Ho, and Singh 2005). Virtually all of the 40 or so pharmaceutical manufacturing firms in Singapore are majority foreign owned (Wong 2005).

To strengthen its appeal for the pharmaceutical companies, Singapore is also marketing the island-state's hospital infrastructure. The hospitals in Singapore offer access to a multiracial population as a potential site for clinical trials. Local hospitals attract wealthy patients from Indonesia and Malaysia ("Can Money Turn" 2005)[27] and are subject to an efficient regulatory regime that can facilitate clinical trials. This effort is being buttressed by a joint venture with Johns Hopkins University to set up the International Medical Center with Singapore's National University Hospital, which will provide patient care and conduct clinical trials in oncology (Wong, Ho, and Singh 2005). The plan also includes moving the Center for Molecular Medicine, with its 150 researchers, closer to National University Hospital to take advantage of the existence of a teaching hospital. The Center for Molecular Medicine will include a facility to mass produce stem cells for clinical research ("Irresistible Force" 2005). Firms such as Pharmacia and Novo Nordisk are exploring the advantages of conducting trials in Singapore, as is GlaxoSmithKline, which opened a preclinical facility in Biopolis to study Alzheimer's disease ("Eastern Rebirth" 2005; Wong, Ho, and Singh 2005). However, the number of clinical trials conducted by those firms is still small, partly because demography and geography limit the scale and number of the trials. Of the three phases of the clinical trials for new drugs, phase I and II trials can be more easily conducted in Singapore (see table 4.4). But the small size of

27. On this front, Singapore faces competition from other countries, notably Thailand and Malaysia (Tan and Phang 2005).

the population—and hence the incidence of particular ailments that a drug targets—may pose a difficulty for conducting phase III clinical trials, which involve thousands of patients with a common medical condition. In this area, Singapore is facing competition from countries such as India and China, where the population size enables researchers to more easily identify a target group of patients and the costs of clinical trials are lower ("India Emerges" 2004).[28]

Inevitably, not all the efforts to attract multinational corporations (MNCs) have worked. For instance, SurroMed, a U.S. firm specializing in molecular barcoding technology, opened a US$25 million R&D center in 2001, with financing from EDB, but the center was dissolved in 2003 (Wong, Ho, and Singh 2005). There are other reasons why tangible evidence of progress has been slow to collect. One reasonably consistent finding across a number of industrial countries is that publicly funded research or research in the leading public laboratories complements rather than substitutes for research done by private entities. At the same time, larger firms appear to derive much more benefit from the spillovers generated by this research and through direct links with government labs. Moreover, firms in the chemical, pharmaceutical, and biotechnology fields have been among the ones most likely to work closely and advantageously with public research institutes (Cohen, Nelson, and Walsh 2002; David, Hall, and Toole 1999; Veugelers and Cassiman 2005). Thus, Singapore's investment in public research institutes could be the basis for collaboration with the private sector. However, the presence of large foreign firms will begin to pay off only if they move some of their basic and early-stage development work to Singapore rather than keeping it closer to their head offices. So far, there is no sign that any firms have done so, because Singapore is still very far from having built up a sizable core of researchers. Furthermore, residual fears exist regarding the loss of intellectual property, which is especially valuable and vulnerable to loss in the pharmaceutical industry. Such fears induce firms to compartmentalize

28. For instance, when Germany's Mucos Pharma GmbH wanted to find 650 patients out of 750 for a clinical trial in India, it visited only five hospitals and took only 18 months to identify those patients. By comparison, the firm took 36 months and visited 22 hospitals to identify the remaining 100 patients in Europe ("India Emerges" 2004). Conducting trials in China could be even cheaper and more efficient. A recently completed trial for an anticlotting drug called Plavix by Bristol-Myers Squibb involved 45,852 patients in 1,250 Chinese hospitals. That trial cost a few million dollars and was expedited by close support from doctors and by the provision of high-quality data (COMMIT 2005). More than 2 million new cases of cancer are diagnosed in China each year—enough to find volunteers for new cancer treatment drugs. The cost of clinical trials in China is about one-tenth of that in the United States ("Cancer Treatment" 2006).

their research and to secure their most vital investigations and intellectual property (Dietz, Lin, and Yang 2005). And after two years, Biopolis still has a deserted air. There are more tenants, but not much "buzz" or sense that it is one of those privileged places where big things are going to happen. That could change.

Star Scientists

Alongside its effort to induce foreign direct investment into biotechnology, the government is also sparing no effort to assemble a team of star scientists to lead the current research and to serve as attractors for other talented people. The lure is ample funding, advanced facilities, a liberal regulatory regime, and the opportunity to engage in stem cell research, which is subject to more stringent checks in Europe and the United States. This program has notched up some early successes.[29] Jackie Ying, formerly a professor at the Massachusetts Institute of Technology (MIT), now heads the Institute of Bioengineering and Nanotechnology of the Agency for Science, Technology, and Research. One of her neighbors in Biopolis is Alan Colman, who worked on cloning Dolly the sheep and now heads a research team in ES Cell International that makes insulin-producing cells from stem cells, with human clinical trials anticipated to start in 2006 ("Asia Jockeys" 2005). Similar work by Bernat Soria on insulin has been ongoing in Singapore since 2002, with the support of the Juvenile Diabetes Research Foundation in the United States. Soria's research was originally conducted in Spain, but the regulatory ban on further work persuaded him to move to Singapore to pursue his research ("Asia Jockeys" 2005).[30] Soria has been joined by Axel Ulrich from the Max Planck Institute in Martinsreid, Germany, who is a leading authority on the treatment of cancer and diabetes and who heads the Onco Genome lab in Biopolis. The interest in insulin-producing cells in Asia is immense because Asia has the largest concentration of diabetics in the world (Parayil 2005). Other leading lights who have taken up residence in Singapore include Sydney Brenner, a Nobel Laureate in medicine; Edison Liu, former director of the U.S. National Cancer Institute; David Lane, one of the codiscoverers

29. Singapore is top ranked among small countries for its ability to attract talent from around the world, according to the *World Competitiveness Report* (Koh and Wong 2005). The reliance on foreign talent stems from the fact that only a few Singapore citizens are working or studying in the biotechnology field ("Can Money Turn" 2005).

30. Although the Spanish government has since relaxed the regulation of stem cell research, Soria intends to stay in Singapore ("Asia Jockeys" 2005).

of the p53 cancer gene;[31] Ian McNeice, an oncologist from Johns Hopkins University in Baltimore; and Yoshiaki Ito, one of the pioneers of chemical carcinogens who is recognized for his research on the Runx genes (Finegold, Wong, and Cheah 2004).

In attempting to become a leading commercial force in the field of biotechnology, Singapore has an advantage over other countries, especially those in East Asia. The official language is English, which facilitates communication among the team members when researchers come from different countries. For instance, a 25-person research team at ES Cell International includes researchers from 15 different countries ("Asia Jockeys" 2005). Without having English as the working language, their collaboration would have been quite difficult to manage. Anecdotal evidence suggests that, for this reason, many recent Ph.D. graduates in Europe consider Singapore to be one of the places where they would be willing to work. However, Singapore needs a stable critical mass of scientists in this field and the ability to retain them until there is a more plentiful supply of homegrown scientists, some of whom have the requisite experience and entrepreneurship ("Can Money Turn" 2005). Currently only 8.2 percent of researchers working at various government research institutes are citizens of Singapore with Ph.D.s (Tan and Phang 2005). Of the 35 principal investigators at the IMCB, only one is a citizen of Singapore. Moreover, patents granted in Singapore to Singapore residents, while rising, are miniscule compared with the number of patents granted to nonresidents (see table 4.5).[32] Although foreign researchers provide a temporary stopgap and might be a partial solution, for the longer term, the depth of basic science and the scale of the effort needed to move forward at the commercial level demand a far greater input of domestic knowledge workers, as is the case in Finland, Ireland, and Israel.

Manpower Planning

The scarcity of homegrown talent has not escaped the planners. Singapore is trying to enlarge the domestic pool of science and technology personnel by encouraging enrollment in biotech-related fields both from within Singapore and from abroad. To expand domestic training, Nanyang Technology University opened the School of Biological Sciences and has invested in state-of-the-art equipment and facilities.

31. The p53 cancer gene is used in a gene therapy for cancer patients in China, the only country where such treatment is available ("Cancer Treatment" 2006).

32. Charter Semiconductor is the only domestic firm among the top 10 filers of patent applications in Singapore.

Table 4.5 Breakdown of Patents Granted in Singapore, 1995–2004

Year	Patents granted to Singapore residents	Patents granted to nonresidents	Total	Domestic share of patents granted (%)
1995	20	1,730	1,750	1.1
1996	30	3,300	3,330	0.9
1997	20	3,100	3,120	0.6
1998	30	2,360	2,390	1.3
1999	50	4,360	4,410	1.1
2000	110	4,980	5,090	2.2
2001	170	7,050	7,220	2.4
2002	240	7,340	7,580	3.2
2003	180	4,160	4,340	4.1
2004	400	5,580	5,980	6.7

Source: Intellectual Property Office of Singapore (http://www.ipos.gov.sg/).

In 2003, the Agency for Science, Technology, and Research budgeted US$286 million in scholarships for doctorate students in biomedical sciences who are willing to commit to working in Singapore for up to eight years upon completing their studies ("Of Mice and Men" 2003). In addition, the school curriculum at tertiary and secondary levels has been modified to provide the younger generation more opportunities to study the life sciences (Koh and Wong 2005). All those efforts are sound investments, but the payoff lies at least a decade or more in the future ("Singapore Aims" 2005).

The quality of university research in biotechnology also needs improving if Singapore is to become a regional biotechnology cluster. Such quality, especially with regard to basic research, was not essential for the electronics industry where applied research and sustained on-the-job training proved sufficient. But biotechnology is a more demanding field, and the research threshold needs to be set higher. Singapore is relying on the strength of its established and well-known university, the National University of Singapore (NUS), to set up either a satellite school or alliances so as to quickly develop research capability in the biomedical sciences. The alliances being cultivated are with Johns Hopkins University, MIT, Duke University, Columbia University, and the Indian Institutes of Technology (Finegold, Wong, and Cheah 2004). Moreover, a thriving homegrown cluster also needs a steady supply of entrepreneurs, and for these, Singapore is deepening on a number of training programs at the NUS.[33]

33. Feldman and Francis (2003) emphasize the role of entrepreneurship in the context of cluster development in the Washington, D.C., metropolitan area.

Regulatory Regime

In East Asia, Singapore's highly streamlined regulatory system is a byword for efficiency and incorruptibility. The regulation of the biotechnology industry is no exception. A single agency, the Health Sciences Authority, defines the rules and orchestrates business activity.

Recognizing the commercial potential and scientific significance of stem cell research, Singapore has adopted a more liberal stance than have some Western countries.[34] The current regime allows extraction of stem cells from aborted fetuses, and human embryos can be cloned and kept for up to 14 days to produce stem cells for therapeutic purposes ("Of Mice and Men" 2003). ES Cell International, which was cofounded by Ariff Bongso from NUS and Monash University, owns 6 of 78 human embryonic stem (ES) cell lines listed on NIH's Stem Cell Registry in 2002 and has supplied more than 140 ES cell lines to researchers around the world ("Asia Jockeys" 2005). Bongso successfully created human ES cells using human feeder cells and nutrients rather than mouse feeder layers in 2002. This achievement is significant because, by doing so, researchers can now use those cell lines for clinical trials, whereas researchers using animal-based cells cannot ("Asia Jockeys" 2005).[35]

Finance

In the early 1980s, EDB set up a venture capital office in the United States to invest in promising dedicated biotechnology firms. The initial purpose

34. In other countries, the regulatory hurdles to conduct stem cell research are quite high. In the United States, research in this field needs to be funded by nonfederal sources, although such rules are changing because of strong public sentiment in favor of broadening research. In Europe, because of the diverse historical and religious backgrounds, only a small portion—€130 million—of the research budget allocated by the European Union agencies in Brussels was devoted to stem cell research between 2002 and 2005, and only €13 million will be available for human embryo research out of a research budget of €17.5 billion for 2002 to 2006 ("Politics May Move" 2005). One indicator of the opportunities for the determined newcomer to the business of health care is that barely 1 percent of the global expenditures on pharmaceuticals are devoted to research on the diseases afflicting the vast majority of the world's population and killing millions each year.

35. The earlier method of relying on mouse feeder layers for the propagation of human ES cells risks introducing animal pathogens; hence, it is not suitable for human clinical trials ("Asia Jockeys" 2005). It seems that the few stem cell lines that are approved in the United States are contaminated with animal cells. This contamination could invalidate the existing and future research based on these cell lines ("Approved Stem Cell" 2005). The only way to ensure that stem cell lines are animal-free is to use newer ones without relying on the mouse feeder. However, at this point, only stem cells existing as of 2001 are usable in the United States for research supported by federal funding ("Approved Stem Cell" 2005).

of this office was to learn about the biotechnology industry through investing. Later on, firms were targeted on the basis of their willingness to establish R&D facilities in Singapore in return for an injection of funds by EDB (Finegold, Wong, and Cheah 2004). For instance, S*Bio was created through equity participation of Chiron, while EDB invested in Chiron in the United States (Finegold, Wong, and Cheah 2004).

Although the venture capital industry has since grown considerably through the entry of foreign firms (Kenney, Han, and Tanaka 2004), the reluctance of private venture capitalists to invest in biotech start-ups led the Singapore government to establish a biomedical venture fund called Bio One Capital, with assets of US$700 million, under EDB. EDB also manages the US$600 million Biomedical Sciences Investment Fund, which invests in pharmaceutical and biomedical ventures in Singapore and abroad ("Singapore: Pharma Industry" 2004). By 2002, US$150 million had been invested in 50 companies (Koh and Wong 2005).

Currently, there are more than 100 venture capital firms in Singapore. However, 20 percent of the capital originates from the government (Tan and Phang 2005), and venture capital firms depend heavily on subsidies from the government to survive.[36] A key reason for this dependence is the small number and size of the deals available in Singapore. Although some firms operate regionally, the pickings are modest. Without a large pool of potential start-ups or opportunities for mezzanine-level and advanced-stage financing, private venture capitalists will have difficulty thriving in the Singapore environment, and the government will have difficulty exiting from the business, especially if it wishes to continue supporting the biotech and other high-tech industries. (Kenney, Han, and Tanaka 2004).

Whether private venture capitalists will finance these firms for 10 years or more is questionable, especially when most venture capitalists in Singapore have invested mainly in electronics or in traditional manufacturing industries for which the exit time is only two to three years. Unless the government is prepared to provide the bulk of long-term risk capital, firms will need a definite business plan in order to sustain a steady revenue

36. The Singapore government has actively promoted the venture capital industry by offering tax and other incentives to attract foreign venture capitalists from around the world, in addition to encouraging the entry of local firms (Kenney, Han, and Tanaka 2004). In the early 1980s, it set up Vertex Management and EDB Ventures. In the late 1990s, it invested US$1 billion in a Technopreneurship Investment Fund to persuade leading global venture capitalists to use Singapore as their regional hub (Tan and Phang 2005). Vertex Management was spun off from Singapore Technologies, a government-owned industrial conglomerate (Kenney, Han, and Tanaka 2004).

flow. In the absence of such plans, few spinoffs will survive. In fact, this has been the experience with spinoffs in Singapore. Currently, there are only a limited number of surviving biotechnology spinoff firms from NUS, Lynk Biotechnologies being possibly the most successful. Lynk Biotechnologies survived the early teething stage because it was able to generate earnings from the sale of cosmetics and nondrug health products, which cover a part of the cost of drug development.

Biotechnology Competitors

Whether Singapore can take a lead in the contested field is debatable, given the volume of funding on stem cell research now forthcoming in California and other states in the United States.[37] In addition, the recent setback experienced by stem cell research in the Republic of Korea raises troubling questions and has provided ammunition to many who are opposed to such research.[38] Dr. Hwang Woo-Suk's team at Seoul National University claimed to have isolated ES cells from cloned human cells ("Asia Jockeys" 2005) and later created stem cells that matched the DNA of donors. This technique, once perfected, could have made it possible to grow replacement tissues without worrying about rejection by the immune system, which is common with implants ("Stem Cells: Big Step" 2005; "Without Apology" 2005).[39] But the findings published by the

37. Because of the ban on new stem cell research using federal funding, the state of California has allocated US$3 billion (US$300 million for the next 10 years) for the research on stem cells in California (Zhang and Patel 2005). The total R&D expenditure on biomedical research in the United States was US$94 billion in 2004, of which 57 percent came from private firms and 28 percent from NIH. (Moses and others 2005).

38. The age of the female donor matters for the efficient production of an ES cell line. Oocytes from women in their 30s yield on average one ES cell line for every 30 attempts at production, whereas only 13 tries are needed to obtain a cell line from younger women. Considering that each donation typically produces 10 oocytes, this finding is significant ("Korean Team Speeds" 2005). Because of the scarcity of eggs and of the health risks associated with extracting eggs, scientists are searching for alternative materials suitable for cloning, including growing eggs in vitro and using eggs from other animals ("Mining the Secrets" 2006).

39. Although more work is needed, Dr. Yuri Verlinsky of the Reproductive Genetics Institute in Chicago, Illinois, was able to create patient-matched stem cells without relying on therapeutic cloning. If this finding is verified, it will bypass the ethical question surrounding the destruction of embryos associated with therapeutic cloning and will be easier than Dr. Hwang's method ("Double Triumph" 2005). The reason for therapeutic cloning is to create replacement organs that will not be rejected by the immune system. However, with the controversies surrounding stem cell research, some scientists are refocusing their efforts on a better understanding of the rejection of foreign organs and ways in which to trick the immune system into accepting those donated organs ("Do We Even Need Eggs?" 2006).

Korean team were shown to have been fabricated. Thus, the challenge facing stem cell researchers is now more daunting, but the work is proceeding apace. Currently, more than 300 researchers are working on stem cell research in Korea ("East Asia Powers Ahead" 2005). More than US$10 billion is likely to be invested in biotechnology activities by Korea in the next five years (Koh and Wong 2005), far more than the investment planned by Singapore.[40]

China is another competitor with an expanding biotech program initiated during the Seventh Five-Year Plan (1986–90) (Wang and Tong 2005). The Beijing Genome Institute, with just US$50 million in public funding, has contributed significantly to the Human Genome Project and has sequenced rice, chicken, pig, and other genomes. It is now regarded as one of the top five sequencing and bioinformatics centers worldwide. ("Eastern Rebirth" 2005). The competition from China takes the form of some 300 firms that are engaged in a subfield of molecular biology and that serve a domestic market valued at US$2.4 billion in 2004, plus make contributions to the exports of reagents and other products. The government is devoting close to US$600 million to R&D, mainly focused in Beijing, Shanghai, and Shenzhen. This effort is building capability, and one Shenzhen-based firm, SiBiono GeneTech, has been certified by the authorities to market a gene-based anticancer drug, Gendicine, that attempts to suppress tumor formation by injecting a gene into the body ("Cancer Treatment" 2006; "Emerging Biotech Giant?" 2005).[41] China's pharmaceutical sector is huge, with a turnover of US$54 billion in 2004. After the United States, it is the second biggest producer of ingredients, and it exported US$4 billion in pharmaceutical products in 2004 ("Pharmaceuticals Sector" 2005). India's US$9 billion pharmaceutical industry is a second competitor with 4 percent of the global market for generics, a growing pipeline of drugs, and multiplying links with MNCs ("Copycats No More" 2005).

Between 300 and 400 Chinese researchers with Ph.D.s are engaged in stem cell research, with at least 80 of them studying ES cells. Although

40. That investment by Korea is in addition to the past and ongoing research programs, some of which are the Biotech 2000 program (1994–2007), with a US$20 billion budget; The 21st Century Frontier R&D (1999–2009), with a US$3.5 billion budget; the Development of Hybrid Biomaterials and Its Application Technology (2000–09), with W 45 billion; and the Biomedical Technology Development Project (2002–09), with W 685 billion.

41. The founder of SiBiono GeneTech, Zhaohui Peng, worked at the University of California–Los Angeles medical school and at a biotech start-up in San Diego before he returned to China to start his own company. The seed money of US$300,000 was provided by the Shenzhen government ("Cancer Treatment" 2006).

lack of information makes it difficult to gauge the progress made by scientists in China, the country has a major advantage over Singapore in its capacity to lure back researchers who were trained in Europe and the United States.[42] CapitalBio, a firm located in the Zhongguancun Life Science Park, is emerging as a world leader in biochips, a device used for biological testing and medical diagnostics that marries biotechnology and electronics. That firm, which was established in 2000,[43] is already exporting to the United States. ("Science and Technology: Scientists" 2005).[44]

Researchers at the Industrial Technology Research Institute in Taiwan (China) are also working on insulin-producing cells ("Asia Jockeys" 2005). Six of the researchers at Academia Sincia have returned from Australia, Europe, and the United States to engage in stem cell research closer to their home region ("Asia Jockeys" 2005). India is a recent entrant, but already start-ups are beginning to blossom in Bangalore and Pune.

Intellectual Property Protection

Singapore offers good intellectual property protection. The government has upgraded its Registry of Trade Marks and Patents to Intellectual Property Office of Singapore in 2001 (Tan and Phang 2005). This effort is a major advance because high-tech industries, including the biotechnology and especially the pharmaceutical industry, are sensitive to the effective enforcement of intellectual property rights. The enforcement of intellectual property rights is not perceived to be as strong in other countries such as China. For instance, a patent on Viagra by Pfizer was invalidated in China in 2004 because the application did not include sufficient data. Pfizer, however, claims that such information was never required nor requested when its application was filed in 1994. In this kind of

42. For instance, Sheng Hui Zhen, a researcher at Shanghai Second Medical University, worked at NIH for 11 years before returning to China to head a 50-person research team on stem cells. The team is funded mainly by the municipal government of Shanghai ("Asia Jockeys" 2005).

43. CapitalBio was spun off from the National Engineering Research Center for Biochip Technology ("Eastern Rebirth" 2005). It was founded in 2000 by Jing Cheng, who was a scientist at Nanogen Inc. in San Diego. With its biochip, CapitalBio has been selected to screen athletes at the 2008 Olympics in Beijing. Using just 25 chips, CapitalBio can check 10,000 samples in a day ("Can China Innovate?" 2005; "World of Opportunities" 2005).

44. The wages of newly graduated researchers in China are about one-fourth the U.S. levels, although many firms offer much higher compensation to attract researchers. That is what CapitalBio has done to attract some of their senior scientists from abroad, especially Chinese expatriates ("Science and Technology: Scientists" 2005).

environment, Pfizer has expressed caution against future expansion of research work in China ("Can China Innovate?" 2005).

READING THE BIOTECH TEA LEAVES

Singapore's strategy to create a commercially viable biotech industry is faithfully adhering to a script that has been tested in the United States. Given that no other country in the region has established a dominant position in medical biotechnology as yet, Singapore is hoping to gain first-mover advantages in the region in competition against Korean and Chinese researchers, who are also pushing the frontiers in similar areas (Parayil 2005). Singapore's strategy builds on an acquired capability in the manufacture of electronics components and in the development, debugging, testing, and prototype production of high-tech electronics parts. That capability has bolstered confidence in the efficacy of industrial policies in the Singapore context, has established the basics of an R&D infrastructure, and has encouraged the authorities to fix their sights on more ambitious targets.

Singapore's technocrats believe that a San Diego–type of medical biotechnology cluster can be called into existence in Southeast Asia through carefully choreographed policies, backed by a large infusion of state-provided resources. Their methodical pursuit of a clear objective has certainly borne some fruit in that many of the building blocks are now in place. The working space is there, teams of scientists are being assembled, MNCs have flocked to Singapore, the incentive regime is one of the strongest anywhere, and there is venture capital from public sources on tap for start-up firms and others. Bit by bit, the considerable investment in human capital and R&D is leading to more scientific publications and patents, and a critical mass of research talent is taking shape in Biopolis. The expenditure on R&D has steadily increased from 0.3 percent of GDP in 1991 to 2.2 percent by 2003, one-third of which comes from foreign firms' R&D operations in Singapore (Wong 2005).[45] The share of biotechnology in overall R&D has increased from 5 percent in the 1990s to more than 10 percent in the period from 2000 to 2003(Wong 2005). From 1999 to 2001, Singapore ranked 11th, ahead of France, Germany, and Japan in the number of published science and engineering articles, with 590 papers per 1 million inhabitants (see table 4.6), as against 433 such papers in 1998

45. Foreign firms account for 60 percent of private R&D spending (Wong 2005).

Table 4.6 Output of Science and Engineering Articles by Economy
(number per 1 million inhabitants)

Rank	Economy	1999–2001
1	Switzerland	1,165.0
2	Sweden	1,139.3
3	Israel	1,055.2
4	Finland	960.5
5	Denmark	932.2
6	United Kingdom	821.9
7	Netherlands	800.5
8	Australia	794.2
9	United States	722.2
10	Norway	720.0
11	Singapore	590.3
12	France	538.6
13	Germany	530.5
14	OECD average	490.3
15	Japan	445.6
16	Ireland	429.9
17	Spain	382.7
18	Italy	371.4
19	Taiwan (China)	330.3
20	Czech Republic	241.4
21	Korea, Rep. of	206.8
22	Portugal	191.3
23	Poland	139.9
24	Russian Federation	116.4
	Worldwide average	108.8

Source: National Science Board 2004.

(Koh and Wong 2005). But the share of biotech patents granted by the U.S. Patent and Trade Office has not kept pace with the increase in inputs. The share of biomedical patents actually declined from 2.7 percent before 2000 to less than 1.8 percent in the period from 2000 to 2003. The dramatic increase in inputs has yet to be matched by commensurate outcomes (Wong 2005).

Furthermore, the entrepreneurial spirit is still weak in Singapore. It ranks 19th out of 21 countries in Global Entrepreneurship Monitor studies covering the period from 2000 to 2002 (Koh and Wong 2005). Not only is the pool of entrepreneurs in Singapore relatively small, but the number of people who are prepared to join these new ventures is also small. Many prefer to work for the government or for established MNCs rather than for companies offering less job security (Wong, Ho, and Singh

2005). The relaxation of a number of regulations to stimulate entrepreneurship, such as allowing the public housing apartments to be used as office and commercial space, has made little difference (Tan and Phang 2005). Furthermore, the link between universities and businesses remains weak. Only 2.6 percent of university R&D was funded from private sources (Koh and Wong 2005).

There are grounds for optimism,[46] but they must be heavily qualified for a number of reasons. The optimism, as we noted above, stems from the signs that the pharmaceutical industry is entering a new phase; the focus is shifting from blockbuster drugs to medications that target much narrower markets, each generating, at most, just tens of millions of dollars each year. The new wave of drugs might target infectious diseases that are the bane of the poor, mainly in lower-income countries, or might tackle rare illnesses or be tailored to the needs of individuals with a specific genetic profile.[47] Such drugs or vaccines could cost less to research, develop, and market than the blockbuster drugs and could thereby facilitate entry of smaller companies germinating in countries such as Singapore. In effect, the assumption is that the recent era, which witnessed the steady consolidation of the pharmaceutical and biotech industries, may be in for a pause or even a reversal, and that both technological and market development will promote the entry of smaller-scale, boutique providers. Alternatively, one might see the spread of complementary relationships between small biotech companies that take the lead in innovation, whether of drugs, vaccines, or medical devices, and large pharmaceutical companies that assist with the financing, development, testing certification, and global marketing of such products.[48] Advertising now absorbs more funds than R&D, and Pfizer, for example, is the fourth-largest advertiser in the United States, spending almost

46. Currently, there are more than 20 dedicated biotechnology firms in Singapore. Seven years ago, there were none. Along with the emergence of those firms, independent contract research organizations have also started to set up R&D facilities in Singapore (Wong 2005).

47. The size of the target population matters because clinical trials are becoming more complex and expensive. Pfizer, for instance, spent US$2.1 billion to test one of its new drugs for heart disease ("Pfizer's Funk" 2005).

48. Even though Pfizer is testing a drug to raise "good" cholesterol (HDL, or high-density lipoprotein) levels at the cost of US$800 million, it is also buying a small biotech firm that is developing another HDL-raising drug at US$1.3 billion ("Pfizer's Funk" 2005). Eli Lilly has a subsidiary that runs a Web site listing some of the problems drug makers are tackling and offering rewards for solutions. Eli Lilly has more than 25,000 registered research teams around the world vying for the rewards, which range from US$10,000 to US$100,000 ("Big Trouble" 2003).

US$17 billion in 2004, twice the amount spent on R&D ("Pfizer's Funk" 2005).[49] Such an apparently fruitful relationship between pharmaceutical and biotech companies can currently be observed between Roche and Biogen Idec. Roche holds a 53 percent stake in Biogen Idec, but it guides Biogen Idec with a relatively light touch. A similar relationship exists between Roche and Genentech, in which the pharmaceutical giant has a 60 percent share. Roche also entered into an arrangement with the biotech company Antisoma for an option on one of its anticancer drugs. Similarly, GlaxoSmithKline entered into product agreements with Exelixis, also for anticancer drugs ("Big Pharma" 2002).

Industrial change that accommodates a thriving boutique segment catering to niche markets in Southeast and South Asia—and where possible, global niche markets as well—would be advantageous for firms in Singapore and for firms in other industrial countries. In fact, if such change does transpire, it would accelerate the pace of innovation and the intensity of competition.

Furthermore, a reading of recent trends suggests that societies and private individuals will continue, at least in the medium run, to give priority to medical expenses and to provide a ready market for the offerings of the biomedical industry. In other words, expenditures on medical services may continue to displace other expenditures, reflecting a high income elasticity and a low price elasticity of demand.[50] In this scenario, if the promise of the life sciences is realized, even in part, countries such as Singapore that have invested substantially in the biotech infrastructure and in specialized human capital stand to make large gains, as long as their homegrown firms produce a steady stream of commercially successful products in the biomedical and related fields. The magnitude of the benefits will depend on

49. The largest advertisers in the United States are General Motors, Procter & Gamble, and Time Warner, in descending order ("Pfizer's Funk" 2005). Drug companies in Europe and the United States also spend lavishly on marketing to doctors, employing tens of thousands of representatives and using other incentives. That expenditure in the United States amounted to US$9.4 billion in 2002 ("Pushing Pills" 2003).

50. A number of the chronic diseases that are the focus of so much research are the partial consequence of dysfunctional lifestyles. As the costs of health care mushroom, the calculus is bound to favor a change in lifestyles over ever-greater reliance on partial cures and therapeutic intervention. The U.S. experience starkly illustrates the limits of medical spending in lengthening life spans or reducing morbidity. The costliness of medical care is putting routine insurance beyond the reach of a sizable minority, the R&D on new drugs is running into decreasing returns even as it raises the costs of drugs used, and life expectancy threatens to decline rather than increase as a result of lifestyle choices that are seemingly impervious to advances in health care, to levels of education, and to the easier access to information on the causes as well as the consequences of chronic diseases.

the local value added, the employment generated, and the spillover effects from the industry, as well as from the somewhat specialized innovation system that is being put in place.

The Singapore authorities are betting on such a payoff and are banking on a biomedical cluster that complements the electronics industry and other high-tech activities while enhancing the prospects of Singapore's hospital services industry. The odds are that Singapore could achieve a degree of success, possibly not on the scale of a San Francisco, but respectable nevertheless. However, there are risks of a fizzle, and they arise from the characteristics of the biomedical industry and the factors influencing the demand for health services.

The big questions for Singapore and for other countries in East Asia that are grooming medical-biotech industries are whether the deciphering of the genome and the flock of specialized fields it has spawned will produce future earnings comparable to the returns obtained by the major pharmaceutical and biotech companies in recent years. If so, what kind of firms will reap the highest rewards and under what circumstances? And can this industry provide the makings of a cluster that will be a significant driver of growth, mainly through exports, and that will generate the volume of employment that Singapore's economy is seeking?

For a number of reasons, it is far from obvious, as yet, that medical biotechnology is likely to deliver high and sustained profits for a sufficient number of entering firms. The experience of the most successful firms, such as Amgen and Biogen, is by no means unequivocally positive, despite the huge profits garnered by their bioengineered drugs. Their achievements have been few and are based on prolonged research to address a few important medical conditions. In Amgen's case, the condition was the anemia that in particular afflicts patients who undergo kidney dialysis (Goozner 2004).

The pipeline of new drugs is relatively meager given the amounts invested in research,[51] the drugs now being introduced are of a more limited therapeutic value, and the largest biomedical firms have been the most prolific. This situation may exist because of learning and of scale economies in such research, but even Amgen has had few new offerings,

51. Alliance and consolidation are becoming critical in keeping the pipeline full. For instance, half of the new drugs in the pipeline that are produced by Amgen, the biggest independent biotech company, with revenues of US$11 billion in 2004, are the result of Amgen's alliances and mergers with others ("Amgen Works" 2005). Roche has a controlling stake in Genentech, and Novartis is maneuvering to take over Chiron ("Amgen Works" 2005; "Novartis Raises" 2005). Sugen, the developer of a major first-in-class anticancer drug was taken over by Pfizer ("Spirit of a Startup" 2005).

although it and its sister firms, such as Genentech, are promising breakthrough medications for cancer and osteoporosis. Despite an ever-deeper understanding of biogenetic processes, the drug companies are also discovering that neither simulation of the actual working of drugs on human cells nor multistage testing can conclusively identify all side effects of and adverse interactions with other drugs or substances an individual might be exposed to. New, expensively produced, high-profile drugs are being withdrawn—or their prescription severely circumscribed—as unexpected findings come to light ("Another Ailing" 2005; "Genentech's Lessons" 2005). Thus, the whole process of conducting tests and winning approval in industrial countries with the most lucrative markets is not becoming easier. Although nearly US$85 billion was invested in the U.S. biotech industry during 1998 to 2003 and sectoral revenues amounted to US$46 billion in 2003, the industry is struggling (Pfeffer 2005). One way forward for newcomers might be to concentrate on biomaterials, where regulatory hurdles may be lower than for drugs. By building up the capabilities in this area first, Singapore may be able to make more headway later in biopharmaceuticals and genetic medicines (Parayil 2005). The current focus on cancer-related drugs, which is highly contested area and thick with regulations, might be less rewarding.

Two other developments now in train threaten to depress longer-term profitability. The lesser of the two is the length of patent protection provided to vital drugs for conditions such as AIDS and, in this context, the increasing threat from generics. Such protection is effectively down to 10 years, and there is less assurance now that important life-saving discoveries will not enjoy the length of protection they once did.

The other and uppermost concern for the pharmaceutical and biotechnology industries derives from the very success of medical advances to date and how these interact with rising longevity to steadily increase the costs of health care. In the industrial countries, health-related spending is already averaging close to 10 percent of GDP. New and generally more expensive drugs, combined with advanced procedures, which are also frequently costlier than the ones they displace, are inexorably pushing up medical costs (Lichtenberg 2001). As the population ages and chronic diseases become more widespread, exacerbated by the global obesity epidemic,[52] the curve of medical expenditures will very probably steepen

52. See Chou, Saffer, and Grossman (2002); Eberwine (2002); Haslam and James (2005); and "Provocative Study" (2005). According to the International Obesity Taskforce referred to by Haslam and James (2005), 1.1 billion people worldwide were overweight, and of these, 312 million were obese.

further. By themselves, these expenditures might be supportable, but in conjunction with rising pension and welfare benefits for the elderly, societies will face some difficult choices.[53] Among such choices will certainly be those regarding the use of expensive therapies to extend long and economically unproductive life spans by another few years and to ameliorate debilitating chronic diseases. Those therapies will constantly raise the technological ante at prices that would generate high profits for the biotech companies and compensate them for the risks they incur and their substantial R&D outlay.[54]

The risks derive from the following four sources. First is the question of scale. Inevitably, the resources—human capital and material—that Singapore can expend on biomedical R&D and commercialization are a small fraction of what the major corporate entities and countries such as the United States are investing in their efforts to find the right molecule or innovation, especially so in the field of oncology. In the biomedical field, much hangs on the quality and depth of basic research, on the breadth of investigation, and on the lucky break. Singapore's resource constraint forces the country to target a narrow range of options, depending in part on the scientific talent it can attract. That constraint reduces the likelihood of anything more than the episodic discovery and makes it hard to think in terms of a continuously replenished pipeline of products from a stream of new entrants or from incumbent firms that grow in size. Given that millions of compounds are screened and only a tiny few are ever developed into drugs, having a large pool of firms of different sizes engaging in such search and development activities is advantageous until a better technology to identify promising compounds at the initial stage emerges.[55] In fact, the experience with the electronics industry, which has a nearly 25-year history in Singapore, suggests that a stream of

53. Without a significant reform of pension and health care costs, the public outlays on those costs could raise the public debt in France, Germany, and the United States to more than 200 percent of GDP by 2050 ("Debt Threat" 2005).

54. It is instructive to know that in 1935, when the U.S. Social Security Law was signed, the life expectancy at birth was 58 years for men and 62 years for women. Only 54 percent of men and 61 percent of women alive at that time were able to survive until the age of 65 to collect Social Security ("Seventy Years of Plenty" 2005).

55. Danzon, Nicholson, and Pereira (2005) find that an alliance between a small and a large firm is conducive to successful phase II and III clinical trials. But unlike in other industries, repeated interactions between small and large firms are fairly scarce, because the smaller firms tend to be highly specialized and, once the successful alliance comes to an end, the larger firms seek out other firms that may enable the larger firms to expand into new territories (Roijakkers, Hagedoorn, and van Kranenburg 2005).

innovations is difficult to generate, given corporate R&D capability, the scale of Singapore's innovation system, and the pool of entrepreneurial talent.

Second, the intense emphasis on commercialization of research findings noted by Professor Yoshiaki Ito has its drawbacks. It can detract from the necessary attention to basic research that feeds innovation, and labs could become closed societies jealously guarding their intellectual property rather than continuing the open and collegial atmosphere of the typical campus ("Asia Jockeys" 2005; Koh and Wong 2005). A stress on the commercial worth of research could also adversely affect the quality and orientation of teaching universities. Moreover, the star researchers who Singapore has attracted include a number of oncologists, which (as noted above) has biased research toward anticancer drugs. That bias might not be to Singapore's advantage, because the largest markets for those drugs are in industrial countries.

Third, a heavy dependence on foreign researchers and on the research labs of MNCs has its drawbacks. Star scientists are a footloose group, and the departure of one can trigger the breakup of a team and the emigration of other key members. Yoshiaki Ito was able to bring 10 of his key researchers when he moved from Kyoto to Singapore. A similar move out of Singapore by a leading scientist could result in an exodus that would quickly erase the capability of an institute. The spillovers from MNC research labs are also uncertain. The evidence that a relationship between itinerant teams of foreign researchers and MNC research facilities will lead to enough spinoffs to form a leading sector is simply not there. So far, generous financing, provision of state-of-the-art facilities, and a relatively lenient regulatory environment have enabled Singapore to attract these foreign scientists. However, questions still remain about how long the foreigners will stay in Singapore after their initial stint and how long Singapore will be able to sustain its attraction for such people, especially as countries such as China and India develop further. Singapore is writing the case law on this particular initiative. For the biomedical industry to serve as a growth pole calls for innovation, industrial initiatives, and corporate marketing capabilities in a number of interlinked subfields that draw on an array of scientific disciplines.[56] Whether Singapore can piece together such an expansive world-class innovation system is unclear.

56. For instance, even though prototypes of equipment can be created in Singapore, actual production takes place elsewhere, delaying the deployment of such equipment. Similarly, some specialized inputs need to be imported, and it takes more time to obtain those inputs in Singapore than in countries such as Japan.

Fourth, the one lesson that the short history of the life sciences has driven home is that there is a lengthy lag between remarkable scientific discovery and some eventual practical outcome. In the United States, the elapsed time from drug discovery to approval typically ranges from 12 to 15 years (Danzon, Nicholson, and Pereira 2005). So far, the pharmaceutical giants and venture capitalists have shown patience and great persistence, because the eventual prizes from the occasional winner have been staggeringly large. But if the number of winners starts to dwindle, then the willingness to commit the volume of patient capital that is needed will be sorely tested. Such a tendency has been noted. The number of drugs launched by the pharmaceutical giants in the United States fell from 59 per year during 1998 to 2002 to 50 per year during 2002 to 2004, and many of these drugs were variants of existing drugs.[57]

Nevertheless, there are some bright spots here for the biotechnology sector: one-third of the 50 to 60 therapeutics launched in the United States during 2003 were from biotech companies, as against one-fourth in 2001 and 7 percent in 1998 ("Demand Far Outstrips Supply" 2002); on average, treatment for chronic conditions using biotech drugs is less costly than treatment using small-molecule pharmaceutical drugs; and the pace of innovation in biotechnology is quickening (Pfeffer 2005, 115). Although the risks are undeniable, it is possible to end on this positive note.

57. About 40 percent of R&D is spent on research to extend the usefulness of the existing drugs, rather than developing new ones ("Big Trouble" 2003). Such strategies work if a firm is the owner of the underlying patent, but otherwise, firms will face significant hurdles. This fact is especially true for newer firms, which may not have enough patent portfolios to trade with their competitors.

CHAPTER 5

MEET ASTRO BOY AND FRIENDS

Neither robotics nor animation are new industries, but advancing technologies, emerging applications, and changing preferences are giving each of those fields a new and potentially much larger role in the postindustrial city.[1] Both industries emerged in Tokyo some decades ago, yet they have occupied relatively small economic niches. Robotics mainly served a handful of manufacturing industries, such as automobile assembly, whereas animation provided the grist for comic books, cartoons, collectibles, and small knickknacks. Now, the footprint of both industries, as measured by forward and backward links, seems set to expand. Moreover, the products of these industries (but robotics more so than animation) could become as intrinsic to daily urban existence as the Internet and in as short a span of time.[2] Why robotics and animation? What is Tokyo's comparative advantage with respect to those industries? And why are such industries important for Tokyo's industrial future?

The case for robotics stems from the huge increase in the applicability of robotic technologies that have arisen from advances in information technology, electronics, mechanical engineering, nanotechnology, and artificial intelligence (AI). Such advances, coupled with major strides spearheaded by Japanese firms in the miniaturization of equipment and the integration of systems, are enabling elements of the robot concept to infiltrate diverse aspects of urban life. For an aging population, various kinds of robotic devices can assist with housekeeping,[3] movement, home

1. The word *robot* was coined by Czech writer Karl Capek in 1920 (Menzel and D'Aluisio 2000).

2. For a readable and quirky account of the state of the robotics science, see Wilson (2005). For a brief review of the development of the field and some of the key challenges, see Perkowitz (2004).

3. The government of the Republic of Korea anticipates that every household in the country will possess a robot helper by 2020 ("Trust Me" 2006).

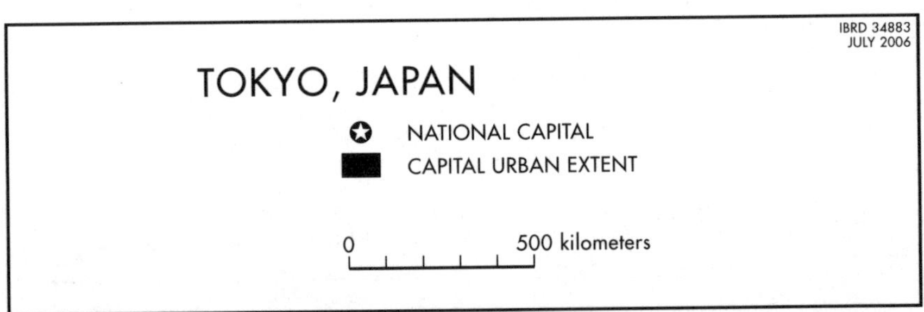
IBRD 34883
JULY 2006
TOKYO, JAPAN
NATIONAL CAPITAL
CAPITAL URBAN EXTENT
0
500 kilometers
120°
50°
RUSSIAN FEDERATION
CHINA
40°
DEM. PEOPLE'S REP. OF KOREA
Sea of Japan
JAPAN
Tokyo
Yellow Sea
REP. OF KOREA
PACIFIC OCEAN
30°
East China Sea
130°
140°

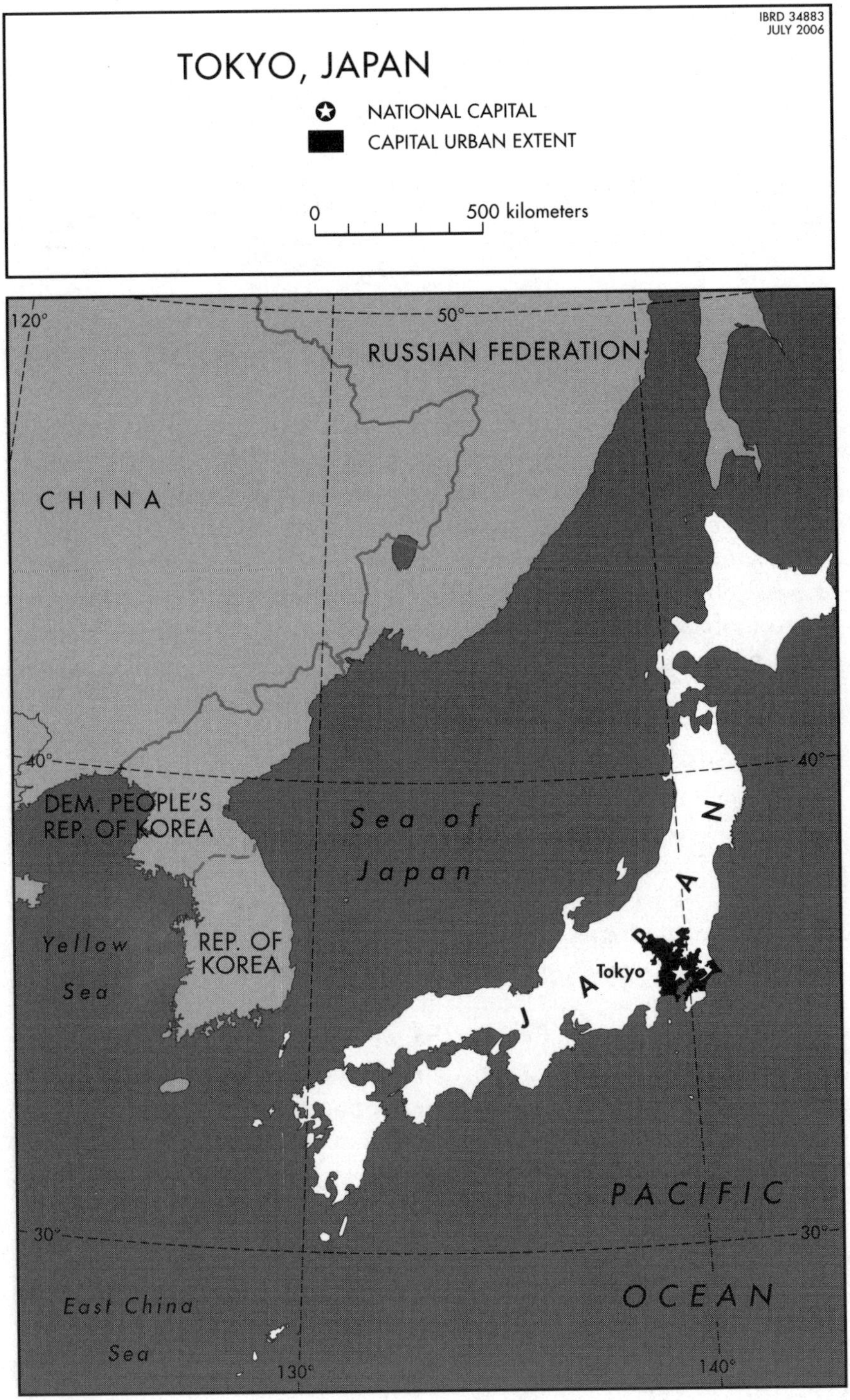

security,[4] and the use of home appliances through programmed instructions or voice activation. For leisure and recreational purposes, humanoid robots have the potential of becoming more companionable and less demanding playmates than other kinds of pets.

The mechanical, sensor, optical, remote-control, and AI technologies being progressively refined by the robotics industry have applications in space exploration (the Mars Rover) and the medical field (in surgery, remote surgery, and physical therapy for recuperating patients, for example) ("Cutting Edge" 2005; "Family of Robots" 2005; "Intelligent Beings" 2006).[5] Robotic devices are critical to the functioning, maintenance, and decommissioning of nuclear facilities, and robots are being perfected to assist with disaster relief in places where, for instance, a snakelike device that has the degrees of freedom to bend in many directions is needed to burrow through debris to locate survivors. Starting with the use of robotic equipment for clearing minefields, the utility of unmanned vehicles and sensor technology for surveillance and for smart projectiles is now widely appreciated. Unmanned airborne vehicles (UAVs), armed unmanned ground vehicles, and underwater vehicles[6] are being embraced by the military in several countries, and the use of UAVs for monitoring fires and weather conditions is being actively explored. As the technology improves and becomes more reliable, the use of UAVs for long-distance operations—monitoring, surveillance, transporting cargo, or attacking low-value, high-risk targets—is bound to become widespread.[7]

4. Currently, 25 percent of the Japanese population is at least 65 years old, and that proportion is expected to increase to 33 percent by 2040. Because the smaller cohort of younger people could dampen the demand for home security, many firms in Japan are developing guard robots for the elderly ("Robot Guards" 2005).

5. The next big step, which is at the experimental stage, will be a marriage of robotics with neuroscience that would allow individuals to manipulate a robotic arm, for example, through impulses passed through electrodes planted in the brain. Researchers at Northeastern University are attempting the transmission of electrochemical impulses from the chest to a robotic arm ("Bionic Sensation" 2006). At the University of Pittsburgh, neural impulses from monkeys have achieved this objective through the mediation of a specially programmed computer ("Food for Thought" 2005).

6. Under contract from the U.S. Navy, a number of companies, including Lockheed Martin, Bluefin Robotics, and Nekton Research, are building autonomous underwater vehicles for conducting surveillance, hunting mines, and inspecting vessels.

7. Establishing standards and rules for certification is ongoing so that UAVs can function as a part of civil aviation ("Atlantic Harmony" 2005; "Common Purpose" 2005). Because of different demand conditions, robots that perform dangerous and dirty duties are developed more in the United States, especially in connection with military applications and space programs (see Wilson 2005). The United States plans to spend between US$9 billion and US$10 billion on UAV programs for ground attack and electronic warfare purposes ("New Vision" 2006). In contrast, robots in Japan are developed by electronics firms and are aimed at consumers.

The revolutions in electronic hardware and programming have also transformed animation. Computer-generated or computer-modulated animation is now woven into movies and other programs, the demand for which is certain to go on rising in line with increased leisure time. It is a staple in advertising and being put to inventive use by the education industry for a variety of classroom purposes as well as for the purposes of distance-learning programs.

Even though we have touched on only a fraction of the uses to which robotics and animation technologies are being put, those examples should suffice to convey their emerging salience and the likelihood of their widening utility during the course of this century. Thus, a city that achieves and sustains a comparative advantage in those technological domains stands to reap large gains through the production and marketing of goods and services with high added value. However, the nature of the robotics and animation industries is peculiarly complex and requires an unusual combination of technical skills, research facilities, and manufacturing capability. Robotics, in particular, straddles so many technical specializations that a world-class innovative industry is inseparable from an agglomeration of activities spanning many different technical disciplines, together with a well-honed corporate capability to perceive commercial possibilities and manage and integrate findings from across a spectrum of technologies. The importance of diverse and highly evolved technological capabilities encapsulating much tacit knowledge and their agglomeration within a metropolitan area that facilitates frequent face-to-face communication cannot be emphasized enough. Robotics and animation, both of which depend on creativity at or near the frontiers of multiple scientific subfields, need a particularly rich urban milieu to flourish.

Tokyo has accumulated those diverse capabilities and, surprisingly, the relatively structured social environment has promoted a kind of disciplined creativity that has produced a succession of disruptive innovations such as the Walkman and the PlayStation 2. Tokyo is the birthplace of Astro Boy, which has a talismanic significance for robotics and for Japanese anime. Can the city maintain its lead, and can those activities achieve the scale of the consumer electronics industry, for instance? That is, of course, the big question, because the history of technology is rarely linear; nevertheless, first-mover advantages can maintain or even widen an initial lead with suitable investment in capabilities.

Astro Boy had a tremendous effect on Japanese society. Until then, anime was confined to the sporadic production of a few feature films and short animated cartoons. Astro Boy's immediate popularity paved the way to serial animation programming on television. But this pioneering work has exerted an influence well beyond Japan's animation industry. Astro Boy and its robotic progeny, such as Mazinger Z, Raideen, and the modular robot in Getta Robot, also aroused interest in robotics in Japan.[8] One characteristic of some of these animations is that they portray a robot living with people and supporting human companions physically as well as emotionally. Thus, exposure to Astro Boy and other similar anime characters has prepared the Japanese for a world in which humans and humanoid robots can coexist.[9] The increasing rootedness of such positive images has stimulated and shaped the Japanese personal robot industry, and they are responsible for the creative and human-friendly products such as Sony's dog-shaped robot, Aibo, which was introduced in 1999,[10] and Honda's humanoid, Ashimo.

The interest in animation shows no sign of waning in Japan. In fact, this fragment of Japanese culture has struck a chord worldwide and has produced rising exports. The estimated market share of Japanese animation in the world is about 65 percent (DCAj 2004). This dominance was recently underscored when Hayao Miyazaki's *Spirited Away* was awarded the 75th Academy Award for long animation in 2003 and the Golden Bear Award at the Berlin International Movie Festival in 2002.[11] Mamoru Oshii's *Innocence* was nominated for the Palme d'Or at the Cannes Film Festival in 2004. *Pokémon*, *Digimon*, and *Yu-Gi-Oh* are household words in the United States, and the penetration of anime in Europe is such that the Italian National Railway Company used a Japanese animation character in one of its advertisements (DCAj 2003).

The interest in robotics has been gaining momentum as advances in information technology make possible the incorporation of more and more of the attributes of an Astro Boy in a functioning robot. The 2005 Aichi Expo in Nagoya is "manned" by robots performing a variety of functions: they guide visitors and clean the facilities. Toyota's Partner robots, which can play the trumpet, have opened a trapdoor into the world of entertainment.

---

8. Another such character, which has been on television since 1979, is Doraemon, a versatile robotic cat from the future that comes to the assistance of a hapless youngster.

9. In the United States and worldwide, the *Star Wars* movies portrayed robots in a favorable light. R2D2 and C3PO were among the stars of those six films and were striking for their playfulness and companionability. They were modeled on two characters from a 1958 Kurosawa movie, *The Hidden Fortress.*

10. Since Aibo's introduction, Sony has sold 150,000 units, but in 2006 it announced the discontinuation of future development and sale of Aibo (Borland 2006).

11. Miyazaki, whose films include *My Neighbor Totoro* and *Princess Mononoke*, released yet another mysterious, fantasy-based animated film, *Howl's Moving Castle*, in 2005.

Many manufactured goods are becoming commoditized through the codifying of technology, and globalization intensifies competition. Japan, therefore, needs to derive its prosperity from new industries by continuously extending the frontiers of comparative advantage. Anime and robot industries are among the two candidate industries that could supplant industries migrating out of Japan. Because both industries are skill intensive and require close interfirm cooperation as well as research inputs from universities and specialized institutes, Tokyo is inevitably where much of the action is going to occur.

ROBOT INDUSTRY

Japan's robot industry is the world leader, and the Japanese manufacturing sector is the largest user of industrial robots. But the industry is in transition. Until recently, the main function of robots was to improve the efficiency of manufacturing processes by replacing workers in certain repetitive jobs and other jobs considered undesirable by human workers. Since the 1990s, however, robots are increasingly being designed for new purposes, including entertainment, and the sensors as well as other technologies being developed for robots are being put to related uses, such as the creation of the "smart house." In the future, this diversification is likely to continue, and the share of the industrial robots will shrink (although in absolute terms, their numbers will remain substantial). By 2025, the markets for commercial and entertainment robots could rival that for household durables.

Evolution of the Robot Industry

Following the invention of the basic robotic technologies in the United States, Japan began importing the early Versatran, Unimate, and Tralfer industrial robots from the United States in 1967. Just three years later, Kawasaki Heavy Industry (KHI) was able to introduce a domestic Unimate principally for the purposes of spot welding and paint spraying. Interestingly, one of the pioneering users of industrial robot technology was Nissan's Zama plant in the Kanagawa prefecture close to Tokyo. Over seven years, KHI and Nissan worked together on the application and maintenance of robots and the perfection of the technology. Researchers and engineers from KHI collaborated with their Nissan counterparts and the Zama plant. The process pulled in and was enriched by the participation of other subcontractors, and it underlined the degree to which the

Table 5.1 Stock of Industrial Robots at Year-End, 2002–08

Location	2002	2003	2004	2008[a]
Japan	350,169	348,734	356,483	390,500
United States	103,515	115,384	125,235	159,900
Europe	233,769	262,025	278,906	348,100
Others	82,652	74,330	87,140	143,200
Total	**770,105**	**800,473**	**847,764**	**1,041,700**

Sources: UNECE 2004, 2005.

a. Estimated

close interaction of the several key players in the Tokyo area contributed to the manifold requirements that enhanced practical application, which greatly expanded market demand. By 1980, more than 130 Japanese companies were engaged in the manufacture of robots—68 in the Tokyo area—and their extensive use had spread not just to the other auto manufacturers, such as Toyota, Honda, and Suzuki, but also to many other kinds of assemblers (Hasegawa 1981; Long-Term Credit Bank of Japan 1981; Sadamoto 1981). The number of industrial robots increased from the 1970s onward, in line with the increased demand for cars, reaching 93,000, or approximately 70 percent of the world total, in 1985. Since 1990, however, as a result of the downsizing and restructuring of companies as well as the transfer of production overseas to lower-wage locations, demand for industrial robots in Japan has stagnated and now is mainly for replacement parts rather than for additions to the stock.

Industrial Robots. The current estimate of the stock of industrial robots worldwide is 850,000, and this number is projected to increase to more than 1 million units by 2008 (see table 5.1).[12] Japan has 356,000 operating industrial robots, or about 329 robots per 10,000 manufacturing employees in Japan, whereas in second-ranked Germany, the ratio is 162 per 10,000 (UNECE 2005).

Worldwide, the automotive sector is the heaviest user, followed by the electronics and semiconductor industries, which are engaged in precision manufacturing. In those industries, there is often more than one robot per ten production workers (the densities are similar in Japan, Italy, and Germany) (UNECE 2004).

12. The estimate is based on an average life of 12 years for these robots. If the average service life of robots is 15 years, as some studies find, more than 1.1 million units of robots were in operation in 2004 (UNECE 2005).

The productivity and the quality of robots have been improving over the years, yet as with computers and other electronic products, the real prices have been on the decline. A robot bought in 2003 cost only one-fourth of a similar but technologically less advanced type of robot in 1990. Meanwhile, industrial wages have been increasing. As a result, in the United States, the relative price of robots (indexed on 1990 prices) to labor cost fell from 100 in 1990 to 28 in 2003. Although data for other countries are not available, the decline in relative prices is a fairly universal phenomenon (UNECE 2004).

The domestic shipment of industrial robots dropped sharply in 1992, and since then it has been hovering at about 4,000 to 5,000 units yearly, mainly to replace existing robots, which have a useful life of between 8 and 10 years. However, the exports of industrial robots have been rising since 1990 and now account for more than 50 percent of the total shipments by Japanese firms (see figure 5.1).

Decreasing domestic demand and relative prices have reduced the number of firms in the industry. Of those remaining, only four firms specialize in industrial robots (Japan Machinery Federation and Japan Robot Association 2001). These firms, together with three firms from the electric and machinery industry, currently dominate the Japanese market. Fanuc, the largest, is the 23rd-most-valuable company in Japan and also the leading global producer of electronic controls ("Green Tea" 2003). The industry

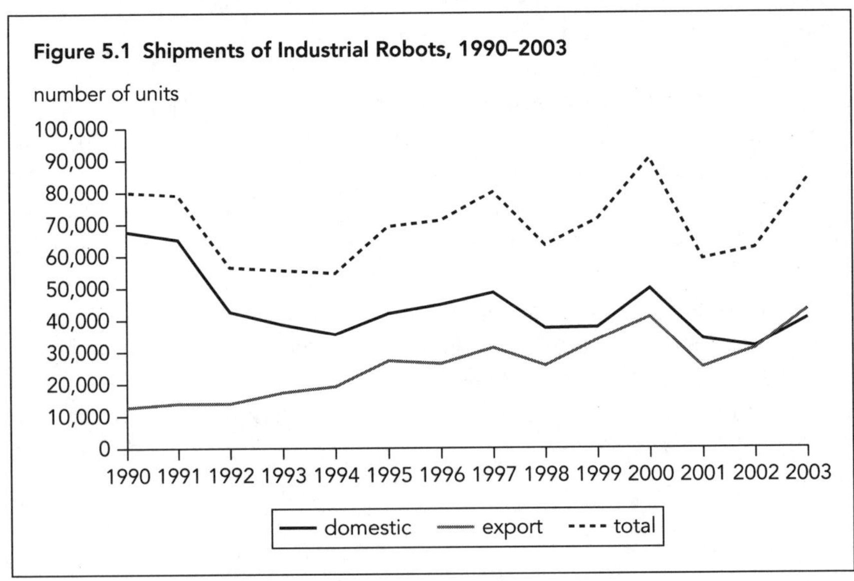

Figure 5.1 Shipments of Industrial Robots, 1990–2003

Source: Japan Robot Association (http://www.jara.jp).

is even more concentrated in other countries. The United States has only one firm that specializes in industrial robots, and Europe has just six. (Japan Robot Association 2000).

Aside from demand factors and the complexity of the technology involved, the increasing size and concentration of firms are associated with the provision of after-sales services to buyers, which the larger firms can more reliably supply over an extended time frame.

Other Kinds of Robots. Increasingly, robots have found uses outside the factory, especially in service industries. Up to 25,000 robots installed worldwide in 2004 supplied "professional services."[13] Underwater robots accounted for 21 percent of those robots, followed by robots for cleaning (14 percent), laboratory work (14 percent), demolition and construction (13 percent), medical purposes (11 percent),[14] mobile robot platforms (11 percent), agricultural work (9 percent), and public safety (defense, rescue, and security) (5 percent) (UNECE 2005).[15] The forecast for 2005 to 2008

13. This fact is contrary to the arguments made by Gordon (2004a). Firms are sparing no effort to replace low-end service jobs with robots. Investment banks, for example, now routinely use automated traders ("March of Robo-Traders" 2005). One way of increasing the demand for industrial robots is to find an alternative use outside the factory floor. One such example is to use industrial robots in amusement parks. Industrial robots can support heavy weights, can swing their arms in many directions, and are programmable to simulate different movements seen in roller coasters ("Factory Robots" 2005). The German firm Kuka has broadened its product range from industrial robots for car assemblers to include robots for theme parks and entertainment purposes. By dint of careful design, its offerings such as the Robocoaster are becoming ubiquitous in amusement parks, making Kuka the world's fourth-largest manufacturer of robots after Fanuc and Motoman of Japan and ABB ("Taking Robots" 2005).

14. Robots have three typical applications in the medical field. The first is to deliver documents, drugs, and other materials within the hospital. The second is to assist doctors and surgeons in improving the accuracy of medical and surgical procedures. For instance, robots are being developed to take blood samples ("Robot in the Right Vein" 1999), to automatically mix necessary ingredients in custom syringes ("Robo-Pharmacist" 2005), to conduct heart surgery (remotely controlled by a surgeon) ("da Vinci Mode" 2004), and to perform breast examinations (remotely controlled) ("Robot Hand" 2005). Third, robots can be used for physical therapy to improve rehabilitation, such as Anklebot, which was developed at Massachusetts Institute of Technology (MIT), and to provide exoskeletons for the weak and disabled as well as for soldiers and firefighters who need to lift heavy loads (E. Thomson 2005; Guizzo and Goldstein 2005).

15. A number of robots are in development for use in Iraq by the U.S. military. iRobot's PackBots, which can dispose of improvised explosive devices and serve as scouts, are widely used in Iraq and Afghanistan (Hines 2005). iRobot is developing a semiautonomous supply vehicle for the U.S. military with John Deere (Kanellos 2004b). A robot with a machine gun remotely controlled by a soldier may be deployed in a battlefield in the future (Kanellos 2004a). iRobot has also developed a prototype system to assist troops by pinpointing incoming rounds from rifles and mortars ("iRobot Unveils" 2005). The U.S. Department of Defense has given US$26.4 million to Carnegie Mellon University and defense contractors to develop a robotic

is that 50,000 new service robots will be installed, with the strong growth coming from humanoid robots, laboratory robots, underwater systems, public safety, cleaning, and mobile robot platform. The growth in demand for medical robots is slower than anticipated (UNECE 2004).[16]

The robots most commonly used by households are floor-cleaning robots and lawnmowing robots.[17] Together, they accounted for 1.2 million units worldwide in 2004. Since then, the number has climbed steeply. According to Helen Greiner, the chair and cofounder of iRobot, the company sold 1.5 million units of the Roomba vacuum cleaner in less than two years.[18] This rate of sales growth is much faster than that for any previous generation of new gadgets. For instance, it took six years to sell 1 million black-and-white television sets and four years to sell 1 million mobile phones (Hines 2005). Robots in household use are projected to reach 7 million units by 2008. Domestic robots (vacuum cleaner, lawnmower, window cleaner, and so forth) are expected to account for 4.5 million units, and entertainment and leisure robots (such as the Wakamaru from Mitsubishi Heavy Industry, the PaPeRo from NEC, and Promet from the Advanced Industrial Science and Technology Institute at Tsukuba and Kawada Industry) and a number of toy robots for the balance (UNECE 2005).[19]

The variance in market forecasts is predictably large, ranging from US$5 billion in 2005 to between US$17 billion ("Robotic Pioneers" 2004) and US$60 billion in 2010, with a total of 56 million units sold ("Ready to Buy" 2004). The overall robot market in Japan is forecast to be ¥8 trillion by 2025, with households generating 50 percent of the demand, a rising proportion of which will be for robots that assist the elderly

military vehicle. The Department of Defense plans to have at least one-third of all combat vehicles operating under robot control by 2010 (Kanellos 2005). To achieve this goal of solving technological problems associated with high-speed travel over unfamiliar terrain by a robotic vehicle, the Department of Defense in 2004 introduced a race called Grand Challenge with an award of US$1 million. The 2004 event resulted in the best vehicle traveling only 7 miles on a 144-mile course simulating the terrain in Iraq and Afghanistan. However, a year later, Grand Challenge 2005 saw four teams finish the race within the allotted time, which greatly exceeded expectations. Many of the teams were from universities and had private sponsors. The team from Stanford won the race and the US$2 million award, followed by vehicles from Carnegie Mellon University (Gibbs 2006; "Stanford Wins" 2005).

16. A wide range of robotic devices ranging from the bizarre to the ingenious are on display in the lavishly illustrated volume edited by Menzel and D'Aluisio (2000).

17. They are produced by Friendly Robotics, among others.

18. At the core of this machine is an "Aware" system that enables the machine to move around in complex or changing environments.

19. See "How Humanoids Won" (2006). Lego announced its next-generation robotic kits based on its Lego building block (Terdiman 2006).

Figure 5.2 Forecast of Robot Market in Japan, 1995–2025

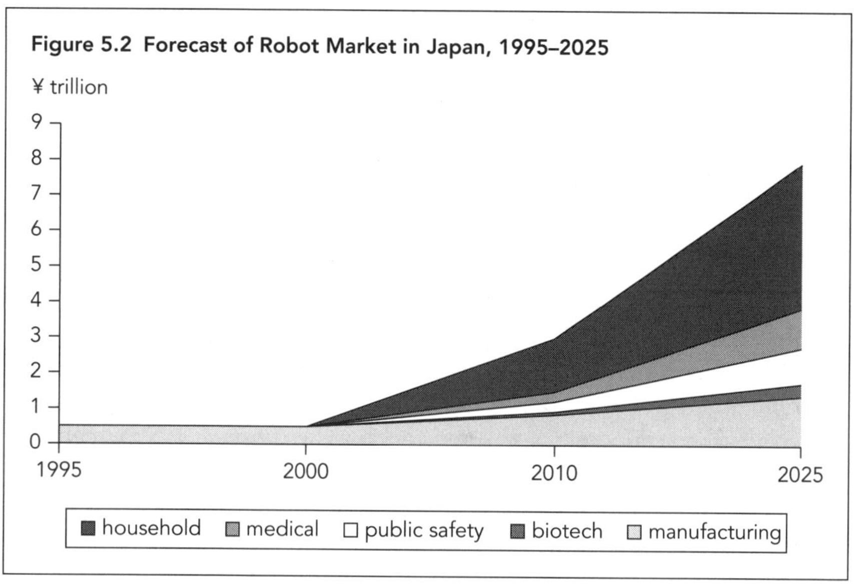

Source: Japan Machinery Federation and Japan Robot Association 2001.

(see figure 5.2).[20] According to a survey by Nikkei, consumers expect robots to house-sit or guard the residence, to clean, and to help with other household chores while costing less than ¥300,000, a price comparable to other household electronics (Matsuhira and Ogawa 2004).

These forecasts are for certain categories of robotic devices, some of which, such as industrial robots, are a known quantity while others, such as helper robots, are still being developed. The basic functions and expectations of household goods such as washing machines are the same across different households (Tanie 2004). For household robots, however, such functions are still not clear-cut. Honda, which is actively engaged in researching the potential of robots, is conscious that people buy a car because they easily see the use for it and they perceive the value in owning it. For household robots, consumers have yet to be convinced that they would be worth owning. Part of this lag is simply because robotic technologies for household use are breaking new ground, and as yet, designers are unable to devise a product that can cope with the complexity of work that consumers expect robots to perform at an affordable price. Currently

20. General Motors now offers as an option a "Sit-N-Lift" power seat that uses a robotic arm to assist elderly passengers ("Ready to Buy" 2004). A number of products, such as an automatic spoon, have been developed and tested to assist the elderly in continuing to live independently.

a “bipedal robot costs more than a Ferrari” (“How Humanoids Won” 2006). Hence, simple-function robots such as Roomba are winning a wider acceptance because they are moderately priced, the consumer knows what the robot can do, and the robot can deliver the desired functions.

Although household and leisure-related robots are attracting the most attention, the largest eventual markets for robotic technologies might well be in the health, transportation, defense,[21] and security fields. For those applications, the embedded software, electromechanical components, various kinds of sensors, communication devices, and voice recognition equipment now being developed in the Tokyo region will be major inputs even if the final product is designed and assembled elsewhere. In fact, the embedded software market for robots, for which firms in Tokyo are well placed to compete, is expected to grow by more than 9 percent per year to reach US$138 billion by 2007 (“Ready to Buy” 2004).

The demand for many types of electronic components is also likely to expand; where robotic applications require mobility, for example, image sensors and extremely robust electromechanical devices will be in strong demand. Those opportunities are but a few of the many available for Tokyo-based firms. But first, a host of technological hurdles must be tackled. In this regard, Tokyo has many advantages over other cities because of the concentration of university and corporate research facilities as well as the numerous subcontractors who can design and manufacture components to exacting specifications.

Technological Challenges

Many technological challenges still exist, including the difficulties of enabling robots to recognize surrounding features, making them mobile, designing them to interact with people, and devising ways for them to be controlled.

Recognition of the Surroundings. One of the major shortcomings of current household and other types of humanoid robots (which is common to some other robotic applications) is that the current sensors and AI technologies embedded in robots is not mature enough to enable robots

21. The development of armed and unarmed UAVs is proceeding apace, and the potential for civilian uses is also being more actively explored. See “Commercial Futures” (2001), “Unmanned Aerial Vehicles” (2004), and “Unmanned Ventures” (2005). The National Aeronautics and Space Administration (NASA) is also developing general types of robots to assist astronauts in space. NASA hopes that such robots can accompany astronauts on shuttle flights soon (“NASA Concocting Robots” 2005).

to take account of relevant features of the surrounding environment (Ozaki and Hashimoto 2004). For instance, although robots can "see" through their optical inputs (in many cases using the same technology as in a digital camera),[22] after the image is inputted, the robot still needs to identify the objects viewed, to determine the distance to the object, to recognize the nature of the object, and to know from its instruction set how to interact with the object.[23] It needs, moreover, touch sensors on its "hands" and "feet" and sensors to enable it to achieve balance, coordinate movement, and sustain orientation.

Most people can quickly assess the surrounding environment and know how to interact (or react to the situation). Thus, for a robot (that is, device) to be truly useful in a household or other setting for which such products are being developed (such as defense and medical purposes), it needs such situational awareness—and some rudimentary social skills. The possible way to cope with the first requirement would be to embed radio frequency identification (RFID) chips into objects the robots will come into contact with; these chips will provide the robot with all the information it requires. Although RFID technology is evolving, this approach might be cumbersome and have other complications as well. Hence, alternative approaches are being explored. Social skills call for advances in AI and learning capabilities.

Because of the complexity of the software required simply to be "cognizant" of the surroundings, many firms need to collaborate to extend

22. For a robot to have a fast reaction time, the optical inputs need to be of high speed. Most actuators can be controlled at a millisecond level. The conventional video input is only 30 frames per second, a rather slow flow of information. If a quicker reaction is required, then faster video input is necessary to improve the speed and accuracy of the reaction by the robot. Otherwise, the robot's reaction will be based on extrapolation from limited inputs (Okada, Oaki, and Kondoh 2004). New technologies allow experimental robots to update information 60 times per second and to achieve better situational awareness through "closed feedback loops" (Wilson 2005, 98). Vision sensors are relatively fragile, confused by changes in lighting and rendered unreliable by vibration. Robots can supplement line-of-sight vision systems with thermal and hyperspectral imaging devices and laser range finders.

23. Suppose a robot is required to close a door. First, it must scan the room and identify where the door is. To do so, it must know what "door" is. Then, when it identifies where the door is, it needs to determine how to get there while avoiding various obstacles on the way, such as tables and chairs. When it is at the door, the robot must determine how to close it (is it "pull" or "push"?) with appropriate force. Closing a window is much more difficult because it can mean moving the window pane down (or up), sliding it sideways, or closing it like the door. Of course, using appropriate force is necessary not to shatter the glass. Even more complicated, the materials of which the object is made change the mode of interaction. For instance, chairs can be made from metal, wood, bamboo, plastics, and paper. Of course, one would not try to sit on the chair made of paper, but how would a robot know it is made of paper?

the utility of a robot. Two ways of achieving this goal exist. One is through the joint development of a product. The other is to make the architecture of the robot somewhat open so that different components can be added, much as is done with a personal computer (PC). Hooking up a monitor to a PC is rather easily done by plugging it in, which gives consumers much more freedom to select among monitors. PC makers need not be concerned with the various options users may choose, as long as they design devices to which other standardized components can be easily added. This approach has made the PC a highly flexible device. Robots need to be able to achieve flexibility and expandability similar to that of a PC that will permit easily adding or swapping components. We will come back to this point later.

Sensor technology is another major hurdle for all manner of uses. A robot designed to entertain through interaction with humans needs to communicate. To do so, such a robot must identify who it is talking to, what they are talking about, and what the moods of its interlocutor are, plus be able to express itself in a "natural" way. To achieve all those functions, a robot would require a good sensor (optical input device) for face recognition (similar to a digital camera), software for rapidly recognizing key facial features, voice recognition (and voice-to-text capability), some understanding of a person's mood from the tone of voice (some elements of psychology are needed), an understanding of what is an acceptable behavior (some element of sociology), and of course, good AI software.[24] If physical contact with humans is a part of their function, such robots need some tactile feedback mechanisms. Once again, the experience with industrial robots provides a foundation for future advance, and research on materials with sensory capacity is lighting the way forward.

At this stage, firms in Tokyo are working on specific aspects of recognition technology, such as voice recognition and the following types of facial recognition:

- Recognizing faces from different angles
- Recognizing faces under different lighting
- Recognizing faces when multiple faces are visible
- Recognizing faces when some portion is obstructed
- Recognizing faces of different sizes

The current technology is adequate for recognizing a single face, located at a predetermined distance from the optical input, under optimal

24. In some instances, especially using evolutionary computing, AI can come up with solutions that are highly innovative ("Thinking Machines" 2000).

lighting. Such a facial recognition system is already used as an entry security measure (for instance, at Toshiba). The entry security system is a good example of the perfect conditions for facial recognition because the lighting can be controlled (in many cases the location is indoors), users can be instructed to stand at a predetermined distance and face in the right direction, and the database of the face is already inputted into the computer. However, for a robot to be able to interact with humans, it needs to be able to recognize faces under varying conditions. It also needs to recognize the person of immediate interest (for instance someone who is talking to the robot) among many visible people. Furthermore, once it identifies the objects of interest, the robot needs to be able to track them and isolate them from other objects (Koga, Suzuki, and Yamaguchi 2004).

The difficulties with voice recognition under a variety of circumstances are also manifold but are also being whittled down little by little. The main difficulty associated with voice recognition is, first, to recognize sound as voice separate from the other noises and, second, to do so without a dedicated input to alleviate this problem. Once a voice is isolated, the robot needs to understand who the speaker is and the content of the speech. Firms are still working on these technologies to make robotic applications more useful.

Mobility. The shift from industrial use to other purposes also confronts problems associated with the mobility of robots. Industrial robots are mostly immobile, fixed installations along the conveyer belt, although some mobile (often guided) robots are used mainly for delivery within a factory or warehouse on a fixed route marked with guiding lines. In addition, safety concerns are mainly met by specifying a perimeter that people are prohibited from entering to minimize the risks from robot malfunction.

For many other uses, however, robots need to be mobile. The type of mobility depends on the application: caterpillars or wheels are appropriate for autonomous vehicle-type robots such as the ones being developed for military and disaster relief purposes, while quadruped or biped mobility is more appropriate for animal- or humanlike robots.[25]

---

25. A key concept for bipedal robots, *zero-moment point,* was developed by a Yugoslavian researcher, Miomir Vukobratovich, who was a close friend of Ichiro Kato, the pioneer of Japanese robotic research in mechatronics, at Waseda University (Menzel and D'Aluisio 2000). Researchers at MIT have a robot called Toddler that can learn to walk in 20 minutes ("Design Lets Robot Walk" 2005). Firms are attempting the difficult feat of creating something resembling humans partly on the basis of the assumption that these machines will be better accepted if they look similar to us (Menzel and D'Aluisio 2000). This tendency is also reflected in the

If a robot is mobile, it needs to have various sensors to gauge distance and to avoid obstacles in its path, as well as various gyroscopes and accelerometers for maintaining balance and orientation when in motion. Various types of sensors can be used, such as infrared, temperature, and vibration. The experience accumulated from industrial robots is a useful guide for the advanced equipment now being developed, but this technology has a long road ahead of it.

Command and Control. How are robots to be controlled? Currently, most commands to robots are sent electronically either with wires or wirelessly. For unmanned ground or airborne vehicles, secure and fail-safe communication mechanisms are critical, and research on these devices continues. For house-sitting types of robots, the predominant mode of sending commands is through cell phones, and in this case, as well, the technology is likely to evolve.

First-generation robots needed to be reprogrammed if a change in their function was required. New programs now permit robots to be taught and to learn. The now discontinued final version of Sony's Aibo model has such learning capability.[26] The capacity to plan, to anticipate responses and contingencies, and to look ahead are all being refined, and some of the chess-playing programs provide a glimpse of what is now feasible. The research on this function, which is vital for the further development of robotics and of AI, is being done through a RobotCub, a collaborative effort among 16 labs in Europe, Japan, and the United States ("Men Are from Mars" 2005). One interesting scenario conjured up by the Ministry of Economy, Trade, and Industry in Japan is to use the Internet and follow strategies similar to open-source software or other highly customizable software to increase the utility of robots.[27] As long as many users are

choice of pets. Dogs do not really begin to resemble their owners; rather, owners tend to choose dogs that resemble them ("Love Me" 2005). However, close resemblance can also highlight the limitations of robots. The lesson from the limited production of NeCoRo (cat robot) by Omron was that users felt disappointed when it could not behave like a live cat, even though NeCoRo looked like a living cat. Building on that experience, the National Institute of Advanced Industrial Science and Technology in Japan developed Paro (a therapy robot), which is modeled after a seal, an animal not as familiar to Japanese users as cats. About 500 of these robots have been sold at several thousand dollars each ("How Humanoids Won" 2006).

26. A robot designed by the Neurosciences Institute in La Jolla, California, has been able to acquire the abilities of an 18-month-old baby through a process of exploring and learning ("Brain Box" 2005).

27. Many computer games allow customization through modification of some aspects of the game by using tools supplied by the game developers. Similarly, some software, such as winamp (for MP3 playback), Opera (for Web browsing), and Firefox (for Web browsing), can be customized with extensions offered by users.

willing to teach robots new functions and they are willing to share such knowledge with others, this approach could have considerable potential for certain kinds of robotic applications. However, this specific type of robot would need to be connected to the Internet, gather information, and update itself automatically. "Smarter" robots that have the software and the neural circuitry to be able to learn will command a far wider market and have numerous applications. They would provide a strong boost to the industry and the research establishment in the Tokyo area and strengthen local comparative advantage.

Main Players and Complementarities

Broadly speaking, four types of firms are in the robotics field in Japan; they come from various backgrounds that have diversified into robotics by leveraging their strengths in other fields. The first group consists of firms producing industrial robots. The second group is drawn from consumer electronics. The third group comes from the automotive sector. The fourth group comprises research institutes supported by venture capitalists. The firms from the industrial robotics arena rely on their experience with factory automation. The main strength of those firms lies in sensor technology and tactile feedback. The electronics firms are building on their strength in miniaturization, packaging of equipment, energy efficiency, power supplies, and design. The point of departure for automotive firms is their mastery of mechanical engineering and the technologies impinging on mobility. The last group of firms tends to specialize in aspects of communication (AI, facial expression, integration with information technology) and special-purpose robots (military, security, rescue).

The new breed of more sophisticated robots will be an amalgam of several complex and rapidly evolving technologies. As we stated earlier, Tokyo's comparative advantage in this field derives from the presence in the metropolitan area of the many players[28] (see table 5.2) that are contributing to the separate strands of technology as well as of firms that can knit these strands together into commercially viable packages.[29] No single

28. Because most of these firms develop robots as an experimental activity, exploring new possibilities, the location of their operations tends to be close to the main office, which in most instances is in the Tokyo area. For instance, the research and development for Ashimo by Honda is done in Wako city (Saitama prefecture, north of Tokyo), separate from the R&D for main automotive research.

29. In the United States, most of the robotic research is conducted with funding from the Defense Advanced Research Projects Agency (Menzel and D'Aluisio 2000). In Japan, much of the research is done by private corporations.

Table 5.2 Firms Involved in Robotics, by Robot Type

Services	Entertainment	Medical	Industrial
Tmsuk (security robots, both commercial and residential) Sougo Keibi Hoshou (security, commercial) Mitsubishi Heavy Industry (house-sitting, health monitoring) Fujitsu (house-sitting) Toshiba (communication and entertainment, vacuum cleaning) Matsushita (vacuum cleaning)	Sony (Aibo) NEC (PaPeRo) ATR (Mu) Honda (Asimo) Sony (SDR-4XII) Toyota (Partner) Mitsubishi Heavy Industry (Wakamaru)	Toshiba and Hitachi (surgical equipment) Paro (therapy robot pet) Secom (robotic hospital room, My Spoon)	Fujikoshi Fanuc Kobe Steel Mitsubishi Jyuko Toyoda Koki Toyo Koken Mitsubishi Electric Denso Automax Ishikawajima Harima Osaka Gas Engineering Yaskawa

firm can internalize all the technologies—success will rest on partnerships and alliances with other firms and with research institutions.

Links with universities such as Waseda (Humanoid Robotics Institute) and Tokyo Institute of Technology are multiplying, and more and more firms are entering into alliances to spread the costs of research and development (R&D) and to benefit from an open research environment. But a tendency remains among the major developers to limit their dependence on other firms, slowing progress and the growth of a robotics cluster in Tokyo.

The relative scarcity of research funding for robotics in general is also squeezing R&D on long-term projects. This limitation has resulted in a tendency to focus on software development rather than on hardware because such research activities are less expensive (Japan Robot Association 2000). From the perspective of industrial change in Tokyo, the robotics industry offers robust growth prospects, but given the technological and market uncertainties, the fate of the industry might depend on policy action in a number of areas.

Stimulating the demand for nonindustrial robots—especially for medical, military, security, and space-related applications—would be one useful step (Japan Machinery Federation and Japan Robot Association 2001). For example, the funding provided by the U.S. government for the development of next-generation medical and military equipment based on robotic technology is an important spur. Some of this work is done by the defense industry, some is commissioned to universities, and some is done through open competitive tendering. Similarly, support by public agencies for space exploration is helping push the frontiers of robotics by promoting innovation and subsequent spillover to consumers. Because this field is still in its infancy, many robots are created without any common platform in which firms can build certain modules. Hence, the setting of standards, possibly with government mediation, in close consultation with the industry, would be another significant step with important antecedents. The rapid diffusion of the PC did not occur until the interface was standardized so that firms specializing in individual components were able to emerge and many new firms were attracted to the PC industry as assemblers of the PC or as component suppliers. At this time, such interchangeability of key components among particular types of robots is not possible. For instance, if an interface (both at the hardware and software level) was standardized, a firm could specialize in producing the bipedal module and another firm could produce wheel-based modules. With standardization, different users would need to change only the lower body parts for the robot to be wheeled or biped, depending on need.

Additional standards and regulations will be required in the interests of safety and to build safeguards for the sake of security. As with any products in the market, robots used in commercial and household settings would need to satisfy safety regulations appropriate for this emerging technology but designed not to deter the development of the industry. The consensus emerging in Japan is that safety issues need to be assessed according to the frequency of direct contact with human beings. For a robot that has minimal contact with humans (most entertainment and household-appliance type robots), a version of the current safety regulations for household appliances, electronics, and toys can be used as the basis, with modifications as needed. As direct contact with humans increases, however, the safety standards will need to be raised substantially to avoid potential harm caused by robotic malfunction. For instance, malfunctions of care robots assisting people with disabilities will pose much higher risks than those of a robot vacuum cleaner. This issue will become especially important when mobile robots with sufficient AI are used in public places.[30]

30. Another important issue is the question of liability in case of damages caused by malfunction. Is it the manufacturer's responsibility? Or because these robots will be highly customizable and programmable by the end-users, is it the user's responsibility? Or is it the robot's responsibility

For certain kinds of robots, safety concerns can be alleviated by setting weight restrictions so that, were a robot to topple, it would cause little harm to people and surrounding objects ("Chat with Roomba" 2004). The required miniaturization and lightweight yet sturdy body will entail advanced technologies in material sciences and mechanical and electronic engineering. Building in redundancy can also lessen the risks associated with failures of motors or of systems.

Adequate and regularly updated safeguards will be needed to avert the intrusion of malicious software, especially into the systems of robots that are expected to be always connected to some form of a network. Likewise, securing the information stored in the robot to protect the privacy of the users would be equally as important as protecting computers and would involve very similar standards and software integrity.

Do We Need Mobile Robots?

For certain household purposes, humanoid robots might be unnecessary. Instead, robotic attributes can be and are being built into houses, and this development, too, will require changing the codes for housing as well as for commercial properties. A "robotic house" using equipment now being developed by Japanese firms could control electronic appliances and provide security. Through the addition of many sensors and input and output devices, the coffeemaker in the kitchen could be turned on by a voice command in the bedroom. To accomplish this task, the computer must know where the instruction originated, differentiate the voice from other noises, process the instruction, and then—if confirmation is necessary—report back by directing the output (in this case, "yes, it is done") to the source of the instruction. The directional output is necessary to avoid echoes and to ensure that the voice of the computer is not heard by others within the room. A smart house needs to have multiple listening stations to determine where the voice came from and multidirectional speakers that will focus a response to a certain person within a room. Multiple cameras will enable the computer to know where the person is (Mizoguchi 2004).

Whereas in the future, homes can be designed to incorporate such features, the existing stock of housing will need to be retrofitted with wiring

if a robot is given sufficient autonomy and learning capability? Currently, the responsibility for the first and the third would be the manufacturer's, but once robots become more complex and their learning skills more advanced, the liability is less clear-cut. These arguments may sound far-fetched, but in fact, they are being actively discussed among policy makers in Japan and by robot-ethicists ("Trust Me" 2006). Without clearly defined rules and the possibility of buying insurance against robot-related accidents, development of the robotics industry will be slowed.

sensors and controllers to accommodate a move toward this kind of truly "smart" home. Mobile robots that have multiple capabilities and considerable dexterity could be a substitute and eliminate the need for a large additional capital investment in the home. Because making the mobile robot useful will have similar requirements to creating smart homes, by developing those robots first, firms can acquire experience and the technological capabilities that can later be incorporated into the smart house of the future.

Many firms (computer, software, consumer electronics, telecommunications, cable, and Internet companies) are looking at a more narrowly defined "digital home" as the potential growth area. One optimistic estimate puts the market for digital homes at US$250 billion in the United States alone and US$1 trillion worldwide by the end of the decade ("Science Fiction?" 2005).[31]

The distinctive feature of a digital home is that all the appliances and electronic gadgets are connected and contents can be shared seamlessly across different devices. For instance, movies can be downloaded and streamed to different machines in various rooms.[32] This technology will move the distribution of goods from the physical to the electronic level. However, consumer demand for this kind of service is still low. One of the major obstacles is the complexity of the technology for making it work. Consumers do not buy systems the way firms do. Consumers buy goods separately and individually, and they need to be able to hook everything up easily without any help. Currently, this option is not available. Two major problems loom: file formats (including codecs for videos) and digital rights management. Too many incompatible formats exist in the market for consumers to choose from, and these standards are not guaranteed to last forever, a major difference when compared to physical goods such as CDs and DVDs that are based on a single global standard.[33] In addition,

31. Some of these ideas are not new. As early as 1900, the *Ladies' Home Journal* predicted that music would be delivered to homes through telephone lines and that refrigerators and central heating and cooling would be widespread ("Time to Put" 2005). The value of the total housing stock in the Untied States in 2005 was US$19 trillion.

32. Sony Pictures Digital has had a movie download service, Movielink, for several years, but with little success ("Download This" 2005). Even the most popular music download service, iTune, accounts for only 1 to 2 percent of the total music sales ("Time to Put" 2005).

33. Currently there are two competing (and incompatible) standards for the next generation of DVD: HD-DVD and Blu-ray. Equipment and contents based on both standards are coming to market supported by two camps of manufactures and movie studios, reminiscent of the early days for video recorders (VHS versus Betamax). Many expect the initial diffusion of next-generation DVD to be slow because of the lack of single standard, unlike the case for CDs and DVDs that were introduced as a single global standard from the beginning.

the general complexity of computer-related products in the marketplace presents a problem ("Time to Put" 2005). The only successful product of this type is TiVo, which is basically a computer but hides all the complexity and presents consumers with simple, easy-to-navigate menus for operation ("Technophobia" 2005).

The backward and forward links of robotics are both deep and diverse. These links make robotics especially suitable for a postindustrial Tokyo. But for those links to materialize fully and exert their pull on the local economy, markets will need to be created, many thorny technological problems solved, standards agreed to, and regulatory hurdles crossed.

ANIME INDUSTRY

The modern form of *manga* (a distinctively Japanese form of cartoons) catering to all age groups was popularized by artists such as Osama Tezuka starting in the late 1940s. Since then it has become staple reading for both male and female readers. An episode in a *manga* resembles a television show or a movie that is frozen onto the page with conversations continuing over several pages that "focus on subtle emotional changes in the characters' faces" (Patten 2004, 236; Carey 2006). The *manga* comics are tailor-made for animation, which made an appearance in the mid-1950s under the aegis of the Toei Animation Company, whose star animator launched *Doodling Kitty* in 1957. Animation found its stride in the early 1960s with *Speed Racer* and a weekly series called *Astro Boy* that debuted on New Year's Day in 1963. This series was followed by many others, each featuring "a mechanical warrior controlled by a human warrior to defend Earth against invading space monsters" (Patten 2004, 280). Astro Boy led to Gigantor to Mazinger Z to Great Mazinger, UFO Robot Grandizer, Space Battleship Yamato, Brave Raideen, Mobile Suits Gundam, and others.[34] The hit movie *Akira*, screened in 1988, opened new vistas, making anime a source of inspiration for producers, most recently of the *Matrix* series and *Kill Bill.*

Relative to robotics, the animation industry occupies less economic space in Tokyo. Nevertheless, it is a creative industry with a promising future in Japan and globally. The products of the animation industry can be divided into three categories: animation for theatrical release; television animation; and software based on the first two, including sales of videos and DVDs.

34. Many future engineers were inspired by these anime. A group of engineers has developed an 11-foot robot controlled by a human pilot much like in the anime.

Table 5.3 Anime Productions of Six Largest Firms in Japan, 1997–2003

Firm	1997	1998	1999	2000	2001	2002	2003
Toei Animation	12,350	10,825	9,269	9,794	14,845	16,031	17,695
Sunrise	5,834	5,000	7,131	6,920	7,038	8,877	8,419
Nihon Animation	2,507	2,360	2,914	2,888	2,276	1,916	
Shinei Douga	2,461	2,829	2,932	2,858	2,984	2,800	
Studio Piero	1,800	2,498	2,154	3,205	2,269	2,729	
Mad House	1,300	2,100	3,000	2,000	1,300	2,500	2,400
Total 6 largest firms	26,252	25,612	27,400	27,665	30,712	34,853	28,514
Total animation industry	163,700	165,100	151,900	159,300	186,000	213,500	191,200
Share of 6 largest firms	16.0%	15.5%	18.0%	17.4%	16.5%	16.3%	14.9%

Sources: Dentsu Communication Institute 2003, 2004.

In 2005, the total turnover of the animation industry in Japan was close to US$2 billion, an increase over the previous year. Two factors were responsible for the double-digit growth. One was the box office success achieved by Miyazuki's *Spirited Away* and *Howl's Moving Castle*, as well Katsuhiro Otomo's *Steamboy* and Mamoru Oshii's *Innocence*. The second was the transition from videocassettes to DVDs.[35] Of the 642 movies shown at Japanese theaters in 2003, 133 were animation films (DCAj 2004).[36] If licensing business and character merchandising are added to the first three categories, the total market size was more than US$18 billion. The estimated total box office receipts and DVD sales of anime films worldwide in 2005 was US$2.5 billion. When all the games, toys, and associated products are included, sales in Japan alone exceeded US$18 billion ("Anime Biz" 2005). Moreover, in 2003, Japan earned US$4.35 billion in merchandise sales and royalties from animation from the United States alone.

In view of the turnover of the industry, it is surprising that most producers are small to medium size. Some 440 studios exist. The biggest, Toei Animation, has 10 percent of the total market, and the share of the six largest firms is just 15 to 18 percent (see table 5.3). The smallest are just cottage-industry-size operations with a handful of people catering to the television business. Typically for an industry such as this one, only about a tenth of the productions bring in significant profits, and the margins are

35. Reproduction of videocassettes accounted for 2 million DVDs.

36. The number of films includes both domestic and imported films.

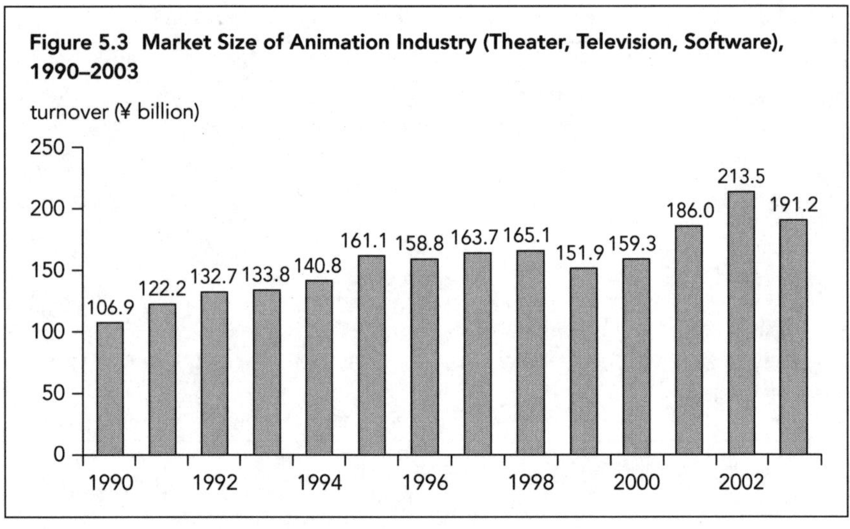

Figure 5.3 Market Size of Animation Industry (Theater, Television, Software), 1990–2003

Source: Dentsu Communication Institute 2005.

modest by the standards of media business in the United States ("Anime Biz" 2005).

Given the nature of the output, each project involves the participation of several entities. The production committee that initiates the project includes a television broadcasting company, a public relations agency, a producer of toys, and the firm responsible for anime production. Makers of toys are important participants in the committee because the marketing of characters in various forms is a lucrative revenue stream for the animation industry (see figure 5.3). At the stage of actual production, the anime production firm takes charge and outsources some of the processes to subconstructors (figure 5.4). For instance, typically eight frames are required to produce a second of moving sequence.[37] In Japan, animations are still mostly hand drawn and colored, which are highly labor-intensive processes, each frame taking at least half an hour to produce. For given moving sequences, frames are classified into two categories: *key* and *in-between*. Key frames are drawn by the lead animator and define the important moments within a motion, whereas in-between frames are fillers to make the motion smooth. For instance, key frames will specify the starting

37. This number is much less than the number of frames used in films (24 frames per second) and videos (30 frames per second). The lower number of frames is used to cut the cost. A half-hour episode of anime costs US$100,000 on average (DCAj 2004).

Figure 5.4 Market Structure of Animation Industry in Japan

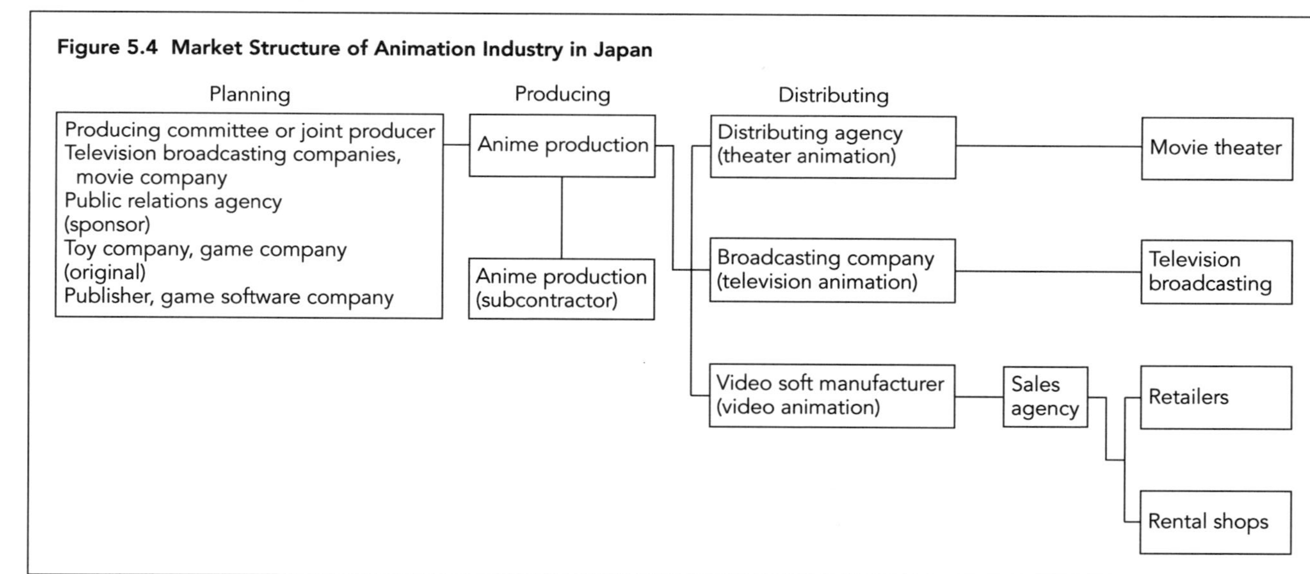

Source: JETRO 2005.

and stopping point of a waving hand, and in-between frames will depict the hands in between those two points. Most animation production firms outsource the in-between cels—increasingly to other countries, such as China, the Republic of Korea, and the Philippines—sometimes along with the coloring of those cels. For example, the film and television programs based on Yu-Gi-Oh were drawn by artists working for the Dangwoo Animation Co. in Korea. Toei Animation digitizes its drawings (key cels) and sends them to a vendor in Manila, which draws and colors the in-between cels and does the filming. Tezuka Production outsources its in-between cels and coloring to China to take advantage of lower labor costs. The trend toward outsourcing together with the adoption of digital technology has led to a reduction in the number of animators in the industry, from 3,500 to 3,000 in 2005, in spite of increasing turnover.[38] Despite the labor-intensive production process, anime sequences are cheaper to produce than cartoons because they have far fewer frames. *Yu-Gi-Oh!: The Movie* cost US$5 million to make compared with US$30 million for *The SpongeBob SquarePants Movie*.

Urban Geography of Firms

Of the 430 anime production firms in Japan, 359 companies are located in Tokyo, with 40 percent in two wards: Nerima and Suginami (see table 5.4). Of the total number of anime production firms, about 50 are main production firms, mostly located in Tokyo. The remaining firms subcontract specific processes within the animation production sequences.

The animation industry germinated in Nerima with the establishment of Toei Animation, which also produced the first theatrical feature-length film, *The White Snake*. The first television animation, *Astro Boy* by Mushi Production, established by Osamu Tezuka, was also produced in Nerima. Thus Nerima is often called the cradle of Japanese animation. Suginami hosts the second-largest concentration of animation companies, about 70. Both wards have established policies that promote and support the animation industry. In May 2004, the Suginami local government opened an Animation Museum that offers visitors a comprehensive overview of the history of the subject.

38. Animation promises to be big business worldwide, and more of it could quickly migrate from Japan to China and India, for example. In 2004, India's animation business already had a turnover of US$550 million and it employed 27,000 professionals in 2001. By one estimate those numbers could swell manifold in the next few years ("On the World's" 2005).

Table 5.4 Location of Animation Firms in 23 Wards of Tokyo

Ward	Number of firms
Nerima	74
Suginami	71
Shinjuku	25
Shibuya	20
Minato	18
Nakano	15
Toshima	8
Chiyoda	7
Setagaya	6
Chuo	4
Meguro	3
Shinagawa	3
Ota	3
Taito	2
Itabashi	1
Kita	1
Bunkyo	1
Arakawa	1
Sumida	1
Adachi	0
Katsushika	0
Edogawa	0
Koutou	0
Total	**264**

Source: Dentsu Communication Institute 2005.

Tokyo's attraction for the animation industry is the strength of its storytelling traditions, both within Japan and within Asia. There are 4,000 publishing firms, with 200 to 300 publishing regularly. They are the main outlets for *manga*, on which many animations are based.[39] About one-third of all magazines publish only *manga* (there are 277 cartoon magazines) and more than two-thirds of all paperback sales are of *manga* (DCAj 2003).[40] Cartoonists are clustered in Tokyo because of the concentration of the

39. The movie industry in Japan is also closely tied to the publishing industry. Tokyo is a host to all major publishers and, through frequent contacts with them, a movie studio can get a first look at upcoming novels, which could be used as the original story for a movie. When a promising story is identified, it needs to be adapted for a screenplay. Such writers are also all located in Tokyo. And other supporting crews, such as recording and sound technicians, are available in Tokyo.

40. Japanese publishers have licensed more than 10,000 titles of Japanese *manga* in East Asia (DCAj 2003).

publishing firms, availability of assistants, and large local market for self-publishers.[41]

With increasing digitization, more of the actual production of animation sequences will likely move overseas, as is happening with manufacturing industries. Nevertheless, the creative core of the industry, which generates the ideas and is responsible for planning and production of key sequences, could stay in Japan, mainly in Tokyo. If animation is able to enlarge its share of the entertainment business in Japan and increase its global following, every likelihood exists that turnover and employment in certain segments of the business could rise. The increasing attendance at the annual anime festival in Washington, D.C.—the Katsucon—suggests that anime is resonating with audiences far and wide.[42] However, a continuing increase in popularity and the global clientele will depend on steady inflow of talent, improvement in the content quality of products, and skillful marketing.

Management and marketing talent will be especially critical for the industry to realize its global potential. But because most studio bosses are artists, the animation industry in Japan worries that it is short of people who understand the changing tastes, intellectual property rights management, legal systems, and financing in the major foreign markets. For this reason, Japanese animation products are rarely marketed outside of Japan without significant success in Japan first, although the situation has started to change slightly in recent years.[43] And no Japanese studio has yet produced a blockbuster to compare with *Finding Nemo*.

The shortage of technical skills has its source in the inadequacy of tertiary-level courses on animation and media content, management, legal topics, and overseas marketing tailored for the anime industry.[44] In

41. The lead cartoonist comes up with a story and then decides on the layouts of each panel and draws in the outline of the characters with pencils. Assistants mainly fill in the details. This process used to be highly labor intensive, but gradually it is being digitized. Unlike the animation industry, however, the cartoon industry has not engaged in global activities yet.

42. *Yu-Gi-Oh* and *Pokémon* are among the most popular cartoon series, and *Pokémon* is shown in 69 countries. The U.S. retail sales of *manga* comics amounted to US$625 million in 2004 ("It's . . . Profitmón!" 2005).

43. For instance, *Innocence* by Production I.G. (the animation firm that produced the animated sequence for *Kill Bill: Vol. 1*) is the first Japanese animation slated for global distribution at the stage of production (Ashahi.com) and *Yu-Gi-Oh!: The Movie* was distributed only outside Japan.

44. Japan is now attracting a large number of foreign students, mainly from Asia, to study animation and technologies used in video games. Those students tend to stay and subsequently work for animation and video game producers ("Japan Emerges as Pop" 2005).

addition, with respect to international business, creative producers knowledgeable about foreign markets and specialists on overseas copyright laws are also scarce. Although 75 tertiary-level institutes with 400 faculty members teach courses on visual content, the number of students graduated and the diversity of subjects taught pales in comparison with the United States and other East Asian countries (DCAj 2004). The United States has several hundred film schools at tertiary level with 4,000 instructors and 70,000 students. The education covers not only production but also management (DCAj 2004). In Korea, more than 300 institutes specialize in training on animation and cartoons (DCAj 2004). In China, 4,000 students are being trained at the Beijing Film Institute alone, in addition to others graduating from Tsinghua University and the Shanghai Industrial Technology University. Moreover, a National Animation School was established in 2001 (DCAj 2004). The University of Tokyo is now attempting to fill this void by creating a department specifically to train people who can take on production and management (DCAj 2004). The Tokyo metropolitan government has held a Tokyo International Anime Fair every year since 2002 to encourage Japanese animators to network with business. Digital Hollywood, a for-profit school to nurture people in the contents industry, has been in operation since 1994 with more than 30,000 graduates (DCAj 2004).

The current relationship between the media firms and the animation firms also handicaps the industry. Typically, producers belong to the distribution arms of media firms, and they identify a particular type of animation to be broadcast and subcontract the creation of such animation to animation production firms. Because of this structure, financing is limited to the expected revenue stream from their main distribution methods, and producers tend not to explore other means of distributing the animation, such as over the Internet, which directly threatens their existing distribution channels (DCAj 2004).

Enlargement of the supply of skills will need to be complemented by greater attention to content to attract younger people from around the world while holding onto older audiences. Because the new content has tended to be thinner, firms are having less success in attracting the younger generation who have not been exposed to the original work. At the same time, in Japan, less space is allocated for television programs aimed at younger people, because the average age of television viewers is on the rise. Thus, firms will need to be more innovative while sustaining the essential esoteric, complex fantasy-based content that is at the heart of anime's appeal. They will need to be able to market more effectively in

Japan and abroad if Tokyo's animation industry is to sustain, if not enhance, its growth.[45]

A NEW DAWN?

The robotics and animation industries have momentum, but theirs is a hesitant and still uncertain advance. No confident prediction can be made, but grounds exist for cautious hope and the makings of two major industrial clusters for Tokyo. Many firms in Tokyo are using the idea of producing humanoid robots to motivate their researchers, many of whom grew up watching robot-themed anime. Finding solutions for the specific functions of different types of robots and integrating components, which draw on multiple disciplines, pose many challenges. But those challenges cannot be avoided. Firms are hoping that research in robotics will yield useful and profitable by-products that they can incorporate in other products or use as standalone products. For instance, visual recognition systems developed for robots can be used for security systems, voice recognition technologies can be incorporated in many consumer and other products, and sensor technology is being used for obstacle-avoidance systems for automobiles. Because of the likely safety concerns, the weight of robots will be restricted, which means that many parts will need to be light as well as durable, energy efficient, and able to work with lighter batteries. Those requirements will lead to further miniaturization, the development of new materials, and better and lighter batteries, all of which can be applied to other goods.

The application of the technologies developed for robots to existing or new products seems to be the main near-term goal of many of the firms engaged in robotics research. For this and other reasons, those firms tend to produce robots entirely in-house, without much collaboration with other firms and research institutes, including universities. A more open and ambitious approach will be needed. Because many of the firms already have R&D facilities in the Tokyo area, robotics research is concentrating in Tokyo to take advantage of the existing production and research facilities and skills available there.

The animation industry is using the recent advances in information and communication technology to increase its overseas productions. This trend is likely to continue, and the source of Tokyo's strength as the

45. Similarly, many movies are now aimed at an older generation of Japanese viewers.

originator of animation will depend on the people who create the original stories, on the people who manage the production processes, on the animators for the key cels, and on people who can market the products worldwide. Although with the increase in the production volume, more animators may be needed, it is in the business services part of their operation that many firms urgently need to increase staffing. If they can do so, the global demand should be forthcoming.

Tokyo needs highly skilled workers for robotics. These people will be mainly drawn from the natural and social science disciplines; for the animation industry, they will come from the professional schools, from the *otaku* subculture, and from professional business services.[46] Whether Tokyo can retain and strengthen its current advantage depends on whether the metropolis can either produce locally or attract from elsewhere the desired combination of skills.

46. Tokyo also needs to attract the young. Many successful cartoonists started out their careers in their late teens by entering contests hosted by the publishers. Such contests are still the predominant form of starting one's career as a cartoonist, along with direct submission of works to the publisher.

CHAPTER 6

FUN, MOVIES, AND VIDEOGAMES

Not much more than a decade ago, Seoul was an industrial city par excellence. Manufacturing was the lifeblood of the city, and key services were geared toward meeting the needs of industry. Manufacturing remains central to the Republic of Korea's prosperity, and autos, transport equipment, electronic components, mobile handsets, and machinery constitute the principal exports. But the manufacturing industry has largely moved out of Seoul and a new industrial ecology is emerging at an amazingly rapid pace. Vestiges of old-style manufacturing can still be found in the Guro industrial district in southern Seoul, with its producers of machinery and textiles, its printing houses, and its food-processing firms now being superseded by firms specializing in information and communication technology (ICT). To the south of the city is a cluster of high-tech manufacturing in the Suwon area, where Samsung's headquarters and laboratories are located (Park 2005). But for the most part, the economy of Seoul revolves around producer services and creative industries.

The downtown area, including Jongno-gu, now houses corporate headquarters and major retail outlets. Like New York, it is also the center of the publishing industry. Some of the leading universities and research institutes have located in Dongdaemun, in the northern part of the city. Across the river in Yoido, one finds the National Assembly, the offices of the three major broadcasting companies, and a concentration of Seoul's many newspaper businesses. The information technology (IT) and multimedia industries and the venture capitalists and providers of other business services are responsible for the affluence of Guro, Seocho, and Kangnam districts in the southeastern part of the city, particularly in the vicinity of Teheran Street, now the center of Teheran Valley (Park 2005; Sohn and Kenney 2005). Kangnam is also where the movie and videogame industries have begun to ripen as a result of

IBRD 34886
JULY 2006

SEOUL, REPUBLIC OF KOREA

NATIONAL CAPITAL
CAPITAL URBAN EXTENT

0 100 200 300 kilometers

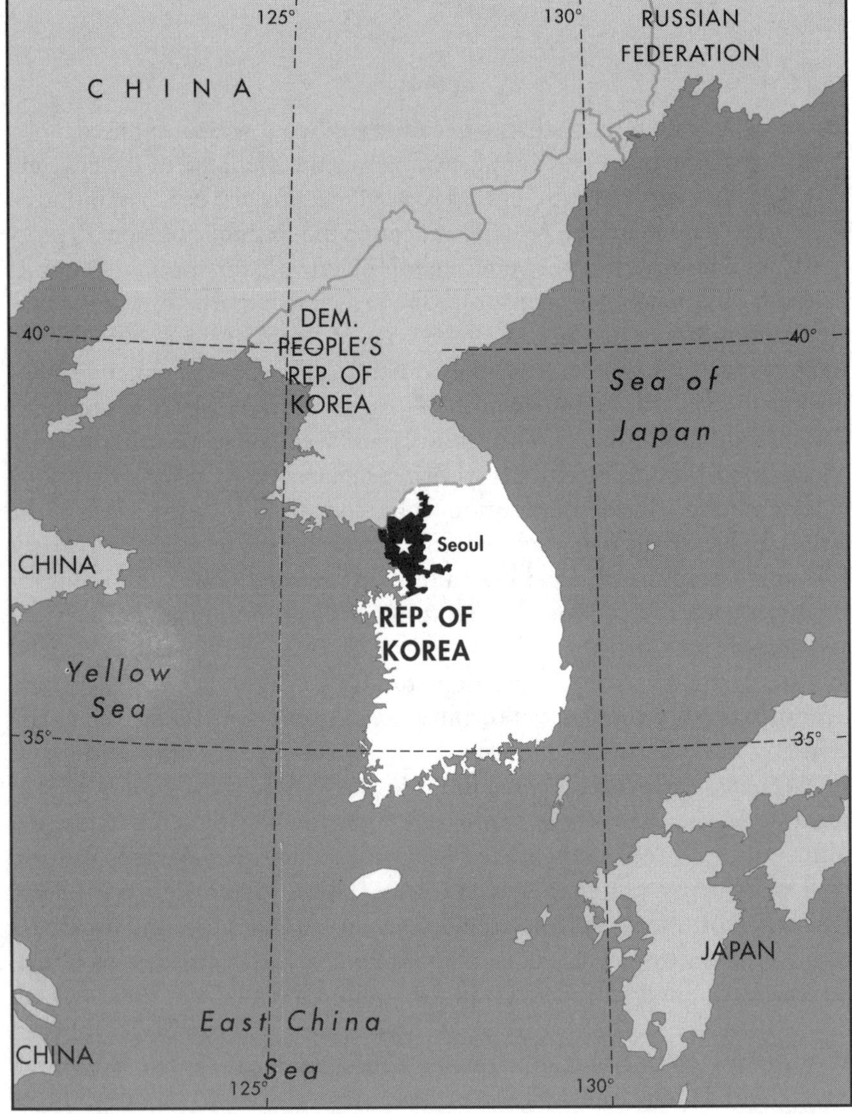

government policies, the backing offered by venture capitalists, and the support of other providers of commercial services.

Among the nascent cultural and creative industries, the media and content industries stand out. They constitute a small cluster so far, but it is a cluster with many links and considerable potential, as is apparent from the experiences of New York and Los Angeles (see chapter 2). It is a type of cluster, moreover, that thrives in large cities with an abundance of diverse skills, "thick" labor markets, and a plentitude of supporting producer services. The media industry relies heavily on a host of other industries for financing and for legal, marketing, advertising, and IT services. It is also a capital-intensive industry that looks to the manufacturers of electronics and telecommunications equipment and the writers of software for essential inputs. In effect, a successful media industry can become an axis for the urban economy.

In recent years, a number of Korean films have won prestigious international awards and are generating substantial export earnings. Producers of videogames, especially online games, are doing equally well. The massively multiplayer online role-playing games (MMORPGs), such as Lineage and City of Hero by NCSoft and The Legend of Mir by WeMade Entertainment, are played by hundreds of thousands of subscribing players around the world every day—especially in China, where on occasion up to 600,000 people log on simultaneously to play The Legend of Mir (H. Lee, Oh, and Shim 2005).

As the ranks of manufacturing industries thin out, the Seoul metro area is pinning its economic hopes on a broad range of services, in particular on a number of creative industries that draw on the cultural resources of the city, other technology-intensive industries, and the IT infrastructure. As we describe below, Seoul has the advantage that a large part of Korea's expertise in electronics and telecommunications is concentrated in the metropolitan area. This expertise includes the major universities and research institutes. In addition, the country's lavish investment in IT hardware has provided households in Seoul with broadband Internet access that is second to none and that triggered the proliferation of IT-based services.[1]

Can those factors support a globally competitive multimedia industry on a significant scale? The Korean government and the Seoul municipality certainly think so. They have the backing of several large conglomerates, which have plowed capital into electronics and telecommunications and are keen to expand into downstream services. Moreover, the past few

1. See *Korea Internet White Paper* (National Computerization Agency 2001).

years have raised the industry's hopes. Korean films have enthused audiences overseas, and videogame developers have notched up some early successes. Whether those successes lead to a further clustering of talent and industry in Seoul and establish the reputation of Korean producers abroad is highly conjectural. In this chapter, we examine the state of the multimedia industry in Seoul and the changes that are sweeping through the longer-term prospects of Korean producers in the global marketplace.

THE FILM INDUSTRY'S DEVELOPMENT IN KOREA

Since the end of the 19th century, production capital, directors, and film technicians from Japan were largely responsible for the initial flowering of the film industry in Korea. From the early 20th century until 1945, production and distribution of films were wholly in Japanese hands. At the end of the World War II, film-related equipment and facilities (mainly in Seoul) were transferred to the Korean authorities.

The outbreak of the Korean War in the 1950s and the damage it inflicted on Seoul led to the temporary dispersion of film production to other cities: Busan, Daegu, Jinhae, and Masan. After the bullets stopped flying and the Armistice Agreement was signed in 1953, filmmakers returned to Seoul. The end of the war ushered in a golden era of growth for the Korean film industry, extending to the late 1960s.

Thereafter, tight regulation of industry and unflagging censorship of the media by authorities led to stagnation through the early 1990s, despite quota restrictions on foreign films that persisted until the early 1980s.[2] The popularity of television also contributed to a decrease in film production as

2. Article 16 of the Motion Picture Law of 1962 specified that to import foreign films, Korean distributors needed to export four movies and earn at least US$20,000. In addition, any domestic films that were shown at least 60 days in overseas markets were given cash awards. Specific legal restrictions were imposed on Japanese imports (Rosen 2003).

The new Motion Picture Law of 1985 (amended in 1987) dissolved the import-export link and allowed foreign companies to produce and distribute films directly in Korea. In the past, movies were imported through Los Angeles-based Korean buyers, importers, regional distributors, and exhibitors. Although imports were allowed, the screen quota remained, with at least 40 percent of screen time allocated to Korean films (146 days). This period was shortened to 106 days in 1996 (Rosen 2003). Restrictions remain on the dubbing of foreign movies and local advertising for foreign retransmission channels. These are part of the Korean Broadcasting Commission's guidelines for implementing the Broadcasting Act. France has a similar quota system, as do a number of other countries. Among the 33 economies studied by Marvasti and Canterbery (2005), France and Italy are the most protectionist with regard to the movie industry; Korea ranked sixth, along with Argentina and Mexico.

Table 6.1 Domestic Market Shares of Korean and Foreign Films, 1991–2004

Year	Korean films (W hundred million)	Foreign films (W hundred million)	Korean film share (%)
1991	321	1,263	20.3
1995	393	1,532	20.4
2000	1,209	2,251	34.9
2001	2,609	2,628	49.8
2002	3,068	3,259	48.5
2003	3,823	3,348	53.3
2004	5,048	3,450	59.4

Source: Korean Film Council 2004.

well as in theater attendance. Women in their 30s and 40s, the majority of the moviegoing audience for local films, took to viewing television. The industry's plight worsened further when color television was introduced at the beginning of the 1980s.[3] The recovery of the film industry over the past decade and its localization in Seoul is largely the result of government policies to reverse the ebbing popularity of Korean films and of efforts under way to transform the composition of Seoul's economy.

The Korean quota system was put in place in 1969 to prevent domination of the domestic market by U.S. films, to maintain cultural diversity, and to balance and regulate exchange between cultures (Marvasti and Canterbery 2005). This system has gone through a number of revisions. The current system, introduced in July 2006, requires that at least 73 days of the year be allocated to domestically made movies, a ruling that will increase the competitive pressure from foreign films and reinforce the trend toward higher-quality Korean movies ("South Korea/US: Film Quotas" 2006) (see table 6.1).[4]

The big turnaround of the domestic film industry came in 1999, when several new directors who were trained in the West and familiar with new techniques became active filmmakers (Rosen 2003). At the same time, funding from the *chaebol* dried up, and venture capitalists became an important source of financing. The new capital proved a godsend, because the production cost of a feature film had increased from an average of

3. When color television was introduced in the United States, theater attendance also decreased. But at the same time, television generated an aftermarket for old movies (Waterman 2005).

4. It should be noted that protection did not contribute to the success of Hollywood. The United States has had no protective or supportive measures for the movie industry (Marvasti and Canterbery 2005), except at the end of World War II, when Hollywood movies were exported to Europe as part of the Marshall Plan package of assistance ("Paris, Texas" 2003).

US$769,000 in 1995 to US$1.7 million in 2000. More important, the marketing cost had also risen, from US$77,000 to US$500,000. Nearly half of all venture capitalists exited the movie industry by 2002, after a series of high-profile flops of big-budget movies, so funds from this source are on the ebb (Rosen 2003). Early-stage venture capital is generally scarce in Korea (Sohn and Kenney 2005).

Although the quota was central to the government's policy toward the film industry, a number of other policy initiatives have also proven important. The Korean Film Council was founded in 1973 as a government-supported body to develop the Korean film industry. With the industry's support, it has taken the lead in establishing film festivals that have placed Korea on the map in the world of moviemaking. Film festivals are a sign of credible commitment by the government to promote the industry and to reach mainstream viewers abroad, not just a specialized audience with a taste for exotic fare and a willingness to sit through a dubbed or subtitled film. (That market is extremely limited.)

The government invested in the Seoul Studio Complex, now in the Kangnam district of Seoul, where some of the best-known Korean movies of recent years have been shot. This US$60 million facility contains 990 square meters of studio space for underwater shooting and special photography; a props room; studios for art design, sound, and visual effects; and an outdoor movie set. Like Universal Studios in Los Angeles the complex also caters to tourists, who are an additional source of income.

In 2002 the government established the Seoul Film Commission to serve as an efficient support system and to assist in designing an urban environment conducive to the development of the film industry in Seoul. The commission assists in obtaining permission (or serves as liaison) for location shooting. It makes available police and fire personnel as well as resources for traffic broadcasting and promotion to mitigate public grievances; arranges parking space with Seoul City or the subcontractors of Seoul City; and maintains an extensive directory of resources for preproduction, production, postproduction, equipment, and public relations and distribution requirements. All films are eligible as long as they apply for support from the commission.

MAKING AND SCREENING MOVIES IN SEOUL

In 2004, the Korean film industry made steady progress. Locally produced films captured 60 percent of the earnings from the domestic market, compared with 53 percent in 2003 and 35 percent in 2000 (table 6.1).

Table 6.2 Number of Films Produced and Imported by Korea, 1991–2004

Year	Produced films	Imported films	Produced films as share of total (%)
1991	121	309	28.1
1995	64	378	14.5
2000	59	404	12.1
2001	65	339	15.5
2002	78	262	22.7
2003	80	271	22.8
2004	82	285	22.3

Source: Korean Film Council 2004.

Table 6.3 Market Share of U.S. Movies in Selected Countries, 2000

Country	Number of films produced	Domestic film industry share (%)	U.S. film industry share (%)
Australia	31	8.0	87.5
France	204	28.9	58.3
Germany	75	9.4	81.9
Italy	103	17.5	69.5
Japan	282	31.8	64.8
Spain	98	10.1	82.7
United Kingdom	90	19.6	75.3
United States	460	96.1	n.a.

Source: Scott 2004.

Note: n.a. = not applicable.

These earnings reflected an increase in the number of films—from 59 in 2000 to 82 in 2004—as well as gains in cinematography and content[5] that have made these movies even more popular among local moviegoers—and a match for movies from Hollywood, which dominate in many other countries (see tables 6.2 and 6.3).[6] Because of the government's efforts to develop the creative industries in Seoul, more than 90 percent of film production

5. In the early 1990s, the ticket prices for foreign films were typically 5 or 6 percent higher than those for domestic films. However, in the past few years, the difference has narrowed to less than 1 percent.

6. Hollywood has not always been dominant. At the beginning of the 20th century, two-thirds of films shown around the world were of French origin. By the end of the century, 80 percent of the movies in Europe were of U.S. origin, while European movies accounted for less than 0.5 percent of the movies in the United States ("Paris, Texas" 2003). In fact, many foreign producers moved to Hollywood. Nevertheless, perhaps because of extensive support from the state, France remains a major producer, releasing up to 200 features each year. In 2005, 73 million people worldwide viewed these movies, and *March of the Penguins*, originally a French film, was a great in hit in the United States ("Channel Hopping" 2006).

Table 6.4 Attendance and Number of Theaters and Screens in Korea by Year, 1991–2004

Year	Population (million)	Total admissions (million)	Theaters	Screens	Screens per theater
1991	43.3	52.2	762	762	1.0
1995	45.1	45.1	577	577	1.0
1997	46.0	47.5	497	497	1.0
2000	47.3	61.7	373	720	1.9
2001	47.3	89.4	344	818	2.4
2002	48.0	105.1	309	977	3.2
2003	48.4	119.5	280	1,132	4.0
2004	48.6	135.2	302	1,451	4.8

Source: Korean Film Council 2004.

companies and related industries are based in the metropolitan area and about 80 percent of Korean films are produced in the capital city.

The popularity of films impinged on the supply of theaters and screens, which decreased until 1998; a turnaround commenced in 1999, when multiplex construction began in earnest (Rosen 2003). Since then, although the number of theaters has continued falling, the number of screens has risen to four per site (table 6.4). The advantage of multiplexes for theater owners is that they can offer movies that appeal to a broad spectrum of tastes, feeding the demand for a diverse mix of movies and promoting both the industry's development and the penetration by movies made by Hollywood (Scott 2004). A similar trend occurred in the United States. In 1980, there were 17,675 screens; the number of screens has increased to 36,264 at 6,979 sites, with an average of 5.2 per theater (Scott 2004).

The intensification of the government's support has a lot to do with the suddenness of the changes in the industry. Ever on the alert for new exports to replace maturing ones and to replace industries that are migrating to other economies, the Korean government has recognized that cultural content (or cultural products) can be successfully exported if it can acquire an international appeal. The government believes that cultural content can contribute to economic growth, not marginally but significantly—so much so that the Korean Culture and Content Agency (KOCCA),[7] a public organization under the Ministry of Culture and Tourism, has fixed its sights on making Korea a cultural industry powerhouse, among the top

7. KOCCA, established in 2001, promotes activities relevant to the development of the Korean cultural content business, including animation, music, characters (for licensed merchandising), comics, mobile and Internet content, and educational material. It also facilitates the involvement of Korean companies in joint ventures and partnerships.

five globally, according to its vision and goal statement. Achieving this status will contribute to achieving the government's per capita income target of US$20,000. Seoul, which has the largest concentration of facilities, creative people, and services, is to spearhead this effort.

To this end, KOCCA has made cultural production part of the national economic blueprint. It is organized as a private corporation run by skilled managers recruited from the private sector. KOCCA's aim is not only to promote Korean cultural products abroad, but also to nurture talent and creativity by offering grants and loans as well as by investing in creative projects. The short-term results have been positive: production value has increased and cultural content is now more diversified. Seoul is on the road to becoming a center of production for the creative industries.

The government's investment and the easing of regulatory constraints are paying off. Since 1992, the lifting of the censorship imposed by the military government in the late 1960s has enabled directors to increase the political and sexual content in their movies, thus contributing to the surge of creative energy (Rosen 2003). The freer climate led to the success of movies such as *Shiri*, which confronted some of the issues arising from the division of the peninsula, a theme that would have been prohibited under the previous regime (Rosen 2003).[8]

Other movies followed. One of the most profitable Korean films to screen in the United States was *Tae Guik Gi*, which grossed a little more than US$1 million at the U.S. box office and about US$70 million globally. Another large export market for Korean movies is Japan. A total of US$3.2 million was paid for the distribution rights to *A Bittersweet Life* in Japan. Show East's film *April Snow* is said to have been presold to a Japan distribution company for between US$7 million and US$8 million. It will be released in China, Hong Kong (China), Indonesia, Japan, Korea, Taiwan (China), and Thailand at almost the same time; Show East claims that it will be the biggest simultaneous release for an Asian film. Sony Pictures Television International has entered into a distribution agreement with CJ Entertainment, a Korean producer and distributor. The deal involves Sony handling the Asian television distribution rights to two movies, but there are also plans for Sony to participate in local production. Without such exports, the Korean movie industry would have lost more than US$20 million in 2004 ("Asian Alliance" 2004).[9]

---

8. Some restrictions remain, such as the requirement to portray the military in a positive light (Rosen 2003).

9. Surprisingly, exports have become the major source of revenue for Hollywood also since the international success of *Titanic* in 1997. In 2005, box office sales in the United States amounted

Table 6.5 Korean Film Exports by Region, 2002 and 2003

Region	2002	Share of exports (%)	2003	Share of exports (%)	Growth rate (%)
Asia	10,499,979	70	19,024,000	61	81
Europe	2,365,500	16	5,724,000	18	142
North America	695,500	5	4,486,000	14	545
Oceania	123,610	1	30,000	0	−76
South America	47,000	0	82,500	0	76
Others	1,206,500	9	1,632,500	5	35
Total	**14,952,239**	**100**	**30,979,000**	**100**	**107**

Source: Korean Film Council 2004.

Korean films have struck a chord in Japan and in China as well, because they are based on human interest stories that are not culturally specific. They enjoy the same advantages as action movies and comedies focused on physical slapstick, because their appeal is relatively uniform across cultures. Korean movies are also appreciated in China, because they offer lighter fare than the often highly didactic movies produced locally (Cowen 2002). Since 2000, the export of Korean films has increased dramatically, mainly to Asia and Europe (table 6.5), with each film earning much more than in the 1990s, although exports in 2001 and 2002 seem to be of lesser quality than those in 2000 and 2003 (table 6.6).

In 2004, Korean filmmakers won major prizes at prestigious international film festivals in Berlin, Cannes, and Venice. Park Chan-Wook won the Grand Prix, second to the main prize of the Palme d'Or, for *Old Boy* at Cannes. Kim Ki-duk won best director awards in Berlin for *Samaritan Girl* and in Venice for *3-Iron*. *The King and the Clown* won critical acclaim in 2005 and has enjoyed considerable commercial success. But more than being recognized for their merit by film festival judges with awards—although that does elevate the profile of particular films and the Korean

---

to US$9 billion versus nearly US$10 billion from overseas. *Brokeback Mountain* and *Hitch* are just two examples of Hollywood movies that have grossed more revenues internationally ("Hollywood Caters" 2006).Without this revenue, many films would not even cover their costs (Scott 2004). The movie industry is adapting to globalization, and no blockbuster big-budget movie is made unless producers are convinced that it will sell overseas. Increasingly, U.S. studios are releasing films simultaneously around the world instead of sequencing their release, as with *The Da Vinci Code* in June 2006, so as to combat piracy. The timing of release in multiple markets has become an important consideration (Marvasti and Canterbery 2005; "Hollywood Caters" 2006). However, foreign movies account for less than 1 percent of box office receipts in the United States, despite the lack of any protection. This figure is down from 10 percent in the 1960s (Marvasti and Canterbery 2005).

Table 6.6 Earnings from Korean Film Exports, 1991–2003

Year	Number of films	Export price per film (US$)	Amount of export (US$)
1991	17	27,815	472,850
1995	15	13,912	208,679
1996	30	13,467	404,000
2000	38	185,625	7,053,745
2001	102	110,289	11,249,573
2002	133	112,422	14,952,089
2003	162	191,228	30,979,000

Source: Korean Film Council 2004.

film industry in general—the films need to appeal to international audiences and to cross over to mainstream taste.

In this effort, Korean films seeking an audience abroad are not alone. A number of East Asian economies are trying to capture the attention of the worldwide audience. China, Hong Kong (China), and Taiwan (China) have all been remarkably successful in breaking into foreign markets, and not just regionally—their performance record in the U.S. film market is quite impressive.[10]

Links with Other Industries

The movie industry typically depends on an extensive array of supporting services. Even in an age when electronics communication is so effortless, a concentration of varied talents, as in Hollywood and now in Seoul, is vital for success. These talents include scriptwriters, musicians, sound technicians, prop constructors, lighting specialists, digital effects specialists, and other professions, including financial and legal ones. The movie industry also contributes to the economy indirectly, mainly by offering leisure activities such as movie-themed amusement parks; by boosting tourism through sales of CDs, DVDs, and other merchandise; by promoting cultural life; and by pulling in foreign direct investment.

The increasing presence of performing artists has substantial multiplier effects and technological spillovers. Aside from material supplies and equipment, musical performers, for example, require a variety of supporting services. Markusen and King (2003, 17–18) note that "musicians [need] people to repair and fine tune [instruments] . . . , back up musicians and craft work ancillary to building sets, . . . [and] more generic service

10. China also protects the domestic industry by limiting to 20 the number of U.S.-made films that can be screened in a single year ("Hollywood Caters" 2006).

Table 6.7 Number of Establishments and Employees in Motion Picture Production in California, 1997 and 2002

Year	Description	Number of establishments	Number of employees	Annual payroll (US$ thousand)
1997	Motion picture and video production	3,321	49,762	3,408,881
2002	Motion picture and video production	4,148	69,820	5,186,938
1997	Motion picture and video industries	16,193		
2002	Motion picture and video industries	19,606		

Source: United States Census Bureau (http://www.census.gov/econ/census02/guide/02EC_CA.HTM).

Note: Data for nonemployers are available only at NACIS5121 (Motion Picture and Video Industries), which includes both production and distribution activities. A *nonemployer* is a business without any paid employees, such as independent contractors.

providers such as accountants and photographers. . . . Artists also generate employment in the distribution of their work. . . . Innovative artists often push the envelope, asking a maker to design an instrument differently or a choir to sing unconventionally. . . . Artists then amplify their economic significance to a region by generating work for others who are supplying their materials and services needs and polishing and distributing their work." In the United Kingdom, for example, the 31,500 full-time employees in the film industry supported an equivalent number of other workers in 2004 (Oxford Economic Forecasting 2005).

In 2002, California had 4,148 firms with about 70,000 workers employed in the motion picture and video production industry, mainly in the Los Angeles area. In addition, 19,606 independent contractors supplied teleproduction and postproduction services; casting bureau services; wardrobe and equipment rentals; talent payment services; and the services of independent writers, directors, and performers (table 6.7).[11] A high percentage are skilled workers commanding premium wages. This is also true for the filmmaking workforce in the United Kingdom, two-thirds of which is in the London area and the southeast.[12]

11. Although they may be independent, many are members of either a union or a guild for collective bargaining purpose ("Lights. Industrial Action!" 2005).

12. In 2004, the film industry in the United Kingdom had a turnover of UK£23 billion, with value added of close to UK£16 billion. When all other sales are accounted for, the direct and indirect contributions of filmmaking to gross domestic product were UK£31 billion. Interestingly, employment in filmmaking alone was equal to that in the publishing industry (Oxford Economic Forecasting 2005).

Without more disaggregated data, it is hard to accurately calculate the multiplier effect of movie production on other industries. Typically, this multiplier is estimated at between 2.0 and 4.6 (Business Research Division 2003).[13]

By comparison, the employment directly generated by the movie and video industry in Seoul is quite small. The 310 establishments in 2002 employed a little more than 2,000 workers (table 6.8).

Collaboration with Foreign Movie Studios

Financing from the *chaebols* contributed to the development of the Korean film industry. Funding from Samsung, Lotte, and CJ Entertainment made a hit movie like *Shiri* (1999) possible. But this source of funding is on the decline, and the Korean venture capital industry now offers scant support, preferring instead to finance established firms in more mainstream activities.

In tune with the globalization of the movie industry and in response also to these modest supplies of local funding, producers in Seoul have been forging alliances with foreign partners, although not to the same extent that their rivals in China have. The pace is affected by foreigners' perception of Seoul and the local movie production business. Partners and investors have yet to be impressed with what the city has to offer. This attitude is beginning to change, with more Japanese financing becoming available because of the interest in Korean films and the costliness of making movies in Japan.

The need to find collaborators is made more urgent by the rising outlay on each film. The average budget of a film is now US$4.5 million, necessitating many coproducers to finance a single movie. By comparison, the average cost of a major Hollywood feature film is US$60 million (Waterman 2005). However, collaboration can also modulate content and style, thereby enhancing the international flavor and appeal. *Daisy*, the latest offering of Korea's iFilm, was written by a Korean; the director was from Hong Kong (China); and the story is set in the Netherlands. In 2001, Hur Jin-ho's *One Fine Spring Day* was coproduced by Korea's Sidus Pictures; Applause Pictures of Hong Kong (China); and Japan's Shochiku Films. It had a budget of US$1.5 million.

13. It is difficult to adequately capture links, especially indirect ones. For instance, an animatronic puppet studio has collaborated with the Massachusetts Institute of Technology to create robots that can be used in movies ("It Came from Hollywood" 2003). Many links such as this one are generally overlooked.

Table 6.8 Establishments and Employees in the Korean Film Industry, 1993–2002

Sector	1993	1996	1999	2000	2001	2002	1993–2002 (Growth)
General motion picture and video production							
Number of establishments	177	194	125	227	225	198	1.25
Number of employees	1,846	1,603	1,012	1,758	1,851	1,564	−1.83
Size of establishments	10.4	8.3	8.1	7.7	8.2	7.9	−0.28
Motion picture and video related service							
Number of establishments	54	59	138	79	93	112	8.44
Number of employees	398	562	1510	468	493	580	4.27
Size of establishments	7.4	9.5	10.9	5.9	5.3	5.2	−0.24
Theaters							
Number of establishments	446	553	341	442	461	469	0.56
Number of employees	2,578	3,648	2,487	3,533	4,449	5,075	7.82
Size of establishments	5.8	6.6	7.3	8	9.7	10.8	0.56
Total (film industry)							
Number of establishments	1,185	3,711	3,457	3,721	3,655	3,644	13.29
Number of employees	15,373	18,218	18,075	22,776	22,752	22,309	4.22
Size of establishments (persons per firm)	13	4.9	5.2	6.1	6.2	6.1	−0.76

Source: Korea Culture Contents Promotion Agency; Korea National Statistical Office 2004.

In 2003, Pandora Film, an independent film production company from Germany, invested W 300 million (more than US$295,000) in Kim Ki-duk's *Spring, Summer, Fall, Winter . . . and Spring*, which had an overall budget of W 1.3 billion (US$1.28 million). The same company expects to partner with LJ Films to produce a movie planned for worldwide release in 2007. That film's production cost is estimated at W 8 billion. LJ Films is also negotiating with Kadokawa Holdings Inc., a Japanese book publishing and film company, to invest in the project. Many more such joint ventures are needed for Seoul to compete with Chinese producers, who are aggressively vying for markets and funding.

Lucrative distribution deals with Hollywood are sometimes more valuable than production deals, because of the entry gained into the American market. After Miramax acquired Chow's *Shaolin Soccer*, marketing the film became a major hurdle. The studio did some slight editing but kept the film on the shelf for two years before releasing it. When the company did release it, though, Miramax realized it had been sitting on a gold mine. Although Asian films are now generally associated with martial arts, Korean fare is more contemporary (though a lot of the films are historical dramas) and reality based and appeals to completely different types of audiences.

Typically, an effort is made to export a film only after it has won approval in the domestic market. So far, no movie has been made with international distribution in mind from its inception. To attract more foreign funding and compete with the Chinese, Korean producers will have to adapt film content and style to establish a Korean brand that is widely appreciated and to win a secure international foothold for their movies.

The Film Industry Workforce

Directors who were born after the 1960s and educated in the 1980s contributed significantly to the development of the film industry in Korea. Many were trained at Chung-Ang University in Seoul. It was one of the first institutions to be licensed as a university (in 1953) and has a Graduate School of Advanced Imaging Science, Multimedia, and Film. It offers courses in scriptwriting, sound and shooting, editing, and acting. Young people drawn to acting inevitably gravitate to Seoul to seek training and a career. Many graduates from Chung-Ang have become prominent in the moviemaking business. Among them are directors Kang Je-Gyu and Hong San-Soo, actress Kim Hee-Sun, and leading actors such as Yoo In-Chon, president of the Seoul Foundation for Arts and Culture, and Park Jung-Hun. Many professors or instructors who are engaged in teaching the performing arts are also from Chung-Ang University. Other schools, all in the Seoul area, include Hanyang University, the Academy of Film Arts, and the School of Film, TV, and Multimedia at the Korea National University.

Prospective directors who have produced short films or are self-taught are increasing in numbers, with the availability of affordable digital video cameras and alternative consumer movie-editing software as effective as the professional ones ("Budding Filmmakers" 2005).[14] As in Hollywood, more of the industry's services providers are working as independent contractors. This trend is likely to continue as the industry evolves and microprocessor technology improves (and multicore chips are introduced) ("Hollywood Sees Power Shift" 2005). The technical skills needed for film production are also more abundant as people educated abroad—in Australia, the United Kingdom, the United States, and elsewhere—return to Seoul, drawn by rising earnings and the opportunity for greater recognition.

However, the number of graduates is still small. To enhance their effectiveness, the film schools need to develop a two-year special school or a graduate school to deepen the knowledge of film production—similar to that imparted, for example, by the American Film Institute and the London Film Institute. Skilled scriptwriters are in short supply. Everyone wants to be a director, not a scriptwriter, because writers do not get the recognition given directors.

The management of stars for film production is another weak spot. Most actors receive income from multiple sources, of which acting in films is only one. Contracting actors and actresses for their services is difficult. For instance, stars not only appear in the movies but also on television shows and in endorsements, and they perform as singers. This system is in stark contrast to that of the United States, in which movie stars tend to concentrate on appearing on big screens, television stars being on TV shows, and singers on recording and performing. In fact, in the United States a movie star's stature and reputation can be diminished by an appearance in a TV feature (Waterman 2005). Of course, there are a number of crossovers, but in general, the number remains small compared with the norm in Korea. This pattern reflects the small size of the talent pool in Korea as well as cultural proclivities perhaps peculiar to Northeast Asia. Japanese stars behave in much the same fashion.

---

14. For instance, the manufacturer of the industry's leading software, Avid, claims that it has been used for 90 percent of the prime time television shows and 85 percent of the blockbuster movies. However, many students feel that the Final Cut product series by Apple can edit movies professionally at a significantly lower price of US$1,300 (even lower with academic discounts) ("Budding Filmmakers" 2005). Also, in place of text- and image-based blogs, the new trend is to have a video weblog ("vlog"), signifying the availability of necessary hardware and software and indicating that the Internet is moving more toward video content ("Blogging" 2005). The interest in video search capabilities by a number of firms attests to this trend ("Google, Meet TiVo" 2005). This trend is not limited to moviemakers. Many independent artists and musicians are using computers and specialized yet affordable software to self-promote and distribute their works instead of relying on their traditional middlemen ("Making Their Own Breaks" 2005).

Korea's Competitors

Films produced in China, Hong Kong (China), and Taiwan (China) have done very well at the box office in recent years. *Crouching Tiger, Hidden Dragon*, released in the United States in 2000, grossed more than US$128 million there and US$213 million worldwide, an impressive achievement for a non-English film. It was nominated for Best Picture and won the Best Foreign Language Film award, as the entry from Taiwan (China), at the 23rd Academy Awards in the United States in 2001. This achievement was followed by the wide release of *Hero* in 2004, which grossed US$54 million in the United States, and *House of Flying Daggers*, which had grossed US$11 million by the end of 2004. They are among the largest-grossing foreign-language films released in the United States. They impressed audiences with stunning cinematography and impressive and colorful visuals. The somewhat unconventional story-telling and presentation became immediately popular, much like Japanese anime, because it seemed so new and fresh to a Western audience.

Korean producers also face competition from India's Bollywood in Mumbai. In terms of the number of feature films produced, India is ranked first, producing twice as many movies as the second-ranking United States ("Power Projectors" 2005). Indian films tend to be highly formulaic. A young, good-looking couple become romantically entangled and, after many changes of costume (every five minutes) and a half-dozen or more lengthy songs and dances, find fulfillment or explore the contours of tear-soaked tragedy (Rosen 2003). The popularity of these films is greatest with an ethnic audience, and in fact, overseas Indians now account for 65 percent of Bollywood film revenues (Rosen 2003). Without them, most films would not cover costs.

China may be Korea's biggest competitor in movies, as it is in other areas. Chinese filmmakers are not neophytes; the Chinese film industry emerged in the early 1900s and flourished in the 1930s, mainly in Shanghai. Hong Kong (China) and Taiwan (China) developed their own film industries and later overshadowed their mainland counterparts. Following the reopening of the Beijing Film Academy in 1978, a new crop of directors came to the fore and launched an exciting new genre that subtly challenged existing movies. Films such as *Yellow Earth*, *Red Sorghum*, *The Big Parade*, *Dove Tree*, and *The Blue Kite* pointed to a remarkable upwelling of talent (P. Clark 2005).

More recently, Chinese movies have shifted toward drama and action, and the political edge is less evident—and perhaps less relevant for today's audiences. Directors such as Ang Lee[15] and John Woo are internationally renowned and have been entrusted with several big-budget Hollywood films, most well received by audiences and critics alike. But beyond the big name directors and recognizable actors, there is in general a renewed interest in martial arts movies, which have been rediscovered by a new generation of moviegoers. In the 1970s and 1980s, Bruce Lee was a popular action hero; however, despite his popularity, his films were countercultural and played mostly underground. Now that genre is both exotic and familiar, and the style has been co-opted, adopted, and imitated in Hollywood action films and even considered mainstream. Even the small action-comedy films of Stephen Chow, who produced, directed, and starred in *Shaolin Soccer* and *Kung Fu Hustle*, did good business. Together, those two films grossed more than US$17 million in the United States and about US$90 million worldwide—besides receiving favorable reviews.[16] Chow's comedic routines, reminiscent of the style of Hong Kong–to–Hollywood crossover star Jackie Chan, are a clear contrast to *Crouching Tiger's* high art approach.

Whether this trend is merely a fad is something to consider, but Hollywood seems to think that it will endure, evidenced by the partnerships Hollywood studios are forging in China. *Hoh Xil: Mountain Patrol*, a movie backed by Hollywood studios, shared the Golden Horse Award for best picture of 2005.

Hollywood is drawn to China for a number of reasons. First, China already has a fairly mature film industry. Second, China offers a huge market that Hollywood wants to break into, recognizing that the country offers the broad domestic base, especially for big-budget movies that is key to Hollywood's success (Waterman 2005). Third, the changing political and cultural climate is making it easier to transact business. Fourth, China and East Asia are becoming fertile sources for movie themes that can be repackaged for American audiences, such as that of *Shall We Dance*.[17]

15. His works in Taiwan (China) include *Pushing Hands*, *The Wedding Banquet*, and *Eat Drink Man Woman*. The most famous of all, *Crouching Tiger, Hidden Dragon*, was financed entirely by Columbia Pictures, shot in China, and coscripted by an American, with stars from China, Hong Kong (China), and Malaysia, and minimal input from Taiwan (China) (Rosen 2003).

16. An *Observer* reviewer described *Kung Fu Hustle* as "Jackie Chan Meets Julie Andrews" ("Jackie Chan" 2005). A *Financial Times* review called Chow's performance "a gem in the film's crown"; he was likewise praised for his camerawork and the film's dialogue and witty one-liners ("Crimes against Hollywood" 2005). At the 42nd Golden Horse Awards ceremony in Taiwan (China) in 2005, *Kung Fu Hustle* won five awards, including the award for the best film.

17. *Shall We Dance* was released in Japan in 1996 and won the Japanese Academy Award for the best picture. It was also released in the United States, although limited to art-house theaters.

So, though many a Chinese actor and filmmaker would like to make movies in Hollywood, Hollywood wants to produce more movies in China and sell to the local audience.[18] Moreover, to maintain its grip on the world market, Hollywood's preference is to produce more expensive movies (with special effects), which raises the entry barriers for newcomers (Waterman 2005).

The Future May Be Digital

The high-definition digital camera is working hard to sever moviemaking's bondage to 35 millimeter celluloid film, with directors such as Bryan Singer, George Lucas, and Robert Rodriguez taking the lead. The transition will have momentous consequences for filmmaking as well as for distribution and screening. Digital high-definition (HD) equipment frees the director from constructing a movie through a series of painstakingly choreographed shots in custom-built and carefully lit sets. Instead, filming can take place before a green screen and background that is added or changed as the director sees fit. The face of a movie star can be digitally scanned and projected onto the faces of stunt performers, lessening the need for actors to be involved in actions for which insurance is expensive. Such a technique helped control costs for the movie *Gladiator* (Epstein 2005). Digital equipment also results in enormous savings of time by minimizing the number of takes and frees the activity of production from the tyranny of lighting in sets. With the digital camera, lighting can be adjusted at will. The digital medium has also progressed to the point where it is providing the palette of colors, the texture, the shading, and the feel of film. At the pace at which technology is moving, the remaining gaps that purists can point to will soon be closed.[19]

Digitized movies and videos have many more delivery options, given the diffusion of broadband connections and plethora of new devices.[20] Distribution through digital media allows subscribers and operators to

---

18. The recent *Memoirs of a Geisha*, starring three famous Chinese actresses, shows that Hollywood's grasp of Asian culture and sensitivities is still quite uncertain.

19. Fruitful technological collaboration between moviemakers and scientists was also responsible for importing artificial intelligence and robotics into filmmaking through the movie *Terminator* ("It Came from Hollywood" 2003).

20. Digitization also raises the risk of piracy. The music industry has been fighting over piracy in the United States and so has the movie industry. Not only does piracy affect theater receipts, but it also threatens to erode the lucrative video and DVD markets in which Hollywood firms make substantial profit. Piracy is also the major concern of filmmakers in Korea, and many have been slow to adopt digital shooting because of this concern.

exercise control more efficiently. It also permits a range of tradeoffs between picture quality and system capacity, which is convenient for multichannel operators feeding both low-resolution and HDTV (high-definition television) channels (Waterman 2005). The widespread distribution of videos over the Internet seems inevitable. For instance, BBC will make 50 percent of its regular shows available online for free ("Your Own World" 2005). And Sony Pictures Digital has introduced movies on memory sticks for viewing on cell phones in the United Kingdom ("Download This" 2005).

To take full advantage of digital technology, video content needs to be digitized not only at the final stage (as in transfer from film to digital) but from the beginning.[21] For instance, CJ Entertainment is financing eight HD-format films over the next couple years. This technology is not confined to the big screen. Cable TV station OCN is planning to produce a US$2.5 million omnibus to be shot in HD.

This shift is as much a response to changing technology as it is financially motivated. Use of this format is expected to slash 30 percent of production and postproduction costs and sharply reduce distribution costs, allowing low-budget niche films such as *Indigo* to enter the market. This movie, which cost US$500,000 to make, grossed US$1.19 million on its first day ("Miniature Could Be" 2005; Ravid 2005).

The power of the computer can also simplify the logistics of the filming process itself. Before shooting the film *War of the Worlds* (2005), Steven Spielberg used animated renderings of the movie to better plan and organize the actual shooting. By doing so, he was able to shoot the movie in 72 days, about half the average time typically required to shoot a blockbuster feature film ("Hollywood Sees Power Shift" 2005; Ravid 2005). Robert Rodriguez's *Sin City* and *The Adventures of Sharkboy* were also shot for a tiny fraction of the cost that conventional technology would have entailed. Digitization of a movie can also change the production processes in the movie industry through more integration of color-generated imagery and other elements of movies (such as backgrounds) on software. Increasingly, postproduction can be and is outsourced (Cook and Wang 2004).[22] The technology for color generation in Korea has improved greatly in the

21. At this moment, only a few programs are shot in HD digital format, even in the United States. Many of the movies shown on HDTV channels are the result of transferring film-based materials to digital format.

22. For instance, the postproduction work on *The Lord of the Rings* trilogy was done in New Zealand, Hollywood, and Germany and that on *Gladiator* in London and Hollywood (Cook and Wang 2004).

past few years. However, much of the equipment necessary for postproduction and color-generation work is still imported.

The adoption of digital technology will depend on the types of films created. Dramas seem not to benefit much from the transition from analog to digital, aside from the transportation cost, because their visual effects tend to be minimal and the sequence of the story tends to be linear. In contrast, for films in which special effects are heavily used or the nonlinear storylines require much heavier editing, the benefits can be far higher. For that and other reasons, George Lucas has become a vocal proponent of the digital format.

To facilitate the change from analog to digital format, exhibition venues need to be able to support digital inputs rather than analog ones. This requirement affects two main venues: movie theaters and homes. The transition to digital projectors from old-style celluloid film projectors is a rather slow and expensive process. In the United States, the transition has not occurred as quickly as expected, with only 19 theaters converting in 2002. Many expect that the transition will not be completed in the United States until 2010 (Cook and Wang 2004).[23] In Korea, it may take even more time because many of the newer multiplex movie theaters began to appear after 1999 and their equipment is still new—although Korea's use of digital projectors is expanding at the fastest pace in Asia ("Power Projectors" 2005). The slow rate of conversion has meant that a movie by Sidus that was shot in a digital camera still needed to be transferred to analog film so it could be shown at the movie theaters, arousing frustration similar to that felt by George Lucas over the screening of his *Star Wars* movies.

The situation could change rapidly if filmmakers adopt a different business model instead of sequencing release windows for different distribution methods (releasing at movie theaters first and then on DVD). Depending on the nature of the movie, firms could simultaneously distribute movies through different distribution channels, including transmission over the Internet, rather than relying on big screens to initiate the "buzz."[24] Using multiple distribution channels could also be a

---

23. The move to digital projectors is estimated to save the film industry US$2 billion on distribution. However, movie studios expect theater owners to bear the cost of conversion (US$150,000 to US$200,000), while the theater owners expect studios to do so (Cook and Wang 2004).

24. MK Pictures experimented with releasing *Desire* (2003) at theaters and online at the same time because that film was shot in digital cameras and only a few theaters had digital projectors. However, the film was not a commercial success—although it was never expected to be. *Bubble*, directed by Steven Soderbergh, was released in the United States in theaters, on subscription television, and on DVD. It is the first of six movies planned for simultaneous release by the director (http://www.stevensoderbergh.net/).

way of combating piracy (Cook and Wang 2004; Ravid 2005).[25] Once the film industry adopts different release practices, theater owners will be forced to adopt the digital projector and other amenities to stay in business. Faced with declining box office receipts (partly the result of rising ticket prices in the United States), studios are now releasing DVDs less than six months after theatrical releases. They are also responding to pressure from Wal-Mart and other retailers, whose DVD business amounted to almost US$18 billion in 2005 ("What's Driving" 2005). In 1998, the average time between theater and DVD release was 200 days. In 2005, the average time was estimated at 137 days. The DVD for *Miss Congeniality 2* was released in 90 days. Many believe that the time will be shorter still in future, further pressuring theater owners ("Building a Better Movie" 2005; "What's Driving" 2005).

To realize the delivery of high-quality video to individual homes, the necessary infrastructure must be in place. The minimum transmission speed for streaming HDTV over the Internet is estimated at 20 to 50 megabits per second (Mbps) even after MPEG-2 compression. High-quality movies (such as *Star Wars* episodes I–III by George Lucas, recorded at 1080p) require 40 to 100 Mbps with MPEG-2 compression.

Korea is ideally suited to initiate this kind of transition, because more than 70 percent of Korean households were connected in 2004 ("Hope Lies" 2005; H. Lee, Oh, and Shim 2005).[26] Anticipating this trend, the Korean government is creating a Digital Media City, where a cluster of digital media technology firms could emerge, including firms specializing in filmmaking and video production, wired and satellite broadcasting, and film release and distribution.

Whether Korean moviemakers can produce a steady stream of movies with international, as distinct from regional, appeal is another question. Currently, the main output of the Korean movie industry is drama, depicting a reality with which audiences can identify. The audience for

---

25. Piracy costs Hollywood between US$5 billion and US$6 billion annually ("Building a Better Movie" 2005). Content producers and consumer electronics (and computer) producers have been at odds for a long time. Content producers wish to limit duplication of their products. Consumer electronics firms tend to promote such duplication, intentionally or unintentionally. The classic example was the "Betamax" case (*Sony v. Universal Studios*) of 1984, and in recent years, multiple court cases have involved peer-to-peer software developers (Cook and Wang 2004).

26. Not only is use of broadband widespread in Korea, but mobile Internet use is high also. There are about 35 million mobile phone subscribers in Korea; 90 percent also access the Internet through their mobile phones (H. Lee, Oh, and Shim 2005).

these movies is culturally fairly specific (Koreans and Japanese). For this reason, the export destinations of Korean films have been concentrated in Northeast Asia, where the cultural ties are stronger.[27] To achieve the global success of American films, Korean films will need to have much broader appeal. It remains to be seen whether low-budget films can compete with Hollywood's products, scale economies, portfolios of global stars, and leveraging of the English language (Marvasti and Canterbery 2005). The challenge now is to find the right content and scale; the other ingredients are more or less in place.[28] The international appeal might be less of an issue with online computer games, which are a second major line of business for Seoul's creative industries.

VIDEOGAME INDUSTRY

The worldwide market for videogames was US$24.5 billion in 2004, exceeding the box office receipts for movies by a comfortable margin in part because games cost so much more than movie tickets.[29] This market is expected to grow to US$55 billion by 2008 ("Game Wars" 2005). The market in the United States alone was US$7.3 billion in 2004, approaching that year's box office receipts of US$9.3 billion ("Hollywood Games" 2005). The profit margin for movie studios is about 10 percent, as compared with 15 percent for the average videogame publisher and 25 percent for those in the lead ("Game Wars" 2005).

The expanding videogame market has caught the attention of other firms in the media industry, which are keen to leverage their intangible assets and reach a wider audience—especially the movie industry, which in the United States is eyeing the game industry as a fulcrum to increase its sales by offering movie-based games. Moreover, the actors involved in

27. One of the reasons Japanese anime attracts a wide audience is because the characters tend to have certain specific attributes. In the words of Stan Winston, the acclaimed makeup and robot artist in Hollywood, "big eyes, a head that is bigger than a body, a cute mouth, and a pug nose [are] considered lovable everywhere" ("It Came from Hollywood" 2003).

28. The organization of the movie industry might also have to shift, as it has in the United States over the past two decades. Independent studios struggling to survive need powerful backers, which generally have their own agendas (Thomson 2004).

29. Johns (2006) estimates that the online videogame industry earned US$23.2 billion in 2003 and projects a market of US$33.4 billion in 2008. The console-based videogame industry earned US$10.5 billion from the sales of hardware and software in 2005 as against US$9.9 billion in 2004, generating apprehension that the market was becoming saturated ("Video Game Industry" 2006). The Xbox 360 and Nintendo's dual-screen handheld console resulted in a pickup in sales of videogames in 2006 ("Signs of Recovery" 2006).

the source movies are lending their voices to add realism to these games,[30] and screenwriters for the movies are offering their services ("Hollywood Learns to Play" 2005).

Other media industries are also using videogames to reach consumers. Faced with declining television viewership, some advertising companies now produce videogames to showcase their products for those who spend more time in front of a computer ("Now, A Game" 2005).[31]

The explosive growth of the videogame industry globally has its echo in Korea.[32] The number of Korean videogame firms has increased from 694 (of which 416 are developers) in 1999 to 2,633 (of which 1,774 are developers) in 2002. Industry jobs also rose, from 13,500 in 2000 to 33,970 in 2002 (H. Lee, Oh, and Shim 2005).

Korean firms are recent entrants, with no earlier association with the videogame industry.[33] In the past, videogames based on specific consoles (such as Atari, Nintendo, Playstation, and Xbox) were the mainstream outlets for game developers. These machines gave rise to a division of labor between producers of hardware and producers of software, with consoles tailored to specific regional markets with their own standards such as PAL (phase alternating lines) or NTSC (National Television Standard Committee) and backed by a sophisticated international network of producers (Johns 2006). Korea missed this stage altogether because the import of such machines from Japan was banned. Given that the console market was dominated by Japanese firms (Nintendo, Sega, and Sony) until 2001, when Microsoft entered the market, none of the Korean firms were able to develop any games for this platform. Japanese popular culture (movies, music, games, video, animation, and broadcasting), which had been banned from Korea, began to be legally imported only after 1998 following the Joint Declaration between Korea and Japan. This opening to Japanese culture has taken effect in stages. In February 2002, for the third stage of the opening up, the import of video console games was permitted. This was also when Sony's Playstation 2 could be imported legally. For the fourth stage, effective January 1, 2004, the remaining bans

30. Including Sean Connery, Al Pacino, and Clint Eastwood ("Hollywood Learns" 2005).

31. Other entities also use videogames effectively. For instance, the U.S. military uses videogames to improve the results of its recruiting effort. The United Nations World Food Programme has a game to raise awareness of hunger around the world ("Now, A Game" 2005).

32. Steve Russell, a student at the Massachusetts Institute of Technology, created the first interactive videogame, called Spacewar!, in 1961 (Johns 2006).

33. For a brief history and interesting review of the videogame industry, see Aoyama and Izushi (2003).

(against playing videogames at home) were also lifted. Before the opening up, the Korean videogame market was barely developed. According to the *Game White Paper* (Korea Game Development and Promotion Institute 2001), arcade games accounted for 61.4 percent, online games for 22.9 percent, and personal computer (PC) games for 13.9 percent of the market, while console videogames accounted for just 1.5 percent.

In 1992, Fox Ranger, developed by Soft Action, became the first commercialized Korean game title for the IBM PC. Although the demand for PC games remains strong with the advent of newer and more powerful consoles,[34] the growing popularity of more interactive games over the Internet has raised the earnings of Korean developers. The precursors of such games date back to the text-based online multiplayer virtual worlds that emerged with the earliest computer networks in the 1970s. The popularity of virtual worlds as in EverQuest has grown to enthrall 73 million gamers around the world in 2003, the largest number in China (Castronova 2005). A number of Korean firms have successfully entered the market for MMORPGs.[35] After just a handful of years, there are now more than 400 online games available and 1,500 online game developers in Korea—and some 20 million players ("Present, Fast, and Future" 2004). According to the Korean Game Development and Promotion Institute, the industry turnover could exceed US$1 billion in 2005, and exports could rise substantially over the US$250 million level reached in 2004 ("South Korea Top" 2004).

The Brief History of MMORPGs

Starting with Dungeons and Dragons, tabletop fantasy-based games evolved into multiuser dungeons, which allowed users to enter "text-based virtual environments hosted on a computer" (T. Taylor 2006, 21–22). The first key differences between the early single-player role-playing game and the MMORPG are the fact that there is no end to the MMORPG; the extraordinary richness of the MMORPG environment; and the deliberate focus on the social interaction of players and, through it, the creation of a forum of game-specific social capital (T. Taylor 2006). Although there are small, preset objectives that a player can achieve, there is no winner and no

34. The release of next-generation machines such as the Xbox 360 (in 2005) and the Playstation 3 (in 2006) stimulated the release of a new round of more sophisticated games.

35. Once the number of players expanded from 8-16 to more than 3,000, the term *massively* was added to MORPG (Castronova 2005).

ultimate goal such as defeating the monster to rescue the princess. There are levels of progress toward accumulating wealth and power but these levels do not evoke much competition with other players (T. Taylor 2006). Therefore, the individual storyline of the single-player game is missing from the MMORPG. Instead, this kind of game is more about guilds, tribes, clans, or nations, emphasizing cooperation with other players. While single-player games entail no more than 40 to 50 hours of game play, MMORPG players can spend 1,000 hours a year playing (Smith 2005).[36] The only way to end the game is through boredom, although interactions with other players maintain the randomness of the events in the game (not scripted by the programmers) and player interest.[37] To reduce the risk of the game becoming stale if it is played intensively for a long period, many expansion packs are offered to open additional avenues for exploration and enhance the play. Expansion packs (new cities or dungeons to explore, new dragons to kill) also encourage the spillover of products into other media and attract new players (Woodcock 2005). Interaction with other players is a key feature, because it allows the game play to vary every day, depending on whom one is interacting with online.

The advent of the game Ultima Online (1997) popularized this genre (T. Taylor 2006). The flat monthly fee of US$10 provided further inducement (currently US$13–US$15 for EverQuest). In 1999, Sony Online Entertainment released EverQuest in the United States, followed later that year by Asheron's Call. T. L. Taylor (2006, 28) states, "What you do in EverQuest is immerse yourself in space. People create identities (Avatars) for themselves, have a variety of social networks, take on roles and obligations, build histories and communities [in which] people live and, through that living, play." The commercial success of these three MMORPGs launched this genre (Castronova 2005).

MMORPGs appeared three years earlier in Korea, starting with a game called Nexus: The Kingdom of the Winds, designed by Jake Song. This

36. In fact, the addictiveness of gaming (EverQuest is known in gaming circles as *EverCrack*) is giving rise to serious psychological problems in Korea, where an estimated 12 percent of the population between the ages of 9 and 39 are suffering from some degree of addiction ("When Escape Seems" 2006).

37. Some games are criticized because of excessively linear game stories. Introducing random events into games is one way of lessening linearity. One innovative product is a game called Boktai, in which the hero's ability will be influenced by the actual sunlight picked up by the solar sensor attached to a portable game console ("Sunny the Vampire-Slayer" 2003). Videogames are not the only ones introducing the element of randomness. Chess960, invented by Bobby Fischer, is another such game. Unlike traditional chess, in which each piece has preset positions, in Chess960 the pieces can take 960 different positions. By introducing the element of chance, this game avoids the standard opening moves that are so exhaustively studied ("Unorthodox Chess" 2005).

game debuted in 1996 and was played by a million subscribers (Wikipedia 2005). His next game, Lineage, published by NCSoft, was released in 1998. It proved to be a bigger hit, drawing 4 million players (Woodcock 2005)[38] and encouraged NCSoft to expand into the global market (Wikipedia 2005). A sequel, "Lineage II," was released in 2003.

By 2002, the initial success of these Korean MMORPGs resulted in a flurry of new entries by other game publishers, even though the overall player population was rising slowly. That sharpened competition among game developers to secure players; only a few games can survive in this environment (Woodcock 2005). Nevertheless, popular games enjoy lasting loyalty. For example, EverQuest still enjoys a huge following, is supported by 1,500 servers worldwide with an underground command center—called *Death star*—in San Diego, and continues to be developed by a team of 50 people while Ultima Online, one of the earliest games, still draws 150,000 subscribers (Castronova 2005; Johns 2006; Kushner 2005, 34–36).

In the current MMORPG market, 85 percent of the games are fantasy based, 9.5 percent rely on sci-fi themes, 1.3 percent are combat simulation games, and 4 percent fall into social and other categories (Woodcock 2005).[39] This market is highly skewed compared with that of other entertainment products, such as movies, where there are more sci-fi stories than fantasy stories. This scenario is likely to change in future, as more games with sci-fi themes are launched in 2006 (Woodcock 2005). The MMORPG also has a more devoted following in Asia, although Final Fantasy XI did well in the United States (Woodcock 2005).[40]

Technical Challenges Posed by MMORPGs

Simply put, the difference between the single-player role-playing game and the MMORPG is that there are many more people playing the game

38. Not all 4 million players pay subscription fees. Many players in Korea play this game at Internet cafés (PC *baangs* in Korea), and the owners of the cafés pay the subscription fees, opening a wedge between the number of players and the number of subscribers (Woodcock 2005).

39. This breakdown is based on U.S. data, so when one includes the market share of Lineage and other Korean games, the share of fantasy-oriented games is much higher.

40. Ultima Online achieved the highest subscription in 2003 with 250,000 subscribers, but by March 2005, the number had declined to 160,000 worldwide, of which 70,000 were in Japan (Woodcock 2005). In March 2005, the subscriber base of Lineage was about 2 million worldwide but only 7,623 in the United States (Woodcock 2005). Lineage II was released in Korea in November 2003 and in the United States in April 2004. In early 2005, it had 2.1 million subscribers worldwide with 65,644 in the United States (Woodcock 2005). The newcomer, World of Warcraft, is hugely successful. Within three months of its launch in China, it attracted more than 2 million customers. The subscriber base for MMORPGs in China is said to be 25 million, with estimated revenues of US$390 million. The expected growth rate is 40 percent over the next three years ("Role-Playing" 2005).

at the same time in a much larger virtual world—one more generously supplied with quests, puzzles, danger, missions, and possibilities for social interaction through economic transactions and gift-giving, made possible by a larger dose of artificial intelligence (AI). Thus, much of the innovation is in the client-server technology, especially the server technology, because of the need to handle massive amounts of information simultaneously while keeping the connection to many players (Kushner 2005).

Each MMORPG requires many servers. They can be grouped in three categories: zone servers,[41] chat servers, and database servers (Smith 2005). Because the key attraction of the MMORPG is the opportunity to interact with other players, chat servers play a crucial role in assisting communications among players. Database servers keep all the information and attributes of every single item available in the game, numbering in the thousands, while zone servers are the main servers that participants use to play and manipulate the objects and other characters in the game. Not only do zone servers keep track of the movements and actions of the players; they also control the other creatures controlled by AI, depending on the players' actions (Castronova 2005; Smith 2005). The graphics files are stored on the clients' computers. The server, by sending small packets of information, tells the files what to do.

Typically, each zone server represents a small predefined location within a larger world. The persistence of the world is another key feature of MMORPGs; hence, the server needs to run continuously (Smith 2005).[42] Because of much longer playing time, the world that participants play in needs to be much larger than it is in the single-player games. The virtual world of EverQuest, one of the most popular MMORPGs, covers an area of 350 square miles—15 times larger than Manhattan. Seamlessly integrating servers to provide smooth game play is a daunting task and supporting technicians have to deal with bugs around the clock (Smith 2005; Kushner 2005).

41. The world of MMORPG can be either *zoned* or *seamless*. In the zoned games, when a player enters a zone, only those data are transmitted and loaded on a player's computer. Thus, when one is moving from one zone to the other, there is a lag and discontinuity in the game. In the seamless world, players can continue traveling from one area to another without such delay. Those different types of world structure affect the memory requirements of client computers, the bandwidth requirements, and server configurations. In a zoned world, typically a server is assigned for each zone, balancing the load, whereas in the seamless world one server handles all the players. Zoned worlds tend to be able to accommodate a much larger number of players at the same time because of this configuration (Wikipedia 2005).

42. This persistence is a key difference from other online games, in which the environment one plays in is not persistent.

These games create an environment for the advancement of personal avatars. They also promote thousands of items that are sold at merchant shops and through auctions among players, so several elements of economic models are integrated and are affected by players' actions.[43] T. L. Taylor (2006, 62) observes that "one of the most fundamental and indeed most powerful design choices made for the game was the creation of many objects and the ability to trade." Game developers need to maintain basic macroeconomic stability as much as real-world policy makers do, especially by curbing too rapid an increase in money supply (Smith 2005).[44]

In the late 1990s, high-end games cost only US$3 million to develop. Currently, development of the average videogame for the latest high-performance consoles such as the Xbox 360 costs anywhere between US$5 million and US$12 million, although there are exceptions ("Gaming Goes to Hollywood" 2004; "Hollywood Learns to Play" 2005; "Delays and Hefty Costs" 2006). For instance, Microsoft spent US$40 million to develop and market its flagship game, Halo 2 ("Game Wars" 2005). By comparison, an MMORPG with more realistic graphics is much larger and more complex than the single-player games and can cost upward of US$40 million to develop (Smith 2005). Some games, notably Final Fantasy XI and World of Warcraft, are part of the well-established franchise of the single-player games. These firms are leveraging the popularity of their original games and extending into the MMORPG arena. MMORPGs based on *Star Trek*, *The Matrix*, and *Lord of the Rings* are in development (Smith 2005).

Videogames Come to Seoul

The videogame industry is similar to the film industry in that it is highly volatile and only a few firms will be successful. For instance, it is estimated

---

43. The real-world EverQuest economy is worth $150 million annually. Where money is involved, crime follows. In Korea half the computer-related crimes committed in 2003 were related to thefts from synthetic worlds (Castronova 2005; Kushner 2005).

44. Hyperinflation is a common problem in these types of games, although it depends on the nature of depreciation of items in the game. The items and other tradable properties collected in the games can be traded in the real economy using real money, typically through eBay. The owner of the Internet café can sell these items collected by others for a profit. Often, the arrangement is that owners of the Internet café receive some small percentage of the earnings in the game. Reportedly, one can make US$100 a day working at the online "sweatshops" in China ("Virtual War Game" 2005; Wikipedia 2005). There are even foreign exchange services, which trade funds from one game to others, including real currencies ("Model Economy" 2005). See Castronova (2001, 2002, 2003) for an interesting analysis of the virtual economy in EverQuest.

that 14 percent of the games generate as much as 70 percent of the revenues (Aoyama and Izushi 2003). The export markets for these games tend to be China, Japan, and Taiwan (China), owing to cultural similarities, low-entry barriers, and the prevalence of online gaming.[45] In the long run, penetration into U.S. and European markets is the goal of Korean producers.

The game industry is going global in order to recoup development costs and also to add variety to the offerings. A high-quality game can cost US$10 million to US$20 million to develop, and this cost is expected to rise further with the introduction of the new generation of game consoles. Although consumer preferences seem to be converging, each market has its particular preferences and customization is needed. Johns (2006, 173) notes that ultimately videogames are cultural products "that are read in specific ways depending upon the locality in which they are produced." The popular online game EverQuest II, by Sony Online Entertainment, was customized to fit the taste of the Asian market in partnership with Taiwanese developer Soga ("American Gamers" 2005).

Licensing games developed elsewhere can add variety to the genres and types of games sold. For instance, the videogame market in the United States is dominated by sports, military,[46] and racing games. Licensing other games, such as puzzle games developed in Japan, can bring different kind of games that may not sell well but will increase the variety of games in the market, keeping gamers interested ("American Gamers" 2005).

Consolidation. Firms in the videogame industry need to have a wide range of games to diversify their risks, similar to movie studios, because only 5 percent of the games will sell more than 1 million copies ("Game Wars" 2005). This situation has led to a concentration of publishers, with the top five firms accounting for 56 percent of the U.S. market ("Game Wars" 2005).[47]

---

45. Some games are developed specifically for the export market. For instance, Mabinogi by Nexon was developed to cater to the Japanese market.

46. The U.S. military is developing virtual reality-based combat simulators for training purposes and is using videogames to hone the skills of its soldiers (Alpert 2006; "Virtual Reality" 2006).

47. For instance, Bandai (the largest toymaker in Japan) took over Namco (a leading videogame developer and the creator of Pac-Man) ("Bandai to Buy Namco" 2005). In many cases, media firms also own game developers. Blizzard, the developer of World of Warcraft, is owned by Vivendi Universal ("Virtual War Game" 2005). Another game publisher, Ubisoft of France, is seeking to merge with a leading media firm (such as Disney or Time Warner) rather than be taken over by Electronic Arts, the leading videogame publisher in the United States ("Hollywood Games" 2005).

A similar pattern of consolidation is surfacing in Korea, with local and some foreign publishers acquiring developers. Rising costs of individual games are supplying an additional push. In fact, the top five firms now account for 80 percent of the market. For instance, Nexon acquired Wizet Corp., the developer of Maple Story; Shanda of China has acquired Actoz, a Korean game-developing firm.[48] Currently, only Chinese firms are interested in acquiring Korean firms in search of content. However, in the future, as U.S.-based firms expand into East Asia, more investment by U.S. firms is likely in Korea. Already close to 40 percent of the shares of NCSoft, the largest online gaming company, are owned by foreigners. NCSoft, in turn, is active in the U.S. market. It acquired ArenaNet in 2002 and distributes games for U.S. developers.[49] NCSoft is planning to establish a branch in Beijing, which would mainly focus on graphic designs and draw on the large number of graduates from universities in the area. The Beijing branch would be in addition to its office in Shanghai, established when it acquired former partner Shina.

Webzen has wholly owned subsidiaries in Shanghai, Taiwan (China), and the United States. The role of the subsidiary in the United States is to localize the products developed in Korea, gather marketing information in the United States, identify promising products in the United States that can be distributed through its client-server technology, and provide customer support. The role of the subsidiary in Shanghai is more development oriented, although the client-server programmers are all Korean. The choice of Shanghai stems from the abundance of developers, mass media, and government agencies there.

The Geography of the Gaming Industry. Firms in the game industry are clustered in the Kangnam area in Seoul, much like the moviemaking firms. Nexon is there, along with its partners (developer firms). The location is advantageous for recruiting client-server technicians and programmers from such prominent universities as Seoul National University. In addition, the availability of producer services, such as marketing, is an advantage, as is the access to government bodies and industry associations.[50]

48. Chinese firms such as Shanda, Netease, and The9 have built up the distribution network to sell prepaid access cards for these games. Most games are licensed from abroad; there are no homegrown Chinese games ("Role-Playing" 2005).

49. ArenaNet is a game development company founded by the team that developed the game network Battle.net, as well as hit games such as Starcraft, Diablo, and Warcraft.

50. Local labor markets are key to the development of clusters of creative industries (Scott 2006).

In terms of infrastructure, Seoul offers the best there is in Korea for high-speed, bandwidth-hungry applications. The reason has to do with the concentration of Internet exchanges (IXs) in Seoul. An IX is a node within the Internet, connecting other IXs (domestic or foreign) or Internet service providers (ISPs). Thus, traffic between two ISPs will most likely pass through an IX (although they can bypass it by connecting directly with each other).[51] The data will have less distance to travel and less chance of being affected by congestion if they are closer to an IX.

Most of the servers are provided by the publishers, although private servers exist. However, the need for the servers to be up continuously, the large storage requirements, and the high bandwidth requirements are the main reasons private servers for MMORPGs are few (Wikipedia 2005). The only exception to this general tendency seems to be in China. There, private servers have sprouted because the 100 Mbps fiber-optic connection can be had for as little as US$30 a month and the operating cost of servers seems to be lower in China (Wikipedia 2005).

Outsourcing. Most game developers tend to specialize in a few upstream areas and outsource other functions, generally to nearby firms, which promotes clustering. These functions include full-motion video, three-dimensional (3D) renderings for showcases, and sound effects. Other firms (such as NCSoft) produce everything in house. Typically the showcase piece requires artistic rendering of the actual game play, combined with music made specifically for it. An example is the showcase piece for SUN (the upcoming game by Webzen), created by the company that made the soundtrack for *Lord of the Rings*. For specific services, developers will search widely and contract the best supplier, wherever the firm may be located.

Research and Development, Innovation. Among the creative industries, producers of videogames devote considerable resources to research and development (R&D) (Aoyama and Izushi 2003). As noted earlier, the strength of the Korean videogame firms lies in the client-server

51. The best way to understand the role of an IX is to think of it as a major airport hub (http://www.linktionary.com/i/internet_arch.html). For instance, imagine a trip from Washington, D.C., to Seoul. One would travel first to Reagan National airport (from your home to an ISP), then to Chicago O'Hare airport (from an ISP to an IX), then to Inchon airport (another IX), then to downtown Seoul (from IX to ISP). As in air travel, one can take many different routes (instead of Chicago, one can use San Francisco or Los Angeles). As with any flight, the more stops you make along the way, the more time it takes in general (a flight from Washington, D.C., to Chicago to San Francisco or Los Angeles, and then to Seoul would take longer).

technology, such as Nexon's hybrid peer-to-peer system. Although this system includes a central server, only selected data are sent to the central server and other data are sent directly to the other PCs. Thus, Nexon eliminates the time lags often seen in action and arcade types of online games. The development of the client-server technology is the result of experience accumulated through learning by doing, especially from managing simultaneous connections to half a million players.

The wide diffusion of broadband connection and a large player base are advantages that Korean firms enjoy relative to other countries. Because of them, the network-oriented technologies tend to be developed in their labs in Seoul. Korean firms also expend considerable effort in developing their own engines or adapting the engines of others. Webzen, for example, purchased the Unreal engine and customized it to avoid royalty payments.

Korean firms also have R&D centers scattered around the world. Nexon has an office in Tokyo to scout for ideas and content suitable for the Japanese market. The reasons Tokyo was chosen are its high concentration of gamers, easy access to information, and availability of supporting firms, although the development of the game Mabinogi took place in Seoul at DevCat Studio (an R&D center for Nexon). NCSoft has an office in Austin, Texas, where many game developers are concentrated and are developing its next game, Tabula Rasa.[52]

Demand for Skills

Making computer games requires a multitude of skills (table 6.9). The skills of programmers are key, but the industry also depends on artists, musicians, and designers who can conceptualize and manage the entire development project. In many respects, videogame production is similar to movie production, which partly accounts for the proximity of the movie and gaming industries in Seoul.

Clearly, a mix of skills is needed to produce commercially viable MMORPGs. Because it is equipment intensive, a MMORPG needs many client-server technicians to ensure a smooth online experience. This type of skill is relatively abundant and most videogame firms in Korea are satisfied with the quality of "pure" programmers coming out of local

52. Austin, Texas, was also where the legendary game developer Richard Garriott (creator of Ultima game series) was located. To break into the U.S. market, NCSoft hired Garriott in 2001 and also bought Seattle-based ArenaNet ("South Korea Top" 2004).

Table 6.9 Occupational Categories and Required Skills in the Videogame Industry

Occupational category	Major tasks	Skills and training required
Game designers	Designers write the blueprint of the game and decide on the mission, theme, and rules of play. Various designers work on concepts, on different levels, and on texts and dialogues.	Required skills include writing and communication abilities; management skills; technical skills, including computer programming and software design. Most designers earn a college degree in English, art, or computer science.
Artists	Artists create graphics. In a two-dimensional game, they draw images on paper and then scan them into the computer; in a three-dimensional game, they create most images on computer. Character artists design and build creatures; animators make them move. Background artists create videogame settings, and texture artists add detail to the surfaces of 3D art.	Required skills include visual imagination, ability to apply basic math concepts, and ability to use modeling and animating software. Most videogame artists have formal training in the fine arts or art-related subjects; bachelor's degrees are an advantage.
Sound designers	Sound designers compose music and sound in a game, research appropriate music options for particular games, and choose creative sound effects with the correct balance of realism and exaggeration so as to optimize the entertainment value.	Required skills include musical creativity, training in audio engineering, and knowledge of the basics of computer hardware and software. Many sound designers have a bachelor's degree in music, and some have education in film scoring.
Programmers	Programmers plan and write videogame software and translate ideas into mathematical equations. Engine programmers write software that makes videogames run. Artificial intelligence programmers write code to make computer-controlled characters act realistically. Graphics programmers, sound programmers, and tool programmers write software for artists and designers.	Required skills include strong math skills and knowledge of computer programming (C and C++). Most programmers have a bachelor's degree in computer science.
Game testers	Game testers play games to find errors in software, graphic glitches, computer crashes, and other bugs. They write reports describing problems they find.	Required skills include an ability to communicate clearly, familiarity with technology, and expert game-playing skills. A formal education is not required, but testers are encouraged to earn computer technician certificates.

Source: Crosby 2000.

universities. "Engine" programmers, who also are in big demand (to define the physics, collision detection, motion, and so forth), can also be found in local universities.

The worry for firms such as Nexon is the lack of content creators. Because the industry is relatively new, the pool of creators with expertise is still small, with only about 10 such people in Korea now. Currently, Webzen sponsors several private game academies, but it feels that universities should shoulder this role. This gap in university offerings is the major issue confronting the game industry in Korea. Universities and vocational education institutes do not provide customized training courses for creators.

Furthermore, continuous technological change on the PC side—especially in the processing power of both the central processing unit and the graphics cards and in the demand for rich content (three dimensional rather than two dimensional)—necessitates continuous upgrading of skills by workers or their replacement by new workers equipped with the latest expertise.[53]

Often neglected in the story is the role played by musicians. Music in videogames now is used in the same as way as in movies: to heighten emotional responses and to signal changes in scenes. In the past, scores could be bought fairly inexpensively (for, say, US$15,000). However, with the increase in sophistication of the music included in videogames, well-made games now contain four to five hours of original music by the likes of the Los Angeles Philharmonic Orchestra, with the cost limited only by the budget ("Play Myst" 2005). Alongside the involvement of Hollywood actors and actresses and directors in the videogames, composers who produced soundtracks for the movies are being hired to provide the in-game music.[54] In Japan, where videogames have been tremendously popular, sales of game soundtracks have been quite robust.

The game industry is largely male dominated[55] in terms of both consumers and developers, but now the leading firms are taking a serious look at the other half of the population, which has been mostly untouched

53. For instance, Lineage II is in 3D.

54. One such example is the music for Metal Gear Solid 2, composed by Harry Gregson-Williams, who also did the soundtracks for *Shrek*, *Spy Game*, and *Armageddon* (Hermida 2002).

55. According to one study, 80 percent of EverQuest players were male; they played an average of 25 hours per week. Most were not students. A separate survey showed that about a fifth of the hard-core players were so immersed in the synthetic world that they treated it as reality (Castronova 2005).

("Female Sensibility" 2005; T. Taylor 2006).[56] The first sign of interest among female players was in The Sims by Electronic Arts. The second came from MMORPGs. Both types of games are social: interactions with other players are the main feature ("Female Sensibility" 2005).

Promoting the Games Industry

For a number of reasons, MMORPGs have acquired a large following in Korea and abroad. First, as mentioned earlier, the highly interactive nature of the games is attractive to consumers, especially in East Asia, where the group mentality still is strong. Games such as EverQuest, for example, by inducing communication among players, "facilitate various forms of social interaction and interdependence" (T. Taylor 2006, 38), supporting the formation of groups, guilds, and collectives. Guilds, for example, are "officially sanctioned organizations of players with a hierarchical leadership structure . . . [and] the high end guilds are very adept at blending instrumental action with social work." (T. Taylor 2006, 43).

Second, as with the movie industry, the Korean government has been lavish with institutional support and some venture capital support to help the industry develop in Seoul. The Korea Game Development Institute, under the Ministry of Culture and Tourism, offers seminars, connects foreign partners with domestic ones, conducts market research, and gives game developers an opportunity to participate in foreign exhibitions. More broadly, the Korea IT Industry Promotion Agency, under the Ministry of Information and Communication, is responsible for policies and infrastructure provisions that may improve the game industry as a whole. It also matches local firms with foreign firms and conducts market trend research. Both associations, in addition, provide a variety of materials and financial support, promote exports, and grant awards. The Korean Association of the Game Industry, meanwhile, acts as the public relations arm for the game companies. Some venture capital has come from the government-owned Hansol venture capital arm, as well as from private providers.

Government support of IT, which made broadband connections available to most urban households, has enabled more Korean consumers to play MMORPGs longer. The broadband connection is always on, and usage is unlimited. By expanding the user base, the proliferation of Internet cafés (PC *baangs*) has contributed significantly to the popularity of this type of game in Korea.

56. Men purchase 70 percent of all video console games; 10 percent of all software engineers are women, but only 4 percent of game programmers are women ("Programmers" 2005).

Third, the new business model, which permits free downloads of the client program with a monthly subscription, eliminated the threat of piracy that plagues computer and console games. Firms have been able to recoup development costs gradually through subscriptions.

Fourth, many game-producing firms are classified as venture capital–supported companies and, as such, were able to secure highly qualified personnel at low wages through the Special Military Service system.[57]

Fifth, the marketing barriers for MMORPGs are, from the firm's point of view, lower than for typical computer-based videogames (although they do present different challenges in the form of client-server management). The underlying engines (for 3D graphics or client-server technology) and middleware (such as adventure-building systems and plug-ins for superior AI effects) can be licensed from other companies (Castronova 2005).[58] There is no preset storyline besides the very simple broad premise on which the game is based. By comparison, many large Japanese game developers painstakingly create a complete storyline for each computer game from beginning to end ("Invaders" 2003). With MMORPGs, the story evolves as the game progresses, through interaction with other players. And because many of the significant characters are controlled by people, there is less need to invest in the development of good AI to mimic human behavior.[59]

Firms are leveraging the experience gained from online games to branch out into other lucrative markets, such as consoles and mobile games. For instance, Webzen is planning to release two new games for

57. As part of their military service, Korean men in their 20s can serve in the Special Military Service, working in companies designated as Special Military Service companies. This system was designed to supply employees to enterprises related to national defense and to support research in the Korea Advanced Institute of Science and Technology in the 1980s. Later, the system expanded and the conglomerates and small and medium enterprises (SMEs) could also use it. It provides benefits such as career recognition and academic continuity to students. For the firms, this system is a stable source of employees at relatively low wages. To hire experts in technology, companies have to pay high wages, which many SMEs cannot afford. However, the Special Military Service system attracts more participants with greater technical capabilities who do not expect higher compensation.

58. For instance, Lineage II is based on the Unreal engine. There are other 3D engines, such as Quake and Source (used in Half-Life 2).

59. This is also true of many first-person shooter games, which are exclusively multiplayer oriented. For these kinds of games, the developer needs to supply a good collection of maps and sound effects and a networking layer without any storylines or creatures controlled by AI. In addition, these types of games can be customized by users (new maps, new textures, new "look" of the people, and so forth) using the tools supplied by the developers, significantly extending the life of a game without using additional resources.

consoles in the next few years. The global market for cell phone games has climbed from US$587 million in 2003 to an estimated US$3.0 billion in 2005 and shortly could exceed the US$3.5 billion market for ring tones.[60] The market has begun attracting the big console game producers, such as Electronic Arts and Activision ("Taking Video Games" 2005). With close to a third of the world's population now carrying cell phones and millions of people having grown up playing console games, it is almost inevitable that the videogame industry will mount a strong push into this lucrative terrain ("Mobile Phone Makers" 2005). However, whether Korean firms can successfully break into this market remains to be seen. Unlike the computer and online games in which they now excel, games optimized for mobile phones present a higher level of difficulty. They need to be written more efficiently, and a new gaming style needs to be adopted to fit into a small screen. Thus far, only old games such as Tetris and Pac-Man had much success. Only 4 percent of cell phone users currently download and buy games ("Tiny Games" 2006). Conceivably, console videogame makers may have an edge in this area with their experience ("Gaming Goes to Hollywood" 2004) and with their capacity to leverage their established franchise in old games (bringing out the old games for a new platform)[61] and hit movies ("Halo Effect" 2004).[62]

THE EMERGING MULTIMEDIA ECONOMY

Technological development and the changing tastes and preferences of the younger generation are leading to a convergence of the film and videogame industries. Seoul, which is Korea's cultural capital and the home for both these nascent industries, stands to benefit from such a convergence and a strong global demand for movies and games.

Both the film industry and the videogame industry are developing rapidly in Seoul. Their prospects depend on how appealing either or both

60. Mobile games sales are expected to grow 60 percent in 2006. By 2010, the market size is projected to reach US$18 billion ("Tiny Games" 2006).

61. There has been a move toward archiving and preserving old video games in a museum. However, this effort has met with a rather cool response from the computer game industry. Part of the reason is that the industry is still relatively young and does not yet appreciate the importance of history ("Arcade Addicts" 2003).

62. For instance, the Spiderman game is already in development for mobile phones by Indiagames in Mumbai. The company also developed a mobile game based on the hit TV series *Buffy the Vampire Slayer* ("Games Become a Global Play" 2005). Disney has acquired Living Mobile, a German-based supplier of games for mobile phones ("Disney" 2005). It is already the largest provider of mobile phone content in Japan, with about 3.3 million subscribers ("Disney" 2005).

of them become globally and how much synergy they can generate. The United States, the world leader in the movie industry, provides a model of how the two industries might jointly develop. American movies have global appeal. An important segment of the videogame industry now rides on the popularity of the movie industry by introducing games based on movies such as *Spiderman*, *Star Wars*, and *X-Men*. Unlike in the past, when movie rights were sold to game publishers as an afterthought, game developers now become involved while the movie is being made ("Gaming Goes to Hollywood" 2004).[63] The process works in reverse as well. Movies are being made that are based on the themes and characters from successful games such as Tomb Raider and Pokémon. Similarly, the popularity of both anime and console videogames are buoying Japanese exports of movies (most of them anime) and videogames.

The videogame industry in Korea differs from that in Japan. There, the industry's strength stems from easy access to hardware makers (Nintendo and Sony), good story-telling capabilities based on *manga* (as described in chapter 5), and the use of graphics and sound effects by the anime industry. Although Korean game firms also acquire ideas from films, comic books, and novels, the links with other industries are much tighter and more integrated in Japan. In Korea, the movie industry is more drama based, with a focus on real-world situations, whereas MMORPGs are more fantasy based.[64] Nexon, for example, does not charge a subscription fee for its game KartRider, but it earns handsome revenues from selling accessories and high-priced avatars. With 12 million Koreans playing *KartRider* and spending at the online store, the earnings start to mount ("Dude" 2005). A vibrant videogame industry will need to have both types of developers: those who are the source of ideas and those who depend on

---

63. Although there is much similarity and collaborative effort between the movie and the videogame industries, a number of differences remain. One is that videogames can be tested and reworked many times before their release, unlike movies. Second, game sequels tend to do much better than movie sequels because games can incorporate new technologies that became available after the release of the previous game, in addition to taking advantage of the availability of more powerful computers every year—for example, EverQuest II ("Gaming Goes to Hollywood" 2004).

64. However, to the player, this fantasy is the reality. Even if the setting of the game is artificial and sometimes fantasy based, to players who are immersed in the game world and in interacting with other people and identifying themselves with their avatars—the digital representations of players online—the world seems real enough. This phenomenon is akin to audiences identifying with the people portrayed in a drama. Results from a survey indicate that a significant portion of people playing EverQuest consider themselves to be living and moving between two worlds: the world of EverQuest and the real world (Castronova 2001, 2005; T. Taylor 2006).

the accumulation of experience and continuous improvements. Hence, the industry will depend on a continuous flow of innovative people and on the accumulation of experience, which that gives the advantage to existing firms.[65]

By having to forgo participation in the production of console games, Korean firms were unable to accumulate expertise in those types of games, where experience counts. However, they were able to quickly capitalize on the popularity of MMORPGs and move ahead of developers in other countries. Whether they can translate this advantage into the next likely platform, the mobile phone, depends on their ability to develop these required conceptual games. Many such puzzle and thumb-twitching games will be (and are) released on this new platform by the existing rights holders. Entering this segment of the industry will be a considerable challenge for Korean firms.

With increasing digitization of the movie production process, the overlap will increase in future. For example, videogame software and a technique called *machinima* make it possible to produce an animated lifelike film on a PC using characters from games, customizing the game environment in 3D, and adding voiceovers ("Deus Ex Machinima" 2004; "Young Spielbergs" 2005). The competitive edge that the Korean game firms currently have over others is in the client-server technology. As with any technological advantage, relying solely on one area is dangerous because others can catch up. At this point, many of the leading game companies are holding on to this technology as their competitive advantage, rather than licensing it out as client-server middleware to other firms. Many believe that the differentiating aspects will be better graphics and creative game concepts and stories. Therefore, tighter integration of the strength of the movie industry—the underlying story-telling component—with the videogame industry is one of the crucial links that the gaming industry in Seoul now needs.[66] Once this happens, the Korean videogame industry can expand into other types of games, thereby increasing the opportunities overall.

65. This statement assumes that the developers retain the talent originally responsible for creating successful games or that, as an organization, they are able to retain the experience. In some cases, however, a major publishing firm may purchase a hit game to create a sequel. The original developing team may depart, leaving the publisher only with the right to produce a sequel, without the necessary knowledge accumulated in developing the game. Hence, some sequels do not perform as well as the original games.

66. For instance, MK Pictures is planning to develop mobile phone games that are based on one of its film characters.

The development of the online game industry in Korea happened in large part because of widespread adoption of broadband connections (78 percent of households) and the availability of broadband access through 30,000 Internet cafés (Shameen 2004). In Korea, the common speed is 10Mbps, with some subscribers at 20Mbps. Even faster 100Mbps services are in trial, and the goal is to migrate most households to this speed by 2010 ("Present, Fast, and Future" 2004; Shameen 2004). These speeds are all offered at prices in the range of US$30 to US$50 per month, making the connection speed in Korea one of the fastest at an affordable price.[67] This access has created the market for online games and, in the future, the scope for distributing movies and broadcasting over the Internet (some Japanese firms are already broadcasting past television programs over the Internet for a fee). Online distribution of movies will also help the niche producers because of the long tail phenomenon (the long downward slope of a probability distribution). The ease and low cost of distribution will allow producers to cater to a wide variety of tastes that are poorly served by the mass market for entertainment that aims for the lowest common denominator ("Long Tail" 2004). Already past television programming can be downloaded in Korea for as little as US$0.40, and Korean movies made in the 1980s and 1990s can be downloaded for US$0.80 (Shameen 2004).

The Korean online videogame industry had a head start. With the experience accumulated through the early stage of online game development, these firms now have the technological capability to manage large online games, including client-server technology. Whether they can keep developing innovative contents to take advantage of their early lead is an open question. The rising expenditure of increasingly sophisticated users is inexorably ratcheting up costs for game producers. In part, also, the pressure on producers comes from the competitive forces unleashed by the music and movie industries, which compete for the same segment of potential buyers ("Games Makers" 2003). Firms in other countries are leveraging their assets in contents. For Japanese firms, the content lies in console games and anime. In the United States, it is PC games and Hollywood movies.[68] As broadband expands in other countries and more firms

67. However, at these government-regulated rates, recouping the cost of investment and earning a healthy profit are a problem for broadband suppliers.

68. There is a concern, however, that too much collaboration with the movie industry may stifle the creativity of the game industry, especially when production costs are soaring. Many game publishers may try to stick with the safer games based on hit movies (and sequels) rather than developing new creative games ("Gaming Goes to Hollywood" 2004).

enter the entertainment industry, the success of Korean game developers—especially in the U.S. market, where Lineage has made few inroads—will depend crucially on the quality of the game and the underlying storyline. The same will be true for the movie industry.

Closer interaction could well enhance the prospects of both industries, although a question hangs over the future of the filmmaking business (not just in Korea), as it faces the prospect of intensifying competition in home markets from foreign movies, as it confronts the implications of lowered entry barriers, as digital production and distribution technology spread, and as it makes the transition to new forms of distribution. The two industries can share many of the same resources—especially the pool of highly specialized and skilled personnel—and work together to improve the technologies. In addition, continuous investment in the infrastructure in the form of faster broadband connections would widen the market domestically and enlarge the clientele abroad.

CHAPTER 7

SILK AND GEMS

The term *fashion* immediately evokes images of two cities—Paris and Milan. After reflection, some might add New York, Tokyo, and London. But only the indulgent would consider extending the list. Clearly, among the creative industries, the high-fashion industry has proven to be geographically the most exclusive and still among the least mobile. This attachment to place is unusual because the fashion industry in the broad sense is widely diffused. The worldwide turnover is vast and relatively impervious to business fluctuations, and the entry barriers do not appear to be especially high, which could make it attractive for industrializing countries such as Thailand that have gained a comparative advantage in the manufacture of garments and jewelry. That Bangkok could become a leading fashion center of East Asia is surely within the realm of the possible, but for the moment the idea remains on the very fringes of the possible. Could it be brought within closer reach, and if so, what will it take for this most delicate of industries to bloom in Bangkok? Could this industry become an engine of growth for postindustrial Bangkok? Are the changing local and global circumstances ripe for a new entry? These are some of the questions addressed in this chapter.

INVENTING FASHION

Almost inevitably one must start with an existing point of reference. Paris is where the fashion industry was born, and by observing the accidental birth and gradual flowering of the Parisian fashion business into a worldwide

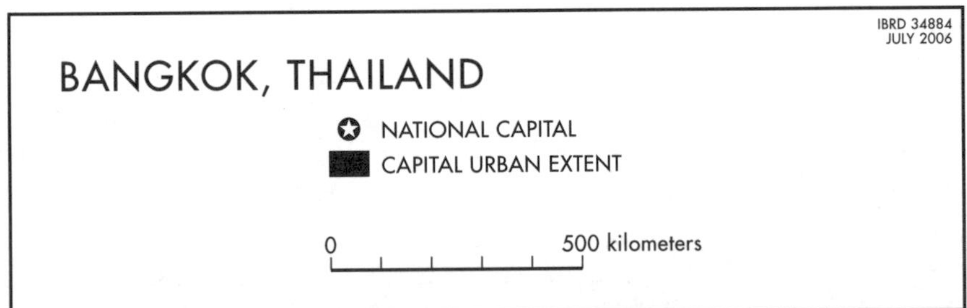
IBRD 34884
JULY 2006
BANGKOK, THAILAND
NATIONAL CAPITAL
CAPITAL URBAN EXTENT
0
500 kilometers
100°
110°
CHINA
MYANMAR
VIETNAM
20°
LAO
P.D.R.
Gulf of
Tonkin
THAILAND
Bangkok
CAMBODIA
Andaman
Sea
10°
Gulf of
Thailand
MALAYSIA
INDONESIA

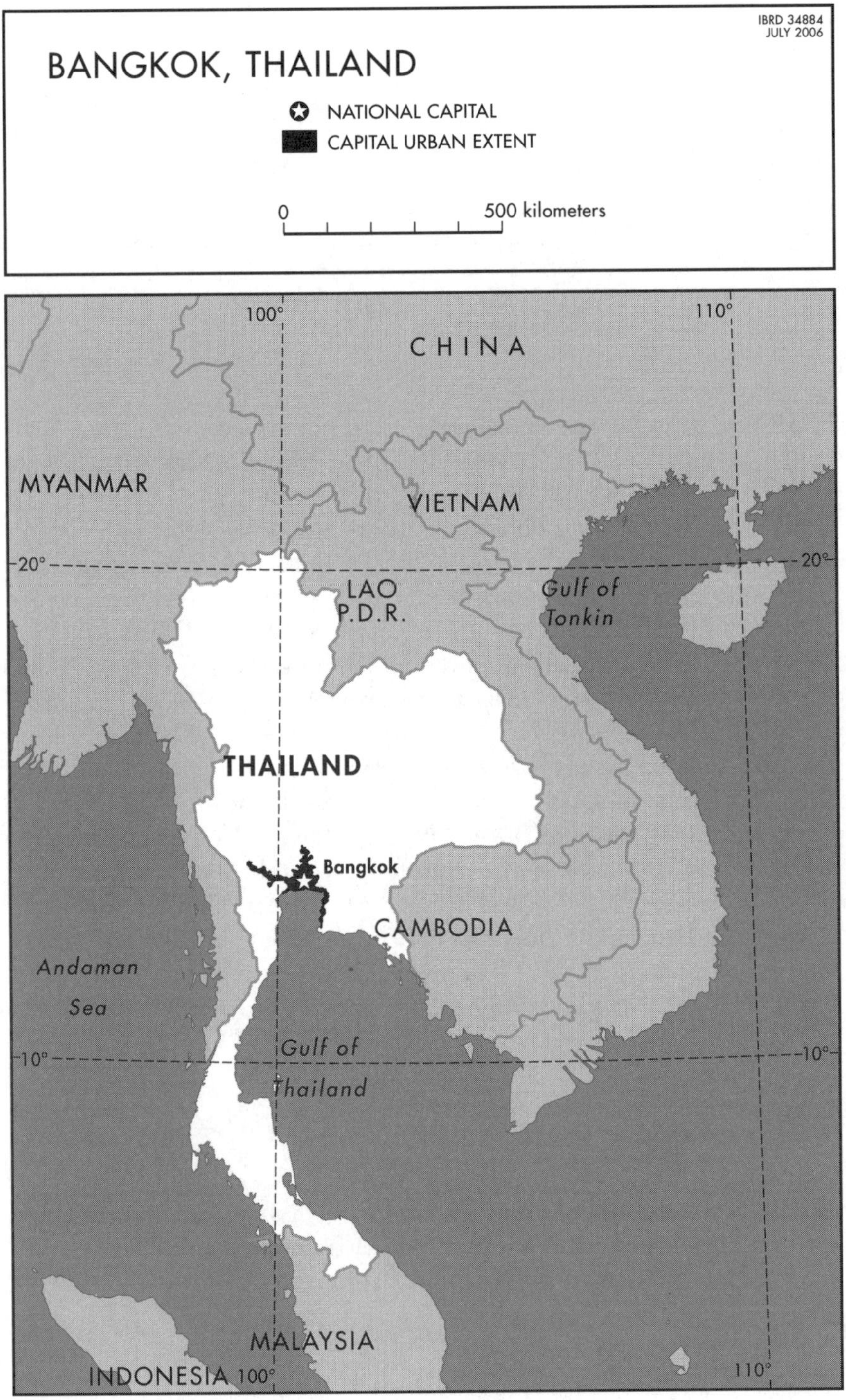

phenomenon, one can find one of several keys in developing a fashion industry that is more than a tiny urban enclave.[1]

The story of fashion as currently perceived begins in mid-17th century Europe (see DeJean 2005). A glance at the paintings from this period suggests that something new had entered the lives of the rich and the cultured. For the first time, their garments and accoutrements began to take on a meaning and significance of their own. The wealthy had discovered fashion, and henceforth it was to become a marker variously of status, distinction, style, and individual wealth. Items of dress and decoration started becoming almost as important as the person depicted in the painting and, therefore, were meticulously selected, coordinated, and presented for maximum effect. Just as people became increasingly conscious of differences in styles of clothing, in materials, and in how those varied from place to place and over the seasons, artists strove to render these newly charged sensibilities and to present the image their subjects were attempting to project. Those many images help us construct an overlapping tableau of changing fashions.

Paris can claim to be the birthplace of the fashion industry because of a king and his overweening ambition. In the mid-17th century, Louis XIV, a monarch with a sedulously cultivated taste for style, sought to elevate France over its European rivals by the sheer grandeur of his court. The king shrewdly came to realize that the pomp and style other monarchies quickly attempted to emulate could become the basis for considerable mercantile strength. With the help of his minister of finance, Jean-Baptiste Colbert, Louis built a small but thriving fashion industry for the aristocratic elite by regulating every aspect of high-end merchandising so that it would favor France's business community—by minimizing imports where possible and encouraging exports (DeJean 2005).

Under the king's patronage and with the help of incentives from the state, industry mushroomed, and by setting the standards, Louis ensured that French products, especially luxury items, became known for their unique designs and high quality. The king's endorsement also made the products more marketable and desirable. This initial success spurred creativity, new professions arose, and entrepreneurs were inspired to pursue fresh ventures. DeJean (2005, 9) notes of that period, "France's national image was the product of a collaboration between a king with a vision and some of the most brilliant artists, artisans, and craftspeople of all time—men and women who were the founding geniuses in domains as disparate

1. Aggregating the direct and indirect economic effect of the fashion industry leads to big numbers. For France as a whole, as much as 8 percent of industrial output and more than 350,000 jobs can be traced to the businesses that produce, display, package, bottle, and market fashion products ("Rags and Riches" 2004).

as wine making, fashion accessorizing, jewelry design, cabinetry, codification of culinary technique, and hairstyling." Paris thus gained first-mover advantages. A concept, a tradition, and an industry were established that survived the French Revolution and quickly found a new patron in Napoleon, whose appetite for ostentatious display was a godsend for the textile producers in Lyon and the dressmakers in Paris.

When, in the mid-19th century, Napoleon III became emperor, fashion found a patron with an even keener penchant for grandeur. His wife, the Empress Eugenie, created the couturier line by commissioning Charles Frederick Worth, the English dressmaker, to design a wardrobe fit for an empress. He did, and the House of Worth was born (Mansel 2005). But Worth did more than father the couturier culture. Imitations were already worrisomely prevalent in those days, and this concern provoked Worth to found the Chambre Syndicale de la Haute Couture[2] in 1868 to safeguard his designs, as well as to promote and market Parisian tailoring. This chamber was joined more than a century later, in 1973, by the Chambre Syndicale du Prêt-à-Porter des Couturiers et des Créateurs de Mode, for ready-to-wear fashion, and the Chambre Syndicale de la Mode Masculine, for menswear. All three chambers make up the Fédération Française de la Couture, du Prêt-à-Porter des Couturiers et des Créateurs de Mode,[3] which fixes the annual fashion calendar and schedules the fashion shows; develops emerging brands; coordinates the activities of the various industry participants (designers, buyers, weavers, subcontractors); tackles issues of intellectual property rights; trains people; and defines the ground rules of the fashion industry ("Fashion's Favourite" 2004).[4,5]

2. *Haute couture* literally means high sewing in French. It is, traditionally, the term used for custom-fitted, handmade, high-quality clothes that use expensive fabrics and materials, with close attention to detail and finish. Legally, only design houses that belong to the Chambre Syndicale de la Haute Couture and have met the conditions set by the chamber are granted the right to use the appellation *haute couture*. The term, though, is also informally used to refer to clothes that are similarly stylish and are of high quality.

3. The Italian chamber responsible for the development of the fashion industry, La Camera Nazionale della Moda Italiana, was established in 1958. With the signing of the Italian-French agreement in Milan, both chambers outlined Italy's leading role in the fashion industry. In 2000, the Italian-French protocol agreement was signed in Paris, detailing the importance of a common policy for the export of luxury goods outside of Europe (see http://www.cameramoda.it/eng/areaistituz/profilo.asp).

4. For example, a fashion house needs to employ at least 20 people in its workshops and must present a minimum of 50 designs at the twice-yearly Paris collections in order to qualify as *haute couture* ("Fashion's Favourite" 2004).

5. Support from the state continues and takes many forms: incentives to couturiers to use fabrics manufactured in France, attention given by state-controlled television to fashion shows, and permission to designers to present their collections at iconic buildings such as the Louvre ("Rags and Riches" 2004).

World War II forced several fashion houses in Paris to either close down or else relocate. Designers who moved their businesses elsewhere went to New York or London, some permanently. This partial relocation of the industry and the slowing down of the business in Paris stirred creativity in those other cities and induced the trade magazines and newspapers to turn away from an almost exclusive focus on Paris. After the war, Paris recovered some of the ground it had surrendered but was no longer the sole arbiter of fashion.

New York was now a force to be reckoned with. A dress and bespoke-tailoring industry had emerged that not only drew on the skills of immigrant hand labor for the rapid execution of ideas but also developed specializations in sportswear—a reputation the city retains—and work wear for women. New York's advantage was strengthened by structural features of the U.S. economy. Because American designs leaned more toward the practical side, a large, ready market of middle- and high-income households was available, made accessible by retail chains that sell luxury products to a wide cross-section of the buying public ("No-Profit Zone" 2005). Paris also had to contend with the appearance of a high-fashion industry in the early 1950s centered on Milan, which was based on regional craft and design skills that had catered to the demands of regional aristocracies over the centuries. Government support buttressed private initiatives in Milan, as it had done in Paris, enabling rich and diverse cultural traditions (with each region having its own specialties in yarns, fabrics, and jewelry) to feed a fashion industry that now commands a growing worldwide clientele.

Two other centers complete the list. London is a leader in fashion design, with some of the most famous training institutes, and is a major force in men's clothing. Since the 1980s, Tokyo has become a pacesetter for midlevel fashion and casual "punk style" fashions (see, for instance, Richie 2003) with a discriminating local market that has set and sustained high standards of quality. Designers such as Hanae Mori and Issey Miyake have a secure place in the highest reaches of the fashion world.

Milan and Tokyo, rather than Paris or New York, might provide pointers to the Thai government and aspiring designers as they attempt to make the fashion industry one of the pillars of the economy, although Paris, with its remarkable marketing apparatus, could play an intermediary role. In Italy, each region developed a strong artisanal specialty, which later evolved into small, flexible industries in line with fashion trends. For instance, Biella is known for its thread, Prato for its woolen articles, and Florence for its leather goods (Martin-Bernard 2006). From these small Italian industries emerged famous brands such as Cerruti, Etro, Loro Piana, and Zegna, specializing in high-quality weaving; Ferragamo in shoe design; Fendi in furs; Brioni in custom tailoring; Gucci, Prada, and

Table 7.1 Percentage of Consumers Who Would Buy a Brand If Money Were No Object

Brand	Percentage
Giorgio Armani	31
Gucci	30
Versace	26
Christian Dior	25
Chanel	23
Ralph Lauren	21
Louis Vuitton	21
Yves Saint Laurent	19
Prada	16
Emporio Armani	15

Source: "Number in the News" 2006.

Trussardi in leather goods; and Missoni in textiles (Martin-Bernard 2006). Unlike the French fashion industry, which focuses on the artistic aesthetics of design, Italian fashion designers never lose sight that creativity must not hinder the final result of their work, which is to sell. In this way, Italy's approach to fashion is better suited for today's world: Italy retains its fashion conscious image while maintaining a strong balance between product design and innovation. The success of this approach is reflected in Italy's standing in the eyes of fashion conscious buyers (see table 7.1).

Recognizing that a late starter must try harder and telescope the stages of development, the Thai government and the monarchy are highly supportive—the king's granddaughter is a fashion designer herself and her collection opened the Bangkok Fashion Week for 2005. They put great store by Thailand's rich cultural and craft traditions. The Bangkok Fashion City marketing initiative, with the backing of both government agencies and the private sector, aims to unite all fashion-related industry (such as textile, leatherwear, and jewelry) and is promoting, coordinating, and developing Bangkok's image as the creative capital of Asia ("Bangkok Fashion City" 2006). Part of this initiative also involves increasing export volume, facilitating enterprise growth, and educating fashion professionals ("Bangkok Fashion City" 2006). Whether government policy backing can be as potent in today's circumstances, as was the case in France and Italy, remains to be seen. Similarly, the appeal of fashion influenced by Southeast Asian culture still has to be tested in the global marketplace. Although at one level many countries with developed textile industries can acquire a foothold in the world fashion market by dint of clever designing and marketing, approaching parity with the industry leaders is a task of an altogether different magnitude. The rules of the game have changed enormously since Milan was rising into prominence in the 1950s. The front-runners are seemingly more entrenched, and fashion is more of a global industry, controlled by giant conglomerates such as LVMH, Richemont, and PPR. But other factors, such as economic prosperity, demographics, and the geographic shift of manufacturing and income, favor newcomers in Asia, as does an incipient disenchantment in East Asia with the overly familiar and largely Western established brands.

The Thai Fashion Industry

Thailand's sericulture and silk traditions go far back into antiquity, although interpreting the archeological evidence is problematic. Nevertheless, the records suggest that sericulture was well established by the Sukhothai kingdom (1238–1438), which traded silk—along with other goods such as ivory, leather, acacia and sapan wood, ceramics, and pepper—with neighboring kingdoms in China and in what is now Cambodia. Those commodities—especially silk—were also used as royal gifts or tributes. Ayutthayan[6] customs indicated position, rank, and status among court officials through designs on silk. Whereas cotton was used for everyday purposes, silk garments were worn on special occasions, such as ordinations, weddings, and festivals. The court of King Narai forged friendly ties with that of Louis XIV, and through a diplomatic mission, the Ayutthayan king sent the French monarch some fine examples of Thai silk handiwork.

This skill in silk weaving, which reaches far back in time, is one of Bangkok's strengths as it attempts to bolster the long-run economic fortunes of the fashion sector. This fashion sector is composed mainly of two industries: (a) garments and (b) gems and jewelry. In both subsectors, Bangkok is a dominant player in Thailand, with 74 percent of jewelry, 48 percent of garments, and 41 percent of leather goods coming from Bangkok in 2002. The fashion sector currently generates over US$12 billion (B 500 billion) annually in both domestic and foreign sales. It comprises nearly 20,000 mostly small enterprises, with a total workforce of about 2 million people ("Designing a Fashion Hub" 2004).

Within this fashion sector, the garments and textile subsector is one of Thailand's most robust, and the majority of production (48 percent) is

6. The kingdom of Ayutthaya lasted from 1350 to 1767. At that time, the capital of Thailand was Ayutthaya, 85 kilometers north of Bangkok.

Table 7.2 Total Value of Exports: Textiles, 1990–2003
(2005 US$ billion)

Economy	1990	1995	2000	2003
China	7.2	13.9	16.1	26.9
Italy	9.5	12.9	12.0	13.6
Hong Kong (China)	8.2	13.8	13.4	13.1
Germany	14.0	14.4	10.9	12.0
United States	5.0	7.4	11.0	10.9
Korea, Rep. of	6.1	12.3	12.7	10.1
Taiwan (China)	6.1	11.9	11.9	9.3
France	6.1	7.5	6.7	7.1
Belgium	—	—	6.3	7.0
India	2.2	4.4	6.0	6.8
Japan	5.9	7.2	7.0	6.4
Pakistan	2.7	4.3	4.5	5.8
Turkey	1.4	2.5	3.7	5.2
United Kingdom	4.4	5.1	4.6	4.8
Spain	1.5	2.8	3.0	3.6
Netherlands	2.9	4.5	2.7	3.1
Indonesia	1.2	2.7	3.5	2.9
Canada	0.7	1.4	2.2	2.3
Thailand	0.9	1.9	2.0	2.2
Austria	2.1	2.1	1.8	2.1

Source: World Trade Organization statistics database.

Note: — = not available. Countries are ranked according to 2003 data. Textiles are Standard International Trade Classification Division 65.

located in the Bangkok metropolitan area. The industry, which employs about 81,000 people, has a 3 percent share of gross domestic product. Clothing and textile exports amounted to US$5.8 billion in 2003 (see tables 7.2 and 7.3), or just over 7 percent of all exports, most of which went to the European Union, Japan, the United States, and Southeast Asia ("Thai Garment Exports" 2005). Although exports have risen steadily, they are less than 2 percent of a global textile and clothing trade valued at US$343 billion in 2003.

Thai firms want to enlarge their market share, and they have begun putting real money behind this aspiration. Between 2001 and 2004, Thailand's textile and clothing industry invested around US$12.5 billion in upgrading its dyeing, finishing, weaving, knitting, and spinning facilities ("High Style" 2005). Machinery was imported from Germany, Italy, Switzerland, Taiwan (China), and Japan. The latest in textile technology is merely one factor in overall competitiveness, however. Textile and garment producers still need to streamline the industry to be able to respond

Table 7.3 Total Value of Exports: Clothing, 1990–2003
(2005 US$ billion)

Economy	1990	1995	2000	2003
China	9.7	24.0	36.1	52.1
Hong Kong (China)	15.4	21.3	24.2	23.2
Italy	11.8	14.4	13.4	16.2
Turkey	3.3	6.1	6.5	9.9
Germany	7.9	7.5	7.3	9.7
Mexico	0.6	2.7	8.6	7.3
France	4.7	5.7	5.4	6.9
India	2.5	4.1	6.2	6.6
United States	2.6	6.7	8.6	5.5
Belgium	—	—	3.9	5.4
United Kingdom	3.0	4.3	4.1	4.4
Bangladesh	0.6	2.0	4.2	4.3
Indonesia	1.6	3.4	4.7	4.1
Romania	0.4	1.4	2.3	4.1
Netherlands	2.2	2.8	2.7	3.7
Thailand	2.8	5.0	3.8	3.6
Korea, Rep. of	7.9	5.0	5.0	3.6
Vietnam	—	—	1.8	3.6
Spain	0.6	1.5	2.1	3.3
Portugal	3.5	3.6	2.8	3.2

Source: World Trade Organization statistics database.

Note: — = not available. Countries are ranked according to 2003 data. Textiles are Standard International Trade Classification Division 84.

quickly and comprehensively to buyers' needs. Such buyers may require large lots on small production cycles, as short as two to three months, so producers must learn to integrate the different processes and optimize the flow of resources in the supply chain using the full potential of information technology and modern logistics. Producers also need to find ways to partner with other parties in the manufacturing process, so that they can share and improve their technology, consolidate resources, reduce production time, and broaden their product range into the high-value end ("High Style" 2005).[7] Very likely, through networked clusters and some consolidation into larger-sized firms, firms could augment their capabilities in areas of design, production, and exports.

7. Growth and innovations as well as obtaining the technology to create and develop technical textiles will also benefit the automobile, medical, construction, sports, and agriculture industries. Each car is estimated to use 10 to 15 kilograms of polyester in upholstery and airbags, but Thailand imports polyester worth about B 4 billion per year from the Republic of Korea, Japan, Taiwan (China), and Europe because domestic supplies are insufficient ("Bt25 Bn Fund" 2004).

Thailand competes with China, India, Malaysia, Vietnam, and other producers, and this competition will become much stiffer now that Multifiber Arrangement quotas have been eliminated, leading to the closure of many producers in several exporting countries, including Thailand. However, buyers looking to moderate their reliance on China, whose share in the textile market is expected to triple to 45 percent in a few years, are turning to other suppliers. Thailand exported an estimated additional 80 million pieces of apparel through the end of 2005 as a result of the U.S.-imposed import restrictions against the flood of cheap textiles coming from China. The European Union, likewise, is limiting the importation of 10 categories of apparel in line with the restrictions that allow Chinese exports to grow only by between 8 and 12.5 percent in each category ("Thailand Benefits" 2005). Even Japan, where Chinese textile and garment imports have taken more than 90 percent of the market, is looking toward other suppliers through bilateral free trade agreements with the Association of Southeast Asian Nations and the individual economies within the bloc, Thailand among them ("Japanese Textile Companies" 2005). All these developments can become stepping-stones to an export structure within which fashion garments account for a larger share.

Thailand needs to forge these partnerships and search for such opportunities. Even with the investment made by the textile and garment sector in recent years, low-end exports are likely to suffer as a result of competition from other suppliers. Hence, diversifying into fashion garments and leveraging the domestic strengths in producing different kinds of silk are all the more necessary.

A Silken Future?

In 1901, King Chulalongkorn invited experts from Japan to upgrade local silk production, and later, in 1903, the Department of Silk Craftsmen was established, which marked the beginning of sericulture and silk-weaving development in the modern era. But those initiatives had run out of steam by the 1930s, and silk-making technology had once again begun to ossify. What sparked a revival in the post–World War II period was the entrepreneurship of Jim Thompson, an ex–U.S. Army intelligence officer. He smelled an opportunity, adopted the profession of a merchant, and set about reviving the art of silk weaving[8] in Thailand and ratcheting up the standards of quality.

8. This skill, particularly the skills needed to weave variants such as mudmee silk, was on the wane at that time.

Thompson's company, the Thai Silk Company, was first established as a small retail store in the late 1940s. At that time, silk production was largely a family activity and a way for farming households to supplement their income. Consequently, little attention was paid to quality because most material was made either for personal use or for the local market. Colors faded quickly with repeated washings because the natural vegetable dyes that were used did not hold very well. Thompson persuaded producers to switch to colorfast Swiss and German artificial dyes. He also introduced weavers to the techniques of making printed silk fabrics, using designs found in paintings, pottery, and old fabrics, and encouraged them to create their own designs.

Thompson introduced tourists to the fabrics he was producing by approaching them in the hotel lobby of The Oriental in Bangkok and asking them to examine the material he had draped over his arm. In 1947, he brought samples of his silk to Edna Woolman Chase, editor of *Vogue*, in New York. The magazine was as influential then as it is now. Chase was impressed with the display and in the pages of *Vogue* declared it a "magnificent new discovery" (http://jimthompsonhouse.com/life/vogue.ASP). Jim Thompson's efforts were reinforced by the interest of the Thai royal family in winning recognition for Thai silk production.

The Thai Silk Company that Jim Thompson launched currently has 27 branch shops in Thailand, 15 of them located in Bangkok, and 14 overseas shops located in London, Brunei Darussalam, Dubai, Malaysia, and Singapore. Their merchandise is also displayed in various shops and showrooms in more than 30 countries. The company has diversified its product line to enhance revenues by producing neckties, handbags, and other accessories, as well as home and furniture collections, all released under the Jim Thompson label.[9]

Queen Sirikit brought mudmee silk to international attention by way of the garments she wore during state visits in the 1960s. These patterned fabrics are among the ones most closely identified with Thai silk and are now widely copied and machine manufactured.[10]

Differences in climate, breed of silkworm, species of mulberry tree, and production methods lend Thai silk specific characteristics differentiating it from silk produced in China, India, and Italy. Thai silk comes in a wide

9. The Jim Thompson corporation also established four restaurants and bars.

10. In 2004, the Department of Intellectual Property Rights of the Thai Ministry of Commerce patented more than 7,000 traditional handwoven textile patterns and presented them to the queen as a birthday gift.

range of prices, types, and quality. Traditionally handwoven, the fabrics tend to be soft, but nubby and imperfect, unlike typical silk, which makes each bolt of material unique. Thai silks are known for their rich and bright colors because the coarse and knotty fibers are able to absorb and hold dyes better, giving them a distinctive luster.[11]

The varieties of Thai silk provide designers with the raw material, and through further innovation, the variety can be continually enlarged. Innovation, however, needs to be routinized in design as well as in perfecting and frequent fine-tuning of the vehicles for marketing these products.

Human Capital Development

Cultivating relevant skills is a necessary step, which has led the Thai Garment Manufacturer's Association to embark on a program to train entrepreneurs. The program imparts management and marketing skills through instruction and practical demonstration—by visiting the production plants and business operations of leading firms in the garment industry. This activity is part of the government's plan to create new entrepreneurs. The plan aims at adding 50,000 entrepreneurs to the current total of nearly 4 million business owners within the next few years ("Training Plan" 2005).[12] A budget of B 12 billion has been earmarked for the whole project. The Thailand Textile Institute is complementing this sum with a B 25 billion investment to create new yarns and fabrics and to develop technical textiles that will provide the raw material for designers.[13]

---

11. *Thai silk*, according to the Thai Silk Association, which oversees the Thai silk industry and industry standards, is defined as pure silk woven in Thailand, including silk woven with dobby or jacquard designs that may contain materials other than silk, but not more than 15 percent by weight. There are several varieties of Thai silk, such as mudmee silk, had saew silk, praewa silk, lai nam lei silk, and sin teen jok. Mudmee, a type of Thai silk also known as *ikat*, is probably the most popular. It comes from the northeast part of Thailand and is characterized by traditional intricate geometric and zoomorphic designs that have been handed down from generation to generation. The designs are made by tying bits of string around a thread mounted on a frame. The thread is dyed, which leaves the tied places uncolored; the dyed and undyed portions appear as a pattern on the fabric as the thread is used for weaving.

12. Entrepreneurs make up 15 to 20 percent of the population in developed countries. The United States has between 30 million and 40 million business owners, and Japan has between 8 million and 9 million ("Training Plan" 2005).

13. One idea being developed by Thai scientists is the bacteria-resistant shirt. Scientists from Chulalongkorn University's Institute of Metallurgy and Material Science have been using nanotechnology to coat fabrics with silver nano, which inhibits the growth of bacteria and fungi, in effect sterilizing and deodorizing fabrics. In a collaboration between the university, the Science and Technology Ministry's National Innovation Agency, and United Textile Mills, B 15 million has already been invested in producing the prototype shirt and another B 200 million is needed to commercialize the product ("Researchers Develop" 2005).

The objective of these schemes is to transform Bangkok's textile and garments industry from just executing designs of foreign name brands to developing local brands and designs that will bring the city recognition in international fashion circles. The local fabrics need to be developed, and indigenous weaving techniques and materials must be used in creating new products and textiles that will stand out from those of the other low-cost and midlevel textile and garments producers.

A number of fashion design schools were established around Bangkok in recent years. Most of these schools are strongly influenced by foreign faculty and links with institutes abroad.[14] Perhaps it is through these links that Thailand will learn and acclimate itself with the challenges, evolving trends, and idiosyncrasies of global consumers.[15]

Although increased capacity and better technology can raise production and quality, Thailand must also move on the organizational front. Either through tie-ups with multinational corporations (MNCs) in the fashion industry or through homegrown firms, Thailand requires organizational vehicles to become a fashion center and to groom a few international brands. Building a reputation for style, good design, fine tailoring, exact execution, up-to-date technology, and other intangible qualities is a necessary condition. But the real test lies in the building of brands and their global marketing.

GEMS: A CITY'S BEST FRIENDS?

For centuries, gems and precious metals have been central to Thai decoration and adornment in artworks, religious figurines and structures, and clothing. Deposits of rubies and sapphires are found in Chantaburi, Trat, and Kanchanaburi. Black spine, pyroxene, amethyst, agate, and carnelian are also mined all over Thailand. Cutting, polishing, and setting of imported diamonds commenced in the early 1990s, building on a long tradition of gemcraft in some rural areas that has supplemented the incomes of farming households. The jewelry industry in Bangkok arose from this cottage industry (Scott 2000a).

---

14. For instance, the Chanapatana Institute, a top internationally recognized design school founded by monk Luangphor Viriyang Sirintharo, is run by Accademia Italiana, a design institute based in Florence. Foreign faculty members teach techniques rather than actual style or design (Barton 2004).

15. Thailand needs to play up to the fashion tastes of global consumers by carefully analyzing fashion trends, by ensuring that product quality meets global demand, and by building a strong fashion database with industry information.

In recent decades, the gem and jewelry business has achieved considerable success, with a turnover of about US$500 million. It employs about 32,000, exports four-fifths of output, and each year has been one of the major industrial investors. Gemstone and jewelry companies are numerous in Thailand, with headquarters mostly located in Bangkok. Bangkok has two jewelry districts, which are adjacent to each other: an older traditional district, which is located around the area of the traditional Chinatown because the business is dominated by ethnic Chinese entrepreneurs, and a newer one, which emerged during the industry's growth in the 1970s. The older district has small workshops and retail outlets that cater mostly to local markets. In the newer district, located in the modern commercial center along the Surawong-Silom Road area, the firms are producing on a larger scale and selling to international markets (Scott 2000a). The industry is a network of complex relationships grounded in family ties, ethnicity, and religion. Scott's (2000a) survey of the industry shows that many of the firms are partnerships in which at least one of the partners is a member of the family. External business relations also involve familial ties, and "it is not unusual to find that inter-firm transactions involve siblings, cousins and other relatives" (Scott 2000a, 55).

Thai gem manufacturers are known for their skillful cutting and they excel in heat treating to enhance color and quality.[16] They also are among the leading producers of synthetic gems. Jewelry manufacturers rely on imported machines and freelance designers, although the bigger ones have in-house designers as well. Small and medium-size firms rely mainly on copying other designs.

Thai firms have penetrated the global market, with offshore subsidiaries catering to different markets. A total of almost 1,100 export firms, most of them small and medium-size, employ approximately 1 million workers, a significant fraction of whom are in the Bangkok region (Scott 2000a).

Jewelry production is a capital-intensive industry with mostly imported equipment. In addition, it is now increasingly reliant on imported stones (see table 7.4), so most manufacturers are foreign-owned businesses or have Thai and foreign partners. Raw materials make up about 75 percent of the total cost of diamond and gem-based jewelry and accessories production (see table 7.5). Still, many manufacturers favor Thailand and have moved their production activities to the country because of low wage rates; the

16. For example, the color of a ruby can be made more intense by adding chromium and heating the stone.

Table 7.4 Imports of Gems, Precious Metals, and Jewelry, 1999–2002
(B billion)

Categories	1999	2000	2001	2002
Pearls	0.4	0.5	0.4	0.5
Diamonds	23.1	31.5	32.7	39.1
Precious and semiprecious stones	3.5	4.3	4.3	4.3
Synthetic stones	1.0	1.0	1.2	1.4
Silver	3.0	3.7	4.5	4.7
Gold	13.4	24.1	36.7	33.1
Platinum	0.5	0.8	0.7	0.6
Articles of jewelry	1.4	2.8	4.1	5.6
Imitation jewelry	0.2	0.2	0.3	0.4
Others	0.2	0.3	0.2	0.3
Total	**46.6**	**69.2**	**85.0**	**89.9**

Source: Gem and Jewelry Institute of Thailand 2003.

Table 7.5 Production Cost Structure of Jewelry and Accessories, 2000
(percentage)

Cost category	Diamond based	Gem based	Accessories
Uncut diamonds	63		
Uncut gemstones		71	
Precious metals			35
Cut gems			30
Other raw materials	8	6	5
Labor cost	15	15	12
Other expenses	14	8	18
Total	**100**	**100**	**100**

Source: Department of Export Promotion 2001 (http://www.thaitrade.com/en/doc/Jewelry%20and%20Accessories.doc).

availability of skilled Thai labor (for example, cutters and designers); and the local expertise in using heat treatment to bring out the color of stones.

Jewelry and accessories, mostly in a cut or worked form valued at B 93 billion, were exported in 2002 (see table 7.6). About one-fourth of exports went to the United States; about 22 percent to the European Union; and the balance to Israel, Japan, Switzerland, and others (see figure 7.1).

However, because certain kinds of stones are either unavailable domestically or in short supply, Thailand imports stones from Australia, Cambodia, the Lao People's Democratic Republic, Madagascar, Myanmar, Sri Lanka, Tanzania, Vietnam, and various countries in Africa and South America. Between 40 and 50 percent of the world's rubies and sapphires are cut in Thailand.

Table 7.6 Exports of Gems, Precious Metals, and Jewelry, 1999–2002
(B billion)

Categories	1999	2000	2001	2002
Diamond	16.2	21.0	22.2	25.3
Precious and semiprecious stones	8.8	9.4	8.9	9.0
Synthetic stones	0.6	0.6	0.6	0.6
Gold	6.5	0.9	0.9	10.2
Articles of jewelry	31.6	33.0	43.8	42.3
Imitation jewelry	2.1	2.5	3.0	3.3
Others	1.3	1.9	1.9	2.3
Total	**67.2**	**69.4**	**81.3**	**93.0**

Source: Gem and Jewelry Institute of Thailand 2003.

Figure 7.1 Gem and Jewelry Exports, by Country, 2002

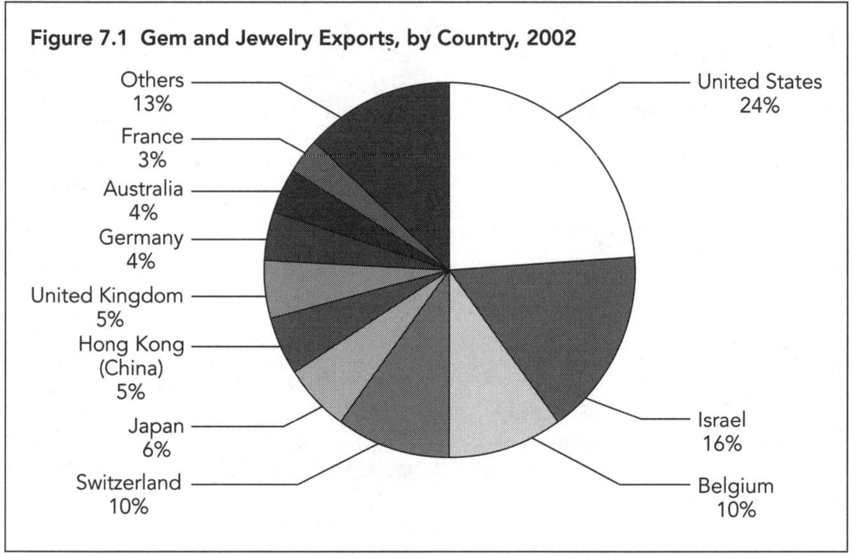

Source: Gem and Jewelry Institute of Thailand 2003.

Although the Thai silver jewelry and gemstones industry has a firm foothold in the international market, it competes against high-end silver and gold jewelry from Italy and also against lower-priced silver and costume jewelry from India and China. Additionally, the thousands of Thai rural workers engaged in the sorting and grading of gemstones risk a loss of jobs from computerized sorting techniques that are more accurate.[17]

17. Cambridge University's Institute for Manufacturing claims to have devised a way to make the grading of diamonds and other precious stones more consistent. (Assessing the value of gems, especially their clarity, involves a certain amount of subjectivity.) The institute automated the

The response to those pressures has been a slew of government and industry-sponsored schemes to try to keep value adding activities in Thailand by staying abreast of technological developments. The Ministry of Industry has allocated B 89.6 million to support the establishment of a skills and technology development program for gem and jewelry manufacturers and exporters. The program is aimed at substantially increasing exports. The Bangkok Fashion City office appointed the Center of Academic Service of Srinakarinwirot University to operate the Jewelry Advanced Research and Development project, one of the subprojects of the Bangkok Fashion City. Its goal is to make Thailand a global gem and jewelry center by 2012, in line with the Bangkok Fashion City plan.

Achieving this goal will depend considerably on the dynamism of the Gemopolis Industrial Estate, a jewelry cluster that is located just 4 kilometers from Bangkok's new airport.[18] A group of gem and jewelry entrepreneurs established Gemopolis in the early 1990s with government support. It was envisioned as a one-stop manufacturing and trading area, a supply-chain cluster where the interrelated components of the industry—such as raw materials, machines and technology, finished products,

process by using a set of rules, distilled from the judgments of four diamond experts, to determine the clarity of 503 "virtual stones"—computer models of stones containing different flaws. When a stone is presented to the computer system, it grades the stones according to how the experts would have done it. Models of gemstones, which are produced by scanning the stones using a desktop x-ray tomography machine, are fed into the system. Automating the process can lead to more accurate valuations. Tests of the machine, called the iGem, showed it could increase the value of a rough stone by as much as 25 percent.

The next step is to automate the physical process of cutting the diamond. Such a method is being developed by Calibrated Diamonds, a company based in Johannesburg, South Africa. The company is using lasers to make rough cuts and to carry out "bruting," the beveling process used to give diamonds their characteristic sharp-edged shapes. The laser-cutting method can make more precise cuts and can even polish the stones. (Traditionally, diamonds are cut and polished using other diamonds.) Combining the automated evaluation system and laser cutting could both reduce waste and shorten the turnaround time from months to days.

18. One early example of a jewelry cluster that enjoyed a long and successful inning was in Providence, Rhode Island. The jewelry industry in Providence was started in the late 18th century by Seril Dodge, the first jeweler to open a shop in Providence, and Nehemiah Dodge, his nephew. They dealt in watches, clocks, and gold and silver jewelry, operating alongside Rhode Island's maritime trade. Their success encouraged other jewelers to join the local market. Nehemiah Dodge, when he opened his own shop, developed an early process of roll-plated gold, which consisted of uniting a thin sheet of gold to a thicker sheet of copper with silver solder and then hammering and rolling it into the desired thickness. Dodge, therefore, became the first "manufacturing jeweler" when he sold his plated gold to other goldsmiths. He also started two trends that the Providence jewelry industry continues to be known for: (a) production of jewelry in lower price ranges and (b) specialization and innovation in the technology of jewelry manufacture.

logistics and distribution services, as well as marketing—are all located close to one another. More than 50 manufacturers have factories in the estate. They are exempt from corporate income tax, import duties, and value added tax for five to eight years, as long as they apply for a license with the Board of Investment. These manufacturers employed more than 10,000 workers and generated exports of US$500 million in 2003, about one-fifth of Thailand's total exports. Currently, more than 80 percent of the companies in Gemopolis are owned by foreigners. Gemopolis houses a factory outlet and retail facility for small to medium-size enterprises, as well as the Bangkok Diamond and Precious Stones Exchange, which is similar to a stock market, on which precious stones are bought and sold. The estate is also being promoted as a tourist destination by the Tourism Authority of Thailand, and the government is planning Gemopolis Habitat, an entire township, with a convention hall plus commercial and residential accommodations.

Meanwhile, the Thai Chamber of Commerce has requested that the government let financial institutions accept raw gems as collateral for loans to entrepreneurs. For this idea to come to fruition, an institute to evaluate the value of the stones must be established to ensure that the gems meet international standards. The chamber hopes that this idea will ease the difficulties traders in raw gems face in gaining access to finance, thereby making the industry more competitive and doubling the value of exports to B 200 billion in the next five years. Thailand's exports of jewelry and ornaments totaled B 104 billion in 2003. Government and industry are also responsible for new courses being introduced by universities that will teach students the use of the latest high-tech tools and machines. Such machines are needed to add more value to the products and to upgrade both the quality and the design of Thai gems and jewelry. The techniques that will be taught are advanced jewelry prototyping using computer-based methods; advanced gemstone and diamond cutting; advanced casting; stone in-place casting; stamping, welding, and tubing; polishing and refurnishing; and plating (Bangkok Fashion City's Jewelry Advanced Research and Development project). Recognizing that technology will always be changing, gem traders are working with scientists to understand how each new process works and then to introduce the process to the industry with full disclosure; the marketplace can then determine its value and properly certify the treated materials.

A number of Thai firms are at the forefront of initiatives to enhance competitiveness. For example, Pranda Jewelry specializes in making affordable gold and silver jewelry set with diamonds and semiprecious stones. The company was established 30 years ago, and its products are sold globally, mostly under the Pranda brand, but also under names such as Prima, Cristalina, and Century. Pranda has about a dozen manufacturing, wholesale, and retail brand distribution subsidiaries around the world. Its factories are located in China, Indonesia, Thailand, and Vietnam, with subsidiaries in France, the United Kingdom, and the United States to provide customer service to international customers. Exports account for 83 percent of Pranda's production. Pranda is planning to invest an additional B 200 million to increase production capacity both in Thailand and abroad. The investment will increase the group's annual production capacity of 5.87 million pieces of jewelry to 6 million pieces. The company worries, however, about the competitive pressures that will arise as a result of free trade agreements with China and India, pressures that will force Pranda to constantly upgrade design and quality or risk losing market share ("Pranda Jewellery" 2005). Such improvements require high-technology equipment, such as laser machines for faster and more accurate cutting of stones and other machines that will allow the creation of more complex designs. In turn, these upgrades entail making heavy capital investments and building specific skills, not only to run the new equipment but also to service the machines when they break down—costs that small and medium-size firms cannot easily afford.

Thaigem, based in Chantaburi, near Bangkok, claims to be the vendor of 90 percent of the gems sold online worldwide. In Thailand, such a huge Web site stands out simply for its clear English and painless navigation. The company was started in 2000 by Don Kogen, who sold a few gems on eBay. Against expectations, more and more people are comfortable buying gems online because the selections are wider, buyers have ample time to choose, the prices are lower, and the purchased item can be tried at home and returned if the customer is dissatisfied. In 2004, 2 percent of all diamond jewelry sales, amounting to US$63 billion, were made online; fine jewelry is one of the fastest-growing items sold online. Europe's biggest online retailer of diamond jewelry, Cool Diamond, has grown sixfold in just six years. Thaigem is successfully exploiting this trend. It is able to keep costs down by slicing away some seven to eight layers of intermediaries, whose commissions ratchet up the colored gem's price on the journey from the mine to the jewelry store. Thaigem's other advantage is cheap labor. Programmers' salaries run about US$750 per month, craftspeople earn US$300 per month, and secretaries' wages are as low as US$150 per month. Revenues were US$4.3 million in 2001 and more than doubled to US$10.3 million in 2002.

The initial challenge that Thaigem faced was Thailand's reputation for credit card fraud and gem scams;[19] a pilfer-prone postal service, unreliable phones, and antiquated banks; and a workforce not known for team spirit or command of English. Kogen bypassed the postal service by negotiating a volume discount with FedEx. And for the first few years, Thaigem overcame customers' reluctance to purchase from a developing country by making use of U.S.-based third-party payment systems, such as Escrow.com and PayPal. In March 2002, when the company's credibility was established, it began accepting direct payments by credit card. Now, Thaigem sources gems from 60 countries, stocking more than 400 gem types. Such high volume enables the company to buy inventory in bulk and resell as single items or in smaller lots.

These two success stories on an international scale are still something of an exception. Most Thai jewelry firms are not innovative and are not aggressively introducing new designs or cultivating a brand image. They prefer instead to service the domestic market or supply foreign buyers. Instead of aiming for branded products, small and medium-size manufacturers, especially, are reluctant to make the big investments required and continue producing jewelry according to their clients' orders and specifications.

This hesitancy is not a recipe for increasing competitiveness or growth. Jewelry firms need to be much more venturesome to enlarge their share of the export market and their contribution to the economy of Bangkok.

A FASHIONABLE BANGKOK

For a new entrant to the fashion industry such as Thailand, this is "the best of times and the worst of times" because of globalization, demographics, industrial concentration, technological change, flux in the fashion business, and an excess of beautiful things vying for the consumer's

19. An incident around 2002 further put the Thai jewelry industry's reputation in doubt. Orange stones that looked like *padparadschas*, precious orange-pink sapphires from Madagascar, started showing up in the market in large quantities. At first they were thought to be the actual Madagascar stones, and gem traders readily snapped them up. But buyers soon became suspicious when the supposedly rare sapphires flooded the market. The stones were discovered to be created by gem burners and part-time farmers from the province of Chantaburi, who introduced traces of beryllium into oil-fired ovens, thereby transforming low-grade stones into orange and gold stones similar to *padparadschas*. Although some imperfect gems are subject to heat treatment in order to enhance their color and quality, some U.S. gemnologists alleged that this new corundum treatment pioneered by Thai burners violated the ethics of the trade—although no law was actually broken—because the provenance of the stones was not disclosed. In an industry that relies not only on precision and expertise but also on trust, the lack of disclosure on the part

dollar. In this world, the challenge, in the opinion of the designer Karl Lagerfeld, is keeping the desire to buy alive.

Fashion has always tended toward the international, and in recent decades this tendency has become far more pronounced, opening the way for designers in cities such as Bangkok. The multiplication and widening of electronic and media-related communication channels are part and parcel of globalization, and they have had a hand in this expansion. In addition to providing information, these channels have contributed to cultural traffic—in particular, the rapid and widespread diffusion of fashion—and to an unprecedented visual pluralism. As it has done for many other handicrafts and folk arts, global demand is imparting new life to the fashion industry, which was on the verge of losing skills passed down over hundreds of years (Cowen 2002). As Hollander (1993, 345) observes,

> The tyranny of fashion has in fact never been stronger than in this period of visual pluralism. The enormous plurality of dress messages in our time has been made possible not only by the expansion and diversity of the clothing business but also by the availability of so much visual information both accumulated and newly generated. . . . The rate of change in fashion has not actually increased, what has increased is the number of fashions, all of them individually subject to change.

The cultural globalization we are experiencing in the early 21st century differs from cultural commerce in earlier eras because,

> Images and practices [are] moving with far greater extensity and at a far greater velocity. . . . The saturation of television, radio, and telephone ownership in the West and their marked increase in [industrializing countries] and the emergence of new domestic technologies of communication have expanded the volume of signs and signification that people are exposed to. This domestic rise in information is coupled with the increasing appearance of foreign symbols and artifacts within national economies introduc[ing] a speed and immediacy to elements of contemporary cultural globalization in a way that is historically distinct. In the past, imperial states, networks of intellectuals, and theocracies were the key agents of cultural diffusion. In the contemporary world their role has been displaced by that of large media industries as well as by greater flows of individuals and groups. MNCs are at the heart of these interconnected processes. In the contemporary world the [cultural] flows continue to be generated primarily in the West and in its

of the burners and the dealers who were in on the process created a crisis of confidence in the industry. Customers began doubting retailers and traders, nobody wanted to lose reputation by certifying stones wrongly, and existing supplies of sapphires were affected because people were unsure of what they were buying. Gem wholesalers were estimated to have lost more than US$30 million ("Gemstone Scandals" 2003).

most powerful cultural institutions. . . . However, flows have begun to be reversed, primarily through migration but also through other cultural forms shifting from South to North and East to West. Music, food, ideas, beliefs and literature from the South and East have been percolating into the cultures of the West, creating new lines of cultural interconnectedness and fracture" (Held and others 1999, 368–69).

This cultural globalization, quite remarkably, has not yet affected the fashion industry's concentration in a very few centers, but that trend could change. Fewer than 10 cities can currently claim to be the points of light in the fashion world, and their number has shown no signs of increasing in the past two decades, although the ideas and designs coming out of those centers are now penetrating every urban corner of the world.

The geographic concentration of the fashion industry reflects historical forces and first-mover advantages. Those advantages might have eroded were it not for the emergence of a small number of MNCs that now dominate the business of fashion and have the resources to sustain brand names and dynamic design strategies; to harness new technologies in the areas of materials, production, logistics, and marketing; and to commit vast sums to advertising their products to underpin the intrinsic merits of the fashions being purveyed. To thrive in a global marketplace, the products of the fashion industry must first and foremost acquire a brand. Moreover, they need to project an image symbolizing quality and, to a degree, exclusivity, and they must be differentiated from other competing products, even when those products are ready-to-wear fashions. Ensuring the quality and appeal of branded products requires ingenuity and large investments for multimedia global coverage and for the use of high-paid celebrities who temporarily enjoy favorable as well as global name recognition. Undoubtedly, designers matter, but the brand comes first.

The necessity of a brand image, of obsessive attention to design and quality, of multinational corporate vehicles for producing and selling goods worldwide, and of relentless high-stakes advertising has made new entry, except on a minor niche basis, extremely difficult. A new entrant can start out as an original equipment manufacturer and a supplier to an MNC with a parcel of brands, and then by dint of investment become an original design manufacturer preparatory to launching its own branded products, initially regionally and then on a global scale. But such an evolution, although it is being pursued by companies such as Esquel and Giordano, requires a long-term strategy for acquiring design skills and the capacity to market and conduct operations globally. Essentially, it is a question of either staying under the wing of an MNC, as most Thai exporters have preferred, or of devising a strategy to become an MNC in the fashion industry. In a business in which fashion can rise and fall in a matter of months, where the fortunes of even the leading apparel companies—such as Vanity Fair, Jones Apparel, Liz Claiborne, or The Gap—are at risk, design and marketing are two necessary ingredients of success. Equally important, however, are the scale of operations and the ability to anticipate future fashion trends and to deliver just the right kind of product in a timely manner. Achieving such scale, in part through acquiring other firms and by building the market expertise, must be part and parcel of a longer-term strategy of Thai companies if they are to achieve global business heft and to contribute significantly to the economy of Bangkok ("Stitching Together" 2005; "Too Many Surveys" 2005).

Although design, quality, marketing, and scale are the keys most critical to success in the fashion business, in this industry as in most others, innovation has become an important determinant of competitiveness. The innovation can take many forms. Most commonly it shows up in design, but it is becoming as important in the area of materials. Whether for clothing or jewelry or leather goods, technology has a growing hand in how those products are constructed. In the case of clothing, how it is cut is affected by technology, and for making jewelry, the way in which metals are treated or combined is at issue. Interestingly, one-third of all men's shirts and suits sold in the United States now incorporate some innovation in the materials that enhances comfort, reduces creasing, increases stain resistance, or introduces other attributes. Innovation extends all the way along the supply chain, from the production and handling of the raw materials to its presentation to the final consumer. Such innovation, which must now be continuous in order to meet market expectations of seasonally refreshed product lines and to parry the innovations of competitors, requires developing in-house capability, outsourcing, collaborating with partner firms, and creating links with research institutes and design houses. Most firms, large and small, rely on a mix of those strategies. The point to be noted is that innovation is now a must, and Thai firms with aspirations to become global players will need to learn to innovate, which lengthens the odds against a newcomer's attaining global stature in the fashion business.

The cultural plurality of the industry adds yet another complication. Designers, whether of jewelry or clothing, draw their inspiration from many sources. They ransack all cultures for styles, techniques, and symbols and evolve unusual hybrids. Jewelry, for instance, can in one season lean heavily on classical Greek and Roman designs; in the next, it can rely on Indian. In other words, with globalization, all cultures are fair game for the designer; specific, ethnically rooted styles or materials cannot be counted on to serve as the basis for enduring success—although Kenzo, Etro, and

Dries Van Noten have defied the odds. A product line with a strong Thai cultural flavor will lack uniqueness and might not attract consumers, whether in Thailand or overseas. If it does succeed in one season, it might not in the next. If it acquires a strong following, it will be imitated by others. Only if the product line builds a strong brand image and a large group of loyal buyers is it likely to be profitable over the longer term. Put differently, not only has the cultural democracy introduced by globalization limited the leverage that a cultural heritage can offer to a local fashion industry with global ambitions; it has also, as is widely noted, led to an incipient homogenization of fashion cultures: designer jeans are being worn virtually the world over.[20]

Not only the global convergence of consumption preferences but also the tenacious survival of regional variations reflecting local cultural proclivities is exemplified by cross-country patterns of beer and wine intake. Wine consumption is increasing irrespective of what is happening to the national production of those beverages, even between France, a traditionally wine-drinking country, and Germany, where beer has long been the preferred tipple. Differences persist among Latin American countries, however, that are related to the cultural heritages carried over from European origins of dominant groups (Aizenman and Brooks 2005). The same tendencies are found in the fashion industry.

Whether fashion clothing and accoutrements are being made for the exclusive high end or the midrange, an intention to market them worldwide almost requires that cultural flavors be toned down to appeal to the largest number of customers. Something that is unusually exotic is likely to have a limited market, and global success would be either a fluke or the result of an extraordinarily inventive marketing effort. Because products designed for the global marketplace must now be aware of and sensitive to many fashion cultures, they lie in the midrange, where many such cultures

20. Building a brand name and then managing it carefully to preserve the exclusivity that commands high prices is probably the only sure route to consistently high returns. However, not all brands are moneymakers, even for LVMH and PPR. Attracting a top designer or designers to design collections that are then displayed in the major centers in Europe and East Asia would be a major plus. This success would need to be backed by the production skills that guarantee the highest quality. Exclusive brands also find it necessary to maintain their own stores in the most fashionable districts of the major cities—even if they operate at a loss. In addition, they must link up with the upscale retail chains, provide additional outlets, and sell and advertise globally through a variety of carefully selected media. They must also maintain a full range of accessories and perfumes to generate adequate revenues—because apparel alone is rarely sufficient—and frequently refresh the various lines being offered to keep in step with the faster tempo of the fashion world.

now intersect. Standing out in this crowded space calls for a carefully cultivated distinctiveness; a sensitivity to the variations in preferences across markets that call for adjustments in size, in colors, and in subtle customization; and tens of millions of dollars of marketing.[21] Even this care is not proof against pirating and imitation, which is the bane of the fashion industry and forces firms to frequently change designs, aside from plowing millions into innovation and legal protection.[22] All these concerns are major hurdles for newcomers.

Several facets of globalization are not advantageous for a new entrant trying to secure a beachhead in the market for fashion products, but others broaden the range of opportunities. First, globalization has immensely increased the scale of the market. Global value chains assist sellers in finding markets for their goods, in finding suppliers of inputs, and in integrating products. In the fashion garment and jewelry businesses, Thailand enjoys the advantages of the latecomer to a globalized world economy in which the infrastructure of mass marketing is already in place. The many channels, including e-marketing, that are now available permit producers to sell in bulk or to exploit the potential of the "long tail" by selling only a few hundred differentiated items. As Cowen (2002, 16) puts it, "Partial homogenization often creates the conditions necessary for diversity to flower at the micro-level." International retail chains such as H&M and Zara provide a potential outlet for promising new designers and established names as they seek to woo the lower budget, fashion- and quality-conscious shoppers in the same way that the online book superstores such as Amazon and Abebooks provide outlets for the small presses ("Good Fit" 2005).

Second, contracting for services from anywhere in the world has become much easier. For instance, if producers in Bangkok need design

21. For example, Coach has found that local research and customer feedback provide valuable leads that enhance sales. For instance, bags sold in Japan need to be smaller than ones aimed at the U.S. markets. The latter also need to have more pockets ("Handbag Invasion" 2003). A brand needs to be able to capture a market through various means, both traditional and nontraditional. Securing pages in fashion and beauty magazines can be very costly, but such magazines reach a large audience. *Cosmopolitan*, the fashion magazine that has the largest circulation in the United States, sells almost 3 million copies; a full-page ad can cost as much as US$175,900. High-end brands not uncommonly have several two-page spreads in a single issue. Fashion brands are estimated to spend as much as 10 percent of total revenue on advertising alone. Building a fashion brand requires promotion, although trendy brands sometimes initiate interest in their products by trying to create some buzz about their products, which may or may not work.

22. The FBI estimates that up to US$250 billion a year is lost to counterfeiting in the United States, and clothing and footwear companies in Europe are estimated to lose about €7.5 billion a year. About 65 percent of the production of counterfeit goods is thought to come from China ("Counterfeiting" 2005).

services or services for constructing garments, they can be purchased from some of the same people who design for leading houses.[23] Local capacity to design no longer needs be a binding constraint, as long as a firm has a good business model that clearly delineates the particular characteristics of designs to be adopted. A Thai firm might add a dash of cultural flavor and use certain kinds of materials to differentiate its products, as the Jim Thompson Thai Silk Company attempts to do.

Third, entry into the fashion midrange is relatively easier, and models exist of companies that have successfully carved out a considerable market share by focusing on affordable ready-to-wear fashion clothing where the designs are frequently refreshed.[24] Chains such as Zara and H&M have clearly signposted the possibilities for others to follow. Each firm has introduced innovations in organization and marketing and has built up the capacity to meet extraordinarily demanding design, production, and delivery schedules.[25] Innovation in these areas would most likely be needed for a Thai firm to enter the world market.

Once deemed inconceivable, the online retailing of high-fashion garments and accessories is now a reality. Web sites such as Net-A-Porter.com, NiemanMarcus.com, and BergdorfGoodman.com do a thriving e-business because they have won the trust of their moneyed and discriminating but time-constrained customers. They have gained this trust by offering the very latest fashion, by providing excellent packaging

23. "The truly successful designer has an instinct for visualizing sharply what is perhaps nebulously and unconsciously desired. Designers exist and work on all levels, not just at the top of the limelight. Most cheap blouses and shoes have been specially designed for the mass market, not copied from high priced versions" (Hollander 1993, 35).

24. Fashion houses normally put out more than one clothing line in order to diversify their clientele. They do couture and also midlevel clothing and prêt-à-porter. Some even target the younger age groups and create clothes for children. Children's wear is a lucrative market for luxury brands in the United Kingdom; it is expected to be worth UK£6.1 billion by 2007, a 26 percent growth, with infant wear being the fastest-growing market segment. The U.S. children's wear market is also growing, but at a slower pace ("Rise of Petite Couture" 2005). Teenagers and young adults are an important market segment because they will be the firm's main customers in 5 to 10 years if the firm has made them familiar with its products and brands.

Men's fashion and couture is slowly starting to become a less marginalized section of the industry, which is typically the domain of tailors and haberdashers. As designers and design houses realize that men's fashion is part of the larger market and can be just as financially rewarding as women's fashion, they now have to reconsider designs and marketing concepts that will appeal beyond the female market and tap into those niche markets that are replete with potential.

25. The Spanish-based Zara is integrated in both retail and production. The entire production process (from design to manufacture) usually takes four to five weeks and rarely restocks old styles as new styles always arrive; H&M, on the other hand, specializes in outsourcing fashion production (Tran 2006).

and delivery, and by agreeing to take back any item that fails to satisfy ("Surfing" 2005). Although the difficulties of creating a thriving business in fashion items should not be minimized, especially for emerging designers, whose materials, sizes, construction, and attention to detail might not be well known to prospective buyers, this new channel is important for prospective Thai fashion houses that are prepared to develop brand image. Net-A-Porter is able to sell anywhere in the world, and sales are being buoyed by strong growth in online shopping in Europe and more recently in the Middle East ("Looking for Luxury" 2005).

Probably the factors that most favor the fashion firms in Thailand's budding creative industries are demographics, urbanization, and economic growth. East Asia is the world's fastest-growing region, and over the next 20 years, the economic center of gravity for the global economy will shift toward Asia. Close to 70 percent of the population will be of working age, and the average age will be below 40 years. With rising incomes and urbanization, an increasing number of households will be able to afford the products of the fashion industry. The passion for name-brand fashion products is particularly noticeable in Japan and now in China, as well as in Southeast Asia and India. Chinese buyers already absorb 5 percent of the luxury goods sold, and between 5 and 20 percent of the revenues of major luxury brands are being derived from China, India, and the Russian Federation ("Rags and Riches" 2004).[26] Clearly, Bangkok is in the right part of the world. Whether it can capitalize on the geographic and economic advantages will depend on a mix of entrepreneurship, innovativeness, and financing, as well as on the building of multimedia marketing services in Bangkok.[27] Currently, in the Southeast Asian region, only Bangkok is in the running, although efforts are under way in both

26. Chinese visitors to Hong Kong (China) were spending an average of HK$5,600 over a three-day visit, and they have strongly buoyed sales of luxury goods ("Chinese Set to Shop" 2004).

27. International exposure will also induce a rethinking of certain cultural and social mores and the devising of appropriate marketing practices for the fashion industry. As an example, a fashion show during Fashion Week 2002 caused a sensation when models—allegedly unintentionally—exposed themselves. The Cultural Surveillance Center gave the organizers a warning, saying that "the incident was not in line with Thai society and norms as a Buddhist country," instead of subjecting them to criminal charges ("Thailand Raps *Elle*" 2003). Showing skin is all too common in fashion shows and fashion shoots, whether by accident or by design. Conservative Thais have rejected the notion that they must be more open-minded about revealing clothes if they want to succeed as a major fashion hub. Subjecting the design industry to censorship could easily limit the range of styles that can be shown and constrain the creativity of designers. Many Thais who hew to conservative traditions and cultural mores may not be ready for change, in which case Thai designers operating from Bangkok may find it less easy to cater to a global clientele.

Singapore and Hong Kong (China) to build a fashion industry. Farther to the west, many Indian designers are testing Western markets. Arguably, Thai firms and designers have a window of opportunity they can exploit. In doing so, they will need to harness talent from around the region, and in this respect Bangkok's ambience and lifestyle offer many attractions.

If those attractions can be enhanced, the kind of creative workers who are responsible for the development of a fashion industry will flock to the city. Likewise, Bangkok-based firms need to build the metropolitan innovation system of universities, research institutes, and design houses to support continuous technological change. The media and publishing business need to be strengthened to buttress the fashion sector. Technical assistance from leading designers, such as Armani and Lagerfeld, and their endorsement of Thai fashion could boost the industry. And firms will have to make effective use of the global value chains that are behind the spread of the fashion industry and provide the logistical and marketing sinews.

The Bangkok Fashion Fair is a means of stimulating the local fashion industry and of bringing local designers into the global limelight. The big retail chains, which are increasingly on the lookout for alternatives to the standard labels, have a growing appetite for such talent and buyers. Taking Bangkok fashion on the road and displaying Thai designs at other fairs, as was done in Milan in 2004, provide additional exposure. These high-profile fashion events and smaller shows by individual designers provide an opportunity to display fine-stitched apparel different from other offerings. They also allow Thai designers to learn about international business models and develop contacts. But such events are pricey, and designers need to be able to raise the funding to display their offerings abroad.

None of the major creative industries offer easy pickings for newcomers. Each requires a marshalling of talent, business acumen, finance, technologies, and production skills. And each presupposes the willingness to market globally and considerable staying power. The rewards are large, however, and the alternatives for the apparel, jewelry, and accessories industries in Bangkok are fairly bleak. The Bangkok industries confront intense competitive pressure from China and India, which are able to match quality and have substantial price advantages. They also confront potential pressure from designers in Singapore and the Republic of Korea, who have their eyes on the same markets.

CHAPTER 8

SCULPTING THE URBAN SKYLINE

Shanghai—with Guangzhou—is the birthplace of the modern manufacturing industry in China. Starting in the late 19th century, cotton and silk textile factories fed by raw materials from farms in Jiangsu province were established in the Suzhou Creek area. Other light industries followed. Although the industry was badly scarred by the wars that gripped China from 1937 onward and was decimated by the emigration of many of the leading mill owners in 1948 and 1949 to Hong Kong (China), it rebounded in the 1950s. Along with light manufacturing, the new government also invested in machinery and metallurgical industries. By the time China's open-door policy was cautiously initiated in 1979, Shanghai had acquired the broadest industrial base of any city in the country and, in particular, was the leading producer of textiles as well as key household durables such as bicycles and sewing machines.

Twenty-five years later, although 50 percent of Shanghai's gross domestic product (GDP) is derived from manufacturing, the entire industrial system is being reshaped. Much of the textile industry has moved into neighboring provinces or the interior parts of the country. Dominating the industrial sector now are production of chemical feedstocks and fibers in the Caojing Park, where both BASF and Bayer have located their new plants; automobile production in the Anting district; steelmaking in Baoshan; shipbuilding in a huge facility being constructed on Changxing Island; information technology–related and biotechnology industries in the Zhangjian High-Tech Park in Pudong, and in Qingpu, and Songjiang; engineering and the production of auto parts and instruments in Jiading; and a mix of high-tech production by companies such as Ricoh, Bosch, Lucent, and Siemens in the Waigaoqiao area, with its deep-water port at the eastern edge of the municipality. The vast industrial system that generates nearly US$45 billion in gross products is still evolving, but Shanghai's planners recognize that manufacturing has passed its

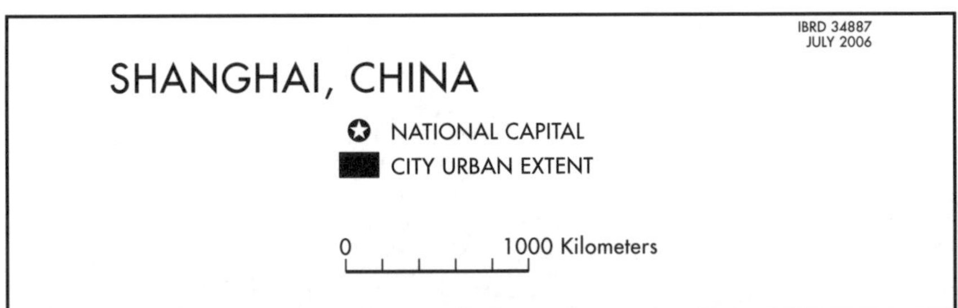
IBRD 34887
JULY 2006
SHANGHAI, CHINA
NATIONAL CAPITAL
CITY URBAN EXTENT
0
1000 Kilometers
105°
120°
135°
45°
30°
15°
RUSSIAN FEDERATION
MONGOLIA
Beijing
DEM. PEOPLE'S REP. OF KOREA
REP. OF KOREA
Yellow Sea
JAPAN
CHINA
Shanghai
East China Sea
VIETNAM
LAO P.D.R.
THAILAND
Philippine Sea
PHILIPPINES

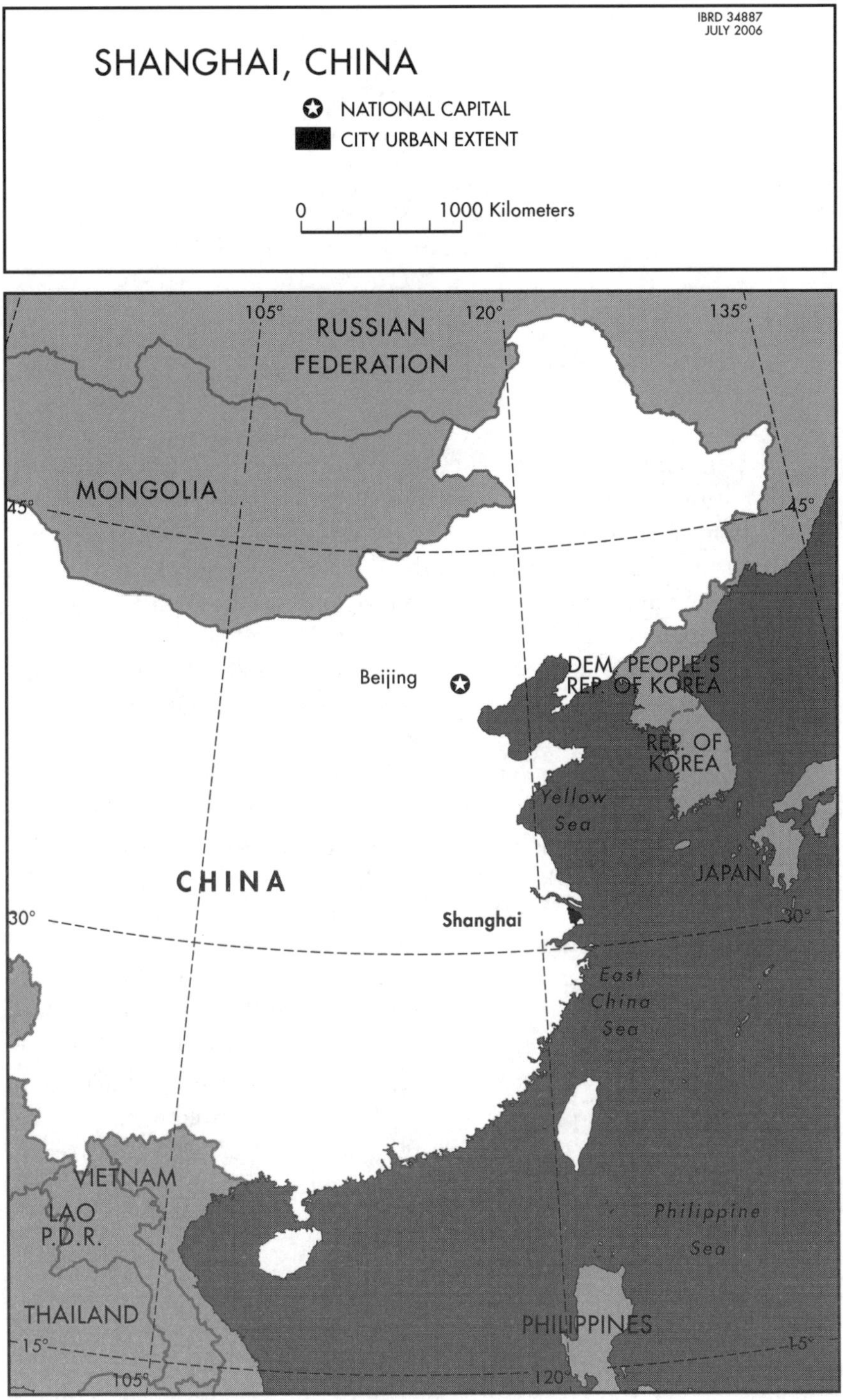

high-water mark and that other producers will follow Intel and Durex to lower-cost locations in places such as Chengdu. In fact, the authorities project a steep reduction in the share of manufacturing to 10 to 15 percent of GDP. Those projections assume an enormous increase in the contribution of services to output and employment.

WHY CONSTRUCTION?

Much of the discussion of the future development of the services sector has focused on finance, insurance, accounting, and consulting services, and Shanghai has attracted many global financial institutions such as Citibank, Standard Chartered, Bank of America, and HSBC (Wei, Leung, and Luo 2006). Financial and legal services are the top-tier business services that account for an important slice of the GDP of London and New York, as well as Hong Kong (China), Singapore, and Tokyo. But in an integrated global economy, those are not necessarily the producer services with the highest growth prospects or the services that will be employing many people in postindustrial cities. On the contrary, organizational and technological trends favor a consolidation of financial, accounting, and legal services in a few large firms headquartered in a small number of metropolitan areas from which they serve a worldwide clientele. Moreover, innovation is promoting the commodification of many financial services, and digital technology has slowed the growth in jobs even as it induces the outsourcing of routinized financial back-office activities, engineering services, software production, and even some retail operations.

We conjecture that other producer services will be occupying the center stage in postindustrial Shanghai alongside finance and accounting. Among them, the architectural design, engineering, construction, and real estate industries will arguably play a leading role. The logistics sector, which is linked to construction, will be of equal importance. This group of activities has, in Shanghai, the potential to contribute the highest growth rate, the most jobs, and a substantial percentage of metropolitan GDP through localized delivery of services and exports to other parts of China as well as abroad. Already the construction and real estate industries combined account for more than 12 percent of Shanghai's GDP[1] as against 10 percent for financial services, and globally the construction business

1. Construction is China's fourth largest industry, with a 7 percent share of the GDP in 2004 ("Brick by Brick" 2005).

has a turnover of well over US$3 trillion.[2] The industry expanded rapidly after 1990, with the average growth rates of 23, 16, and 14 percent for the 1990–95, 1995–2000, and 2000–03 periods, respectively.[3] There are at least five reasons why its share could expand.[4]

First, there is the huge volume of investment in urban infrastructure and in intercity transportation facilities that will be required over the coming decades as a large chunk of the Chinese population that is currently classified as rural—57 percent—enters the urban world. The geography of migrant streams in China and the experience of other industrial economies suggest that the migrants from the rural areas will prefer living in coastal cities,[5] which means that intensive construction activities in the expanding metropolitan areas and along the transportation arteries will continue far into the future. The growth rate of the homebuilding market in China was 18.7 percent in the period from 2000 to 2004, although this rate is expected to decline to 9.2 percent from 2004 to 2009 (Datamonitor 2005d). The urban face of China and the spatial distribution of the population as we know it today will change beyond all recognition, and the construction industry will intermediate this transformation.[6]

We foresee a second factor at work that will contribute a further surge of activity entailing large inputs from the design, engineering,[7] and materials industries.[8] Chinese cities, as well as cities outside of China, are being rebuilt and expanded with little thought given to residential quality, energy efficiency, the consequences of rampant water use, and the implications of a warming climate subject to extreme swings in the weather that could impinge, for instance, on the available supplies of water and on the susceptibility of some coastal areas to typhoons. The numerous high-rise buildings and residential complexes that dot the

2. The upward revision of the national accounts in 2005 suggests that the share of real estate might be significantly higher in Shanghai as well.

3. These are simple average annual growth rates calculated from the *Shanghai Statistical Yearbook* (Shanghai Municipal Statistical Bureau 2004) and the *China Construction Yearbook* (Ministry of Construction 2003).

4. According to the Shanghai Statistical Bureau, Shanghai invested Y 88.6 billion in urban infrastructure in 2004, a 31.7 percent increase from 2003 (Shanghai Municipal Statistical Bureau 2005).

5. According to China's 2000 census, the coastal provinces received close to 60 percent of interprovincial migration flow (Fan 2004).

6. Most of the leading Chinese cities have undergone one round of changes since the mid-1980s, but a second and more extensive round is now under way.

7. China accounts for 18 percent of the engineering market in Asia (Datamonitor 2005c).

8. China consumed 54 percent of the global concrete output in 2004 (Datamonitor 2005f).

metropolitan area are being constructed with scant attention paid to cultural and recreational amenities, green spaces, the requirements of a leisure-oriented population that in the future will be appreciably older on average, and an urban environment that is both safe and more user friendly. Neither the urban infrastructure inherited from the pre-1980s nor much of the development since is likely to be viewed as satisfactory by urban dwellers a couple of decades in the future, and especially so in China's most advanced and affluent cities such as Shanghai.[9] Hence, we anticipate a major redesign of the city and its partial reconstruction to create a more thoughtfully planned urban space that is culturally more vibrant, apart from being better suited to the conditions and demographics of the future—what one author describes as "slow cities in a fast world" (Knox 2005).[10] Thus the pell-mell construction of the past decade could well lead to echo effects in Shanghai and other cities that will sustain the tempo of construction.

The industrial restructuring of the city to increase the share of technology-intensive industries, to relocate the shipbuilding and port facilities along the Huangpu River, and to make Shanghai into a major regional logistics hub will be a third source of long-term demand for construction services frequently of a specialized nature. Electronics and biotech firms require customized facilities that call for a high level of expertise, and the products' short life cycles presage steady demand, as long as the industries remain in the Shanghai area. The continuing exodus of old engineering and shipbuilding enterprises and of the docking facilities from the Huangpu riverfront frees up prime land for other uses, thereby opening up opportunities for creative mixed-use urban developments comparable to those planned for London and those implemented in Tokyo and in Baltimore, Maryland, for example. Furthermore, the ambitious 50-berth Yangshan port project, the ongoing expansion of Pudong International Airport, and the associated transport infrastructure all point to the intensive construction activity extending well into the future.

9. Two recent books that describe the physical and architectural evolution of Shanghai during the past century are Denison and Ren (2006) and Rowe and Kuan (2004).

10. A good example is Xintiandi, a two-hectare complex of restaurants, bars, and shops in an open low-rise style built along narrow alleys. The developer for this US$170 million project was Shui On Holdings Ltd. from Hong Kong (China), with architects from Wood + Zapata, based in Boston, Massachusetts ("Building the Country" 2005). That complex is a part of the Taipingqiao redevelopment project, with luxury apartments and commercial centers that are adjacent to Xintiandi ("Remaking Shanghai" 2004).

A fourth reason that construction has all the makings of a leading sector is that it is rich in links and can become a driver of technological change. Already almost 20 percent of China's GDP is absorbed by construction and real estate. That percentage is likely to be sustained, with a significant part of the finance and insurance sectors remaining keyed to the fortunes of the construction industry and its affiliated activities. Backward links from construction reach into a host of manufacturing industries extending from cement and glass to ceramics, air-conditioning equipment, and construction machinery. Forward links are equally numerous, affecting the appliance, furniture, ceramics, and textile furnishings industries, to name only a few. The real estate sector is a huge employer, contributing vitally to the development, sale, leasing, and maintenance of properties. The engineering design and materials wings of the construction sector give rise to a host of technological advances in the use of computerized techniques in designing more cost-efficient structures, in making buildings more energy and water efficient, and in helping to introduce prefabricated modules. Other advances in construction methods are stimulating innovation in materials to enhance aesthetic appeal, reduce costs, and raise the quality of construction as well as the functionality of structures. In short, design, engineering, and construction trigger technological advances across a wide spectrum of industries, and the accruing gains in efficiency can make a major contribution to the growth of total factor productivity. Viewed from that perspective, the construction sector, in its totality, is technologically one of the most dynamic industries and is potentially a core competence for the Shanghai metropolitan area.

Shanghai's comparative advantage in construction activities is buttressed by its geographic location in the Yangtze Delta. That location enables China's leading industrial city to bid for the diverse, extensive, and long-term construction requirements in the Yangtze Valley region, which, in addition, guarantee stable demand, offer plenty of scope for learning by doing, and provide opportunities to experiment with new technologies. The comparative advantage also derives from the broad base of manufacturing industries in the metropolitan area and in the near vicinity of Shanghai that "internalize" most of the linkage effects. That comparative advantage could also be enduringly supported by the supply of skills from local universities, the technological inputs from research facilities, and the accumulating expertise of local developers and project contractors. A deepening of the core competence in the vital area of producer services would further support a range of industries and services in the metropolitan area and would give Shanghai-based firms the skills to design and build the kinds of cities that will be better tailored to China's emerging requirements.

There remains a fifth reason for focusing on construction services in Shanghai. That multifaceted sector generates numerous and varied jobs, many of which are relatively well paid, and it is hospitable to firms of all sizes.[11] In 2003, there were more than 2,000 firms in the construction industry. As we noted in chapter 1, postindustrial cities face widening income disparities as manufacturing migrates to other locations, taking away midrange blue- and white-collar jobs. With a large construction industry, however, a metropolitan area is assured a secure base of employment for highly paid architects and engineers as well as for skilled craftspeople engaged in the building trades, an army of real estate agents, employees of manufacturing firms servicing the building industry, and the unskilled or semiskilled workers who toil on construction sites. In Japan, for example, close to half a million firms are engaged in the construction industry, and one in seven members of the workforce are some way linked to the construction sector, which still absorbs 15 percent of total investment. Similarly, in the United States, the construction industry employs 7.2 million workers,[12] three-fifths working in small companies with fewer than 20 employees. The fortunes of the construction industry are a good barometer of the health of the U.S. economy, with housing starts serving as one of the most closely followed indicators. Architecture and engineering services are among the three leading producer services and are one of the key industries in world cities such as New York.

THE CONSTRUCTION INDUSTRY IN SHANGHAI

The role of the construction industry in Shanghai needs to be viewed against the backdrop of the city's phenomenal transformation since the early 1990s. Economic growth has averaged between 10 and 14 percent

11. The world's construction materials market is fragmented, with the top five firms accounting for only 13.3 percent of the global market share. Consolidation is likely in the future, especially as many firms are trying to diversify from their current dependence on the U.S. market (Datamonitor 2005f). Some construction materials firms have invested in China already. The French company Saint-Gobain, which ranked 106th in the Fortune 500 for 2005, invested US$27 million in building a glass-fiber factory in Yixin, the pottery city that is located in Jiangsu province and that has plenty of raw materials and a skilled local workforce. (http://www.aaart.com.cn/cn/news/show.asp?news_id=11605). Similar fragmentation is also present in the construction and engineering sector. No firm has more than 5 percent of the market share in Asia. Most leading firms in Asia are large Japanese firms, such as Kajima, Taisei, Shimizu, and Obayashi (Datamonitor 2005a).

12. That figure includes both full-time and part-time workers.

Table 8.1 Infrastructure in Shanghai at a Glance, 1990 and 2004

Type of infrastructure	1990	2004
Road area (square meters per capita)	2.28	12.3
Rail transit (kilometers)	0	125[a]
Living area (square meters per capita)	6.6	14.2
Green area (square meters per capita)	1.02	10.0
Wastewater treatment rate (%)	0	65.3

Source: Gao 2005.

a. Data are for 2003.

per year since 1995, driven by investment in infrastructure and industry. This growth has not only rejuvenated the manufacturing sector but also stimulated a boom in services and, almost as a footnote, created an impressive new skyline ("China: Leading City" 2005). In 1990, the road area was only 2.28 square meters per capita, public green areas were a mere 1.0 square meter per capita, and living area was just 6.6 square meters per capita (Gao 2005). By 2004, those numbers had risen to 12.3, 10.0, and 14.2 square meters, respectively (see table 8.1). In 2004, Shanghai added 330 million square meters of housing ("Architecture Watchdog" 2005), and it has 34 million square meters of office space.[13] The city has 4,000 skyscrapers (twice the number in New York) and plans to add 1,000 more by the end of this decade ("China Builds Its Dreams" 2005). A major expansion of the road network and the completion of two ring roads, six bridges over the Huangpu River, and two tunnels and a subway network of 310 miles add breathtaking detail to the city's achievement and reflect the extraordinary prowess of the construction sector.

As an aside, it is worth noting that the magnetic levitation train from Pudong International Airport to the Puxi area, is the world's fastest train;[14] that the longest underwater pedestrian tunnel runs under the Huangpu River; that the Jinmao Tower in Pudong houses a Hyatt hotel with the highest elevation of any hotel in the world; and that local companies built all these structures ("Building the Country" 2005).

13. The data for office space are from 2003 (Shanghai Municipal Statistical Bureau 2004). Between 1990 and 1997, Shanghai added 8.3 million square meters of office space. Considering that it took Hong Kong (China) 20 years—from 1976 to 1996—to create 5.8 million square meters of office space, the pace of development in Shanghai is quite high (Zhu 2002).

14. It is also the first commercial maglev train in operation (Cho 2004).

Because the construction industry, broadly defined, accounts for well more than one-tenth of Shanghai's GDP[15] and is a major employer, the performance of that industry will have a large effect on labor productivity and the pace of growth in the city.[16] In 2004, Shanghai spent Y 67.3 billion on building highways, bridges, government offices, and parks and other amenities ("China: Leading City" 2005).[17] In addition, because infrastructure is long-lived, it will also influence appearance, livability, and efficiency. Not only is the construction industry itself very large, but as noted above, it is linked to numerous other industries, including the production of steel and other materials, the production of electric goods, and the financial and insurance services.

It is clear from the experience of more advanced countries that the sophistication of the construction industry will have a lasting effect on the environment. China faces a number of environmental challenges. Many of them deserve to be tackled early on, especially through buildings that have a life extending over several decades. Putting in the right kind of structures now will enable Shanghai to minimize energy costs that are trending upward. In the United States, for example, buildings account for 65 percent of electricity consumption, 36 percent of total energy use, and 30 percent of greenhouse gas emission ("Rise of the Green" 2004).

The ongoing boom in the construction business is a good time and place for the domestic industry to acquire the necessary capabilities through learning by doing and, at the same time, give companies the opportunities to experiment with new methods and innovative materials.[18] By encouraging those activities, the construction sector can become one of most efficient and innovative industries in Shanghai.

A STATISTICAL PROFILE

Commercial and residential construction has brought into an existence a burgeoning real estate industry across China and notably in Shanghai, which accounts for about 2,600 firms, or 8 percent of the total number of

15. When the real estate sector is included, construction can account for as much as 20 percent of Shanghai's GDP ("China: Leading City" 2005).

16. Shanghai has remained the top place in China in terms of labor productivity in construction industry since 2002 (National Bureau of Statistics of China 2005). The latest figure is Y 28,769 in 2004.

17. That money is in addition to the more than Y 300 billion invested in infrastructure in the 1990s (Wei, Leung, and Luo 2006).

18. The homebuilding market in China is the largest in Asia, with a 40 percent share of the construction market. It is followed by Japan, with 36 percent (Datamonitor 2005b).

Table 8.2 Composition of Real Estate Firms in China, 2002

Location	All firms	Domestic firms	State-owned firms	Collectively owned firms	Firms from Hong Kong (China), Macao (China), and Taiwan (China)	Foreign firms
China						
Number of firms	32,618	28,657	5,015	2,488	2,884	1,077
Percentage of total firms	100.0	87.9	15.4	7.6	8.8	3.3
Shanghai						
Number of firms	2,588	2,308	420	184	197	83
Percentage of total firms	100.0	89.2	16.2	7.1	7.6	3.2
Percentage of firms in Shanghai	7.9	8.1	8.4	7.4	6.8	7.7

Source: Ministry of Construction 2003.

firms in China (see table 8.2). Shanghai is second only to Guangdong, which has 3,806 firms, or 12 percent of the total number of firms. Furthermore, the sector's dynamism in Shanghai has been enhanced by the increasing proportion of non-state-owned firms, which include 280 firms from outside mainland China, representing 11 percent of the total. Of these firms, 70 percent are from Hong Kong (China), Macao (China), and Taiwan (China).

By 2002, employment in the real estate industry had risen to 79,392, 7 percent of the national employment in this sector. As can be seen from table 8.3, relatively more people were employed by foreign firms and firms from Hong Kong (China), Macao (China), and Taiwan (China).

The bulk of the investment completed in 2002 was in housing units (see table 8.4). Relative to other cities in China, Shanghai has a disproportionate share of the real estate investment in single family homes and luxury condominiums, reflecting the higher incomes of the average family. The average cost of housing in Shanghai is also close to twice the national average, costing Y 2,137 per square meter in Shanghai as opposed to only Y 1,184 per square meter in China on average. The strong demand for housing and the higher quality of the units constructed make Shanghai a highly profitable place for the real estate industry (see table 8.5).

Although the majority of Shanghai-based construction firms are mainly active in the metropolitan area only, some firms operate in other cities also.

Table 8.3 Composition of Real Estate Employees, 2002

Location	Total	Domestic firms	State-owned firms	Collectively owned firms	Firms from Hong Kong (China), Macao (China), and Taiwan (China)	Foreign firms
China						
Number of employees	1,134,009	1,014,254	208,722	89,739	85,449	34,306
Percentage of total employees	100.0	89.4	18.4	7.9	7.5	3.0
Shanghai						
Number of employees	79,392	65,991	13,590	4,090	8,355	5,046
Percentage of total employees	100.0	83.1	17.1	5.2	10.5	6.4
Shanghai's share of total employees in China (%)	7.0	6.5	6.5	4.6	9.8	14.7
Average number of employees per establishment	30.7	28.6	32.4	22.2	42.4	60.8

Source: Ministry of Construction 2003.

For instance, the Shanghai Construction Group worked on the National Theater in Beijing, along with some foreign contractors (Tuchman, Reina, and Kemp 2004). A small number of Chinese contractors are active abroad. In 2000, exports of foreign economic cooperation (FEC) businesses, which cover contract engineering, labor services, and design consultation, amounted to US$9.3 billion, by far the largest service exports of China (see table 8.6). By the end of 2001, the central government had issued FEC business licenses to about 2,000 Chinese contractors to stimulate the export of construction services (Chen and Mohamed 2002).[19]

Close to 50 Chinese construction firms are listed among the top 225 international contractors, and 12 design firms have risen to the ranks of

19. China is following the lead of construction firms from the Republic of Korea. Since the first foray into the international market by Hyundai in 1965, Korean construction firms have been active in construction works globally, especially in the Middle East. Those international activities greatly expanded the market for Korean firms. For instance, Hyundai's contract for Jubail port in Saudi Arabia was worth 25 percent of Korea's national budget in 1976. Without those activities, Korean firms would have faced a much smaller market, limiting the scope for their growth.

Table 8.4 Investment by Building Types, 2002

Location	Completed investment	Houses	Single-family houses and luxury condos	Economic housing	Office buildings	Business commercial building	Other
China							
Amount of investment (US$ billion)	94.1	63.1	6.2	7.1	4.6	11.3	15.1
Percentage of total types	100.0	67.1	6.6	7.6	4.9	12.0	16.0
Shanghai							
Amount of investment (US$ billion)	9.04	6.86	0.96	—	0.40	0.75	1.03
Percentage of total types	100.0	75.8	10.6	—	4.5	8.3	11.4
Percentage of investment in Shanghai	9.6	10.9	15.4	—	8.8	6.7	6.8

Source: Ministry of Construction 2003.

Note: — = not available.

Table 8.5 Revenue of Real Estate Firms, 2002

Location	Total business	Land transfers	Merchandise housing sales	Housing rents	Other revenue	Business taxes and other affiliated fees	Business profit
China							
Revenue (US$ billion)	85.5	2.7	74.2	1.7	6.8	4.5	3.1
Percentage of total revenue	100.0	3.2	86.8	2.0	7.9	5.2	3.6
Shanghai							
Revenue (US$ billion)	16.1	0.7	12.4	0.7	2.3	0.8	1.1
Percentage of total revenue	100.0	4.6	77.0	4.2	14.3	4.7	6.7
Percentage of revenue in Shanghai	18.8	27.1	16.7	38.2	33.7	16.9	35.3

Source: Ministry of Construction 2003.

Table 8.6 China's Export of Construction Services, 2000

Market	Revenue (US$ billion)	Share (%)
Asia	6.74	72.2
Africa	1.29	13.8
Europe	0.54	5.8
America	0.60	6.4
Oceania	0.17	1.8
Total	9.34	100.0
Share of gross output of construction industry		6.19
Share of service exports		82.47

Sources: Chen and Mohamed 2002; National Bureau of Statistics of China 2002.

the top 200 international designers.[20] Among the leading Chinese international contractors, two are located in Shanghai.[21] Compared with the construction industry in other countries, Chinese firms are on average smaller, and the degree of domestic market concentration is low. The exception is Shanghai, where the market is dominated by large firms such as the Shanghai Construction Group,[22] which comprises 300 affiliates and has a turnover of Y 26 billion. The Shanghai Construction Group, the Shanghai Urban Construction Group, and the Shanghai Baosteel Engineering and Construction Corporation were ranked the 6th, 16th, and 60th largest contractors in China, respectively ("Top Chinese Contractors" 2006). If the experience from other countries is a guide, then consolidation of the industry may be needed to scale up the size of these firms sufficiently. Here Shanghai-based firms could take a lead and establish a nationwide presence.

Engineering and Architectural Services

The engineering and architectural services sector can be broken down into three components: (a) planning and architecture design, (b) construction engineering, and (c) project management and execution. Foreign

20. The ranking of international contractors and designers is based only on international contracts expressed in U.S. million dollars in 2003. The global ranking is based on both international and domestic contracts.

21. The lists of top-ranking firms in 2004 were obtained from the *Engineering News-Record*, http://www.enr.com.

22. The main line of business of those firms is to provide construction and engineering services as well as advisory services, manufacturing of equipment, and material (Datamonitor 2005d).

firms tend to contribute most significantly to the first and third components, generally by way of joint ventures with local design bureaus and construction companies. The division of labor between foreign and domestic firms arises from differences in their capabilities.[23] Foreign firms have more experience and capabilities in integrated planning and design,[24] whereas domestic firms have the engineering talent to do the detailed design and construction engineering and are also much more familiar with the local regulations and building codes.[25] Usually a domestic firm charges a design fee equal to about 0.5 percent of the total project cost, whereas a foreign firm typically charges about 3 percent and even higher for more complicated and highly visible projects.[26] The price differentials reflect the levels of services provided by those firms. Foreign firms are usually superior to the domestic firms in the quality of their designs and their attention to functional details. Domestic firms tend to ignore such features, which cost more time and money. Therefore, in the construction market, domestic firms usually are responsible for the bulk of the middle- to low-tier building projects, and foreign firms generally are involved with upper-tier building projects. Many of the most conspicuous high-rise buildings in Shanghai were designed or developed by foreign firms—as well as those from Hong Kong (China)—in partnership with Chinese firms. Those foreign firms tend to draw on their relationships with global architectural and design firms and harness talent from around the world.

There are five Shanghai-based design firms that are highly rated by *Engineering News-Record*: Shanghai Xian Dai Architectural Design (Group) Co., Ltd. (rated 3rd); SINOPEC Shanghai Engineering Company Limited (rated 15th); Shanghai Municipal Engineering Design Institute (rated 19th); Shanghai Urban Construction Design and Research Institute (rated 45th); and the Shanghai Investigation, Design, and Research Institute (rated 59th) ("Top Chinese Design Firms" 2006).

---

23. In China, most medium-size and large design firms (those with a staff of 1,000 or more) are state owned. The management and operation style of those firms is rooted in the old planning system. To raise the efficiency of those firms, the government is encouraging partnerships with foreign firms, which could help change management style and organizational structure.

24. Foreign firms tend to have better knowledge of technology not only in the areas that they are immediately involved in but also in the other areas that may be relevant to construction of a building. Identification of new technologies and integration of such technologies on a project basis are complex and complicated tasks. The technological hurdle seems to be much higher now with the need to overlay older technologies with newer ones (Gann and Slater 2000).

25. The involvement of foreign firms at the initial stage is used as a marketing tool for real estate developers, reflecting the consumer preference for foreign products.

26. See http://house.sina.com.cn/n/s/2002-12-02/16668.html.

The Shanghai Xian Dai Architectural Design (Group) Co., Ltd., was established in 1998 through a merger of the East China Architectural Design and Research Institute and Shanghai Institute of Architectural Design and Research. It has more than 20 subsidiaries and employs one-third of Shanghai's licensed architects and structural engineers. It has completed more than 30,000 design or consulting projects, which include participation in some iconic buildings in Shanghai such as the Shanghai TV Tower, Jin Mao Building, Shanghai Grand Theatre, Shanghai Stadium, and Shanghai Pudong Airport.[27] In addition, some emerging private design firms set up by famous Chinese architects are trying to compete with the big design institutes. For example, Ma Qingyuan, an architect educated at the University of Pennsylvania, established the firm Ma Design and Associates in Shanghai in 1999.

Another area in which foreign firms excel is in the development of communities. In a city like Shanghai, residents now want more than just living space. They are demanding various amenities in the buildings and the surrounding areas. Many real estate developers are taking note of those preferences and offering such communities ample amenities, which were neglected in the past. For example, buildings are being situated along bodies of water, near a fountain, and between small, human-made forests. Western architectural styles and cultural nuances are attractive to the upper income groups in particular.

Luxury community development—*jin guan*—is a trend that is gaining ground in Shanghai. The recently released rankings of Shanghai's Top 10 Luxury Residential Buildings and its Top 10 Commercial Buildings reflect the mounting competition among builders, and there is pressure to construct buildings of a higher quality.

Typically, a real estate development company will establish a project company for each development project so as to minimize financial and other risks. For residential development, the project company will be disbanded once the construction is finished. For commercial properties, the companies generally remain to manage the leasing of buildings. The business of long-term management of residential and commercial properties is still in its infancy in China, and there is considerable scope for expansion of and improvement in services provided. It is sure to remain a growth industry for some time.

Such is the strength of demand in the Shanghai housing market that Shanghai-based community design firms are the biggest employers of

27. This information comes from the company's Web site, http://www.xd-ad.com.cn/.

Table 8.7 Capital Sources for Real Estate Firms, 2002

Location	Total	Funding within national budgeting	Domestic loan	Bonds	Foreign capital	Foreign direct investment	Self-provided funding	Other[a]
China								
Capital (US$ billion)	117.75	0.14	26.82	0.03	1.90	1.50	33.07	55.80
Percentage of total capital source	100.00	0.12	22.77	0.02	1.61	1.27	28.09	47.38
Shanghai								
Capital (US$ billion)	12.18	0	2.75	0	0.39	0.26	3.24	5.80
Percentage of total capital source	100.00	0	22.57	0	3.22	2.13	26.61	47.60
Share of Shanghai (%)	10.3	0	1.0	0	20.7	17.3	9.8	10.4

Source: Ministry of Construction 2003.

a. Other includes investments by other firms.

architectural designers, providing jobs for 60 percent of recent recruits.[28] Design firms from Europe, Hong Kong (China), Japan, and the United States are especially active. They are looking for employees who can assimilate their design ideas, are familiar with computer-based designing, have good aesthetic judgment, and have a couple years of local experience in the details of designing. There are few such people in Shanghai today, but the numbers are growing with experience.

Large domestic firms, such as the East China Architecture Design and Research Institute, are involved in the development of residential and general commercial buildings. Some of the large state-owned contractors have their own architectural and design division; others—especially smaller businesses—contract with specialized architectural firms. The big state-owned enterprises also are engaged in the manufacture of materials (Chen and Mohamed 2002).

Financing

Nationwide, firms in the real estate sector procure finance from a variety of sources (see table 8.7). Close to half of the funding takes the form of

28. See http://www.aaart.com.cn/news/show.asp?news_id=11443.

Table 8.8 Foreign Construction and Real Estate Developers in Shanghai, 1996–2000

Year	Total number of developers	Total number of foreign developers and developers outside mainland China	Number of developers from Hong Kong (China), Macao (China), and Taiwan (China)	Percentage of developers from Hong Kong (China), Macao (China), and Taiwan (China) among foreign developers
1996	2,030	256	93	36.3
1997	2,398	264	129	48.9
1998	2,601	307	206	67.1
1999	2,595	301	208	69.1
2000	2,549	285	201	70.5

Source: Zhu, Sim, and Zhang 2006.

investment by other firms and investors. Another 30 percent of the financing comes from the cash flow of the firm. About 18 percent is made of loans from banks, whereas foreign direct investment (FDI) accounts for the balance of about 2 percent. At this stage, firms do not rely on bond issues to raise necessary funding. As table 8.7 shows, Shanghai-based firms adhere to a pattern of financing that closely resembles the national average, although they rely more on FDI than firms elsewhere in China.

Involvement of Foreign Firms

In 2000, of the 285 foreign firms (and other firms outside mainland China) that were engaged in the construction and real estate business in Shanghai, 70 percent were from Hong Kong (China), Macao (China), and Taiwan (China) (see table 8.8). These firms have a vital role in the transfer of technology and tacit knowledge. Such firms—especially those from Hong Kong (China)—are involved in the planning and development of the more upscale real estate projects (Zhu, Sim, and Zhang 2006).[29] For example, 76 percent of the office space in Jiang'an and 91 percent in Huaihai was

29. The comparative advantage of firms from Hong Kong (China) in those areas arises because such firms are not at the forefront technologically. Many developers from Hong Kong (China) do not use prefabricated construction materials even though they can greatly reduce costs and increase the quality of the resulting building. In addition, such firms do not invest much in research and development, whereas Japanese construction firms spend 3 percent of their revenues on research and development each year (Chinag and Tang 2003).

developed by firms from Hong Kong (China) (Zhu, Sim, and Zhang 2006), whereas 74 percent of the office space in Lujiazui in Pudong was built by local developers, many of them state-owned enterprises.

Before China's accession to the World Trade Organization, many foreign design and engineering firms operated within China on a project-by-project basis. Following accession in November 2003 and the subsequent steps to liberalize the construction industry, expectations among foreign firms were running high on the prospects of expanding their operations in China because wholly owned foreign subsidiaries are to be allowed for the first time in the construction industry (Tuchman 2003). However, the so-called liberalization, which was implemented well ahead of schedule, has imposed high capitalization requirements (up to US$1 billion in capital is required for a US$5 billion project by foreign firms); has required foreign firms to hire 300 technical and managerial personnel if they are constructing a class I building; has resulted in the repeal of laws that had earlier qualified foreign engineering and construction firms; and has imposed certification requiring experience in China only and not globally, effectively making the sector more restrictive than ever before ("Brick by Brick" 2005; Walton 2004).[30] Those requirements plus the opacity of the tendering process and the long delays in finalizing contracts could slow the entry of foreign firms as well as technology diffusion. More likely, given the attraction of the Shanghai market, the conditions will further pressure foreign companies to seek local partners and impart the technology that the locals are seeking.

Links with Other Industries

The rapid growth of construction activity in China is translating into a surging demand for heavy machinery. The sale of wheel- and track-type hydraulic excavators in China exceeded 55,000 units in 2005. By comparison, in 2003, 26,000 units were sold in North America and 66,000 units in Europe (Hampton 2004). That vast demand has brought the major international producers to China, where they have, for the most part, entered into joint ventures with Chinese companies. The Chinese domestic market is currently dominated by firms from the Republic of Korea and Japan. The top two firms, Daewoo and Hyundai, held 20.3 and

30. The Regulation on Management of Foreign-Invested Urban Planning Service Enterprises allows joint venture and wholly foreign-owned investment in urban planning, but it limits foreign investment in "microlevel urban planning" without adequately defining what constitutes microlevel urban planning as opposed to comprehensive urban planning (Walton 2004).

20.0 percent, respectively, of the market share in 2003, while Komatsu and Hitachi held 16.7 and 15.0 percent, respectively. Together those firms accounted for three-fourths of the market in hydraulic excavators in China (Hampton 2004).[31] Caterpillar also has about 10 subsidiaries in China in partnership with local construction equipment companies. In 1995, Caterpillar entered into a partnership agreement with Xuzhou Engineering Equipment Group Inc., China's largest construction equipment supplier. Caterpillar also introduced the heavy construction equipment rental business, which is a new procurement and finance trend in China's construction industry (Datamonitor 2005e).[32]

The growth of construction and FDI is drawing more Chinese firms, judging by the increased participation in trade shows (Hampton 2004). An important new manufacturing sector is on the march. The links from construction activities extend to a number of other high value added items as well, all produced within the Shanghai municipality. Baoshan Steel, by expanding its capacity and adding new products lines, is now able to meet most of the construction industry's requirements for steel structures. Schindler, the world's largest producer of elevators and escalators, has been induced to operate the world's largest escalator manufacturing factory in Shanghai, and Carrier, a leading supplier of air-conditioning equipment, uses Shanghai as a base for production and research. Some of the leading manufacturers of glass, ceramic products, and tile are also distributed around the metropolitan region and in nearby cities, with both Toto and American Standard meeting the needs of Shanghai builders. All of those enterprises are extending Shanghai's industrial base in directions that will be increasingly valuable down the road because their products are technology and design intensive and the local value added is high.

Links with Universities and Other Tertiary Institutes

Since the early 1990s, the construction industry has been strengthening its links with universities. Local universities supplied the engineers, architects, designers, and managers, whose energy and effort have changed the face of Shanghai. Although the state-owned construction firms have been downsizing since 1990, they still employ more than 11,000 engineers and

31. Caterpillar had 12.2 percent of the market (Hampton 2004).

32. See http://china.cat.com, http://News.chinabyte.com/253/2114253.shtml, and http://www.quote123.com/usmkt/FinanceNews_Special.asp?ClassID=5&SubID=56689&TableName=NewsHeadline.

Table 8.9 Share of Engineers and Technicians in State-Owned Construction Enterprises, 1990–2003

Types of employees	1990	1995	2000	2003
Total employees	210,300	176,600	77,400	61,900
Engineers and technicians	15,600	20,400	14,000	11,500
Percentage of total employees	7.4	11.6	18.1	18.6

Source: Ministry of Construction 2003.

technicians, and the share of those skilled workers employed by firms is increasing over time (see table 8.9).

That link is now being supplemented by other links with research in universities and in institutes in Shanghai and elsewhere. The Institute of Research on Construction at Jiaotong University is one instance, but there are others as well, such as the Civil Engineering and Architectural Design Institute of Tongji University,[33] where research on materials, design, and construction techniques is beginning. The Civil Engineering and Architecture Design Institute employs 661 professionals, including 98 architects and more than 200 engineers, who can provide services ranging from intelligent building design to bridge engineering, geotechnical investigation, landscaping, and ancient monument restoration and protection. It earned US$71.4 million in 2004.

The promotion of faculty members at Tongji University is tied to outside experience. Many staff members will leave academia for a few years, work for construction firms to gain practical experience, and then return to the university, sometimes in professional positions. Such experience is indispensable in creating the networks that strongly influence the effectiveness of their research. The flow between academia and firms resembles

33. The integrated setting of the Civil Engineering and Architectural Design Institute, with about 10,000 square meters of floor space, permits all technical work to be completed in-house, including detailed drawings using the most advanced computer-aided design systems. The institute was founded in 1958 as the Architectural Design and Research Institute. In March 2001, Tongji University merged the Architectural Design and Research Institute of Tongji University and the Shanghai-Tongji Planning and Architectural Design and Research Institute to form the new Civil Engineering and Architecture and Design Institute of Tongji University. Tongji University became the main shareholder by equity transfer. The ranking of the institute in the General Appraisal of Shanghai Exploration and Design Units rose from sixth position in 2000, to fifth in 2001, and to third in 2002. The Civil Engineering and Architectural and Design Institute is accredited with several class A design certificates issued by the State Ministry of Construction for China. Its design products include office buildings, education buildings, hotel and health buildings, sports facilities buildings, residential buildings, planning and urban design, and protected and converted buildings.

the circulation of talent between Stanford University and the firms based in Silicon Valley.

Labs from the Civil Engineering School and the College of Architecture and Urban Planning at Tongji University actively engage in small commercial and public projects. The labs are typically headed by one or two professors, and their networking skills are critical for securing those contracts. The university encourages commercial involvement of faculty members because the lab and the university share the revenue from such contracts. On the demand side, many firms are willing to contract with those labs because the labs are relatively inexpensive and can provide the requisite expertise. Tongji University owns 20 companies, of which 7 are in the construction industry. The university also has equity shares in other companies—mainly limited liability companies. Tongji University's sister institution, Shanghai Jiaotong University, also owns construction firms. One of them is Shanghai Jiaotong Engineering Construction Ltd., which was established in 1993 with Y 5 million in registered capital. It is funded by both the Shanghai Jiaotong University and the China International Construction Company of the State Ministry of Construction of China. This company provides construction consulting services rather than construction services. It has grown 20 percent every year in the past decade. Of the 600 projects that the company has engaged in, more than 30 percent were important public projects and foreign-funded projects.[34]

Inevitably, research and innovation have not been a priority in the rush to build. However, as the industry has begun to mature and become more conscious of energy efficiency, for example, interest in innovation has started to stir. This budding interest is reflected in the activities at Tongji and Jiaotong Universities. Until recently, universities also were neglecting project management, but that too is changing.

INNOVATION IN THE CONSTRUCTION INDUSTRY

There is a wide scope for innovation in all parts of the construction and real estate sectors, but as long as competitive pressures, market demand for improved quality, and government regulations were weak, technological change was slow to occur. Nevertheless, even in this environment, innovation is occurring in many areas.

34. See the Shanghai Jiaotong University Web site, http://www.sjtu.edu.cn/.

New Materials

The construction of the Jinmao Tower, the TV tower, the Science Museum, the maglev track, and the various bridges has introduced builders to the most complex technologies for laying foundations, pumping concrete to great heights, assembling large steel frames, and installing the plumbing and electrical work for huge structures. Still to come—and the time may be approaching—is the greater use of plastics, a construction material whose reliability has been proven in Europe and North America. Although that technology has been available for a long time, civil engineers around the world have only recently felt comfortable in using plastics to construct bridges. The benefits of the technology are manifold. First is the low maintenance requirement. The life expectancy of bridges built with plastics can be as long as 60 years without major rehabilitation, compared with 10 to 20 years for concrete and steel bridges. Moreover, unlike concrete and steel, plastics do not suffer from corrosion, frost, mold, and damage from insects.[35] A bridge can be constructed from recycled plastics such as the one in New Jersey ("Bridge Too Far?" 2005). Other materials can also be recycled. Constructors find that, in some cases, recycled paper and fabrics provide more effective insulation than traditional insulation ("Rise of the Green Building" 2004). Even concrete can now be made from recycled waste. For instance, 45 percent of the concrete that will be used for the One Bryant Park building in New York will come from leftover waste generated from iron processing, thereby preventing the release of about 50,000 tons of carbon dioxide, which would have been discharged had the building been constructed with new concrete ("54-Story Air Filter" 2005).[36]

The use of the Internet has added an extra dimension to innovation in the construction sector. A computer-integrated project management system can streamline project operations and increase the efficiency of managing complex production systems, which can involve hundreds of subcontractors of various types (Gann and Slater 2000).

35. The InfraCore Bridge, by the Coposieten Team in Rotterdam, Netherlands, offers a simplified way of building bridges—bridges that are made of plastics and are standardized so that ordering is rather simple. The bridges are customized to customer's preference. The customer chooses the size, the color, and options such as handrails, and the bridges can be delivered within a week ("Bridge Too Far?" 2005).

36. Technology related to concrete is also growing. Sensors can now measure the temperature of curing concrete, accurately gauging the maturity level. That ability has led to a two-day reduction in concrete production ("What's Next" 2004).

"Smart," "Green" Buildings

Looking forward, we see that some of the biggest challenges for the engineering and construction industry will be to ensure that the structures and practices adopted are flexible enough to accommodate advances in information technology (IT) and to observe environmental and energy standards. Most new buildings and structures are being designed to be IT ready, with built-in space for telephone lines, broadband connections, and a variety of sensors.

The drive for greater energy efficiency in buildings is not new. The Crystal Palace in London, which was built for a great exhibition in 1851, and the Galleria Vittorio Emanuele II in Milan, which was built in 1877, both used a roof ventilation system and underground air-cooling chambers to regulate the temperature inside ("Rise of the Green Building" 2004). Modern buildings use similar principles. For instance, the One Bryant Park building in New York will use an air ventilation system located on the eighth floor to produce fresh air, which will be filtered to remove dust and other particles, and will use groundwater to regulate the inside temperature ("54-Story Air Filter" 2005).

Although building codes clearly specify energy-efficiency requirements, only 5 percent of office and residential buildings meet the minimum energy-conservation standards in China ("Wasteful Ways" 2005).[37] Since 2001, Chinese cities have enacted new building standards that aim for 50 percent less energy use per square foot, but enforcement remains weak, as does the integration of environmental management techniques in construction ("Wasteful Ways" 2005).[38] Reducing energy consumption of a building by 50 percent is feasible with better designs and the use of advanced technology, as was demonstrated, for example, by the Swiss Re Tower in London ("Rise of the Green Building" 2004). As another example, the Conde Nast Building in London uses special glass to allow all but ultraviolet light to pass through.[39] A gas turbine fuel cell powers the

37. China's Ministry of Construction is in talks with the U.S. Green Building Council to develop a rating system similar to the one used in the United States (Gonchar 2004).

38. Shanghai promulgated its own construction energy saving plans in 2005, but implementation has been slow. The plan for energy saving released in May 2006 set the target to reduce the energy consumption as a coefficient of GDP by 20 percent and to reduce energy consumption in the construction industry by 15 percent during the 11th five-year plan ("Shanghai's Energy-Saving Policies" 2006).

39. By allowing only visible light to come through, the glass helps to keep the temperature warm during the winter and prevents rooms from becoming too warm during the summer. Many new buildings are now adopting those kinds of windows ("54-Story Air Filter" 2005). New kinds of glass will also minimize the adhesion of dust and dirt, cutting down on the costs of exterior cleaning.

building at night, and the exhaust from the fuel cell is used to heat the building and the water used. Solar panels on the roof provide additional power, and motion sensors regulate the use of fans and lights. By incorporating those and other technologies, designers and engineers were able to reduce energy consumption by 30 to 40 percent compared with similar buildings without those technologies.

Buildings can save on energy through clever design and the use of new materials, as well as the use of power generators. The blueprint for the Freedom Tower in New York includes 25 wind turbines to generate electricity, in addition to solar panels to produce about 1 megawatt of power, enough to supply 20 percent of the projected power requirement ("Energy Answer" 2004; "Rise of the Green Building" 2004).[40] The One Bryant Park building in New York will compost wastes generated on site to make methane or biodiesel fuel. Those fuels will feed the power generator ("54-Story Air Filter" 2005).

A survey of green buildings in the United States reveals that by adopting green technologies, building owners were able to reduce the energy consumption by 30 percent on average. The costs of complying with those standards typically adds only 2 percent to construction costs, so that the marginal increase in the cost of building can be recouped from lower running costs within a few years, especially when energy prices are high ("Rise of the Green Building" 2004). For the One Bryant Park building, a comparatively ambitious effort, construction costs will increase by 6.5 percent, but the building is actually expected to save about US$3 million in energy costs and is projected to generate US$7 million through increased productivity. If those assumptions are realized, the additional costs of incorporating green technologies would be paid off in seven years ("54-Story Air Filter" 2005).[41]

The adoption of green technology and alternative construction materials have benefited from the shift in the selection process of construction options and incentive policies.[42] In the past, the initial building cost was the main consideration. Now, the emphasis is more on the total cost of ownership, including maintenance and energy costs ("Science and

---

40. One Bryant Park in New York also will feature a wind turbine for electricity ("54-Story Air Filter" 2005).

41. By using 200 waterless (and odorless) urinals in the One Bryant Park building, the building owner can save an estimated 40,000 gallons of water a year ("54-Story Air Filter" 2005). The building also features rainwater collection facilities. Water collected that way will be treated and then used for toilets and watering of plants.

42. On these policies and barriers to the adoption of new technologies, see Zerkin (2006).

Technology: Composites" 2005). That emphasis has encouraged the further integration of smart building technologies, even though the initial construction costs may be higher. The effective incorporation of plants and trees into the interior space has been shown in Frankfurt, Germany, to enhance comfort, air quality, and health benefits for workers.

Shanghai is receiving help from Hamburg, its sister city in Germany. Pujiang Intelligence Valley is an industrial park consisting solely of research and development and office facilities in an ecological surrounding in Minhang district. The office buildings use various energy-efficient technologies, such as wall activation, geothermal heat and cold, insulation, ventilation technologies, and sunshading technologies designed by Dittert & Reumschüssel (of Hamburg and Hannover) in cooperation with MUDI (Munich Urban Design International). The project is scheduled to be finished in August 2006. There are also a number of the projects that are still at the stage of conceptual design.[43]

The only problem is that much more planning and coordination is needed to construct a green building than a traditional building ("Rise of the Green Building" 2004).[44] The need for such close coordination among designers, engineers, and contractors increases the advantages arising from agglomeration of an industry in a locale. Once such an agglomeration is achieved and firms can lock in the gains from design, planning, and project management, competitors will find that the lead position is hard to challenge. Now is the window of opportunity for the construction industry in Shanghai to quickly establish its position as a leading city regionally, if not globally.

CURRENT STATUS AND PROGNOSIS

What is the future of the construction industry in Shanghai? Clearly, the past decade has provided an auspicious start (table 8.10), and as we have argued, there is much building and rebuilding in store in the metropolitan areas in the Yangtze Valley basin and across China. Many of the supplies and services providers for the construction projects in Shanghai are located in the metropolitan region or in neighboring cities so that within

43. This information comes from http://www.green-shanghai.com/eng/projects.html.

44. There are software packages to simulate the energy and water usage based on shape, heating and cooling systems, orientation to the sun, and geographic locations with three-dimensional modeling ("Rise of the Green Building" 2004).

Table 8.10 Output of the Construction Industry in Shanghai and China, 1990–2003

	1990	1995	2000	2002	2003
Construction industry value added					
China (US$ billion)	179.8	457.4	711.1	846.0	988.1
Shanghai (US$ billion)	7.5	13.3	25.0	30.4	32.0
Share (%)	4.2	2.9	3.5	3.6	3.2
Construction industry growth rate					
China (%)	1.2	12.4	5.7	8.8	12.1
Shanghai (%)	5.1	25.0	3.0	6.4	1.3
Number of construction firms[a]					
China	13,327.0	24,133.0	47,518.0	47,820.0	48,688.0
Shanghai	360.0	682.0	1,586.0	1,679.0	2,009.0
Share (%)	2.7	2.8	3.3	3.5	4.1
Total construction industry employment					
China (thousands)	10,107	14,979	19,943	22,452	24,143
Shanghai (thousands)	340	411	359	420	505
Share (%)	3.4	2.7	1.8	1.9	2.1
Gross output value of construction industry					
China (US$ billion)	281.4	693.9	1,509.4	2,237.6	2,787.9
Shanghai (US$ billion)	15.8	46.9	76.3	99.3	144.4
Share (%)	5.6	6.8	5.1	4.4	5.2
Real estate industry value added[b]					
China (US$ billion)	—	126.8	204.2	253.4	—
Shanghai (US$ billion)	0.8	10.9	30.4	45.1	56.0
Share (%)	—	8.6	14.9	17.8	—
Real estate industry growth rate					
China (%)	—	—	7.1	9.9	—
Shanghai (%)	—	—	—	14.5	14.1
Total investment in real estate development in Shanghai					
Total investment in real estate development (US$ billion)	1.7	55.8	68.4	90.4	108.8
FDI in real estate development (US$ billion)	n.a.	4.2	2.0	2.6	2.1
FDI ratio in total real estate investment (US$ billion)	n.a.	7.5	2.9	2.9	1.9
Construction and real estate value added					
China (US$ billion)	—	584.2	915.3	1,099.4	—
Shanghai (US$ billion)	8.3	24.2	55.4	75.5	88.0
Share (%)	—	4.1	6.1	6.9	—
Exchange rate used (US$1 to yuan)	4.78	8.35	8.28	8.28	8.28

Sources: National Bureau of Statistics of China 2004; Shanghai Municipal Statistical Bureau various years.

Note: — = not available.

a. Because the construction industry is counted as a part of the secondary industry, the real estate industry is usually excluded from this total.

b. The real estate industry is counted as a part of the tertiary industry.

a 100-mile radius, there now exists a cluster that is approaching self-sufficiency in everything from research in materials to air-conditioning equipment. Some types of construction machinery, exterior decoration for buildings, and electrical controls for building utilities are still imported, but little by little, FDI or licensing by domestic producers is bringing those products to the industrial belt around Shanghai. The soft infrastructure of construction regulations and codes has also been taking shape along with modest progress in developing the machinery of enforcement.

The construction industry is vast but is not yet close to its potential productivity, and it is far from being innovative. Still, the scope for achievement is enormous. The hundreds of cranes in the Yangtze Valley demarcate the biggest and the most ambitious construction site in the world, with the most diverse assortment of projects, which have links extending in many directions. At least through the end of the decade, both the manufacturing activities and the services that feed the construction sector are likely to remain and possibly even expand. Further down the road, Shanghai's ability to hold on to the key elements of the construction sector will be a function of selective specialization in the most skill- and knowledge-intensive parts of the construction business. Other parts of the business will most likely move to locations where the production costs are lower.

Currently, Shanghai produces some of the more capital- and skill-intensive products consumed by the construction industry—for example, iron and steel products, heating and cooling equipment, and elevators and escalators. There is little reason to expect the manufacture of such products to move elsewhere. Shanghai has substantial capacity in the areas of architectural design and engineering, but world-class capability is lacking, and those two activities remain fairly compartmentalized. By and large, both design and engineering practices are conservative, structures are overengineered, and—except for the occasional exterior flourish ("the big roof") with respect to high-rise buildings—Chinese architects and engineers hew to well-established and proven techniques. Because labor is cheap, construction methods tend to be immensely labor intensive, even when mechanical equipment is available, which detracts from the quality of the finish, especially with the run-of-the-mill construction. Low wages of engineers also mean that some activities, such as physical modeling of structures, are far more common. There is plenty of room here for upgrading architectural techniques and engineering practices and, through greater interaction, bringing those services close to the state of the art in the most advanced countries. Such deepening in capability is entirely feasible given the ready supply of local skills, the increasing involvement of foreign firms, and the reflux of Chinese trained abroad, all of which are contributing to the diffusion of the latest technologies. Moreover, the entry of many small new architectural and engineering firms is sure to stimulate experimentation and adventurousness in design.

In five areas, however, Shanghai's construction and architectural design lags, and unless remedied, that delay could constrain the competitiveness of the sector, possibly within China and certainly in a future race to win overseas business.

First, Rowe (2005, 17) observes that "rising expectations with regard to building quality, material integrity, and technological performance, as well as similarities in building programmes that substantially transcend in both size and scope traditional ways of building, have led inexorably to a sameness in contemporary built environments throughout the world, save perhaps, for superficial decoration and adornment of structures to suit the tastes, or to conform to expressive norms of a local culture." He (154) goes on to note that, "unlike many cities in Europe, where there is a constant display or palette of urban architecture on offer from other eras, a far less well-conserved and reused residue remains in most East Asian cities" (154). Rowe (144) finds that "Most problematic is the lack of any deeply felt cultural connection between the sign of past tradition and the reality of contemporary modern practice." This tendency is most apparent in China, although it pervades the region. Rowe ascribes it to the "wholesale appropriation and then combining of styles borrowed from abroad." He (34) believes that this practice is responsible for, "the jarring outlandish, downright ugly, or 'over the top' aspect to parts of the urban landscape" in some Chinese cities. Shanghai has its share of outlandish buildings as well as drab and utilitarian ones. Certainly there is much catching up to do in architectural design and in harmonization with urban design to convey some distinct cultural overtones. One observer has remarked that wholesale demolition and rebuilding as practiced in Shanghai is not good for design, "especially if what is replacing it is a bad idea" ("Brick by Brick" 2005, 53).

Second, the more complex projects require close attention to overall project management and systems integration in the interests of efficiency, safety, cost-effectiveness, and timely completion. In the case of China, the emphasis is on meeting deadlines, and in fact, a surprising number of projects are completed on or ahead of schedule. However, cost-efficiency, quality of installation and finish, and safety are sacrificed. The weakness of local expertise in that regard has created opportunities for foreign firms that can define a process from the inception of the project through design and completion and can ensure that all the individual pieces come together when they should. Foreign firms are transferring crucial project-management technologies, safety standards, and craftsmanship. However, unlike with manufacturing techniques, software and tacit knowledge diffuse gradually, and China needs to fill an entire missing generation of project managers and systems integrators. Although there is no dearth of raw talent, moving along the learning curve might take time because integration skills take a while to soak in and foreign firms are in no hurry to share the tacit knowledge, which is the key to their competitiveness.

Third, construction of a project must frequently be complemented by subsequent management of the complete structure for short or long periods. That management calls for different sets of skills if the emphasis is on ensuring quality of services, building customer relationships, acquiring a reputation, and adopting a long-term business perspective. In any strong construction and real estate sector, there is a need for a number of major firms that serve as pacesetters and help to establish industrywide norms and standards to which other firms can adhere to a greater or lesser extent. Such firms have yet to emerge in Shanghai.[45]

The fourth area is the state of financing for construction activities. Shanghai has mobilized huge sums for its infrastructure and housing development, and significant strides have been made in mortgage finance in less than a decade. But too much of the financing of long-lived projects is still sourced from banks, municipal budgets, or informal sources. The intertwining of construction and finance is such that the two sectors need to evolve in step. Thus, the growth and sophistication of bond markets and other term finance markets that support the construction sector will be part and parcel of the maturation of the construction industry. That development should be easily within Shanghai's reach. However, the experiences of China's neighbors suggest that financial deepening, even in a globalizing world, is paced by institutional and cultural changes, which are always gradual.

Fifth, there is innovation abetted by research and development. Innovation covers the gamut of construction-related activities, from design to lending. But the salience of energy-, environment-, and IT-related issues means that some of the most significant gains associated with long-lived and increasingly wired structures are going to accrue from innovations in those areas. Advances in materials development and in the design of structures and their effective assimilation by the industry promise continuing

45. Raising quality standards and acquiring the capacity to assess risk are also areas in which the bigger firms could take a lead (Hoenig 2004).

improvements in productivity, resource conservation, structural characteristics, quality, and project completion times. The older stock of housing and commercial space in China is notoriously energy inefficient. That failing has been only partially remedied in newer structures. Energy losses remain huge, and over the lifetime of a building, they compound China's energy burdens. Shanghai has the opportunity to take a lead in this area by instituting more stringent design standards and codes, by backing them with credible enforcement, by encouraging the use of new materials, and by giving developers incentives to incorporate technologies that use passive methods of heating and cooling as well as renewable energy sources, as long as these methods pass the test of cost-efficiency.

With IT soaking into virtually every corner of urban life, especially in major cities such as Shanghai, the construction industry needs to take full advantage of the new avenues it opens and move quickly to establish standards that permit widespread use across a variety of processes (Chun and others 2004). Moreover, buildings and other structures must be designed to take full advantage, where appropriate, of new digital and telecommunications technologies. Because those technologies are bound to evolve and enlarge their potential to make structures "smarter," current designs need to be flexible enough to allow new wirings and sensors and equipment to be incorporated. As noted in chapter 5, anticipated advances in robotics will gradually change the nature of urban spaces indoors and outdoors, making them more user friendly, interactive, amenity intensive, and safer. In the race to develop, many of the structures being constructed in Shanghai lack that flexibility and down the road may need to be expensively retrofitted or demolished and replaced. Such waste can be avoided, and structures can be designed from the onset to anticipate and accommodate energy-saving, IT, and robotics features that will enhance their utility and prolong their useful life.

Throughout the industrial world and by slow degrees in China, IT through the Internet has begun making inroads into the trading of products at the wholesale and retail levels. Thus, for certain products and services, the bidding for contracts, invoicing, payment, and fulfillment of contracts can be done online. That operation of e-business and the setting up of marketing portals are delivering gains in efficiency that contribute to the price competitiveness of markets while easing the entry of firms. The construction industry is a natural candidate for e-business, and some progress has been made in Europe and the United States, but relatively little in China thus far, even in areas such as project design and the purchase of materials. By taking a lead, firms in Shanghai could steal a march over others.

The scope of innovation in the construction sector is wide because so many different technological advances can be folded in. Thus, the smart building or the smart transportation system[46] or the safe environment rich in amenities will depend on research spanning many disciplines among which materials, robotics, electronics, and IT would rank as the leading contenders. The link between research and the construction industry has yet to be explored and exploited in Shanghai. That link is rich in possibilities, and down the road it could ensure that Shanghai is able to field a clutch of new high-tech construction-related activities commanding global markets. Such advances may require a push from the authorities through the setting and progressive raising of standards and support for experimental technologies. It will also depend on enduring alliances among developers, producers, and researchers to extend the frontiers of technology while keeping a close eye on the direction of the emerging wants of urban dwellers.

In postindustrial cities, the quality and resilience of urban spaces and infrastructures in the context of a harsher physical environment will undoubtedly determine a city's standing in the pecking order of global urban centers. Shanghai's engineering and construction industries, allied with other industries in the city and in its dynamic neighborhood, could achieve remarkable outcomes. But there is much ground to be covered before that highly appealing goal can be reached.

46. An efficient and sustainable transportation system will be essential to the livability and energy efficiency of a city. See Goldman and Gorham (2006) and Turton (2006).

CHAPTER 9

GOLD IN SILICON

The electronics industry is the poster child for the new economy that around the turn of the 21st century promised the start of another technological epoch. The promise proved to be exaggerated but not false. The growth of productivity, which had slackened during the 1980s, has accelerated in a number of industrial and industrializing countries. This acceleration has been spearheaded by the adoption of information technology (IT) by the retail, wholesale, and finance industries; however, the manufacture of electronic products has provided a sizable share of the gains achieved. The allure of the new economy has faded; that of electronics remains, and rightly so.

The narrow definition of the subsector covers equipment and components; in 2004, this hardware accounted for US$730 billion in global production, and exports of electronics were valued at US$1.1 trillion. Production and exports grew by 4.0 percent and 4.4 percent, respectively, between 2000 and 2004. East Asia's share in total electronics exports reached 62 percent, with China alone responsible for 15 percent (Datamonitor 2005g, 2006).[1] Electronics hardware is the leading export, by far, of countries such as Malaysia, Singapore, and the Philippines. In China, products in this category accounted for 35 percent of exports (US$208 billion) in 2004, but total production and trade is climbing rapidly, with foreign direct investment (FDI) continually shifting more production capacity to Chinese cities ("Quarterly Chronicle" 2005).[2] Asia's IT sector is projected

---

1. See also WTO Trade Statistics at http://www.wto.org. More than 87 percent of China's 2004 exports of "new and high-technology products" are produced by foreign-invested firms ("China's Challenge" 2005).

2. China is now the largest exporter of consumer electronics and the second largest market after the United States ("Quarterly Chronicle" 2005).

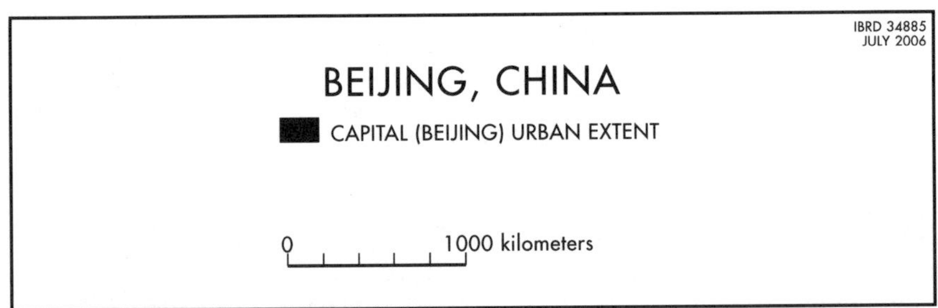
IBRD 34885
JULY 2006
BEIJING, CHINA
CAPITAL (BEIJING) URBAN EXTENT
0
1000 kilometers
RUSSIAN FEDERATION
MONGOLIA
Beijing
DEM. PEOPLE'S REP. OF KOREA
REP. OF KOREA
Yellow Sea
JAPAN
CHINA
East China Sea
VIETNAM
LAO P.D.R.
THAILAND
Philippine Sea
PHILIPPINES
105°
120°
135°
45°
30°
15°

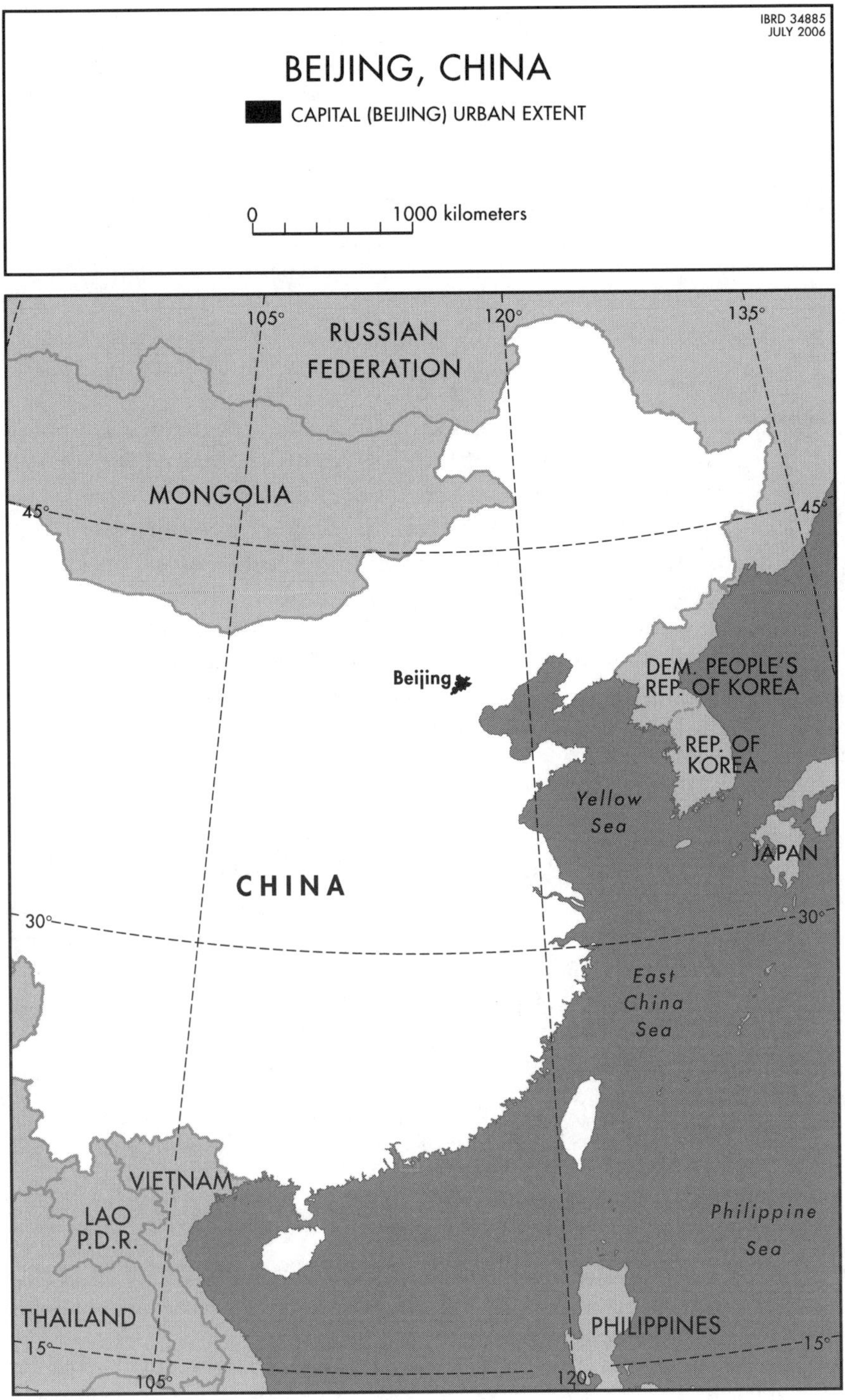

to grow by nearly 9 percent annually through 2009 and account for 2 percent of regional gross domestic product (GDP).[3] This definition focused on manufacturers is increasingly outdated, because electronics is becoming inseparable from various kinds of software, some embedded in equipment, with a variety of associated information services. These new electronics are being joined by an expanding range of multimedia applications and products such as videogames (discussed in chapter 6). Thus, a broadening of the definition to recognize the protean and expanding nature of the industry is clearly warranted.

It is not at all surprising, in view of the salience of this industry and its technology intensity, that Beijing is seeking to become the prime mover of innovation and upstream development in China's electronics and IT industries. The potential for technological advances in electronics and associated IT, biotech, materials, and nanotech industries is vast. Beijing—along with other leading cities such as Guangzhou, Shanghai, Chengdu, Shenzhen, Jinan, Xian, and Shenyang—is investing in a metropolitan innovation system that could maximize the high-value rewards from introducing new products and services, while allowing mass production of commodified products that are based on codified technologies to migrate to other cities. For Beijing, this system may be the only feasible objective. A focus on labor- or land-intensive manufacturing would make little sense, because such manufacturing is a part of the value chain that will gravitate away from urban areas, where wage costs and overhead are lower and water plentiful.[4] The exodus of light manufacturing from Beijing and Shanghai is already well advanced and, although it was initiated by the government, inevitable. By intensifying research and development (R&D), Beijing is pursuing a comparative advantage in innovation, which it hopes will induce multinational corporations (MNCs) to locate their regional research activities in the city, leading to many start-ups as well as to the emergence of globally competitive national companies.

Many cities in Asia are vying for similar roles. Only a small number will be successful on a scale that matters for a metropolitan economy where the population exceeds 5 million. The rest will have to be satisfied with, at best, a few niches that generate modest revenues, little employment, and few spillovers and that do not develop the networked and intersecting

3. These forecasts are based on a study by ICD reported in "America Trails" (2006).

4. Per capita water availability in China is 2,219 cubic meters, only one-fourth of the world average. The water stress is much more severe in northern China, where only 762 cubic meters of water are available per person (Yusuf and Nabeshima 2006a).

clusters spanning multiple industries supported by providers of professional services that have contributed to the growth of urban regions like Silicon Valley and the Boston metro area.

What are the odds in Beijing's favor, and how likely are the nascent subsectors being groomed by the government to flourish and contribute to a long-term growth spiral that is sustained by innovation?

BEIJING'S SILICON CREDENTIALS

Being China's capital city confers great advantages in the national context, because of the government's close involvement in directing industrial change and building an innovation system that will steadily improve technological capability. The Chinese approach closely approximates that of other East Asian economies, in almost all of which industrialization has radiated outward from the capital cities. Governments have been at considerable pains to showcase their industrial prowess by deepening capabilities first in the vicinity of the capital cities, by using the guiding hand of industrial policies and the hidden hand of (managed) market forces.[5] Bangkok, Kuala Lumpur, Seoul, Taipei, and Tokyo are among several notable examples.

China, a relatively late entrant on the East Asian stage and a much larger country than its neighbors, focused industrial reforms initially on the distant southeastern corner of the country—in the Pearl River Delta adjacent to Hong Kong (China)[6]—to test their efficacy. Having determined that the mixed approach to modernizing industry was workable and not disruptive of the political economy, China has applied the new recipe widely, with special attention to Beijing, Shanghai, and a few other major cities. In this approach, Beijing should lead the modernization drive and demonstrate China's gathering strength in key areas of technology, the global yardstick for economic competitiveness. Beijing is also the urban crucible for displaying not only some of the most striking remnants of the old Chinese culture but also the evidence of a new cultural upwelling—an upwelling that could help bolster China's claim to being a cultural pole as

5. The central government decided on Beijing, Guangdong, Jiangsu, and Shanghai, as the national production centers of IT products in 1986 (Wang and Tong 2005).

6. See Yusuf (2005) for a discussion of the factors responsible for the remarkable performance of the Pearl River Delta region since 1979.

well as an industrial one, in a world where "soft power" counts as much if not more than other kinds of power.[7]

The electronics and IT industry neatly supports Beijing's aspirations of becoming a technological powerhouse. It is an industry that has experienced widespread geographic (networked) dispersion following a process of standardization, modularization, vertical specialization, and outsourcing, the proliferation of highly specialized component producers, and diversification into closely linked subfields (Ernst 2002). It is an industry whose growth has been paced by the efficient elaboration of the international supply chain and by rapid advances in the capacity of key components and that has been greatly aided by the rising utility of IT equipment, from an expansion of the base of users, and the resulting networking externalities.

An important characteristic of the industrial dynamic for Beijing is that dispersion is going hand in hand with the concentration of electronics production in a few specialized clusters, with such concentration being especially notable for the most innovative capital- and knowledge-intensive components and software. Electronics and its spreading penumbra of linked IT activities concentrate highly skilled "symbolic workers" and entrepreneurs in the metropolitan area. Their presence can encourage new start-ups while diffusing new technologies to other manufacturing and creative industries and stimulating the cultural life of the city. A richer urban culture would give Beijing the glamour and buzz that cities such as New York, San Francisco, and London have worked hard to cultivate. If there is a mobile and discriminating creative class for whom the world is an oyster, as Florida (2002) persuasively argues, then the electronics industry would be the start of an upward spiral for Beijing. The current base of manufacturing and research could result in a constellation of creative activities, revolving around a core of "anchor firms," universities and science parks.

WHEN IT ALL BEGAN AND HOW

Like much industrial development in China and East Asia during the past three decades, the recent proliferation of electronics and IT firms in Beijing was barely anticipated in the early 1990s. A few large, state-owned

---

7. See Nye (2004) on the concept of soft power and its significance in a globalized environment. Some observers contest whether China is on the road to acquiring such power.

electronics enterprises producing radios, television sets, and other equipment were located in Beijing at the start of the 1980s. The first shoots of a modern electronics industry only began appearing autonomously in the early 1980s, with an initial wave of firms focusing on the software for word processing and printing using Chinese characters. Twenty years ago, there was little awareness of what it takes to create a high-tech cluster and what the implications of such an entity are for urban development.

The tempo of activity began to acquire economic significance in the 1990s. By 1994, the number of IT firms had risen to 4,300. There were several reasons. First, during this period, China's industrial growth accelerated sharply, led by investment and exports—many produced by the consumer electronics industry. As a consequence, the star of the electronics industry began burning brighter. Both domestic and foreign demand for Chinese products perked up. Second, signs that China's vast domestic market might be awakening and the increasing attractiveness of China as a platform for exports both enlarged the flow of FDI, especially into the manufacturing sector. The electronics industry, already a force in several East Asian economies, was viewed as one of the most promising candidates, and it began to attract foreign and local capital. Third, the start of the IT boom contributed to the enthusiasm for the electronics industry and encouraged the central government to redouble its support. Fourth, Silicon Valley was on everyone's mind. As one observer remarked, "Only Silicon Valley was not trying to become like Silicon Valley." Silicon Valley symbolized the IT revolution, and every industrializing or industrial country felt that a desirable economic future required a homegrown miracle in silicon. It soon became evident that silicon appeared to flourish best in a sophisticated and attractive urban locale[8] equipped with a few anchor firms with advanced industrial capability and amply furnished with elite universities, which supply the human capital for the technology-intensive industries that could become the source of commercially viable innovations (Agrawal and Cockburn 2003). Beijing, in the mid-1990s, lacked some of the physical and industrial attributes of a Silicon Valley, but it was endowed with China's leading universities and rich in talent. The central government decided to leverage this talent pool and to grow silicon in Beijing's university belt.

8. However, Hsinchu Park near Taipei is atypical in this respect. It functions very much like an industrial estate. Despite its undoubted success as a high-technology center, the park has not attracted social amenities or contributed to the social infrastructure of its immediate surroundings or to that of Taipei.

China's efforts to build an electronics industry commenced in the 1980s, but the emergence of the subsector in Beijing dates back to the mid-1970s (Sigurdson 2005). It all started with the demand for an electronic publishing system in Chinese. In those days, printing was still done using lead typesetting, which required workers to select each Chinese character manually from a shelf of thousands. Needless to say, this process was—and where it survives still is—highly laborious.[9]

The most advanced technology available at that time was a cathode ray tube (CRT)–based phototypesetting system, developed by the German company Hell. The basic principle was to generate the page layout on the screen of a high-resolution computer monitor, to photograph the onscreen image of the page layout, and then to develop the film for offset printing. The font used to generate the onscreen page layout was stored in the computer memory in dot-matrix format. This process works well for alphabetic languages with a small number of characters, but the technology was stretched to the limit in China because each font required 7,000 Chinese characters. For professional printing, at least four fonts were required, quadrupling the storage requirement in the computer memory to 20 megabytes. Although this requirement seems negligible today, the internal memory of a minicomputer 30 years ago was only 64 kilobytes. Use of other storage devices such as hard drives was rendered impractical by their slow speed and limited storage capacity (Lazonick 2004; Lu and Lazonick 2001).[10]

A junior professor at Beijing University, Wang Xuan, came up with the idea to compress the Chinese characters by relying on their contours and to reproduce the entire character rather than storing the dot-matrix image of the character. This innovation reduced the storage requirement by a factor of several hundred. Research to realize these ideas was approved in 1976 and funded by Program No. 748, which also created the Institute of Computer Science and Technology at Beijing University and germinated an enterprise called Founder (Lu and Lazonick 2001). Because of the complexity of the characters, Wang opted to develop a laser typesetter to record the page layout directly on film (Lu and Lazonick 2001).[11]

9. A similar procedure was used in Japan, and the desire to reduce this tedious drudgery provided the impetus for developing Japanese word processors.

10. The access time of a hard drive is still slow today, relative to that of a memory chip. The seek speed of a hard drive is measured in milliseconds; that of a memory chip is measured in nanoseconds.

11. Such a laser-based system was not widely adopted in the West until 1986 (Lu and Lazonick 2001).

Once the technology was approved for commercial use, it was introduced to the news agencies (which were all state-run) with funding from the state, instantly giving rise to a large market. The key was the raster image processor embedded in a chip. The intellectual property related to this printing system resided with Beijing University; on the basis of it, the University formally spun off the company called Founder in 1993. By 1995, Founder had acquired a 75 percent share of the domestic Chinese electronic publishing systems market.[12] Founder's chip, introduced in 1995, displaced the international heavyweights Hell, Dainippon Screen, Scitex, and Crossfield from the Chinese market (Lazonick 2004).

The success of Founder can be traced to the deliberate policy of the government to make technology development an integral part of postgraduate education. This policy was responsible for a number of innovations by the graduate students of Beijing University's Institute of Computer Science and Technology and for the progressive deepening of the innovation system in Beijing, as well as in other metropolitan areas (Lazonick 2004).

Three other well-known Chinese computer firms that emerged in the 1980s—Stone, Lenovo, and Great Wall—share a similar university-based lineage. Stone was founded in 1984 by alumni of Tsinghua University in Haidian district as a collectively owned enterprise.[13] Stone's first product was a low-cost electronic printer capable of outputting Chinese characters, a task that previously only an imported and expensive Toshiba printer could perform. Stone also reverse-engineered and modified the printers manufactured by Brothers so that they could output Chinese characters. The reengineering was done by two scientists at the Computing Center of the Chinese Academy of Science (CAS) who were moonlighting for Stone. Because Stone was the sole distributor of the machine, it quickly captured the market. Buoyed by the success of its printers, Stone entered the word-processing market, initially in collaboration with Japanese firms. The

12. At that time, foreign computer companies had not yet mastered the problem of Chinese-language word processing. Because the Japanese script shares a number of Chinese characters, Japanese firms would likely have been able to do so in a few years (Lazonick 2004). But Chinese firms seized the opportunities to enter the market and establish a highly recognizable international brand.

13. These founders used to work for government research labs (such as the Chinese Academy of Science) and institutes, as well as in state-owned computer enterprises. They quit their positions to establish Stone, but it was formally owned by Evergreen township, which provided the seed money of Y 20,000 (to be paid back in one year) along with free office space equipped with a phone (Lazonick 2004).

trading company Mitsui was responsible for the design and manufacture of the hardware (although actual manufacturing was outsourced to a contract manufacturer, Alps Electronics of Japan); Stone was responsible for the software development only.[14] Subsequently, Stone entered the electronic cash register market just when the value added tax was introduced, which immediately produced a spike in the demand for such machines (Lazonick 2004).

The second firm, now known globally as Lenovo, was originally called the New Technology Development Company of the Research Institute of Computing Technology of the CAS. It was established in 1984, initially to check and maintain the institute's imported IBM computers and to train the staff. Chuanzhi Liu and the 11 founding members were CAS employees and they remained so (Chen and Kenney 2005; Sigurdson 2005).[15]

The company's first major success was the production and servicing of a computer add-on card (the Hancard) to give an ordinary personal computer (PC) Chinese word-processing capability (Sigurdson 2005). The company also sold motherboards and other computer-related items and established relationships with Motorola and Texas Instruments. Its products were sold under the Legend brand, which is what the company was called until recently. It entered the PC business as a sole distributor of Acer computers with Legend's own Chinese word-processor add-on cards. This position gave Legend a foothold in PC distribution, and in 1988, it decided to enter its own brand into the PC market through a joint venture with a Hong Kong firm that had ample financial resources and international legal expertise. Sales of the Legend computer, introduced in 1990, expanded quickly, backed by highly effective nationwide distribution and service centers throughout China. Legend sold only 2,000 PCs in 1990; by 1995, sales had risen to 100,000. With the proceeds, Legend focused on R&D to strengthen competitiveness with R&D centers in Beijing, Hong Kong (China), Shenzhen, and Silicon Valley. Legend's subsequent success can be traced to the skillful integration of hardware and efficient services. With the creation of the Legend Chinese Word-Processing System Users' Association, the company turned its users into advocates for its products

14. Later, Stone entered a joint venture with Mitsui to develop the next generation of Chinese word processors. Through this joint venture, Stone was able to send its managers and technicians to be trained in Japan (Lazonick 2004).

15. The CAS also provided the seed money of Y 200,000, along with the offices and research facilities (Lazonick 2004).

and valuable sources of feedback for further product development (Lazonick 2004).[16]

Unlike Stone and Lenovo, Great Wall was state owned and state run. From the outset, the other two had broad managerial autonomy, even though they were officially characterized as collectively owned enterprises. Not so at Great Wall. Initially, the enterprise tried to enter into a joint venture with IBM, but that attempt failed. However, during the negotiations with IBM Japan, Great Wall was able to gain an understanding of IBM's structure and mode of operation. Even though IBM's product development was done in-house, production of actual hardware was outsourced to several Japanese manufacturers; IBM retained control over marketing and distribution.

Great Wall emulated this business model and set up a subsidiary enterprise in 1984 with a dozen or so engineers and technicians and seed money of Y 300,000 from the Computer Industry Association's R&D budget. About half the staff members were sent to Hong Kong to learn about high-resolution Chinese font display technology. The other half went to Tokyo to work with IBM Japan on a Chinese word processor. A PC that could display Chinese fonts was introduced in 1985. Following the initial market success with a word processor and a PC, the Computer Industry Association set up another company, Longxing Electronics. Longxing organized production for Great Wall computers by outsourcing assembly to 13 state-owned enterprises, which in turn sourced parts from 10 second-tier suppliers. Longxing also set up a nationwide dealership, which had more than 100 stores by 1987. Initially this original equipment manufacturing arrangement worked well, but the sales of Great Wall PCs slowed significantly in the late 1980s as a result of competition from Stone, Legend, and Founder.

16. The strength of Japanese electronics firms partly depends on the sophisticated user base in Tokyo, which evaluates products and provides valuable feedback to manufacturers on their viability (see chapters 1 and 5; Fujita and Hill 2005). Going one step further, firms can actively engage with consumers in their quest for improvements and innovation. Recent examples of innovations proposed by consumers include prototype telematics for BMW and various add-ons created by users for computer games ("Rise of the Creative Consumer" 2005). Although the active involvement of consumers in product development is not new, the advances in IT and the availability of user-friendly development tools (often provided by the manufacturers) have spurred these activities. Products based on such consumer innovation tend to be more successful than products developed in a traditional way ("Rise of the Creative Consumer" 2005). Three-fourths of traditional product development projects fail. By actively seeking creative consumers to generate ideas, to serve as lead users, and to help develop a community of other users, firms are attempting to focus their research and reduce the cost of development (Franke and Shah 2003; "Rise of the Creative Consumer" 2005).

In 1994, Great Wall entered into a joint venture agreement with IBM. By this time, IBM was willing to partner with Great Wall, having failed to penetrate the domestic Chinese market. IBM saw the arrangement as a way of producing and selling high-end computers in China (Lazonick 2004).

Other firms that emerged during this period included a Chinese start-up, Stone Rich Sight Information Technology Company, which was launched by Wang Zhidong and marketed Chinese-platform software compatible with the Windows environment and Zhongxin Micro Electronic Co., which produced the multimedia "China Chip." (Stone Rich merged with Sinanet.com in Silicon Valley in 1998 to form SINA.com, which became one of the most popular Chinese portal sites.) All of these firms succeeded because of the science and technology (S&T) talent and resources concentrated in Beijing. Without their links with the research institutes, the firms would have lacked the human resources, financial resources, incentives, and general office spaces to begin operations. Equally important was the ability of the scientists and engineers who started these firms to identify the latent consumer demand in the emerging computer industry: the ability to compose and output documents in Chinese.

By the mid-1980s, a few firms were springing up in the Zhongguancun area, a part of the Haidian district, on a stretch of road running from Beijing University to No. 2 Zhongguancun Primary School. As the number of enterprises grew from 11 in 1983 to 90 in 1985, the name Electronic Street gained currency. The small electronics shops and businesses attracted attention because such private entrepreneurial activity was still relatively rare in Beijing. Few saw them as anything more than an epiphenomenon, possibly transient. Still, some reformers sensed the potential of firms such as Founder and Stone and, in keeping with the spirit of that time, were prepared to experiment. Hence, the central government created the Zhongguancun Park in 1988, adjacent to the key universities and research centers—the first of many steps, including the nationwide Torch Program, to bring high-tech industry to Beijing.[17]

17. Funds from the Torch Program were used to support start-ups and larger enterprises including Stone, Lenovo, and Founder. Although the exact effect of the loans is hard to assess, being selected to receive funds from Torch Program acted as a seal of approval, enabling firms to secure funding from other sources (Segal 2003; Sigurdson 2005). A description of the several major research programs launched by the government, such as the "863" and "973" programs, can be found in Sigurdson (2005).

ELECTRONIC ZHONGGUANCUN

Zhongguancun is close to leading universities such as Beijing University, the People's University, and Tsinghua University. In all, there are 58 universities in the area, which together graduated more than one-third of China's college students annually (Hamaguchi and Kameyama 2005).

Zhongguancun High-Tech Zone (ZGC) consists of seven high-tech parks: Haidian Park, Fengtai Park, Changping Park, Dianzi City, Yizhuang Park, Desheng Park, and Jianxiang Park, each of which has its own special function and mix of industries (see table 9.1). The total planned area of the zone is close to 3 million square kilometers, and in 2005, the industry in ZGC accounted for one-sixth of Beijing's GDP (Beijing Municipal Commission of Development and Reform 2006; Xia and others 2004). The majority of the parks are located right in and around the four corners of the fourth-ring road. Future development will focus on building two arms stretching out to the northeast (Changping district and Yanqing county) and northwest (Shunyi district, Huairou district, and Miyun county) (Beijing Municipal Commission of Economics 2005).

The Yizhuang Park, also known as Beijing Economic-Technological Development Area, is the manufacturing base of Beijing and home to several MNCs, including Nokia, Foxconn, and SMC, and to many leading domestic high-tech firms, such as China Aviation, BOE Technology Group Co., and Jin Changke (Beijing Municipal Commission of Development and Reform 2006). The emphasis is on telecommunications, liquid crystal display (LCD) panels, and integrated circuits (ICs).[18]

Nokia and other leading firms in mobile phone business have invested US$1.2 billion since 2001 in the Esoteric Mobile Architecture Plan to build a mobile phone industrial park, which now holds more than 20 cell phone firms (Beijing Municipal Commission of Development and Reform 2006). In addition, Semiconductor Manufacturing International Corporation, a Shanghai-based leading semiconductor foundry in China, plans to invest US$3 billion in two 12-inch IC production lines (Beijing Municipal Commission of Development and Reform 2006). Other major firms include the BOE Technology Group, the largest domestic and the ninth-ranked global thin film transistor LCD manufacturer. This firm acquired the core technology on thin film transistor LCD through the producer, Hynix, a company from the Republic of Korea, for a fee amounting to

18. Silicon Valley owed its beginnings and early momentum to the fruitful nexus established between large corporations such as Lockheed, Hewlett-Packard, and Varian and Stanford University (S. Adams 2005; Lecuyer 2005).

Table 9.1 Industry Distribution in Parks within Zhongguancun

Parks	Industries	Function highlights
Haidian Park	Telecommunication, biotech, optical, mechanical and electronic integration, and new materials industries	High-tech, research and development intensive functions; close to universities and the CAS
Fengtai Park	Optical, mechanical and electronic integration, biomedicine, and advanced manufacture industries	High-tech manufacture functions
Changping Park	New medicine, biotech, environmental protection, telecommunication, new materials, and advanced manufacture industries	Biotech manufacture functions
Dianzi City	Telecommunication, computer software, computer monitor, color display tube, and digital audio and video industries	New technology and high-tech products manufacture functions; reformed from the old industry base
Yizhuang Park	Optical, mechanical and electronic integration, and biomedicine industries	External economy; technology-intensive manufacture functions; national economic technology development district
Desheng Park	High-tech distribution services, high-tech incubator industry, and high-quality technology and industry development services	Upscale, national, well-known high-tech companies and initial public offering companies' research center, sales center, and business center
Jianxiang Park	Technology exhibition, human resources, conferences, marketing, information consulting services	International technology communication, networking, business services, and extended component-based development functions

Source: Xia and others 2004.

US$80 million in 2003. Spearheaded by BOE's efforts on thin film transistor LCD, the cumulative investment of the 16 firms in Yizhuang Park reached US$800 million in 2005 (Beijing Municipal Commission of Development and Reform 2006).[19]

19. The so-called fifth-generation technology that BOE bought is outdated, and the firm's current performance and capacity to upgrade is uncertain.

The individual parks are further subdivided by specialties ranging from the life sciences to agriculture to nanotechnology (see table 9.1). Electronics is prominent across several of the parks, but it rubs shoulders with other industries. In fact, one of the most important characteristics of Zhongguancun that could buttress its long-run success is the diversity of high-tech industries being groomed by the government and the presence in their midst of major anchor firms such as Lenovo, Microsoft, and Nokia.

One lesson that the authorities have drawn from international experience is the cross-disciplinary nature of many innovations, such as the widening contribution of electronics to numerous subsectors, ranging from transportation to health. Hence, it can be a great advantage for producers of electronic products to be next door to firms engaged in developing new materials that can be incorporated into electronic components; to producers of software, which can add value to electronic items through embedded or application software; to biotech firms, which use electronic chips for a host of purposes and contribute to the advance of information technology as well; and to suppliers of producer services, which are major users of electronic hardware as well as application-specific software.

Now that the multifaceted nature of a dynamic electronics industry is more fully perceived than was the case in the 1980s, the planners in Beijing are aiming for an assortment of clusters that derive an innovative focus from electronics and IT. The point to remember about the electronics industry taking shape in Beijing is that, much like biotechnology in Singapore and moviemaking in Seoul, the industry is largely a creature of the central government's industrial policy, as is the Zhongguancun Park. Its fortunes for the time being are wholly tied to a generous regime of industrial incentives, the government's innovation policy, and the efforts under way to "fix" the industry in the Beijing metropolitan area by promoting cultural as well as recreational amenities.

The demonstration effect of the tiny number of pioneering enterprises that started in Zhongguancun 20 years ago attracted a wave of newcomers, whose numbers exceeded 12,000 firms by 2003, employing 48,000 workers. The overwhelming majority of firms are relatively small, with an average of fewer than 10 employees. The large firms, such as Founder, Great Wall, and Lenovo, now being joined by foreign MNCs such as Nokia and IBM, are most directly responsible for the spillovers that have contributed to the proliferation of firms and to Zhongguancun's reputation within China and beyond. They are the equivalents of the Hewlett-Packards, the Fairchilds, and the Lockheeds of Silicon Valley, which provided the lion's share of employment for hundreds of start-ups. Large firms employing more than 500 workers account for 1 percent of the total number of firms but are responsible for 20 percent of the park's turnover. They are the ones that have achieved superior productivity, attained greater profitability, are more innovative on balance, and—because of size as well as demonstrated performance—have found it easier to mobilize resources to finance growth. The larger firms in Zhongguancun, much like similar firms in Europe,[20] also work most closely on technologies with university researchers and very possibly, as in Silicon Valley, will have a decisive influence on future technological capabilities.

Zhongguancun's workforce has impressive academic credentials. Close to 38 percent of workers have a bachelor's degree, and almost 9 percent have a master's degree or a doctorate. Many, if not most, were trained in local universities and have either stayed on to work in local firms or, after a stint at a foreign university, returned to seek their fortunes in Beijing. The chief executive of a start-up firm, which is typically private (*minban* or *minying kejiqiye*), usually has received postgraduate training overseas and may have had some work experience abroad as well.[21] Such chief executives are usually in their thirties.[22] They have returned to the country, often pulled by the generous terms offered by central and municipal authorities, to try to commercialize a research finding or a new licensed technology that is underpinned by a business model that passes muster with the Zhongguancun administration and is sufficiently attractive to mobilize the first round of financing.

Zhongguancun Park offers the new start-up an impressive array of incentives and one-stop administrative and other approvals, which partly—perhaps largely—explains the growth in output and the number of firms. The benefits include tax exemptions, preferential tax rates on corporate income of 15 percent, and tax deductions for R&D expenditures; lower tariff rates on imports of machinery and intermediate inputs; grants to assist companies during the start-up stretch; low-interest bank financing; and assistance with raising money from securities markets at later stages (Segal 2003; Yusuf, Wang, and Nabeshima 2006). In fact, a significant percentage of the grants under the "863" program have been awarded to firms in the park (Sigurdson 2005). Park authorities provide space for

20. See Soete (2006) and Foray (2006) on the Netherlands and Switzerland, respectively.

21. From 1978 to 2003, the government estimates that 700,000 Chinese studied abroad ("We've Got Solid Grounding" 2005).

22. Examples are Zhonghan Deng, the founder of Zhongxin Micro Electronic Co.; Ziping Dong of Keya, a biotech firm; and Jian Zhou of Kesen Technology, an information technology firm.

promising start-ups in one of the incubators or commercial buildings, a form of assistance that is often critical for new businesses, and help with housing as well as access to schooling for families coming back from overseas. Park authorities, recognizing the weaknesses of many new and small enterprises, offer a measure of administrative support to smooth out the many bureaucratic obstacles that dot China's economic landscape. They are a source of information on legal, accounting, financial, consulting, and marketing services. Although most firms do not have much difficulty finding staff from the rich pool of trained workers in the vicinity of the park—another major attraction—the administration can assist firms in finding appropriate human resources and, in some cases, managerial skills. In these respects, the park administration is beginning to fulfill some of the functions of venture capital and angel investors, who assist with managerial and technical advice and provide new firms with contacts that are often essential for gaining traction in the market.

Innovative firms look for intellectual property protection and, to a degree, such protection is also becoming available. Since introducing such laws in the mid-1980s, China has, on paper at least, one of the better intellectual property systems in the world. The cost of enforcement through the courts is a relatively modest US$50,000 to US$120,000, compared with US$500,000 in the United Kingdom. One sign of the increasing robustness of the system is that domestic patent applications are increasing by 25 to 40 percent; Chinese universities are already taking out as many as 6,000 local patents per year ("Chinese Poised to Outstrip" 2005). However, the level of distrust among firms and the level of discontent with intellectual property protection remain high, indicating that there is plenty of room for improving patent rights.

The distrust impedes networking, one of the central characteristics of a dynamic cluster. In current circumstances, smaller firms in particular have extremely limited options if their intellectual property is stolen. In fact, rampant piracy is the bane of IT development in China and a problem that is still a long way from being deterred and contained by the legal system, a point we return to below.[23] As Judson (2005) observes, a respect for intellectual property has yet to germinate, copyright and trademark protection is almost nonexistent, and plagiarism in the sciences is rampant.

23. China adopted modern intellectual property law in 1898 at the end of the Qing dynasty. The law was modeled after those of other industrial countries at that time. However, enforcement was weak (Wang and Tong 2005). A Trademark Law was adopted in 1982, a Patent Law in 1984, and a Copyright Law in 1990. Those laws have been amended and updated (Walsh 2003).

Table 9.2 Business Software Piracy Rates by Economy, 2000

Economy	Rate (%)
Vietnam	97
China	92
Indonesia	88
Russian Federation	87
Bolivia	81
Thailand	79
Greece	64
India	62
Brazil	59
Hong Kong (China)	58
Korea, Rep. of	57
Poland	54
Taiwan (China)	52
Italy	46
South Africa	45
France	40
Japan	38
Germany	23
United Kingdom	22
United States	21

Source: Saxenian 2003.

Piracy is also a problem for the MNCs, which often complain about the lack of intellectual property protection in China. A number of high-profile cases have highlighted the problem. In one survey conducted in 2000, 26 percent of domestic software firms identified piracy as the major obstacle to the development of the industry (Segal 2003). Indeed, business software piracy rates are higher only in Vietnam (table 9.2).

CONSTRUCTING A METROPOLITAN-SCALE INNOVATIVE SYSTEM

By 2000, these incentives, strongly reinforced by the "973" program and broader efforts by the state to develop China's innovation system and catch up with advanced countries, were producing results. Most of the budget for S&T was spent in just a few urban centers—one-fourth of the total public spending and 30 percent of China's aggregate R&D spending for 2000 being allocated to Beijing. By 2004, outlay on S&T in Beijing had risen to Y 51 billion from Y 23 billion in 2000, and R&D expenditure had increased from Y 13 billion to Y 30 billion (see table 9.3). The more than

Table 9.3 Research and Development Spending in Beijing, 1999–2004

Year	Research and development personnel	Science and technology expenditure (Y billion)	Research and development expenditure (Y billion)	Technology contract value (Y billion)
1999	240,000	23.0	10.6	9.2
2000	240,000	23.0	13.9	14.0
2001	261,000	30.5	15.6	19.1
2002	250,000	37.0	18.0	22.1
2003	274,000	45.8	25.3	26.5
2004	290,000	51.0	30.0	42.5

Source: Chen and Kenney 2005.

370 research institutes in Beijing spent one-third of all the resources allocated to R&D by such entities, and one-fifth of the R&D funding for universities flowed to Beijing.[24] Out of this funding, as table 9.4 shows, more than 11 percent was devoted to basic research, close to 28 percent to applied research, and more than 61 percent to technology development, in line with the emphasis on making knowledge usable (Judson 2005). As a result, Beijing-based institutions were responsible for between 17 percent and 21 percent of all patents issued during 1995 to 2000 and received one-fifth of the revenues for contractual research. This share was more than twice that for second-ranked Liaoning and more than three times that of Shanghai. As table 9.5 shows, Beijing also generated more than twice as many patents as Liaoning during 1995–2000 and more than three times as many as Shanghai.

During the period of the Eighth Five-Year Plan (1991–95), the Beijing Municipal government disbursed US$1.3 billion for technology development. Most of this went to independent research institutes rather than to large and medium-size state-owned enterprises. The Ninth Five-Year Plan (1996–2000) doubled the technology budget (Segal 2003). The municipal government was not the only entity investing in technology development. Firms in Zhongguancun on average plowed 8 percent of their income into R&D in 2000 (Segal 2003), far in excess of the 1 percent invested by the average IT firm in China ("China's Challenge" 2005).[25]

24. The government funded 71 percent of the research by institutes in 2003, compared with 53 percent in 1991—a fivefold increase in the volume of resources committed.

25. Some firms, of course, spend more. For instance, ZTE and Huawei spend 10 percent or more on R&D ("China's Challenge" 2005).

Table 9.4 Breakdown of Research and Development in Beijing, 2000

Place of research and development	Total research and development expenditure (Y billion)	Basic research		Applied research		Development	
		Y billion	Percentage	Y billion	Percentage	Y billion	Percentage
Total	14.0	1.6	11.1	3.9	27.6	8.6	61.3
Research institute	7.5	1.1	14.1	1.9	25.2	4.5	60.7
University	1.7	0.4	23.4	1.0	58.6	0.3	18.1
Company	4.8	0.1	2.2	1.0	20.3	3.7	77.5

Source: Chen and Kenney 2005.

Table 9.5 Number of Invention Patents by Regions, 1995–2000

Region	1995	1996	1997	1998	1999	2000
Beijing	328	246	281	309	573	1,074
Liaoning	131	118	131	131	224	458
Shanghai	72	74	88	97	189	304
Jiangsu	72	98	106	85	167	341
Shandong	84	84	96	91	172	363
Guangdong	56	57	49	77	123	261
Country	1,530	1,383	1,472	1,574	3,097	6,177
Beijing as a share of country (%)	21.4	17.8	19.1	19.6	18.5	17.4

Source: Chen and Kenney 2005.

The Beijing government also established technology funds available to promising start-ups, totaling US$120 million in 2001.

By 2002, the universities associated with Zhongguancun had more than 26,000 employees engaged in S&T activities, yielding close to half of all scientific publications from the metropolitan region and 36 percent of the patents. In 2000, universities were actively engaged with firms in more than 1,500 collaborative research projects and in almost 800 technology services contracts. The leading universities were also achieving some success in launching start-ups through their incubators and science parks. Tsinghua University, China's leading technical institution, was managing, through its holding company, 39 technology-based spinoffs in 2003, including Tsinghua Tongfang, one of China's largest producers of consumer electronics, and an equal number of companies offering a range of services. Tsinghua Holding's turnover in 2005 was Y 25 billion (US$3 billion). Beijing University, meanwhile, was equally successful in generating resources from spinoffs. In fact, the turnover of the Founder

Table 9.6 Main Indicators of Different Parks in 2003

Indicator	Haidian Park	Fengtai Park	Changping Park	Dianzi City	Yizhuang Park	Desheng Park
Number of enterprises	8,733	1,287	1,232	395	260	123
Profit (Y million)	9,325	1,772	1,393	1,883	3,568	68
Profitable enterprises (%)	45.21	51.75	43.75	56.71	31.54	43.90
Share of total enterprises (%)	72.59	10.71	10.24	3.28	2.16	1.02
Share of total revenue (%)	58.89	10.42	6.37	8.98	15.02	0.32
Share of total industry output (%)	48.11	6.57	8.41	13.94	22.83	0.14
Share of tax collected (%)	59.11	8.15	7.35	9.65	15.47	0.27
Share of export revenue (%)	28.79	5.28	3.01	16.95	45.85	0.12
Share of R&D expenditure (%)	78.28	2.47	6.85	8.19	2.83	1.38
Share of new product sales revenue (%)	70.28	3.20	9.99	15.21	1.29	0.04
Share of employees	61.22	10.78	10.24	10.30	6.78	0.69

Source: People's Government of Beijing Municipality Administration Committee of Zhongguancun Park 2004.

Note: Jianxiang Park was established in 2003.

Group alone was US$2.8 billion in 2003 (Hamaguchi and Kameyama 2005). It should be noted, though, that some of these enterprises are not high-tech operations and were created to find employment for university employees who could not be laid off. Recently, Tsinghua University set up a four-person office solely to negotiate projects with overseas R&D partners such as General Electric, Lucent, Alcatel, and BP. Foreign firms typically provide equipment and research dollars in research collaborations, and professors and students may work for several years on a dedicated project. ("We've Got Solid Grounding" 2005).[26]

These aggregate numbers are certainly impressive (see table 9.6 for the main indicators of the parks within Zhongguancun). They reflect the striking buildup of technological capacity in Beijing in not much more

26. Microsoft helped set up five laboratories, including one at Tsinghua, focusing on multimedia and networking ("We've Got Solid Grounding" 2005).

than 15 years, following the government's big push on S&T development and its decision to make Beijing the nation's science capital. This progress could yield substantial long-term dividends if innovation flowers and becomes perennial.

The importance of R&D can be seen from the experience in Taiwan (China). Both the IC industry and the PC industry were created by the government, with the state-owned Industrial Technology Research Institute laying the technological foundations, especially for the IC industry. Initially the IC foundry industry did not spend much on R&D (5 percent of sales between 1993 and 1997, when other firms were spending close to 15 percent). To compensate for the paucity of local R&D funding, Taiwan (China) sought support from foreign firms, in particular IBM. These firms played a key role in helping local IC producers move from the 6-inch wafer to the 8-inch wafer. However, firms in Taiwan (China) have steadily increased their spending on R&D and personnel, and they were able to introduce 12-inch wafer production through their own research efforts (Fuller 2005).

The rise of the foundry industry in Taiwan (China) also prompted the development of fabless design companies such as VIA, which focus purely on the design of the ICs and let foundries do the actual manufacturing processes. Some of those design firms are now the world leaders in codec chips for optical drives, Ethernet, and motherboard chipsets (Fuller 2005). The IC industry has steadily invested and upgraded its R&D operations, as is evident in the number of U.S. patents awarded to firms in Taiwan (China). These patents are predominantly granted to IC firms (Fuller 2005).

Cross-country research uncovers a robust relationship between R&D spending and patenting, innovation, and productivity gains.[27] The early findings from Beijing are consistent with experience elsewhere, but it is too early to say that electronics and IT can thrive once the hothouses provided by the state in Beijing are dismantled, as eventually they must be. In fact, some data for Zhongguancun through 2003 belie the statistics on patents and the evidence on R&D activities. In three major product categories, only 4 percent of the production is exported, which suggests that the innovativeness or competitiveness of the products is limited in the global market. Furthermore, parkwide data show that foreign-invested enterprises constitute less than 3 percent of the total pool of enterprises but account for 80 percent of industrial output and half of total assets.

27. For a review of this evidence, see Mohne, Mairesse, and Dagenais (2006) and Wieser (2005).

In effect, although a large number of start-ups are supported by generous incentives, much of the turnover of the Zhongguancun Park comes from a few foreign firms that have been attracted by the incentives and the abundance of skills.[28] They and a few Chinese firms, such as Founder, Daheng,[29] and Lenovo, form the backbone of the park. Although these firms are engaged in research and customization of electronics and IT products for the Chinese market, neither the local nor the foreign-invested firms are conducting research at the frontiers of their fields. By and large, most firms are adapting and developing products for the domestic market. The pure research quotient is low, as is the level of technology. Some of the most successful IT firms are concentrating on multimedia, emphasizing innovation and marketing, which will generate quick returns. The new entrepreneurs are young and ambitious, but they are not equipped to push the frontiers of technology, and the local market is not ready either.

Although the number of firms in the Zhongguancun Park is large, the evidence of clustering and networking that would multiply links and enhance coordination of research and partnerships among firms is fairly thin. Surveys find that firms come to Zhongguancun to benefit from the incentives and to tap the labor pool, but they have established few links, and there is minimal interfirm networking associated with synergy in clusters (Lawlor and others 2002). The problem of mistrust we referred to above poses an additional hurdle. The anchor firms have not yet begun to provide technological leadership. Having acquired IBM's PC business, Lenovo is now attempting to strengthen the ThinkPad brand image, add new design features to its product range, broaden the coverage of market segments, and deepen its penetration into markets such as India's. But little of the research and production undergirding this strategy is done in Beijing. As the Haidian district at the core of the park has become prosperous, developers have put up expensive buildings, and rental costs have risen. Many firms are having to move farther out, with the result that the geographic contiguity of the electronics and IT businesses, their proximity to universities, and the colocation of manufacturing with R&D

28. Close to 90 percent of high-tech exports of China come from export processing activities—mainly assembling imported materials with rather low local value added (Wang and Tong 2005). Overall 62 percent of all Chinese patents registered with the U.S. Patent and Trademark Office are held by foreign-owned enterprises or by joint ventures (Wong 2006b).

29. Daheng's main products include mechanical computer-aided design and system integration, laser processing devices, television network broadcasting equipment, and semiconductor components. Its revenue was Y 3 billion in 2004, with an R&D budget of Y 159 million ("China's Top 100" 2005).

activities are being compromised by the realities of extremely rapid urban development and skyrocketing real estate values. The same problem is seen in other cities: rising rental costs and desire to convert urban land to other uses first drive out manufacturing but then can also push out the creative industries, as happened in New York with multimedia firms.

Even with the financial support that the park administration offers to selected start-ups, most of these firms fairly quickly face cash flow issues, unless they can generate a revenue stream either from their principal product or services or from an interim offering. Although the 1985 Decision Concerning the Reform of the Science and Technology Management System improved the access of high-tech firms to bank financing, in practice much of the lending goes to state-owned enterprises. This situation continues to constrain the financing available to small and medium enterprises (SMEs) (Segal 2003; Yusuf and Nabeshima 2006b). In the absence of much mergers and acquisitions activity involving small firms or a buoyant initial public offering market, if small firms are to survive they must develop relatively minor innovations that can be commercialized quickly.

Stone, Lenovo, and Founder were able to do so initially by being the first firms to offer certain kinds of software. Their incomes were also supplemented by distribution agreements with foreign producers of PCs and word processors. However, as the import quotas were lifted on computers, distribution agreements did not generate much-needed cash flow, and competitive pressures exacerbated the problem. Founder remains the second-ranked PC producer in China, and it has diversified into ICs and circuit boards, but the company has also entered completely unrelated fields, such as steel, medical products, chemical engineering, and real estate ("Diversity and Design" 2005). Stone also has entered the real estate and cement businesses and has even started producing chocolate snack pies (Segal 2003). The strategies pursued by the leading Chinese electronics firms point to the intensity of competition in electronics, but they also suggest that the region's innovation capability remains fairly limited. Though Beijing might be plowing a lot of resources into R&D with a corresponding sharp increase in patent applications and in published articles, the results might take years to materialize.

AN ELECTRONICS AND INFORMATION TECHNOLOGY CAPITAL?

These are relatively early days for the electronics and IT industry in Beijing, and it is too soon to offer firm views on the efficacy of policy initiatives and whether they will lead to the jelling of a dynamic local innovation system. For the sake of electronics and IT development, the Chinese government is requiring companies that produce and market equipment in China (for example, Alcatel, Siemens, Nokia, and NEC) to transfer technology to local partners. This approach borrows from the past practices of Japan and the Republic of Korea. It involves plowing public funds into R&D by research institutes and universities and encouraging R&D by state enterprises. It is supported by efforts to make intellectual property rights more accessible, cheaper to maintain, and legally easier to enforce, something that among the East Asian countries only Japan, Singapore, and now Korea convincingly offer. The government is attempting to create domestic standards for mobile technology—the TD-SCDMA (Time Division–Synchronous Code Division Multiple Access) standard along with standards for video compact discs (VCDs), digital versatile discs (DVDs), and high-definition television (HDTV)—by leveraging the potential of China's huge market. This effort takes a page from the experience of Nokia, for example. The government is also grooming national champions equivalent to Samsung and the big Japanese companies—or to Nokia—which could become global technological and manufacturing powerhouses (see Linden 2003, 2004).

Some encouraging results are already apparent. The trend in spending on R&D nationwide and especially in Beijing is upward, and that expanding volume of resources is a necessary condition for achieving innovativeness. In 2004, China allocated 1.3 percent of GDP to R&D.[30] This share is projected to reach 2.0 percent of a much larger national product in 2015.[31] If 30 percent of this amount continues to be spent in Beijing, the incentives to conduct research and to innovate and the means to commercialize new findings will be considerable.[32] The funding would complement the growing stock of S&T workers in the metropolitan area—the largest single labor market for technical skills in China and another necessary condition for a competitive electronics industry. Beijing has the

30. When this figure is scaled using purchasing power parities, China was classified by the Organisation for Economic Co-operation and Development as the country with the third largest spending on R&D in 2003. At the current pace, R&D spending in the European Union will rise from 1.93 percent of GDP in 2003 to 2.2 percent in 2010. R&D spending in China is growing rapidly and will be on par with that in the European Union by 2010 ("Chinese Poised to Outstrip" 2005).

31. Beijing is the center of R&D activities in China, with 6 percent of GDP devoted to R&D (see chapter 3).

32. In 2000, total R&D spending in China was Y 63 billion, of which Y 21 billion was spent in Beijing and only Y 5 billion in Shanghai (Wang and Tong 2005).

additional advantage of attracting some of the best students from across China (Sigurdson 2005). Already more than 300,000 students graduate with engineering degrees in China every year ("China's Challenge" 2005). In 1975, China produced almost no science and engineering doctorates. In 2003, there were 13,000 doctorates, about 70 percent of them in science and engineering (Freeman 2005). From 30,000 in 1980, the number of scientists and technicians increased to 1.3 million by 2004 ("Long March" 2005).[33]

An increasing number of Chinese and foreign companies (more than 400 by 2004) are setting up research facilities in Beijing and some production units as well.[34] This trend is helping Beijing to develop strong capabilities, including IC design and system-on-a-chip design with assistance under the "863" program. Foundries and IC production units have been established by Beijing and Tsinghua Universities by SMIC, NEC-Shougang, Yangdong, and others (Sigurdson 2005).[35] Nokia, for example, has a large telecommunications production and research facility at Xingwang Industrial Park in the Beijing Municipal Development Zone. One of Nokia's neighbors is GE Hangwei Medical Systems, which started a joint venture in 1991 and in 2003 opened a 60,000-square-meter facility for designing, engineering, and producing medical imaging equipment. In 2003, Microsoft established the Advanced Technology Center in the Haidian district, on the same floor as Microsoft Research Asia, which opened in 1998. The purpose of the center is to transfer the technology developed at the Beijing research center to product development faster than in the past. Started with only 20 staff members, the center now has more than 200, recruited from all over China. Some technology developed in Beijing, such as video editing, has been incorporated in standard

33. Building basic infrastructure, health care, social security systems, and better schooling is likely to occupy many of China's best brains for years ("China's Hi-Tech Success" 2005).

34. Foreign R&D centers in China numbered 750 at the end of 2004 and employed 500,000 people ("Long March" 2005). According to McKinsey, only 10 percent of Chinese graduates are good enough to work for MNCs ("China's Hi-Tech Success" 2005). Although many MNCs recognize the quality of Chinese graduates, they find that creative thinking is not yet a strength. The graduates are good at solving closed-ended questions but not open-ended ones. MNCs' R&D labs urge staff members to ask questions about the whys and hows of research to stimulate more creative thinking. The response in China is still weak ("We've Got Solid Grounding" 2005).

35. A major new Chinese company, LHWT, was established in 2000 by seven Chinese nationals who studied in Japan. LHWT is making headway in the design and development of latent semantic indexing technologies. One-fifth of China's 500 software design houses were located in Beijing in 2004 (Sigurdson 2005).

Microsoft software distributed worldwide. Eventually the center will handle technologies developed elsewhere, making Beijing an important link in Microsoft's innovation strategy ("Microsoft: Getting from 'R' to 'D'" 2005).

These experienced outsiders, the lynchpins of global electronics and IT value chains, play an important role in raising the quality and productivity of research by pulling local research in specific fields closer to the frontier, bringing leading foreign researchers to Beijing, placing experienced research managers in charge of local research centers, linking researchers in the metropolitan area more closely with labs around the world, and providing local producers with points of entry into global markets. Greater openness and heterogeneity would enhance the innovativeness of electronics and the scope for fruitful intertwining of technologies from different fields—for instance, electronics and biotechnology.

Current measures that improve the physical and cultural ambience of Beijing, reverse the worsening traffic congestion, and broaden the options for recreation reinforce the government's efforts to make Beijing a creative city.[36] A city richer in amenities and in the quality of social services—one that offered a more attractive environment, to boot—could pull in the regional headquarters of MNCs seeking a base in China.

It is also possible that China—specifically Beijing—could benefit from the bandwagon effect. Should key research communities come to view Beijing as one of the meccas for their disciplines, the circulation of national and international talent through Beijing will accelerate.[37] The likelihood of this possibility occurring increases if spending on R&D or government incentives weakens in Organisation for Economic Co-operation and Development countries or if economic prospects in Europe and Japan remain tepid, thereby inducing talented people to look for brighter lights.[38]

In East Asia, but not in other parts of the world, the determined pursuit of industrial policy objectives (those that initially appeared misjudged, such as the development of the steel, shipbuilding, auto, petrochemical, and dynamic random access memory industries in Korea) over many years

---

36. Some of these measures are the direct outcome of Beijing's selection as the site for the 2008 Olympics.

37. Beijing is seen as an attractive place for R&D operations. For instance, Hon Hai of Taiwan (China) set up an R&D lab in Beijing even before setting up one in Taipei (Fuller 2005).

38. An outflow of S&T workers from Europe to the United States has been going on for some time. Although a redirection of the stream to China in the near future is highly unlikely, over the longer term it is not inconceivable.

has frequently yielded some striking successes. Who would have thought that China would be the second largest producer of electronic and IT products today and the biggest exporter? Who would have thought that Beijing, Chengdu, Dongguan, Foshan, Guangzhou, Shanghai, Shenzhen, and Suzhou would so quickly achieve manufacturing capability in a broad swath of electronics products and come to be viewed as having the potential to join the leading centers of research? Much of this has happened because of the (in some quarters) unanticipated outcome of industrial openings that emerged in the 1990s, reinforced by central and local industrial policies and now by innovation policies.

A vision that encompasses centers of economic excellence that conduct cutting-edge R&D, the growth of IT and biotech-related services and of prototype or small-scale manufacture of high-value items, and the expansion of affiliated business services is certainly consonant with China's recent trajectory and Beijing's place in China's metropolitan pantheon. This vision is also consonant with the impending departure of the remaining traditional manufacturing industries (with the encouragement of the government) and the push exerted by rising labor costs and stiff environmental regulations.

But a number of imponderables relate to the urban environment in general and the electronics industry in particular. Beijing's innovativeness—for that matter, the innovativeness of any Chinese city—ultimately depends on its openness to ideas and to knowledge workers from around the world. It depends, as Judson (2005) noted, on successful implantation of the ethos of science and the willingness to pursue basic science without getting fixated on the desire for quick technological findings. It will be influenced by the business friendliness of the regulatory regime and by whether it creates an environment that promotes a technological spiral through the entry and growth of electronics firms and the swift exits of unsuccessful ones.[39] It is likely to be intertwined with the growth of the metropolitan economy, itself a function of population and other changes in the metropolitan area, as well as in the hinterland. The area is faced with intensifying water shortages and problems of desertification, which might be ameliorated only in part by the South-North water transfer scheme, which will bring Yangtze River water to the Beijing area.

39. Close to 50 percent of the start-ups in Silicon Valley did not survive (Zhang 2003). The failure of firms is already tolerated in Beijing, especially if they are not governmental firms. The successful computer firms (Lenovo, Founder, and Stone) are aware of this attitude of the local government (Segal 2003).

Beijing faces competition from other cities that are advantageously located in lower latitudes and on or close to the coastline. Cities such as Guangzhou, Shenzhen, and Shanghai also have relatively abundant supplies of skilled workers and are strengthening their university and research infrastructure. They offer cultural amenities that are at least equal, if not superior, to Beijing's, and unlike the capital city, they have been more ready to promote openness. Guangzhou, Shanghai, Shenzhen, and their surrounding cities have resources and are attracting enough foreign investment in their innovation systems to match the resources poured into Beijing's S&T infrastructure by the central government. Beijing could still emerge as China's leading center of innovation in electronics, IT, and affiliated disciplines. But it could be eclipsed by one of the cities of the south.

These factors qualify Beijing's prospects, but in the Chinese context, its chances of becoming a bastion of high-tech development are at least comparable with those of other contenders. The presence of the central government and leading research institutes partially counterbalances the disadvantages of a weaker hinterland. Arguably, the more troubling questions arise from the dynamics of the electronics industry and its potential for generating innovations with as well as from Beijing's emerging technological capability.

Several aspects of the electronics industry deserve attention because they have a bearing on its future geography. Electronics is in the grip of furious technological change, with product life cycles that are measured in months (Agarwal and Gort 2001).[40] It is an intensely competitive industry because modularization and the speed of codification have resulted in a high degree of contestability.[41] The result is that project margins are thin and successful firms depend not only on their innovativeness but equally

40. Within a matter of four years, the semiconductor industry has moved from circuits of 130 nanometers to circuits of 65 nanometers and is now setting its sights on circuits of less than 30 nanometers ("IBM Set to Unveil" 2006).

41. Many Chinese firms, especially the visible ones, are expanding rapidly into the global market. Lenovo, ZTE, and BOE, all makers of thin-film transistor liquid crystal displays, have expressed the need to go abroad to survive in this fiercely competitive market ("Starting a Walk" 2005). For this reason, among others, local technologies such as the Wired Authentication and Privacy Infrastructure (WAPI) standard, TD-SCDMA standard, and the enhanced versatile disc (EVD) have been received with little enthusiasm even by domestic firms, which doubt whether these standards will be adopted by international bodies ("Home-Grown Standard" 2005; "Ticklish Issue" 2005). Such skepticism is warranted from past failure to push domestic standards against emerging global ones. Japan and Korea tried to create their own versions of PCs without using Intel's central processing unit and Microsoft's operating system but without much success. They were never able to gain significant market share domestically, let alone globally (Fuller 2005).

on the scale of their production and their willingness to invest in capital-intensive facilities, on the efficiency of their logistics, and on marketing as well as services, which can be bundled with products.[42] So intense is the pressure on all participants to meet the most exacting standards of production efficiency, quality, and delivery that an industry leader such as Dell has to worry about the fraction of a minute—in the four minutes needed to assemble a PC in 2005—that is required to attach the "Intel inside" sticker ("Critical Mass" 2005). The latest silicon foundries for making semiconductors with circuits 65 nanometers in diameter entail an investment of US$5 billion. Texas Instruments and IBM have unveiled even costlier technologies, which will reduce circuit diameters by one-third to one-half. Although this example is extreme, modern electronics factories are becoming increasingly pricey ("IBM Set to Unveil" 2006).

In these circumstances, one trend that stands out is consolidation. This trend has greatly concentrated the share of the leading 8 to10 firms in key products and services such as hard disk drives, motherboards, and application-specific software. Consolidation of certain production activities has gone hand in hand with a greater readiness to outsource specific components, software, and services to specialists and to constantly shop for suppliers that offer the best package of attributes.

The offshoot of this process of consolidation and outsourcing in conjunction with the technological characteristics of the industry is that electronics and IT production is dispersed and constantly in motion. In not much more than 25 years, an industry centered mainly in a few parts of the United States has seen its center of gravity shift to Japan, Korea, and Taiwan (China) and more recently to China, India, Israel, and several European and Southeast Asian countries. Leading producers of hardware, such as Intel and Motorola, have plants scattered around the world, as do the contract manufacturers such as Solectron, Flextronics, and Hon Hai Precision. Software producers and suppliers of IT services are even more dispersed. IBM, Oracle, and Microsoft have footholds in a half dozen countries.

But so far, despite all this globalization of production and the wide distribution of IT products, the research that drives the industry—the fabrication of the most high-value components and the design, integration, and customizing of the core software—has remained very highly

42. Software and services will account for 35 percent of Chinese technology spending in 2009, up from 26 percent in 2004. Such an increase can give local firms opportunities to enter the market, which is currently dominated by foreign firms ("Open Source" 2005).

concentrated in a few cities in North America, Western Europe, Japan, and Israel, as well as, more recently, India, Korea, and Taiwan (China). The heartland of the electronics industry is in those very few cities. They are where the bulk of the research is done and where the results of scattered research from around the world are integrated into new products, whose production is then farmed out. The cities where the upstream work is done are no longer centers of manufacturing, although most retain some production facilities; however, they have specialized in R&D, software, design, and prototyping and in an array of profitable producer services that are coextensive with the IT industry, such as multimedia, entertainment, and consulting. IBM earns more from consulting than it does from the sale of hardware.

The cities that rank as global centers in the electronics and IT industry are also the ones with the world's leading research universities. Cities such as Boston and San Francisco in the United States; Tokyo in Japan; Cambridge, Stockholm, and Geneva in Europe; and Tel Aviv in Israel derive handsome benefits from the IT industry because they are the brains of the electronics industry and generate tens of thousands of highly paid jobs, mainly for knowledge workers.

Is Beijing ready to compete? And can a top-down strategy underwritten by central government funding propel the city into the ranks of the favored few? Our sense is that the strategy could work, but it might take a decade or more before it begins to show results. The key to success will be flexibility, in terms of both objectives and the means used to realize the objectives. The electronics and IT industry is changing so fast that the target is bound to shift. Maintaining forward momentum will require a flexible response from industry and research establishments, with help from policy makers. Whether and how Chinese researchers participate in the development of new technologies to extend the applications of CMOS (complementary metal-oxide semiconductor) silicon microprocessors and find alternatives to silicon through biotechnology, the neurosciences, and nanotechnology might determine the course taken by the industry in Beijing ("Silicon Down" 2005).

Urban and industrial policies have produced remarkable results in China against considerable odds, but autonomy granted (sometimes inadvertently) to individual actors has had a large role as well, starting with agricultural reforms in the late 1970s. Policy can contribute a lot more to strengthening the electronics industry in Beijing by deepening the research capabilities of universities, by enhancing the quality of the urban environment, by promoting promising technologies such as digital media, by instituting telecommunications policies that assist the industry (as in

Scandinavia), by defining standards that coordinate and focus the efforts of local industry, and so on.

Still, policy efforts alone may be insufficient. The corporate sector must also do its bit through ceaseless, incremental organizational innovation that complements advances in technologies. These organizational skills are concentrated in the large MNCs, which is why the significant presence and active involvement of such large organizations have become vital for the electronics and IT industry. The MNCs bring together research and supporting services of a sufficient scale—both their own and that of associated entities. They provide tested business models, and they have the organizational wherewithal to manage complex operations across the world.

China, including Beijing, still lacks these corporate entities. Observing their emergence elsewhere in East and South Asia, it is far from obvious how their development can be accelerated. Size is not enough. Organizational capability and innovativeness are more important. Without those characteristics, pouring money into R&D and physical infrastructure will have a limited payoff in the short term. Continued over a decade or more, the returns could begin to climb. Beijing can afford to keep trying, and it has time on its side—we think.

CHAPTER 10

SUMMING UP

The economic future of cities hinges on the scale, mix, and competitiveness of their industries. Increasing prosperity demands a steady expansion in jobs, with rising value added and the production of goods and services commanding ready national and international markets. Cities are not self-sufficient entities. They depend on a myriad of imports. Even a brief interruption in the flow can precipitate a crisis. All these imports must be paid for through exports or fiscal transfers from higher levels of government, through remittances, and through direct investment. Temporary imbalances of the urban current account can be offset by borrowing. Long-term imbalances are far harder to sustain, unless they can be financed by capital inflows. In most cases, cities that are unable to correct persistent current account imbalances are pushed into economic contraction and declining incomes. Rising employment and incomes are a function of the productivity and innovativeness of existing industries and the emergence of new tradable activities capable of generating better-paid jobs.

The message of this book is that most of East Asia's leading cities benefited from the industrial revolution that swept through the region in the 1960s. Bangkok, Beijing, Seoul, Shanghai, Singapore, and Tokyo all saw their economic fortunes rise with the growth of internationally competitive, export-oriented, light manufacturing industries. The success of these exporters in domestic and overseas markets led to rising urban incomes through the 1990s.

As incomes rose, two forces began changing the industrial composition of these cities, starting with Tokyo. First, the labor-intensive manufacturing activities began moving out, initially to the periurban fringes and then farther out into the hinterland or to other countries where labor was cheaper. Second, because the income elasticity of demand universally favors services, consumption in these cities shifted toward services, and the nature of employment opportunities began to change.

The East Asian crisis, which sent a shockwave through the economies of the region, underscored the challenges posed by globalization, accelerated the geographic redistribution of industry, and—in conjunction with the information technology (IT) revolution—focused attention on productivity growth and innovation. All six cities, which had attained levels of per capita income well above their respective national averages, were faced with the need to make an industrial transition. Manufacturing industries of different stripes remained part of the urban landscape, but rising land and labor costs decreed that the scale of those industries diminished and that the cities moved, willy-nilly, toward a postindustrial world—a world where manufacturing activities account for a minor share of urban gross domestic product and employ a small fraction of the workforce. This trend is irreversible, and it accords closely with the experience of major urban centers in Western Europe and North America.

If the per capita incomes in the six cities are to continue climbing—or even maintain their current levels—new, more productive, and more innovative activities must replace the ones that have relocated or have been driven out of business.

IDENTIFYING POSTINDUSTRIAL CITIES

The six cities in our sample are distinctive in certain respects and better placed than most to forge ahead in a globalizing environment. First, they are large and populous cities with diversified industrial bases.[1] As such, they benefit from the agglomeration economies associated with size and industrial breadth—economies that boost productivity and can underpin competitiveness (Henderson 2004a; Rosenthal and Strange 2004). Second, five are capital cities and administrative axes of the national economies. The sixth, Shanghai, is China's leading industrial and commercial center. These positions confer numerous advantages, not the least of which is the pull that capital cities exert on businesses because of lower transaction costs, greater scope for networking, and superior infrastructure.[2]

1. For instance, Tokyo's industrial base embraces 122 of a possible 125 three-digit subsectors (Yusuf and Nabeshima 2006a).

2. This has been and is especially true in East Asia, where governments actively intervene in managing economic activities (Fujita 2003).

A third advantage related to urban and administrative dominance in the national context is the degree to which these cities are connected to other centers in their nations and globally. For a postindustrial city increasingly dependent on the export of services, on foreign investment, and on the international circulation of knowledge workers, such connectedness—predicated as it is on the quality of the information and communication technology, transportation facilities, and soft infrastructure—is vital.

Fourth, these cities have the greatest concentrations of learning facilities and research institutes. As a consequence, they are richly supplied with skills from local institutions and from the steady stream of migrants attracted to these cities. The deep and diverse pools of skilled labor first supported the growth of manufacturing industries. Now the base of skills will, to a significant extent, determine the composition and competitiveness of the new breed of industries.

Local universities are the principal source of trained workers. However, in the postindustrial stage, they are also becoming sources of new technologies and ideas with commercial spillovers. Thus, university-industry links, where they are forged through the initiatives of businesses, universities, and governments, could be decisive for the future success of many activities that will drive the postindustrial city.[3] The reservoir of skills and the fruitfulness of the links between businesses and researchers are also likely to affect the resilience of the urban economy and its capacity to overcome shocks, as well as its ability to seek new industrial loci of competitive advantage.

All six cities, even Singapore and Tokyo, continue to derive entrepreneurial energy, dynamism, spending power, and an increase in labor supply from the influx of migrants. Each remains a city where populations are growing. This fifth factor has a bearing on the cities' growth prospects and on the age structure of the workforce.

Sixth, industrial progression in these cities is aided by the capacity of local financial systems and the logistics infrastructure, as well as by the efforts of the state to develop advanced telecommunication facilities. Together these characteristics contribute to industrial change, to productivity increases, and to the increasing export of services.

These six factors frame the postindustrial prospects of East Asian cities. But robust economic growth will depend on the kinds of industries that flower in these cities and, in particular, on their competitiveness in export markets, domestic as well as foreign.

---

3. For discussion of university-industry links in East Asia, see Indjikian and Siegel (2005).

SELECTING URBAN INDUSTRIAL ENGINES

We have examined a number of potentially promising candidates for the postindustrial urban stage in East Asia's leading cities. Our choices were guided by seven criteria necessary to the efficacy of new engines of mega-urban economies and broadly suited to the dynamic comparative advantages of the cities in our sample.

1. The factor requirements of these industries must broadly conform with available factor supplies and the capacity to augment these supplies.
2. The industries must produce tradables—whether services or manufactures—with substantial (potential) global markets that recent trends and developments suggest are likely to grow well into the future.
3. The industries are technology or knowledge intensive and derive a good part of their competitiveness from innovation and creativity. Moreover, their competitiveness is not significantly affected by labor costs, making them suitable for postindustrial cities with rising wages.
4. Because they are technology intensive, the industries all draw heavily on the skills of workers. They also rely to a greater or lesser extent on links with local universities and research institutes for technical workers and technology development.
5. The industries have multiple backward and forward links with other providers of manufacture and components. They are particularly suited to the environment of a megacity, which is industrially diverse and can support activities that require a mix of technologies and input producers.
6. The industries have the potential to generate large turnover and employment. Their economic footprint in the city is such that they can function as leading sectors.
7. For each industry, there are proven business models to guide newcomers and a fund of experience with enabling institutions and policies that can light the way forward.

On the basis of those criteria, we identified one or two industries that can serve as engines of growth for each of these postindustrial cities. Except for biotechnology in Singapore, the industries are not newcomers. More important, they are all far from having realized their full potential and, hence, can add momentum to the urban economy for some time.

The robot industry in Tokyo has a 45-year history and a developed network of subcontractors. But research on humanoid robotics and technologies tailored for smart houses, unmanned aerial vehicles, submersibles, robotic ground vehicles, medical devices, and helper robots offers relatively new, exciting, open, and fresh commercial vistas. Both robotics and animation tap into Tokyo's vast reserves of accumulated expertise in multiple areas and its continuously upgraded skills mix. With an economy the size of India's and of Mexico's, Tokyo also provides a testing ground for new technologies before they are exported (Fujita and Hill 2005). It hosts the corporations and research centers that are spearheading development in these areas. Unlike some of the other industries we discuss, neither robotics nor animation depends on government policy or financial support.[4] Their futures rest on the capabilities inherent in a mature corporate sector and the resources of a postindustrial megacity with an open economy heavily dependent on trade.

Seoul's film industry also has existed for several decades, although the online game business is of relatively recent origin. Moviemaking was protected and had few prospects until regulations were eased in the 1980s and new directors came to the fore. The industry has since notched up a string of successes and could become an exporter of some standing, equivalent in scale to the movie industries of France or the United Kingdom. Similarly, by leveraging its client-server and game engine technologies, Seoul could make the massively multiplayer online role-playing games (MMORPGs) a major and lucrative part of its multimedia sector. Whether these industries do so will depend on several factors—in particular, the effectiveness of government policies, which have provided both businesses with critical assistance. In the case of MMORPGs, investment in broadband infrastructure was the key to success. Such factors as the use of digital techniques in moviemaking and distribution will be influential, as will, most vitally, the flow of talent into both industries. Last but not least, Korean filmmakers will need to respond innovatively—and by differentiating their products—to the intense competition, not only from Hollywood but also from China and India, whose movie industries are becoming more active on the global scene.

The IT and electronics industry is seemingly a natural growth pole in Beijing, given the stage the city is at and its resource endowment. Two decades of developmental work in IT and multimedia and work with the assembly of personal computers and computer peripherals, coupled with a vast university infrastructure and broad-ranging government support for technology development, provide a strong push. Were IT and electronics to put down deep roots, they would be a strong force in Beijing's economy. But thus far, both the basic research to provide the underpinnings for a

4. Basic safety regulations concerning the use of robots outside factories need to be clearly specified for this industry to develop.

dynamic sector and the innovativeness that would lead to and sustain commercial success on a global scale are missing. Those resources could be grown in time with sufficient investment and incentives, just as China has succeeded in building substantial Beijing-based corporations that specialize in electronics (for example, Founders and Lenovo).

Still, resources are only one essential ingredient. For a creative industry, an urban environment that encourages openness and traffic in new ideas is another. And there are still more. Postindustrial Beijing is exploring a number of industrial combinations; although the government's will and ambition are obvious, whether the IT and electronics sector is the right urban champion is not clear.

There can be little doubt, though, that construction, real estate, and engineering could be a major and enduring industrial cluster in Shanghai. This traditional cluster of industries nevertheless offers the widest possible opportunities in China and around the world, with much scope for technological progress. Construction is unique in several respects. It has numerous links with other industries; it is a huge employer of skilled workers; it is relatively less subject to cyclical fluctuations than some industries are; and it offers a great deal of scope for creativity in design and execution, as well as for technological change, particularly with respect to energy and environmental conservation and new materials.

Shanghai started out with a sizable construction sector. The sector has grown to huge proportions, has linked back to suppliers of materials, and has begun exporting its services. As it builds expertise in multiple intersectoral areas, Shanghai could easily become the center of China's construction and engineering industries and from this jumping-off point penetrate markets throughout the world.

Like construction in Shanghai, jewelry making and garment manufacture in Bangkok are industries of long standing. However, in the postindustrial context, they have a new role to play—and unless they adopt this role, these industries will soon migrate from the metropolitan area. Both industries must upgrade in order to grow and contribute more to Bangkok's economy. Upgrading translates to an unwavering focus on design, quality, and finish; on technological refinements that improve materials and quality, assist with design, and lower production costs; and on the marketing and building of brand names that command global recognition.

Government policies and actions taken by the Bangkok metropolitan authority can be a means to realizing these objectives, but much of the initiative and the bulk of the investment must come from the corporate sector. In fact, changes in industrial organization and in strategy will very likely be key to the future scale of these two industries in Bangkok.

The foundations are there, but the fashion industry is a difficult one to break into, and niche-level penetration yields only modest returns. Can Bangkok-based companies succeed in the face of mounting competition from other East Asian players? The answer is far from clear; however, with the demand for fashion products rising steeply in the Asia region, the opportunities are better than ever.

The biotech industry being grown in Singapore represents a fairly radical departure—and a risky one. But success, even on a regional scale, would bring rich rewards to the city-state. Singapore's options are constrained by its size, by its industrial base, and by the supply of skills. The emergence of biotech clusters in San Diego, San Francisco, and Austin in the United States suggests that it is possible to jump-start such development through a series of carefully sequenced investments.

Singapore has gone through a checklist of necessary conditions, allocating physical space, attracting star scientists, building hospital and training facilities, drawing in multinational corporations (MNCs), committing venture capital, and providing determined leadership. It has avoided putting all its eggs in one basket by embracing several subfields in biotechnology, although the emphasis is on drugs and products for combating cancer. Whether these subfields will prove sufficient and, if so, how long it might take for them to become so are big questions. Drug discovery is a chancy business. Piloting drugs, vaccines, and implants through trials is becoming ever more expensive and demanding. And for biotechnology to become an engine of growth, it must acquire a substantial scale, achieve a high turnover, and employ considerable numbers of skilled workers. Singapore's MNC-dominated and thriving pharmaceutical sector offers grounds for hope, but much will depend on whether Singapore can assemble and retain world-class talent and achieve a succession of lucky breaks that will give it a lead over China, India, and the Republic of Korea, its closest competitors.

ENGINE DRIVERS

This industry-eye view of postindustrialism in East Asia's megacities has highlighted the role of three participants. First and foremost are the governments, both national and municipal. Without their policies on the national innovation system (including intellectual property), on urban land use, and on skill development and without their fiscal and financial support, the technology-intensive industries examined here would have difficulty taking root and achieving a high-growth trajectory.

Second are corporations. In each industrial subsector, it is evident that the corporate contribution, in the context of globalization, is of ever-increasing importance. The future of robotics in Tokyo, of moviemaking in Seoul, and of biotechnology in Singapore is entwined with the strategy and dynamism of corporate entities. Japan has an abundance of powerful corporations with a global reach, and Korea has a few. The other countries have still some catching up to do.

Third are universities. All the most attractive candidate industries for postindustrial cities are skill intensive to varying degrees and dependent on innovation for international competitiveness. For both skills and innovation, the quality of universities will matter more and more. In all five countries, the universities—even the elite ones—have given little attention to the quality of education and to basic or applied research. This must change, and in Beijing, Shanghai, and Singapore it is changing at great speed. Other countries need to follow suit.

A transition to a postindustrial economic system is in the cards for these six cities, and for Guangzhou, Kuala Lumpur, Taipei, and others. A transition that does not break the economic momentum that these cities have achieved requires a well-thought-out strategy and the active cooperation of several key players, led by the government, the corporate sector, and the universities.

REFERENCES

Adams, Christopher P., and Van V. Brantner. 2004. "Estimating the Costs of New Drug Development: Is It Really $802m?" Working Paper. Washington, DC: Federal Trade Commission.

Adams, James. 2002. "Comparative Localization of Academic and Industrial Spillovers." *Journal of Economic Geography* 2 (3): 253–78.

Adams, Stephen B. 2005. "Stanford and Silicon Valley." *California Management Review* 47 (1): 29–51.

"After the Fall." 2005. *Economist*, February 17.

Agarwal, Rajshree, and Michael Gort. 2001. "First-Mover Advantage and the Speed of Competitive Entry, 1887–1986." *Journal of Law and Economics* 44 (1): 161–77.

Agrawal, Ajay, and Iain Cockburn. 2003. "The Anchor Tenant Hypothesis: Exploring the Role of Large, Local, R&D-Intensive Firms in Regional Innovation Systems." *International Journal of Industrial Organization* 21 (9): 1227–53.

Aguiar, Mark, and Erik Hurst. 2006. "Measuring Trends in Leisure: The Allocation of Time over Five Decades." NBER Working Paper 12082, National Bureau of Economic Research, Cambridge, MA.

Aizenman, Joshua, and Eileen L. Brooks. 2005. "Globalization and Taste Convergence: The Cases of Wine and Beer." NBER Working Paper 11228, National Bureau of Economic Research, Cambridge, MA.

Alpert, Mark. 2006. "My Virtual War: A Disturbing Stroll through a Virtual Battlefield." *Scientific American*, February.

"American Gamers Get Their Adventures Direct from Japan." 2005. *Financial Times*, October 25.

"America Trails Asia's IT Growth." 2006. *Financial Times*. March 1.

"Amgen Works on the Formula for Profitable Science." 2005. *Financial Times*, November 4.

Amsden, Alice H. 1989. *Asia's Next Giant: South Korea and Late Industrialization*. New York and Oxford: Oxford University Press.

Amsden, Alice H., and Wan-wen Chu. 2003. *Beyond Late Development: Taiwan's Upgrading Policies*. Cambridge, MA: MIT Press.

Anderson, Chris. 2006. *The Long Tail: Why the Future of Business Is Selling Less of More*. New York: Hyperion Books.

"Anime Biz: Still an Adolescent, The." 2005. *BusinessWeek*, June 27.

"Another Ailing Miracle Drug." 2005. *BusinessWeek*, March 14.

Aoyama, Yuko, and Hiro Izushi. 2003. "Hardware Gimmick or Cultural Innovation? Technological, Cultural, and Social Foundations for the Japanese Video Game Industry." *Research Policy* 32 (3): 423–44.

"Approved Stem Cell Line Contaminated." 2005. *New Scientist*, January 29.

"Arcade Addicts Joust with Past." 2003. *Wired*, August 8.

"Architecture Watchdog Does a Demolition Job on Builders." 2005. *Financial Times*, June 18.

"Asia Jockeys for Stem Cell Lead." 2005. *Science*, February 4.

"Asian Alliance." 2004. *Hollywood Reporter*, May 24.

Askew, Marc. 2002. *Bangkok: Place, Practice, and Representation*. London: Routledge.

"Atlantic Harmony." 2005. *Flight International*, September 6–12.

Baily, Martin N. 1998. "The East Asian Miracle and Crisis: Microeconomic Evidence from Korea." Paper presented at the Microeconomics Meeting for the Brookings Papers on Economic Activity, Washington, DC, June 19.

Bairoch, Paul. 1988. *Cities and Economic Development*. Chicago: University of Chicago Press.

"Bandai to Buy Namco for $1.6 Billion." 2005. *Financial Times*, May 3.

Bangkok Fashion City. 2006. "Bangkok Fashion City." http://www.bangkokfashioncity.com/en/pressrelease/viewitem.aspx?ItemID=15.

Bangkok Metropolitan Administration. Various years. "Annual Report." Bangkok Metropolitan Administration, Bangkok.

Bangle, Chris. 2001. "The Ultimate Creativity Machine: How BMW Turns Art into Profit." *Harvard Business Review* 79 (1): 47–55.

Barton, Jack. 2004. "Bangkok's Fashion School." Agence France-Presse, March 28.

Basant, Rakesh, and Pankaj Chandra. 2005. "Role of Educational and R&D Institutions in City Clusters: An Exploratory Study of Bangalore and Pune Regions in India." Paper presented at the Conference on University Industry Linkages in Metropolitan Areas in Asia, World Bank and Social Science Research Council, Washington, DC, November 17.

"Beijing Digs Deep in Quest for Green Energy." 2005. Xinhua News Agency, July 21.

Beijing Municipal Commission of Development and Reform. 2006. "The Development in 2005 and Prospects for Beijing's High-Tech Industry." *China Venture Capital and High-Technology* (January): 18–20.

Beijing Municipal Commission of Economics. 2005. "Plan on Beijing's Industrial Restructuring." http://www.bjinvest.gov.cn/xmzj/zfzj/2005_1/zcfg/200511/P020051114614172475836.doc.

Beijing Municipal Statistics Bureau. Various years. *China Statistical Yearbook*. Beijing: China Statistics Press.

———. 2004. *Beijing Statistical Yearbook*. Beijing: China Statistics Press.

Bell, Daniel. 1976. *The Cultural Contradictions of Capitalism*. New York: Basic Books.

Benton-Short, Lisa, Marie Price, and Samantha Friedman. 2004. "Global Perspective on the Connections between Immigrants and World Cities." George Washington

Center for the Study of Globalization Occasional Paper CSGOP-04-32, George Washington University, Washington, DC.

Berry, Christopher R., and Edward L. Glaeser. 2005. "The Divergence of Human Capital Levels across Cities." NBER Working Paper 11617, National Bureau of Economic Research, Cambridge, MA.

"Big Pharma Woos Its Upstart Cousin." 2002. *Financial Times*, December 9.

"Big Trouble for Big Pharma." 2003. *The Economist*, December 6.

"Bionic Sensation." 2006. *BusinessWeek*, January 9.

"Biotech, Finally." 2005. *BusinessWeek*, June 13.

Biotechnology Information Institute. 1994. "Federal Labs and NIH Are Number One in Bio-Technology Transfer." Press release, Biotechnology Information Institute, Rockville, MD, September 8. http://www.bioinfo.com/fed_biotech_transfer_study.html.

"Blogging + Video = Vlogging." 2005. *Wired*, July 13.

Blonigen, Bruce A., Christopher J. Ellis, and Dietrich Fausten. 2005. "Industrial Groupings and Strategic FDI." *Japan and the World Economy* 17 (2): 125–50.

Bloom, David E., and Jeffrey G. Williamson. 1997. "Demographic Transitions and Economic Miracles in Emerging Asia." NBER Working Paper 6268, National Bureau of Economic Research, Cambridge, MA.

"Brick by Brick." 2005. *Shanghai Business Review*, November.

"A Bridge Too Far?" 2005. *Economist*, June 9.

Bryson, John R., Peter W. Daniels, and Barney Warf. 2004. *Service Worlds: People, Organizations, Technologies*. New York: Routledge.

"Bt25 Bn Fund to Upgrade Thai Textiles." 2004. *Nation* (Thailand), October 16.

"Budding Filmmakers Crave a Break." 2005. *Wired*, July 14.

"Building a Better Movie Business." 2005. *Fast Company*, December.

"Building the Country." 2005. *Economist*, March 10.

Bureau of Industrial and Labor Affairs. 2005. *Graphic Industry and Employment in Tokyo 2005*. Tokyo: Bureau of Industrial and Labor Affairs, Tokyo Metropolitan Government.

Bureau of Labor Statistics. 2002. "Work at Home in 2001." News Release USDL 02-107, U.S. Department of Labor, Washington, DC.

———. 2004. "BLS Releases 2002–2012 Employment Projections." News Release USDL 04-148, U.S. Department of Labor, Washington, DC.

———. 2005. "Work at Home in 2004." News Release USDL 05-1768, U.S. Department of Labor, Washington, DC.

———. Various years. *Consumer Expenditure Surveys*. Washington, DC: U.S. Department of Labor.

Business Research Division, Leeds School of Business. 2003. *The Impact of the Film Industry on Colorado*. Boulder: University of Colorado at Boulder.

"Business's Digital Black Cloud." 2005. *Economist*, July 16.

Campos, Jose Edgardo, and Hilton L. Root. 1996. *The Key to the Asian Miracle*. Washington, DC: Brookings Institution Press.

"A Cancer Treatment You Can't Get Here." 2006. *BusinessWeek*, March 6.

"Can China Innovate?" 2005. *Time International Asia*, May 16.

"Cangen Finds Niche in Cancer Fight." 2005. *Washington Post*, June 9.

"Can Money Turn Singapore into a Biotech Juggernaut?" 2005. *Science*, August 30.

Carey, Peter. 2006. *Wrong about Japan*. New York: Vintage International.

Carlile, Lonny E., and Mark Tilton, eds. 2005. *Is Japan Really Changing Its Ways? Regulatory Reform and the Japanese Economy*. Washington, DC: Brookings Institution Press.

Carlsson, Bo. 2006. "Internationalization of Innovation Systems: A Survey of Literature." *Research Policy* 35 (1): 56–67.

Castells, Manuel, and Martin Ince. 2003. *Conversations with Manuel Castells*. Cambridge, U.K.: Polity Press.

Castronova, Edward. 2001. "Virtual Worlds: A First-Hand Account of Market and Society on the Cyberian Frontier." CESifo Working Paper 618, Center for Economic Studies and Ifo Institute for Economic Research, Munich, Germany.

————. 2002. "On Virtual Economies." CESifo Working Paper 752, Center for Economic Studies and Ifo Institute for Economic Research, Munich, Germany.

————. 2003. "The Price of 'Man' and 'Woman': A Hedonic Pricing Model of Avatar Attributes in a Synthetic World." CESifo Working Paper 957, Center for Economic Studies and Ifo Institute for Economic Research, Munich, Germany.

————. 2005. *Synthetic Worlds: The Business and Culture of Online Games*. Chicago: University of Chicago Press.

Chang, Chen-Tung. 1976. "The Changing Socio-Demographic Profile." In *Singapore: Society in Transition*, ed. Riaz Hassan, 271–89. Kuala Lumpur: Oxford University Press.

Chang, Sen-Dou. 1998. "Beijing: Perspectives on Preservation, Environment, and Development." *Cities* 15 (1): 13–25.

"Channel Hopping: How French Films Crossed Over." 2006. *Financial Times*, March 8.

"A Chat with Roomba Man." 2004. *BusinessWeek*, July 19.

Chen, Kun, and Martin Kenney. 2005. "University/Research Institute–Industry Linkages in Two Chinese Cities: Commercializing Technological Innovation." Paper presented at the Conference on University-Industry Linkages in Metropolitan Areas in Asia, World Bank and Social Science Research Council, Singapore, May 24.

Chen, Le, and Sherif Mohamed. 2002. "China's Foreign Economic Cooperation Development: Exporting Chinese Construction Services." Paper presented at the First Annual Conference on Creating a Sustainable Construction Industry in Developing Countries, International Council for Research and Innovation in Building and Construction, Stellenbosh, South Africa, November 11.

"China Builds Its Dreams, and Some Fear a Bubble." 2005. *New York Times*, October 18.

"China: Challenge from Increasing Communications." 2005. *Oxford Analytica*, January 21.

"China: Demographic Trends Will Add to Fiscal Strains." 2004. *Oxford Analytica*, October 7.

Chinag, Yat-Hung, and Bo-Sin Tang. 2003. "'Submarines Don't Leak, Why Do Buildings?' Building Quality, Technological Impediment, and Organization of the Building Industry in Hong Kong." *Habitat International* 27 (1): 1–17.

"China: Labour Market Remains Underdeveloped." 2004. *Oxford Analytica*, October 8.

"China: Leading City Needs New Sources of Growth." 2005. *Oxford Analytica*, June 8.

"China's Challenge Changes the Rules of the Game." 2005. *Financial Times*, October 19.

"China: Share Sale Scheme to Capture More Companies." 2005. *Oxford Analytica*, August 24.

"China's Hi-Tech Success Is Not Patently Obvious." 2005. *Financial Times*, October 25.

"China's People Problem." 2005. *Economist*, April 16.

"China's Top 100 Electronics and IT Enterprise for 2005." 2005. Xinhua's China Economic Information Services, June 28.

"China to Quench Growing Petrol Thirst." 2005. *Financial Times*, June 29.

"Chinese Poised to Outstrip Europe on R&D." 2005. *Financial Times*, October 10.

"Chinese Set to Shop Till They Drop." 2004. *Financial Times*, July 10.

Chiu, Stephen W. K., and Tai-Lok Lui. 2004. "Testing the Global City-Social Polarisation Thesis: Hong Kong since the 1990s." *Urban Studies* 41 (10): 1863–88.

Cho, Aileen. 2004. "Engineers Are Absorbing Lessons from Shanghai's Express Train: First Commercial Magnetic Levitation System Is Judged a Success." *Engineering News-Record* 252 (7): 34.

Chou, Shin-Yi, Henry Saffer, and Michael Grossman. 2002. "An Economic Analysis of Adult Obesity: Results from the Behavioral Risk Factor Surveillance System." NBER Working Paper 9247, National Bureau of Economic Research, Cambridge, MA.

Chun, Hyunbae, Jung-Wook Kim, Jason Lee, and Randall Morck. 2004. "Patterns of Comovement: The Role of Information Technology in the U.S. Economy." NBER Working Paper 10937, National Bureau of Economic Research, Cambridge, MA.

Ciccone, Antonio, and Elias Papaioannou. 2005. "Human Capital, the Structure of Production, and Growth." CEPR Discussion Paper 5354, Centre for Economic Policy Research, London.

Citron, Paul, and Robert M. Nerem. 2004. "Bioengineering: 25 Years of Progress—But Still Only a Beginning." *Technology in Society* 26 (2–3): 415–31.

Clark, Paul. 2005. *Reinventing China: A Generation and Its Films*. Hong Kong (China): Chinese University Press.

Clark, Terry Nichols. 2004. *The City as an Entertainment Machine*. Oxford, U.K.: Elsevier.

Cohen, Barney. 2004. "Small Cities, Big Problems." *Issues in Science and Technology* 20 (3).

Cohen, Wesley M., Richard R. Nelson, and John P. Walsh. 2002. "Links and Impacts: The Influence of Public Research on Industrial R&D." *Management Science* 48 (1): 1–23.

Coleman, Margaret S., Nalinee Sangrujee, Fangjun Zhou, and Susan Chu. 2005. "Factors Affecting U.S. Manufacturers' Decisions to Produce Vaccines." *Health Affairs* 24 (3): 635–42.

Colombo, Massimo G., Marco Delmastro, and Luca Grilli. 2004. "Entrepreneurs' Human Capital and the Start-up Size of New Technology-Based Firms." *International Journal of Industrial Organization* 22 (8–9): 1183–211.

"Commercial Futures." 2001. *Flight International*, May 8.

COMMIT (ClOpidogrel and Metoprolol in Myocardial Infarction Trial). 2005. "Addition of Clopidogrel to Aspirin in 45,852 Patients with Acute Myocardial Infarction: Randomised Placebo-Controlled Trial." *Lancet* 366 (9497): 1607–21.

"Common Purpose." 2005. *Flight International*, September 6–12.

Cook, David A., and Wenli Wang. 2004. "Neutralizing the Piracy of Motion Pictures: Reengineering the Industry's Supply Chain." *Technology in Society* 26 (4): 567–83.

Cooke, Philip. 2005. "Rational Drug Design, the Knowledge Value Chain, and Bioscience Megacentres." *Cambridge Journal of Economics* 29 (3): 325–41.

"Copycats No More." 2005. *BusinessWeek*, April 18.

"Cost of Living Index." 2005. *Economist*, July 7.

"Counterfeiting: Fighting the Fakers." 2005. *Drapers Record*, May 14.

Cowen, Tyler. 2002. *Creative Destruction: How Globalization Is Changing the World's Cultures*. Princeton, NJ: Princeton University Press.

"Crimes against Hollywood, Chinese Style." 2005. *Financial Times*, June 23.

"Critical Mass Weighs on Dell's Growth Record." 2005. *Financial Times*, November 2.

Crosby, Olivia. 2000. "Working So Others Can Play: Jobs in Video Game Development." *Occupational Outlook Quarterly* 44 (2): 3–13.

Cullen, Julie Berry, and Steven D. Levitt. 1996. "Crime, Urban Flight, and the Consequences for Cities." NBER Working Paper 2737, National Bureau of Economic Research, Cambridge, MA.

"Cutting Edge." 2005. *Newsweek*, December 19.

Dabla-Norris, Era. 2004. "Issues in Intergovernmental Fiscal Relations in China." Paper prepared for the *Report on the 11th Five-Year Plan of China*, World Bank, Washington, DC.

Danzon, Patricia M., Sean Nicholson, and Nuno Sousa Pereira. 2005. "Productivity in Pharmaceutical-Biotechnology R&D: The Role of Experience and Alliances." *Journal of Health Economics* 24 (2): 317–39.

Datamonitor. 2005a. "Construction & Engineering in Asia-Pacific." London, Datamonitor.

————. 2005b. "Homebuilding in Asia-Pacific." London, Datamonitor.

————. 2005c. "Construction & Engineering in China." London, Datamonitor.

————. 2005d. "Homebuilding in China." London, Datamonitor.

————. 2005e. "Global Construction & Farm Machinery & Heavy Trucks." London, Datamonitor.

————. 2005f. "Global Construction Materials." London, Datamonitor.

————. 2005g. "Global Consumer Electronics." London, Datamonitor.

————. 2006. "Global Computers & Peripherals." London, Datamonitor.

David, Paul, Bronwyn H. Hall, and Andrew A. Toole. 1999. "Is Public R&D a Complement or Substitute for Private R&D? A Review of Econometric Evidence." SIEPR Discussion Paper 99-1, Stanford Institute for Economic Policy Research, Stanford, CA.

"The da Vinci Mode." 2004. *Washington Post*, April 27.

Davis, Deborah. 2005. "Urban Consumer Culture." *China Quarterly* 183: 692–709.

Davis, Donald R., and David E. Weinstein. 2001. "Market Size, Linkages, and Productivity: A Study of Japanese Regions." NBER Working Paper 8518, National Bureau of Economic Research, Cambridge, MA.

————. 2002. "Bones, Bombs, and Break Points: The Geography of Economic Activity." *American Economic Review* 92 (5): 1269–89.

DCAj (Digital Content Association of Japan). 2003. *Digital Content White Paper 2003*. Tokyo: Digital Content Association of Japan.

————. 2004. *Digital Content White Paper 2004.* Tokyo: Digital Content Association of Japan.

"Debt Threat." 2005. *Economist*, March 23.

DeJean, Joan. 2005. *The Essence of Style: How the French Invented High Fashion, Fine Food, Chic Cafés, Style, Sophistication, and Glamour*. New York: Free Press.

"Delays and Hefty Costs Disrupt Game Industry." 2006. *International Herald Tribune*, June 20.

"Demand Far Outstrips Supply." 2002. *Financial Times*, November 12.

Denison, Edward, and Guan Yu Ren. 2006. *Building Shanghai: The Story of Building China's Gateway*. Seattle: Academy Press.

Dentsu Communication Institute. 2003. *A Research for Information and Media Society*. Tokyo: Diamond Press.

————. 2004. *A Research for Information and Media Society*. Tokyo: Diamond Press.

————. 2005. *A Research for Information and Media Society*. Tokyo: Diamond Press.

Department of Export Promotion (Thailand). 2001. http://www.thaitrade.com/en/doc/Jewelry%2520and%2520Accessories.doc.

"Designing a Fashion Hub." 2004. *Bangkok Post*, March 21.

"Design Lets Robot Walk Much as a Human Does." 2005. *Washington Post*, February 18.

"Deus Ex Machinima." 2004. *Economist*, September 16.

Dietz, Meagan C., Sarena Shao-Tin Lin, and Lei Yang. 2005. "Protecting Intellectual Property in China." *McKinsey Quarterly* 3: 6–8.

"The Digital Hospital." 2005. *BusinessWeek*, March 28.

DiMasi, Joseph A., Ronald W. Hansen, and Henry G. Grabowski. 2003. "The Price of Innovation: New Estimates of Drug Development Costs." *Journal of Health Economics* 22 (2): 151–85.

"Diseases Remain a Global Threat." 2005. *Oxford Analytica*, June 2.

"Disney in Mobile Games Purchase." 2005. *Financial Times*, November 7.

"Diversity and Design Are the New Watchwords." 2005. *Financial Times*, October 19.

"Does IT Improve Performance." 2005. *McKinsey Quarterly Chart Focus Newsletter*, June.

"Double Triumph in Stem Cell Quest: As Korean Cloners Grab the Limelight, a Chicago Team Is Claiming an Easier Route to Embryonic Stem Cells." 2005. *New Scientist*, May 28.

"Do We Even Need Eggs?" 2006. *Nature*, February 9.

"Download This." 2005. *Newsweek*, September 26.

Downs, Anthony. 2004. *Still Stuck in Traffic*. Washington, DC: Brookings Institution.

"Drugs Get Smart." 2005. *BusinessWeek*, September 5.

"Dublin Thinks Big over Biotech." 2003. *Financial Times*, March 24.

"Dude, Where's My Digital Car?" 2005. *BusinessWeek*, July 4.

"East Asia Powers Ahead on Stem Cell Research." 2005. *Financial Times*, January 26.

"Eastern Rebirth of the Life Science." 2005. *Financial Times*, June 10.

"Eat Your Own Laboratory." 2003. *Financial Times*, May 9.

Eberwine, Donna. 2002. "Globesity: The Crisis of Growing Proportions." *Perspectives in Health* 7 (3): 6–11.

Economist Intelligence Unit. 2005. "The 2005 E-Readiness Rankings." London, Economic Intelligence Unit.

————. 2006. "China: Transport and Communications." London, Economist Intelligence Unit, January 27.

Ellerman, David. 2005. "How Do We Grow? Jane Jacobs on Diversification and Specialization." *Challenge* 48 (3): 50–83.

"An Emerging Biotech Giant?" 2005. *China Business Review*, May.

"Energy Answer: Blowing in the Wind." 2004. *IEEE Spectrum*, February.

Epstein, Edward Jay. 2005. *The Big Picture: The New Logic of Money and Power in Hollywood*. New York: Random House.

Ernst, Dieter. 2002. "Electronics Industry." In *The IEBM Handbook of Economics*, ed. William Lazonick, 319–39. London: Thomson.

Etzkowitz, Henry. 2002. *MIT and the Rise of Entrepreneurial Science*. New York: Routledge.

"Exotic Pursuits." 2003. *Economist*, January 30.

"Factory Robots Retooled as Amusement Park Ride." 2005. *News.com*, August 3.

"A Family of Robots for Rehabs." 2005. *BusinessWeek*, July 25.

Fan, C. Cindy. 2004. "Migration in China: A Review of Recent Findings and Policy Recommendations." Paper prepared for *Report on the 11th Five-Year Plan of China*, World Bank, Washington, DC.

Farlow, Andrew. 2005. "Over the Rainbow: The Pot of Gold for Neglected Diseases." *Lancet* 364 (9450): 2011–12.

"Fashion's Favourite." 2004. *Economist*, March 6.

Feldman, Maryann, and Johanna Francis. 2003. "Fortune Favours the Prepared Region: The Case of Entrepreneurship and the Capitol Region Biotechnology Cluster." *European Planning Studies* 11 (7): 765–88.

Feldman, Maryann, Johanna Francis, and Janet Bercovitz. 2005. "Creating a Cluster While Building a Firm: Entrepreneurs and the Formation of Industrial Clusters." *Regional Studies* 39 (1): 129–41.

Feldman, Maryann, and Roger Martin. 2004. "Jurisdictional Advantage." NBER Working Paper 10802, National Bureau of Economic Research, Cambridge, MA.

"A Female Sensibility." 2005. *Newsweek*, September 26.

"The 54-Story Air Filter." 2005. *Popular Science*, March.

Fine, Charles H. 1998. *Clockspeed: Winning Industry Control in the Age of Temporary Advantage*. New York: Perseus Publishing.

Finegold, David, Poh Kam Wong, and Tsui-Chern Cheah. 2004. "Adapting a Foreign Direct Investment Strategy to the Knowledge Economy: The Case of Singapore's Emerging Biotechnology Cluster." *European Planning Studies* 12 (7): 921–42.

Florida, Richard 2002. *The Rise of the Creative Class: And How It's Transforming Work, Leisure, Community, and Everyday Life*. New York: Basic Books.

————. 2005. *The Flight of the Creative Class: The New Global Competition for Talent*. New York: HarperCollins.

"Food for Thought." 2005. *Popular Science*, May.

Foray, Dominique. 2006. "University-Industry Knowledge Transfer in Switzerland." In *How Universities Can Promote Economic Growth*, ed. Shahid Yusuf and Kaoru Nabeshima. Washington, DC: World Bank.

"Foreign Patients and Overseas Focus Help." 2005. *Bangkok Post*, April 11.

Forman, Chris, Avi Goldfarb, and Shane Greenstein. 2005. "Technology Adoption in and out of Major Urban Areas: When Do Internal Firm Resources Matter Most?" NBER Working Paper 11642, National Bureau of Economic Research, Cambridge, MA.

Franke, Nikolaus, and Sonali Shah. 2003. "How Communities Support Innovative Activities: An Explanation of Assistance and Sharing among End-Users." *Research Policy* 32 (1): 157–78.

Freeman, Richard B. 2002. "The Labor Market in the New Information Economy." *Oxford Review of Economic Policy* 18 (3): 288–305.

————. 2005. "Does Globalization of the Scientific/Engineering Workforce Threaten U.S. Economic Leadership?" NBER Working Paper 11457, National Bureau of Economic Research, Cambridge, MA.

Friedmann, John. 2005. *China's Urban Transition*. Minneapolis: University of Minnesota Press.

Fujita, Kuniko. 2003. "Neo-Industrial Tokyo: Urban Development and Globalisation in Japan's State-Centered Developmental Capitalism." *Urban Studies* 40 (2): 249–81.

Fujita, Kuniko, and Richard Child Hill. 2005. "Innovative Tokyo." Policy Research Working Paper 3507. World Bank, Washington, DC.

Fuller, Douglas B. 2005. "The Changing Limits and the Limits of Change: The State, Private Firms, International Industry, and China in the Evolution of Taiwan's Electronics Industry." *Journal of Contemporary China* 14 (44): 483–506.

Gallagher, Kelly Sims. 2006. "Limits to Leapfrogging in Energy Technology? Evidence from the Chinese Automobile Industry." *Energy Policy* 34 (4): 383–94.

"The Game Is On." 2004. *New Scientist*, September 18.

"Games Become a Global Play." 2005. *Financial Times*, March 22.

"Games Makers Cut to the Chase." 2003. *Financial Times*, January 28.

"Game Wars: Who Will Win Your Entertainment Dollar, Hollywood or Silicon Valley?" 2005. *BusinessWeek*, February 28.

"Gaming Goes to Hollywood." 2004. *Economist*, March 25.

Gann, David M., and Ammon J. Slater. 2000. "Innovation in Project-Based, Service-Enhanced Firms: The Construction of Complex Products and Systems." *Research Policy* 29 (7–8): 955–72.

Gao, Guofu. 2005. "Urban Infrastructure Investment and Financing in Shanghai." Shanghai: Shanghai Chengtou Corporation.

Gem and Jewelry Institute of Thailand. 2003. *Thai Gem and Jewelry Industry*. Bangkok: Gem and Jewelry Institute of Thailand.

"Gemstone Scandals." 2003. *Wall Street Journal*, April 17.

"Genentech's Lessons for Big Pharma." 2005. *BusinessWeek*, May 9.

Gibbs, W. Wayt. 2006. "Innovations from a Robot Rally." *Scientific American* 294 (1): 64.

Glaeser, Edward L. 2005a. "Reinventing Boston: 1640–2003." *Journal of Economic Geography* 5 (2): 119–53.

————.2005b. "Review of Richard Florida's *The Rise of the Creative Class*." *Regional Science and Urban Economics* 35 (5): 593–96.

————. 2005c. "Urban Colossus: Why Is New York America's Largest City?" NBER Working Paper 11398, National Bureau of Economic Research, Cambridge, MA.

Glaeser, Edward L., Hedi D. Kallal, José A. Scheinkman, and Andrei Shleifer. 1992. "Growth in Cities." *Journal of Political Economy* 100 (6): 1126–52.

Glaeser, Edward L., and David C. Mare. 2001. "Cities and Skills." *Journal of Labor Economics* 19 (2): 316–42.

Glaeser, Edward L., and Albert Saiz. 2003. "The Rise of the Skilled City." NBER Working Paper 10191, National Bureau of Economic Research, Cambridge, MA.

Glen, Jerome, and Theodore J. Gordon. 2004. "Future S&T Management Policy Issue: 2025 Global Scenarios." *Technological Forecasting and Social Change* 71 (9): 913–40.

Glosser, Stuart, and Lonnie Golden. 2005. "Is Labour Becoming More or Less Flexible? Changing Dynamic Behaviour and Asymmetrics of Labour Input in U.S. Manufacturing." *Cambridge Journal of Economics* 29 (4): 535–57.

"Glow in the Dark." 2005. *Economist*, December 10.

"Golden Boys and Girls." 2004. *Economist*, February 14.

Goldman, Todd, and Roger Gorham. 2006. "Sustainable Urban Transport: Four Innovative Directions." *Technology in Society* 28 (1–2): 261–73.

Gonchar, Joann. 2004. "'Green' Builders Tackling Sensitive Technical Issues." *Engineering News-Record* 253 (20): 15.

"A Good Fit? Designers and Mass-Market Chains Try to Stitch Their Fortunes Together." 2005. *Financial Times*, October 25.

"Google, Meet TiVo." 2005. *Economist*, June 9.

Goozner, Merrill. 2004. *The $800 Million Pill: The Truth behind the Cost of New Drugs*. Berkeley: University of California Press.

Gordon, Robert J. 2004a. "Five Puzzles in the Behavior of Productivity, Investment, and Innovation." NBER Working Paper 10660, National Bureau of Economic Research, Cambridge, MA.

————. 2004b. "Why Was Europe Left at the Station When America's Productivity Locomotive Departed?" NBER Working Paper 10661, National Bureau of Economic Research, Cambridge, MA.

Graham, Stephen, and Simon Marvin. 2000. "Urban Planning and the Technological Future of Cities." In *Cities in the Telecommunications Age*, ed. James O. Wheeler, Yuko Aoyama, and Barney Warf, 71–98. New York: Routledge.

"Green Tea with Yellow Robots." 2003. *Financial Times*, September 5.

Greenwood, Jeremy, and Guillaume Vandenbroucke. 2005. "Hours Worked: Long-Run Trends." NBER Working Paper 11629. National Bureau of Economic Research, Cambridge, MA.

Guiso, Luigi, and Fabiano Schivardi. 2005. "Learning to Be an Entrepreneur." CEPR Discussion Paper 5290, Centre for Economic Policy Research, London.

Guizzo, Erico, and Harry Goldstein. 2005. "The Rise of Body Botn." *Spectrum*, October.

Hall, Peter 1998. *Cities in Civilization: Culture, Technology, and Urban Order*. London: Weidenfeld and Nicolson.

————. 2000. "Creative Cities and Economic Development." *Urban Studies* 37 (4): 639–49.

"The Halo Effect." 2004. *Economist*, November 11.

Halpern, Laszlo, and Balazs Murakozy. 2005. "Does Distance Matter in Spillover?" CEPR Discussion Paper 4857, Centre for Economic Policy Research, London.

Hamaguchi, Nobuaki, and Yoshihiro Kameyama. 2005. "The Comparative Study of Knowledge-Based Industrial Clusters in East Asia." Paper presented at the Second Asian Development Conference on ICT Industrial Clusters in East Asia, Kitakyushu, Japan, December 12.

Hampton, Tudor. 2004. "China May Lead Production of Machines by Decade's End." *Engineering News-Record* 252 (15): 16.

"Handbag Invasion." 2003. *Financial Times*, August 2.

"Hangover Cure." 2005. *Economist*, May 5.

Harwit, Eric. 2005. "Telecommunication and the Internet in Shanghai: Political and Economic Factors Shaping the Network in a Chinese City." *Urban Studies* 42 (10): 1837–58.

Hasegawa, Yukio. 1981. "The Future of Industrial Robots." In *Robots in the Japanese Economy: Facts about Robots and Their Significance*, ed. Kuni Sadamoto. Tokyo: Survey Japan.

Haslam, David W., and W. Phillip T. James. 2005. "Obesity." *Lancet* 366 (9492): 1197–209.

"Health Spending." 2003. *Economist*, June 28.

Heffler, Stephen, Sheila Smith, Sean Keehan, Christine Borger, M. Kent Clemens, and Christopher Truffer. 2005. "U.S. Health Spending Projections for 2004–2014." *Health Affairs* 24 (2): 570–71.

Held, David, Anthony McGrew, David Goldblatt, and Jonathan Perraton. 1999. *Global Transformations: Politics, Economics, and Culture*. Stanford, CA: Stanford University Press.

Henderson, J. Vernon. 2004a. "Issues Concerning Urbanization in China." Paper prepared for the *Report on the 11th Five-Year Plan of China*, World Bank, Washington, DC.

————. 2004b. "Scenarios Concerning Urban Growth." Paper prepared for the *Report on the 11th Five-Year Plan of China*, World Bank, Washington, DC.

"Here Comes the Wal-Mart Wannabes." 2005. *BusinessWeek*, April 4.

Hermida, Alfred. 2002. "Movie Soundtracks Come to Gaming." *BBC News*, March 5.

"High Style in Thailand: Part 2." 2005. *Just-Style*, April 20.

Hines, Matt. 2005. "Robotics Industry Hypes Drive to Market." CNET News.com, http://news.com.com/Robotics+industry+hypes+drive+to+market/2100-1022_3-5702377.html.

Hinman, Alan R. 2005. "Addressing the Vaccine Financing Conundrum." *Health Affairs* 24 (3): 701–04.

Hoenig, Jay. 2004. "Building in China." *The China Business Review* 31 (2): 56–57, 61.

"Ho, Ho, Hao." 2003. *Economist*, December 20.

Hollander, Anne. 1993. *Seeing through Clothes*. Berkeley: University of California Press.

"Hollywood Caters to a Ravenous Global Appetite." 2006. *Washington Post*, May 27.

"Hollywood Games." 2005. *Financial Times*, May 17.

"Hollywood Learns to Play the Video Game." 2005. *Financial Times*, May 10.

"Hollywood Sees Power Shift from Film-Set to Desktop." 2005. *Financial Times*, June 20.

"Home-Grown Standard Fights for a Role." 2005. *Financial Times*, October 19.

"Hope Lies in Tinseltown's DVD Woes." 2005. *Financial Times*, July 7.

Hospers, Gert-Jan. 2003. "Creative Cities: Breeding Places in the Knowledge Economy." *Knowledge, Technology, and Policy* 16 (3): 143–62.

"How Hong Kong Stays King." 2006. *International Freighting Weekly*, June 19.

"How Humanoids Won the Hearts of Japanese Industry." 2006. *Financial Times*, July 3.

Howe, Christopher. 1996. *The Origins of Japanese Trade Supremacy: Development and Technology in Asia from 1540 to the Pacific War*. Chicago: Chicago University Press.

Hu, Albert G. Z., and Adam B. Jaffe. 2003. "Patent Citations and International Knowledge Flow: The Cases of Korea and Taiwan." *International Journal of Industrial Organization* 21 (6): 849–80.

Huebner, Jonathan. 2005. "A Possible Declining Trend for Worldwide Innovation." *Technological Forecasting and Social Change* 72: 980–86.

Huff, W. G. 1994. *The Economic Growth of Singapore: Trade and Development in the Twentieth Century*. Cambridge, U.K.: Cambridge University Press.

Hutchings, Graham. 2001. *Modern China: A Guide to a Century of Change*. Cambridge, MA: Harvard University Press.

Huws, Ursula. 2003. *The Making of a Cybertariat: Virtual Work in a Real World*. New York: Monthly Review Press.

"IBM Set to Unveil Key Microchip Advance." 2006. *Financial Times*, February 21.

Indergaard, Michael. 2004. *Silicon Alley: The Rise and Fall of a New Media District*. New York: Routledge.

"India Emerges as New Drug Proving Ground." 2004. *Wall Street Journal*, February 19.

Indjikian, Rouben, and Donald S. Siegel. 2005. "The Impact of Investment in IT on Economic Performance: Implications for Developing Countries." *World Development* 33 (5): 681–700.

"Industrial Metamorphosis." 2005. *Economist*, October 1.

"In Search of the Ideal Employer." 2005. *Economist*, August 18.

"Intelligent Beings in Space!" 2006. *New York Times*, May 30.

International Telecommunication Union. 2004. *ITU Internet Report 2004: The Portable Internet*. Geneva: International Telecommunication Union.

"In Tokyo, a Ghetto of Geeks." 2005. *Washington Post*, June 7.

"Invaders from the Land of Broadband." 2003. *Economist*, December 11.

"iRobot Unveils Sniper Detector." 2005. *News.com*, October 4.

"An Irresistible Force." 2005. *Nature*, August 11.

"It Came from Hollywood." 2003. *New Yorker*, December 1.

"It's . . . Profitmón!" 2005. *Fortune*, December 12.

"Jackie Chan Meets Julie Andrews." 2005. *Observer*, June 26.

Jakobsen, Stig-Erik, and Knut Onsager. 2005. "Head Office Location: Agglomeration, Clusters, or Flow Nodes?" *Urban Studies* 42 (9): 1517–35.

Jansen, Marius B. 2000. *The Making of Modern Japan*. Cambridge, MA: Harvard University Press.

"Japan Emerges as Pop Culture Classroom." 2005. *Daily Yomiuri*, October 6.

"Japanese Mobile Phone Sales Down 10.5 Pct. in '04." 2005. *Jiji Press*, March 23.

"Japanese Textile Companies Look for ASEAN Suppliers." 2005. Thai News Service, June 10.

Japan Machinery Federation and Japan Robot Association. 2001. "Report on Technology Strategy for Creation of Robot Society in 21st Century." Japan Machinery Federation and Japan Robot Association, Tokyo.

Japan Patent Office. 2004. *Annual Report on Patent Administration 2004*. Tokyo: Japan Patent Office.

"Japan: Population Trends Weigh on Policy." 2005. *Oxford Analytica*, October 20.

Japan Robot Association. 2000. "Report on Issues on Advancement of Robot Industry for 21st Century." Japan Robot Association, Tokyo.

Jenkins, J. Craig, Kevin T. Leicht, and Heather Wendt. 2006. "Class Forces, Political Institutions, and State Intervention: Subnational Economic Development Policy in the United States, 1971–1990." *American Journal of Sociology* 111 (4): 1122–80.

JETRO (Japan External Trade Organization). 2005. "Industrial Report: Japan Animation Industry Trends." *Japan Economic Monthly*, June.

Jiang, Juan, and Yuko Harayama. 2005. "University Local Industry Linkages: The Case of Tohoku University in Sendai Area." Paper presented at the Conference on University-Industry Linkages in Metropolitan Areas in Asia, World Bank and Social Science Research Council, Washington, DC, November 17.

Johns, Jennifer. 2006. "Video Game Production Networks: Value Capture, Power Relations and Embeddedness." *Journal of Economic Geography* 6 (2): 151–80.

Johnson, Linda Cooke. 1995. *Shanghai: From Market Town to Treaty Port, 1074–1858*. Stanford, CA: Stanford University Press.

Jones, Benjamin F. 2005a. "Age and Great Invention." NBER Working Paper 11359, National Bureau of Economic Research, Cambridge, MA.

———. 2005b. "The Burden of Knowledge and the 'Death of the Renaissance Man': Is Innovation Getting Harder?" NBER Working Paper 11360, National Bureau of Economic Research, Cambridge, MA.

Judson, Horace Freeland. 2005. "The Great Chinese Experiment." *Technology Review* 108 (11): 52–61.

Kanellos, Michael. 2004a. "Army to Deploy Robots That Shoot." CNET News.com, December 4. http://news.com.com/Army+to+deploy+robots+that+shoot/2100-7348_3-5473191.html.

———. 2004b. "iRobot Readies for War." CNET News.com, October 24. http://news.com.com/iRobot+readies+for+war--and+the+household/2100-1041_3-5424307.html.

———. 2005. "Defense Dept. Funds Carnegie Mellon Battle Robot." CNET News.com, February 14. http://news.com.com/Defense+Dept.+funds+Carnegie+Mellon+battle+robot/2110-1008_3-5575773.html.

Keller, Wolfgang. 2002. "Geographic Localization of International Technology Diffusion." *American Economic Review* 92 (1): 120–42.

Kenney, Martin, Kyonghee Han, and Shoko Tanaka. 2004. "Venture Capital Industries." In *Global Change and East Asian Policy Initiatives*, ed. Shahid Yusuf, M. Anjum Altaf, and Kaoru Nabeshima, 391–428. New York: Oxford University Press.

Kiyota, Kozo. 2005. "Services Content of Japanese Trade." *Japan and the World Economy* 17 (3): 261–92.

"Knockout Malaria Vaccine?" 2005. *Nature*, January 13.

Knox, Paul L. 2005. "Creating Ordinary Places: Slow Cities in a Fast World." *Journal of Urban Design* 10 (1): 1–11.

Kodama, Fumio, and Jun Suzuki. 2005. "How Japanese Companies Brought New Sciences for Restructuring Their Businesses: Characterizing Receiver-Active National System of Innovation." Paper presented at the Conference on University-Industry Linkages in Metropolitan Areas in Asia, World Bank and Social Science Research Council, Washington, DC, November 17.

Kodama, Toshihiro. 2005. "An Intermediary and Absorptive Capacity to Facilitate University-Industry Linkages Based on Empirical Analysis for TAMA in Japan." Paper presented at the Conference on University-Industry Linkages in Metropolitan Areas in Asia, World Bank and Social Science Research Council, Washington, DC, November 17, 2005.

Koga, Toshiyuki, Kaoru Suzuki, and Osamu Yamaguchi. 2004. "Face Recognition Technology for Home Robot." *Toshiba Review* 59 (9): 33–36.

Koh, Winston T. H., and Poh Kam Wong. 2005. "Competing at the Frontier: The Changing Role of Technology Policy in Singapore's Economic Strategy." *Technological Forecasting and Social Change* 72 (3): 255–85.

Kohli, Atul. 2004. *State-Directed Development: Political Power and Industrialization in the Global Periphery*. Cambridge, U.K.: Cambridge University Press.

Korea Culture Contents Promotion Agency. "Analysis of Labor Structure and Function of Culture Contents Industry." Seoul: Korea Culture Contents Promotion Agency.

Korea Game Development and Promotion Institute. 2001. *Game White Paper*. Seoul: Korea Game Development and Promotion Institute.

Korea National Statistical Office. 2004. *Report on the Census on Basic Characteristics of Establishments*. Seoul: Korea National Statistical Office.

Korean Film Council. 2004. *Korean Cinema 2004*. Seoul: Korean Film Council.

"Korean Team Speeds Up Creation of Cloned Human Cells." 2005. *Science*, May 20.

Kotkin, Joel. 2005. *The City: A Global History*. New York: Modern Library.

Kremer, Michael. 2000. *Creating Markets for New Vaccines*. Cambridge, MA: Harvard University, Brookings Institution, and National Bureau of Economic Research.

Kushner, David. 2005. "Engineering EverQuest." *Spectrum*, July.

Kwon, Won-Yong, and Kwang-Joong Kim. 2001. "Introduction." In *Urban Management in Seoul*, ed. Won-Yong Kwon and Kwang-Joong Kim, 1–14. Seoul: Seoul Development Institute.

Laursen, Keld, and Ammon Salter. 2004. "Searching High and Low: What Types of Firms Use Universities as a Source of Innovation?" *Research Policy* 33 (8): 1201–15.

Lawlor, Andrew, Herman Chein, Jason Conway, and Yanyan Zhang. 2002. "Cluster Development in Beijing and Shanghai." Background Paper for the East Asia Project. World Bank, Washington, DC.

Lazear, Edward P. 2002. "Entrepreneurship." NBER Working Paper 9109, National Bureau of Economic Research, Cambridge, MA.

Lazonick, William. 2004. "Indigenous Innovation and Economic Development: Lessons from China's Leap into the Information Age." *Industry and Innovation* 11 (4): 273–97.

Leamer, Edward E., and Michael Storper. 2001. "The Economic Geography of the Internet Age." *Journal of International Business Studies* 32 (4): 641–65.

Lecuyer, Christophe. 2005. *Making Silicon Valley: Innovation and the Growth of High Tech, 1930–1970*. Cambridge, MA: MIT University Press.

Lee, Heejin, Sangjo Oh, and Yongwoon Shim. 2005. "Do We Need Broadband? Impacts of Broadband in Korea." *Info* 7 (4): 47–56.

Lee, Kuan Yew. 2000. *From Third World to First: The Singapore Story: 1965–2000*. New York: HarperCollins.

Lee, Soo Ann. 1976. "The Economic System." In *Singapore: Society in Transition*, ed. Riaz Hassan, 3–29. Kuala Lumpur: Oxford University Press.

Leman, Edward. 2002. "Can Shanghai Compete as a Global City?" *China Business Review* 29 (5): 7–15.

Lichtenberg, Frank R. 2001. "The Benefits and Costs of Newer Drugs: Evidence from the 1996 Medical Expenditure Panel Survey." NBER Working Paper 8147, National Bureau of Economic Research, Cambridge, MA.

———. 2002. "Sources of U.S. Longevity Increase, 1960–1997." NBER Working Paper 8755, National Bureau of Economic Research, Cambridge, MA.

———. 2004. "The Expanding Pharmaceutical Arsenal in the War on Cancer." NBER Working Paper 10328, National Bureau of Economic Research, Cambridge, MA.

Lichtenberg, Frank R., and Suchin Virabhak. 2002. "Pharmaceutical-Embodied Technical Progress, Longevity, and Quality of Life: Drugs as "Equipment for Your Health." NBER Working Paper 9351, National Bureau of Economic Research, Cambridge, MA.

Light, Donald W., and Rebecca N. Warburton. 2005. "Extraordinary Claims Require Extraordinary Evidence." *Journal of Health Economics* 24 (5): 1030–33.

"Lights. Industrial Action!" 2005. *Economist*, January 22.

Lincoln, Edward J. 2001. *Arthritic Japan: The Slow Pace of Economic Reform*. Washington, DC: Brookings Institution Press.

Linden, Greg. 2003. "Optical Storage in China: A Study in Strategic Industrial Policy." Report 2003-01. Information Storage Industry Center, University of California–San Diego.

———. 2004. "China Standard Time: A Study in Strategic Industrial Policy." *Business and Politics* 6 (3), article 4.

Lindsay, Colin. 2005. "Employability, Services for Unemployed Job Seekers, and the Digital Divide." *Urban Studies* 42 (2): 325–39.

"Listen: The Sound of Hope." 2005. *BusinessWeek*, November 14.

Lo, Fu-chen, and Yue-man Yeung, eds. 1998. *Globalization and the World of Large Cities*. New York: United Nations University Press.

"Long March to Become a Centre of Technological Innovation." 2005. *Financial Times*, October 19.

"The Long Tail." 2004. *Wired*, October.

Long-Term Credit Bank of Japan. 1981. "Industrial Robots in Japan." In *Robots in the Japanese Economy: Facts about Robots and Their Significance*, ed. Kuni Sadamoto. Tokyo: Survey Japan.

"Looking for Luxury." 2005. *International Herald Tribune*, December 16.

"Love Me, Love My Dog." 2005. *Economist*, February 10.

Lowe-Lee, Florence. 2003. "Korea's Aging Population: Economic and Social Challenges." *Korea Insight* 5 (10): 1–3.

Lu, Hanchao. 1999. *Beyond the Neon Lights: Everyday Shanghai in the Early Twentieth Century*. Berkeley: University of California Press.

Lu, Qiwen, and William Lazonick. 2001. "The Organization of Innovation in a Transition Economy: Business and Government in Chinese Electronic Publishing." *Research Policy* 30 (1): 55–77.

"Making Their Own Breaks." 2005. *Newsweek*, September 26.

Mansel, Philip. 2005. *Dressed to Rule: Royal and Court Costume from Louis XIV to Elizabeth II*. New Haven, CT: Yale University Press.

"Manufacturing on the Move?" 2005. *Shanghai Business Review*, April.

"The March of Robo-Traders." 2005. *Economist*, September 17.

"A Marginalised Market." 2005. *Economist*, February 24.

Markusen, Ann. 1996. "Sticky Places in Slippery Space: A Typology of Industrial Districts." *Economic Geography* 72 (3): 293–313.

Markusen, Ann, and David King. 2003. "The Artistic Dividend: The Arts' Hidden Contributions to Regional Development." Minneapolis, MN: Humphrey Institute of Public Affairs.

Martin, Brian G. 1996. *The Shanghai Green Gang: Politics and Organized Crime, 1919–1937*. Berkeley: University of California Press.

Martin-Bernard, Frédéric. 2006. "La Suprématie de l'Italie." *L'Express*, April 27.

Marvasti, Akbar, and E. Ray Canterbery. 2005. "Culture and Other Barriers to Motion Picture Trade." *Economic Inquiry* 43 (1): 39–54.

Matsuhira, Nobuto, and Hideki Ogawa. 2004. "Trends in Development of Home Robots Leading Advanced Technologies." *Toshiba Review* 59 (9): 2–8.

McCloskey, Donald. 1985. "The Industrial Revolution 1780–1860: A Survey." In *The Economics of the Industrial Revolution*, ed. Joel Mokyr, 53–74. Totowa, NJ: Rowman and Allenheld.

McCombie, John, Maurizio Pugno, and Bruno Soro, eds. 2002. *Productivity Growth and Economic Performance: Essays on Verdoorn's Law*. New York: Palgrave Macmillan.

McKendrick, David G., Richard F. Doner, and Stephan Haggard. 2000. *From Silicon Valley to Singapore: Location and Competitive Advantage in the Hard Disk Drive Industry*. Stanford, CA: Stanford University Press.

McKinsey Global Institute. 2001. "U.S. Productivity Growth, 1995–2000, Section VI: Retail Trade." New York: McKinsey Global Institute.

Meijers, Evert. 2005. "Polycentric Urban Regions and the Quest for Synergy: Is a Network of Cities More Than the Sum of the Parts?" *Urban Studies* 42 (4): 765–781.

"Men Are from Mars, Robots Are from Mitsubishi." 2005. *Financial Times*, December 9.

Menzel, Peter, and Faith D'Aluisio. 2000. *Robosapiens: Evolution of a New Species*. Cambridge, MA: MIT Press.

Messner, Steven F., Jianhong Liu, and Susanne Karstedt. 2005. "Economic Reform and Crime in Contemporary China: Paradoxes of a Planned Transition." Paper presented at the conference on Urban China in Transition, New York University at Albany, New Orleans, LA, January 15, 2005.

MEXT (Japan Ministry of Education, Culture, Sports, Science, and Technology). 2004. *School Basic Survey 2004*. Tokyo: MEXT.

"Microsoft: Getting from 'R' to 'D.'" 2005. *MIT Technology Review*, March.

"Miniature Could Be Hollywood's New Monster Hit." 2005. *Financial Times*, December 13.

"Mining the Secrets of the Egg." 2006. *Nature*, February 9.

Ministry of Construction (China). 2003. *China Construction Yearbook 2003*. Beijing: China City Press.

Ministry of Education (China). 2005. "Abstract on the Job Placement of University Graduates in 2004." http://edu.sing.com/ca/2005-04-12/ba110917.shtml. Accessed June 21, 2006.

————. 2006. "Notice on the Job Placement of the 2006 University Graduates." http://www.myjob.edu.ca/news_files/2006666693.html. Accessed June 21, 2006.

Ministry of Education, Culture, Sports, and Science (Japan). 2004. *Basic Report on Education*. Tokyo: Ministry of Education, Culture, Sports, and Science.

Ministry of Public Management, Home Affairs Posts, and Telecommunications (Japan). 2003. "Communications Usage Trend Survey in 2003 Compiled." Ministry of Public Management, Home Affairs Posts, and Telecommunications, Tokyo.

Ministry of Trade and Industry (Singapore). 2004. *Economic Survey of Singapore*. Singapore: Ministry of Trade and Industry.

Mizoguchi, Hiroshi. 2004. "Sound Spot Forming Technology for Robotic Home." *Toshiba Review* 59 (9): 37–41.

"A Mobile Page Turner." 2005. CNN.com, March 21. http://www.cnn.com/2005/TECH/ptech/03/21/cell.phone.novels.ap/index.html.

"Mobile Phone Makers Eye Booming Games Market." 2005. *Financial Times*, September 1.

"A Model Economy." 2005. *Economist*, January 20.

Mohnen, Pierre, Jacques Mairesse, and Marcel Dagenais. 2006. "Innovativity: A Comparison across Seven European Countries." NBER Working Paper 12280, National Bureau of Economic Research, Cambridge, MA.

Mokyr, Joel. 1990. *The Lever of Riches*. New York: Oxford University Press.

Mommaas, Hans. 2004. "Cultural Clusters and the Post-Industrial City: Towards the Remapping of Urban Cultural Policy." *Urban Studies* 41 (3): 507–32.

Monjon, Stéphanie, and Patrick Waelbroeck. 2003. "Assessing Spillovers from Universities to Firms: Evidence from French Firm-Level Data." *International Journal of Industrial Organization* 21 (9): 1255–70.

Moote, A. Lloyd, and Dorothy C. Moote. 2004. *The Great Plague: The Story of London's Most Deadly Year*. Baltimore, MD: Johns Hopkins University Press.

Morley, John David. 1985. *Pictures from the Water Trade: An Englishman in Japan*. New York: St. Martin's Press.

Morris-Suzuki, Tessa. 1994. *The Technological Transformation of Japan: From the Seventeenth to the Twenty-First Century*. Cambridge, U.K.: Cambridge University Press.

Moses, Hamilton III, E. Ray Dorsey, David H. M. Matheson, and Samuel O. Thier. 2005. "Financial Anatomy of Biomedical Research." *Journal of American Medical Association* 294 (11): 1333–42.

Mowery, David C. 1990. "The Development of Industrial Research in U.S. Manufacturing Firms." *American Economic Review* 80 (2): 345–49.

Muller, Larissa. 2005. "Localizing International Investment: The Advertising Industry in Southeast Asia." In *Service Industries and Asia-Pacific Cities: New Development Trajectories*, ed. P. W. Daniels, K. C. Ho, and T. A. Hutton, 131–49. New York: Routledge.

Murphy, Kevin M., and Robert H. Topel. 2005. "The Value of Health and Longevity." NBER Working Paper 11405. National Bureau of Economic Research, Cambridge, MA.

Nabeshima, Kaoru. 2003. "Raising the Quality of Secondary Education in East Asia." Policy Research Working Paper 3140, World Bank, Washington, DC.

Naquin, Susan. 2005. *Peking: Temples and City Life, 1400–1900*. Berkeley: University of California Press.

Narin, Francis, Kimberly S. Hamilton, and Dominic Olivastro. 1997. "The Increasing Linkage between U.S. Technology and Public Science." *Research Policy* 26 (3): 317–30.

"NASA Concocting Robots for Space Flight." 2005. *News.com*, October 10.

National Bureau of Statistics of China. Various years. *China Statistical Yearbook*. Beijing: China Statistics Press.

National Computerization Agency. 2001. *Korea Internet White Paper*. Seoul: Ministry of Information and Communication.

National Science Board. 2004. *Science and Engineering Indicators 2004*. Arlington, VA: National Science Foundation.

National Statistical Office (Thailand). Various years. *Statistical Yearbook Thailand*. Bangkok: National Statistical Office.

————. 1980. *Population and Housing Census 1980*. Bangkok: National Statistical Office.

————. 2000. *Population and Housing Census 2000*. Bangkok: National Statistical Office.

Nayyar, Deepak. 2006. "Globalisation, History, and Development: A Tale of Two Centuries." *Cambridge Journal of Economics* 30 (1): 137–59.

"New Vision." 2006. *Aviation Week and Space Technology*, April 3.

Niosi, Jorge, and Marc Banik. 2005. "The Evolution and Performance of Biotechnology Regional Systems of Innovation." *Cambridge Journal of Economics* 29 (3): 343–57.

"The No-Computer Virus." 2005. *Economist*, April 30.

"No-Profit Zone." 2005. *Newsweek*, July 25.

Nordhaus, William D. 2006. "Baumol's Diseases: A Macroeconomic Perspective." NBER Working Paper 12218. National Bureau of Economic Research, Cambridge, MA.

Nouët, Noël. 1990. *The Shogun's City*. Folkestone, U.K.: Paul Nurbury Publications.

"Novartis Raises Offer for Chiron." 2005. *Financial Times*, November 1.

"And Now, A Game from Our Sponsor." 2005. *Economist*, June 9.

"Number in the News: Fantasy Fashion." 2006. *Financial Times*, May 22.

Nye, Joseph S. 2004. *Soft Power: The Means to Success in World Politics*. New York: Public Affairs.

OECD (Organisation for Economic Co-operation and Development). 2004a. *OECD Science, Technology, and Industry Outlook*. Paris: OECD.

————. 2004b. *Understanding Economic Growth*. Paris: OECD.

————. 2005. *OECD Territorial Reviews: Seoul, Korea*. Paris: OECD.

———.2006. *Innovation in Pharmaceutical Biotechnology: Comparing National Innovation Systems at the Sectoral Level.* Paris: OECD.

"Off with a Bang." 2003. *Economist*, December 20.

"Of Mice and Men: Lab Rats in Singapore Biotech Drive." 2003. *International Herald Tribune*, August 23.

"Often Footloose, Bangalore Clubs Are Now Dancing-Free." 2005. *Wall Street Journal*, November 7.

Okada, Ryuzo, Junji Oaki, and Nobuhiro Kondoh. 2004. "High-Speed Computer Vision System for Robots." *Toshiba Review* 59 (9): 29–32.

O'Mara, Margaret Pugh. 2005. *Cities of Knowledge: Cold War Science and the Search for the Next Silicon Valley*. Princeton, NJ: Princeton University Press.

"One Sick Patient." 2005. *Economist Intelligence Unit*, October 3.

"On the World's Movie Map." 2005. *India Today International*, August 8.

"Open Source Likely to Open More Doors." 2005. *Financial Times*, October 19.

"Organic LEDs Look Forward to a Bright, White Future." 2005. *Science*, December 16.

Ottaviano, Gianmarco, and Giovanni Peri. 2004. "The Economic Value of Cultural Diversity: Evidence from U.S. Cities." NBER Working Paper 10904, National Bureau of Economic Research, Cambridge, MA.

Overseas Economic Cooperation Fund. 1996. "Measures of Promoting Urban Improvement in Bangkok." OECF Research Paper 11. Tokyo: Overseas Economic Cooperation Fund.

Oxford Economic Forecasting. 2005. *The Economic Contribution of the UK Film Industry*. Oxford, U.K.: Oxford Economic Forecasting.

Ozaki, Fumio, and Hideki Hashimoto. 2004. "Open Robot Controller Architecture (ORCA), the Robot Platform." *Toshiba Review* 59 (9): 20–24.

Parayil, Govindan. 2005. "From 'Silicon Island' to 'Biopolis of Asia': Innovation Policy and Shifting Competitive Strategy." *California Management Review* 47 (2): 50–73.

"Paris, Texas." 2003. *New Yorker*, February 17.

Park, Sam Ock. 2005. "ICT Clusters and Industrial Restructuring in Korea: The Case of Seoul." Paper presented at the Second Asian Development Conference on ICT Industrial Clusters in East Asia, Kitakyushu, Japan, December 12.

"Part-Time Workers." 2005. *Economist*, July 2.

Patten, Fred. 2004. *Watching Anime, Reading Manga: 25 Years of Essays and Reviews*. Berkeley, CA: Stone Bridge Press.

Pauly, Mark V. 2005. "Improving Vaccine Supply and Development: Who Needs What?" *Health Affairs* 24 (3): 680–89.

People's Government of Beijing Municipality Administration Committee of Zhongguancun Park. 2004. *Zhongguancun Science Park Development Report*. Beijing: People's Government of Beijing Municipality.

Perkowitz, Sidney. 2004. *Digital People*. New York: Joseph Henry Press.

Pfeffer, Cary G. 2005. "The Biotechnology Sector—Therapeutics." In *The Business of Healthcare Innovation*, ed. Lawton Robert Burns, 103–89. Cambridge, U.K.: Cambridge University Press.

"Pfizer's Funk." 2005. *BusinessWeek*, February 28.

"Pharmaceuticals Sector Has Unrealised Potential." 2005. *Oxford Analytica*, September 8.

"Philadelphia to Be City of Wireless Web." 2005. *Washington Post*, October 5.

Pisano, Gary P. 2002. "Pharmaceutical Biotechnology." In *Technological Innovation and Performance*, ed. Benn Steil, David G. Victor, and Richard R. Nelson, 347–66. Princeton, NJ: Princeton University Press.

"Play Myst for Me." 2005. *Washington Post*, July 8.

"Politics May Move Stem-Cell Scientists." 2005. *Wall Street Journal*, January 26.

"Population Ageing Requires Broad Reform." 2005. *Oxford Analytica*, October 18.

"Power Projectors." 2005. *Foreign Policy*, July.

"Pranda Jewellery Stays on Sales Growth Path." 2005. Thai News Service, January 31.

"Preparing for a Mature Society." 2004. *BusinessKorea*, November.

"Prescription for Change: A Survey of Pharmaceuticals." 2005. *Economist*, June 18.

"Present, Fast, and Future Broadband Is Transforming Korea's Creative Sector." 2004. *Financial Times*, November 30.

"A Prognosis of Healthy Profits." 2006. *Financial Times*, February 10.

"Programmers: Video Games Need Female Touch." 2005. *Associated Press Wire*, July 23.

"Provocative Study Says Obesity May Reduce U.S. Life Expectancy." 2005. *Science*, March 18.

Puga, Diego, and Daniel Trefler. 2005. "Wake Up and Smell the Ginseng: The Rise of Incremental Innovation in Low-Wage Countries." CEPR Discussion Paper 5286, Centre for Economic Policy Research, London.

"Pushing Pills." 2003. *Economist*, February 15.

"Quarterly Chronicle and Documentation." 2005. *China Quarterly* 183: 745–75.

Rae, Douglas W. 2003. *City: Urbanism and Its End*. New Haven, CT: Yale University Press.

"Rags and Riches." 2004. *Economist*, March 4.

Ramey, Valerie A., and Neville Francis. 2006. "A Century of Work and Leisure." NBER Working Paper 12264, National Bureau of Economic Research, Cambridge, MA.

Ravid, S. Abraham. 2005. "Film Production in the Digital Age: What Do We Know about the Past and the Future?" In *A Concise Handbook of Movie Industry Economics*, ed. Charles C. Moul, 32–58. Cambridge, U.K.: Cambridge University Press.

Rawski, Thomas G. 1989. *Economic Growth in Prewar China*. Berkeley: University of California Press.

"Ready to Buy a Home Robot?" 2004. *BusinessWeek*, July 19.

"The Real Reasons You're Working So Hard . . . and What You Can Do about It." 2005. *BusinessWeek*, October.

Reardon, Marguerite. 2005. "China to Trump U.S. in Broadband Subscribers." CNET News.com, May 4. http://news.com.com/China+to+trump+U.S.+in+broadband+subscribers/2100-1034_3-5695591.html.

Reinhardt, Uwe E., Peter S. Hussey, and Gerard F. Anderson. 2004. "U.S. Health Care Spending in an International Context: Why Is U.S. Spending So High, and Can We Afford It?" *Health Affairs* 23 (3): 10–25.

"Remaking Shanghai." 2004. *Asia Inc.*, August.

"Researchers Develop Bacteria Resistant Shirt." 2005. Thai News Service, September 1.

Richie, Donald. 1992. *A Lateral View: Essays on Culture and Style in Contemporary Japan*. Berkeley, CA: Stone Bridge Press.

————. 2003. *The Image Factory: Fads and Fashions in Japan*. London: Reaktion Books.

Riley, James C. 2005. "Estimates of Regional and Global Life Expectancy, 1800–2001." *Population and Development Review* 3 (1): 537–43.

"The Rise of Petite Couture." 2005. *Financial Times*, August 13.

"The Rise of the Creative Consumer." 2005. *Economist*, March 10.

"The Rise of the Green Building." 2004. *Economist*, December 2.

Roberts, John. 2004. *The Modern Firm: Organizational Design for Performance and Growth*. New York: Oxford University Press.

"Robo-Pharmacist and Toxic Lawsuits." 2005. *BusinessWeek*, January 24.

"Robot Guards for Shops and Offices." 2005. *News.com*, June 23.

"Robot Hand Performs Remote Breast Cancer Checks." 2005. *New Scientist*, July 5.

"Robotic Pioneers Wait for the Market to Steer Them." 2004. *Financial Times*, October 28.

"A Robot in the Right Vein." 1999. *New Scientist*, April 17.

Roijakkers, Nadine, John Hagedoorn, and Hans van Kranenburg. 2005. "Dual Market Structures and the Likelihood of Repeated Ties: Evidence from Pharmaceutical Biotechnology." *Research Policy* 34: 235–45.

"Role-Playing in 3D Starts to Take Off." 2005. *Financial Times*, October 19.

Rose, Richard. 2004. "Governance and the Internet." In *Global Change and East Asian Policy Initiatives*, ed. Shahid Yusuf, M. Anjum Altaf, and Kaoru Nabeshima, 337–64. New York: Oxford University Press.

Rosen, Stanley. 2003. "Hollywood, Globalization, and Film Markets in Asia: Lessons for China?" University of Southern California, Los Angeles.

Rosenthal, Stuart S., and William C. Strange. 2004. "Evidence on the Nature and Sources of Agglomeration Economies." In *Handbook of Regional and Urban Economics: Cities and Geography*, Vol. 4, ed. J. Vernon Henderson and Jacques-François Thisse, 2119–71. Cambridge, MA: Elsevier.

Rowe, Peter G. 2005. *East Asia Modern: Shaping the Contemporary City*. London: Reaktion Books.

Rowe, Peter G., and Seng Kuan. 2004. Shanghai: Architecture and Urbanism for Modern China; New York: Prestel Publishing.

Sadamoto, Kuni. 1981. "Problems Involving the Introduction of IRs: Case Studies." In *Robots in the Japanese Economy: Facts about Robots and Their Significance*, ed. Kuni Sadamoto. Tokyo: Survey Japan.

Santos, Filipe M. 2003. "The Coevolution of Firms and Their Knowledge Environment: Insights from the Pharmaceutical Industry." *Technological Forecasting and Social Change* 70 (7): 687–715.

Sassen, Saskia. 2001. *The Global City: New York, London, Tokyo*. 2nd ed. Princeton, NJ: Princeton University Press.

————, ed. 2002. *Global Networks, Linked Cities*. New York: Routledge.

Saunders, Norman C. 2005. "A Summary of BLS Projections to 2014." http://www.bls.gov/opub/mlr/2005/11/art1full.pdf. Accessed June 20, 2006.

Saxenian, AnnaLee. 2003. "Government and Guanxi: The Chinese Software Industry in Transition." Development Research Centre Working Paper 19, Centre for New and Emerging Markets, London Business School, London.

"Science and Technology: Composites in Construction." 2005. *Oxford Analytica*, January 11.

"Science and Technology: Scientists in the Region Have Begun to Make a Global Impact." 2005. *Financial Times*, June 9.

"Science Fiction?" 2005. *Economist*, September 3.

Scott, Allen J. 2000a. *The Cultural Economy of Cities*. Thousand Oaks, CA: Sage.

————. 2000b. "The Cultural Economy of Paris." *International Journal of Urban and Regional Research* 24(3): 567–82.

————. 2004. "Hollywood and the World: The Geography of Motion-Picture Distribution and Marketing." *Review of International Political Economy* 11 (1): 33–61.

————. 2006. "Creative Cities: Conceptual Issues and Policy Questions." *Journal of Urban Affairs* 28 (1): 1–17.

Screech, Timon. 1999. *Sex and Floating World*. London: Reaktion Books.

Segal, Adam. 2003. *Digital Dragon: High-Technology Enterprises in China*. Ithaca, NY: Cornell University Press.

Seoul Development Institute and Nomura Research Institute. 2003. *Can Seoul Become a World City? Comparison and Analysis of Northeast Asia's Six Cities: Seoul, Tokyo, Hong Kong, Beijing, Shanghai, and Singapore*. Seoul: Seoul Development Institute and Nomura Research Institute.

Seoul Metropolitan Government. 2004. *Seoul Statistical Yearbook*. Seoul: Seoul Metropolitan Government.

Sergeant, Harriet. 1991. *Shanghai*. London: John Murray.

"Seventy Years of Plenty." 2005. *Economist*, August 18.

Shameen, Assif. 2004. "Land of the Wired." *Asia Inc.*, April.

Shanghai Municipal Statistical Bureau. Various years. *Shanghai Statistical Yearbook*. Beijing: China Statistics Press.

"Shanghai's Energy-Saving Policies in the Eleventh Plan." 2006. *China Economic Times*, May 22.

"Shanghai Surprise." 2005. *New Yorker*, December 26.

Shin, Chang-Ho, and Chang-Heum Byeon. 2001. "New Industrialization in Seoul: Industrial Restructuring and Strategic Responses." In *Urban Management in Seoul*, ed. Won-Yong Kwon and Kwang-Joong Kim, 125–46. Seoul: Seoul Development Institute.

Siegel, Fred. 2002. "The Death and Life of America's Cities." *Public Interest* 148: 3–23.

"Signs of Recovery for Games Makers." 2006. *Financial Times*. July 15/16.

Sigurdson, Jon. 2005. *Technological Superpower China*. Northampton, MA: Edward Elgar.

"Silicon Down to the Wire." 2005. *Nature*, July.

Simon, Curtis J. 2005. "Industrial Reallocation across U.S. Cities, 1977–1997." *Journal of Urban Economics* 56 (1): 119–43.

"Singapore Aims to Be a Biotechnology Hub." 2005. *Financial Times*, June 10.

"Singapore: Hong Kong Overtaken as Busiest Port." 2005. *Oxford Analytica*, October 13.

"Singapore: Pharma Industry Set for Expansion." 2004. *Oxford Analytica*, November 30.

"Singapore: Reform Needed to Spur Further Growth." 2005. *Oxford Analytica*, August 17.

Singapore: Singapore Department of Statistics. 1980. *1980 Census of Population*. Singapore: National Department of Statistics. http://www.singstat.gov.sg/.

————. 2000. *2000 Census of Population*. Singapore: Department of Statistics.

————. 2002. *Yearbook of Statistics Singapore, 2002*. Singapore: Department of Statistics.

"Singapore's Man with a Plan." 2004. *Economist*, August 12.

"Smart Way to Ride." 2005. *BusinessKorea*, February.

Smilor, Raymond, Niall O'Donnell, Gregory Stein, and Robert Welborn. 2005. "The Research University and the Development of High Technology Centers in the U.S." Paper presented at the Conference on University-Industry Linkages in Metropolitan Areas in Asia, World Bank and Social Science Research Council, Washington, DC, November 17.

Smith, Will. 2005. "MMORPGs." *Maximum PC* 10 (5): 26–32.

Smitka, Michael J. 1991. *Competitive Ties: Subcontracting in the Japanese Automotive Industry*. New York: Columbia University Press.

"A Smoother Operation at the Digital Hospital." 2005. *Financial Times*, March 18.

Soete, Luc. 2006. "Notes on UIL-Related Polices of National Governments." In *How Universities Promote Economic Growth*, ed. Shahid Yusuf and Kaoru Nabeshima. Washington, DC: World Bank.

Sohn, Dong-Won, and Martin Kenney. 2005. "Universities, Clusters, and Innovation Systems: The Case of Seoul, Korea." Paper presented at the Conference on University-Industry Linkages in Metropolitan Areas in Asia, World Bank and Social Science Research Council, Washington, DC, November 17.

Solow, Robert M. 2001. "NCN Summit 2001: Information Technology and the Recent Productivity Boom in the U.S." Massachusetts Institute of Technology, Cambridge, MA. http://web.mit.edu/cmi-videos/solow/text.html.

"South-East Asia: Population Ageing Will Strain Budgets." 2004. *Oxford Analytica*, October 20.

"South Korea: Ageing, Slowing Population Is of Concern." 2005. *Oxford Analytica*, September 1.

"South Korea Top for Online Gaming." 2004. *Financial Times*, December 31.

"South Korea/U.S.: Film Quotas Will Halve." 2006. *Oxford Analytica*, January 26.

"The Spirit of a Startup Lives On." 2005. *BusinessWeek*, November 21.

Srinivas, Smita, and Kimmo Viljamaa. 2003. "BioTurku: 'Newly' Innovative? The Rise of Bio-Pharmaceuticals and the Biotech Concentration in Southwest Finland." MIT IPC-LIS Working Paper 03-001, Massachusetts Institute of Technology Industrial Performance Center, Cambridge, MA.

"Stanford Wins $2 Million in Robotic Car Race." 2005. *News.com*, October 9.

"Starting a Walk on the Wide Side." 2005. *Financial Times*, October 19.

Statistics Bureau of Japan. 1980. *1980 Census*. Tokyo: Statistics Bureau of Japan.

————. 2000. *2000 Census*. Tokyo: Statistics Bureau of Japan.

"Stem Cells: Big Step for a Controversial Science." 2005. *Newsweek*, May 30.

Stiglitz, Joseph E., and Shahid Yusuf. 2001. *Rethinking the East Asian Miracle*. New York: Oxford University Press.

"Stitching Together an Apparel Warehouse." 2005. *Business 2.0*, May.

"Study: 'Texting' on the Rise in U.S." 2005. CNN.com, March 17. http://www.cnn.com/2005/TECH/ptech/03/17/text.messaging.ap/index.html.

"Sunny the Vampire-Slayer." 2003. *Economist*, September 25.

"Surfing for Haute Couture." 2005. *Economist*, May 12.

Tabellini, Guido. 2005. "The Role of State in Economic Development." *Kyklos* 58 (2): 283–303.

Takayasu, Ken'ichi, and Minako Mori. 2004. "The Global Strategies of Japanese Vehicle Assemblers and the Implications for the Thai Automobile Industry." In *Global Production Networking and Technological Change in East Asia*, ed. Shahid Yusuf, Kaoru Nabeshima, and M. Anjum Altaf, 209–54. New York: Oxford University Press.

"Taking a Page from Toyota's Playbook." 2005. *BusinessWeek*, August 22.

"Taking Robots for a Ride." 2005. *Business 2.0*, August.

"Taking Video Games to the Next Level." 2005. *BusinessWeek*, May 9.

Tan, Kim-Song, and Sock-Yong Phang. 2005. "From Efficiency-Driven to Innovation-Driven Economic Growth: Perspectives from Singapore." Policy Research Working Paper 3569, World Bank, Washington, DC.

Tanie, Kazuo. 2004. "Toward Expansion of Robot Industry Market and Creation of New Robot Business." *Toshiba Review* 59 (9): 9–14.

Taylor, Alan M. 2006. "Globalization and New Comparative Economic History." *NBER Reporter* 6 (Winter): 18–21.

Taylor, Peter J. 2005. "Leading World Cities: Empirical Evaluations of Urban Nodes in Multiple Networks." *Urban Studies* 42 (9): 1593–608.

Taylor, Peter J., David R. F. Walker, Gilda Catalano, and Michael Hoyler. 2002. "Diversity and Power in the World City Network." *Cities* 19 (4): 231–41.

Taylor, T. L. 2006. *Play between Worlds: Exploring Online Game Culture*. Cambridge, MA: MIT Press.

"Technophobia, Impenetrable User Manuals, and Other Reasons the High-Tech Home Is Still a Science Fiction for Most." 2005. *Financial Times*, October 7.

"Technopolis Found." 2005. *Popular Science*, March.

Terdiman, Daniel. 2006. "Lego Mindstorms No Kids' Toy." CNET News.com, January 5. http://news.com.com/Lego+Mindstorms+no+kids+toy/2100-1041_3-6020603.html.

"Thai Garment Exports Seen up 12 Pct. as Quotas End." 2005. *Reuters News*, March 4.

"Thailand Benefits from U.S. Move against Textile Imports from China." 2005. Thai News Service, June 30.

"Thailand Raps *Elle* Magazine over Bare-Breasted Fashion Show." 2003. Agence France-Presse, November 18.

"These Pills Will Earn AstraZeneca More Than $2bn This Year . . . but Is It a Triumph of Marketing, or of Science?" 2003. *Financial Times*, October 22.

"They Came, They Cooked, They Conquered." 2006. *BusinessWeek*, February 13.

"Thinking Machines." 2000. *BusinessWeek*, August 7.

Thomson, David. 2004. *The Whole Equation: A History of Hollywood*. New York: Knopf.

Thomson, Elizabeth. 2005. "MIT Develops Anklebot for Stroke Patients." MIT News Office, Cambridge, MA, June 30.

Thorpe, Kenneth E. 2005. "The Rise in Health Care Spending and What to Do about It." *Health Affairs* 24 (6): 1436–45.

"Ticklish Issue of Whether to Go It Alone or Adhere to International Rules." 2005. *Financial Times*, October 19.

"Time to Put the Digital House in Order." 2005. *Financial Times*, October 7.

"Tiny Games for a Giant Market." 2006. *BusinessWeek*, July 3.

Tokyo Metropolitan Government. Various years. *Tokyo Statistical Yearbook*. Tokyo: Tokyo Metropolitan Government.

———. Bureau of General Affairs. Various years. http://www.toukei.metro.tokyo.jp/.

"Too Little, Too Late." 2006. *Nature*, March 30.

"Too Many Surveys, Too Little Passion?" 2005. *BusinessWeek*, August 1.

"Top Chinese Contractors 2005." 2006. *Engineering News-Record*. http://qa.enr.construction.com/people/topLists/chinaCont/topChinaCont_1-60.asp.

"Top Chinese Design Firms 2005." 2006. *Engineering News-Record*. http://qa.enr.construction.com/people/topLists/chinaDesignFirms/topDesignFirms_1-60.asp

"The Town of the Talk." 2005. *Economist*, February 17.

"Training Plan for Garment Makers." 2005. *Nation* (Thailand), June 7.

Tran, Yen. 2006. "Industrial Dynamics in the Fashion Industry: How Companies Enter the Hall of Fame and Then Fall from Grace?" Copenhagen, Denmark: Danish Research Unit for Industrial Development.

Triplett, Jack E., and Barry P. Bosworth. 2003. "'Baumol's Disease' Has Been Cured: IT and Multifactor Productivity in U.S. Services Industries." *FRBNY Economic Policy Review* 9 (3): 23–33.

Trohman, Richard G., Michael H. Kim, and Sergio L. Pinski. 2004. "Cardiac Pacing: The State of the Art." *Lancet* 364 (9446): 1701–19.

"Trust Me, I'm a Robot." 2006. *Economist*, June 10.

Tsai, Ming-Chih, and Chin-Hui Su. 2005. "Political Risk Assessment of Five East Asian Ports: The Viewpoints of Global Carriers." *Marine Policy* 29 (4): 291–98.

Tuchman, Janice. 2003. "Business Rules Are Changing for Contracting in China." *Engineering News-Record* 251 (25): 14.

Tuchman, Janice, Peter Reina, and Ding Kemp. 2004. "Beijing's National Grand Theater Transforms the Cityscape." *Engineering News-Record* 253 (21): 22.

Turton, Hal. 2006. "Sustainable Global Automobile Transport in the 21st Century: An Integrated Scenario Analysis." *Technological Forecasting and Social Change* 73 (6): 607–29.

UNECE (United Nations Economic Commission for Europe). 2004. "UN Issues Its 2004 World Robotics Survey." Press Release ECE/STAT/04/P01, UNECE, Geneva.

———. 2005. "UNECE/IFR Issues Its 2005 World Robotics Survey." Press Release ECE/STAT/05/P03, Geneva.

"Unmanned Ventures." 2005. *Aviation Week and Space Technology*, May 30.

"Unorthodox Chess from an Odd Mind." 2005. *Wired*, July 19.

USDA (United States Department of Agriculture). 2003. "Thailand Food Processing Ingredients Sector Report." Global Agriculture Information Network Report TH3005. Foreign Agricultural Service, USDA, Bangkok.

———. 2005. "Thailand Exporter Guide Report 2005." Global Agriculture Information Network Report TH5104. Foreign Agricultural Service, USDA, Bangkok.

van der Panne, Gerben. 2005. "Proximity and Knowledge Spillovers: Evidence from New Product Announcements in the Netherlands." Paper presented at World Bank–Cambridge-MIT Workshop on University-Industry Linkages in Europe and North America, Cambridge, U.K., September 26.

Van der Voort, Haiko, and Martin De Jong. 2004. "The Boston Bio-Bang: The Emergence of a 'Regional System of Innovation.'" *Knowledge, Technology, and Policy* 16 (4): 46–60.

Vernon, John A., and W. Keener Hughen. 2005. "The Future of Drug Development: The Economics of Pharmacogenomics." NBER Working Paper 11875. National Bureau of Economic Research, Cambridge, MA.

Veugelers, Reinhilde, and Bruno Cassiman. 2005. "R&D Cooperation between Firms and Universities: Some Empirical Evidence from Belgian Manufacturing." *International Journal of Industrial Organization* 23 (5–6): 355–79.

"Video Game Industry May Be Going off Boil." 2006. *International Herald Tribune*, February 7.

"Vietnam's War on Flu." 2005. *Nature*, January 13.

"Virtual Reality Prepares Soldiers for Real War." 2006. *Washington Post*, February 14.

"Virtual War Game That Has Delivered Pots of Real Gold." 2005. *Financial Times*, May 23.

Wade, Robert. 1990. *Governing the Market: Economic Theory and the Role of Government in East Asian Industrialization*. Princeton, NJ: Princeton University Press.

Wakeman, Frederic Jr. 1995. *Policing Shanghai 1927–1937*. Berkeley: University of California Press.

Walcott, Susan M. 1999. "High Tech in the Deep South: Firm Clusters in Metropolitan Atlanta." *Growth and Change* 30 (1): 48–74.

"The Wal-Mart Effect." 2002. *McKinsey Quarterly*, January.

Walsh, Kathleen. 2003. *Foreign High-Tech R&D in China: Risks, Rewards, and Implications for U.S.-China Relations*. Washington, DC: Henry Stimson Center.

Walton, Julie. 2004. "At Your Service." *China Business Review* 31 (5): 8–13.

Wang, Feng. 2003. "Housing Improvement and Distribution in Urban China: Initial Evidence from China's 2000 Census." *China Review* 3 (2): 121–43.

Wang, Jici, and Xin Tong. 2005. "Sustaining Urban Growth through Innovative Capacity: Beijing and Shanghai in Comparison." Policy Research Working Paper 3545, World Bank, Washington, DC.

Wang, Zuogiong. 2006. "Fewer Cars on Road Give Air Quality a Breather." *China Daily*, June 5.

"Wasteful Ways." 2005. *BusinessWeek*, April 11.

Waterman, David. 2005. *Hollywood's Road to Riches*. Cambridge, MA: Harvard University Press.

Webster, Douglas. 2004. "Bangkok: Evolution and Adaptation under Stress." In *World Cities Beyond the West: Globalization, Development, and Inequality*, ed. Josef Gugler, 82–118. Cambridge, U.K.: Cambridge University Press.

Webster, Paul. 2006. "Controlling the Costs of U.S. Health Care." *Lancet* 367 (9511): 639–40.

Wei, Yehua Dennis, Chi Kin Leung, and Jun Luo. 2006. "Globalizing Shanghai: Foreign Direct Investment and Urban Restructuring." *Habitat International* 30 (2): 231–44.

"We've Got the Solid Grounding, Now for Creative Thinking." 2005. *Financial Times*, October 19.

"What's Driving the Box Office Batty." 2005. *BusinessWeek*, July 11.

"What's Next? Innovations Are Ready for Trial and Adoption, but Great Gains Will Take Major Change." 2004. *Engineering News-Record*, June 21.

"When Escape Seems Just a Mouse-Click Away." 2006. *Washington Post*, May 27.

Whittaker, D. H. 1997. *Small Firms in the Japanese Economy*. New York: Cambridge University Press.

"Why Everyone Loves Austin." 2005. *Financial Times*, May 7.

Wikipedia. 2005. "MMORPGs." http://en.wikipedia.org/wiki/MMORPG.

Wilson, Daniel H. 2005. *How to Survive a Robot Uprising: Tips on Defending Yourself against the Coming Rebellion*. New York: Bloomsbury USA.

"Without Apology, Leaping Ahead in Cloning." 2005. *New York Times*, May 31.

Wong, Poh Kam. 2005. "Commercializing Biomedical Science in a Rapidly Changing 'Triple-Helix' Nexus: The Experience of the National University of Singapore." National University of Singapore, Singapore.

————. 2006a. "Approaches to University-Industry Linkages: The Case of the National University of Singapore." In *How Universities Can Promote Economic Growth*, ed. Shahid Yusuf and Kaoru Nabeshima. Washington, DC: World Bank.

————. 2006b. "The Role of Global MNCs vs. Indigenous Firms in the Rapid Growth of East Asian Innovation: Evidence from U.S. Patent Data." Paper presented at the SPRIE Workshop, Beijing, May 20–21.

Wong, Poh Kam, Yuen Ping Ho, and Annette Singh. 2005. "Singapore as an Innovative City in East Asia: An Explorative Study of the Perspectives of Innovative Industries." Policy Research Working Paper 3568, World Bank, Washington, DC.

Woodcock, Bruce Sterling. 2005. "Analysis." http://www.mmogchart.com/analysis.html.

World Bank. 1999. *Entering the 21st Century*. New York: Oxford University Press.

————. 2002. *China: National Development and Sub-National Finance: A Review of Provincial Expenditures*. Report 22951-CHA. Washington, DC: World Bank.

————. 2005. *Policies for 11th Plan of China*. Washington, DC: World Bank.

"A World of Opportunities: Patent Law Booms as S.D.-China Deals Bloom." 2005. *San Diego Business Journal*, April 25.

Xia, Yingqi, Liping Wang, Junwei Chu, Weidong Liu, Yi Cao, Jingyan Wu, Xin Liu, Zhong Du, Jiajia Zeng, and Yuhong Zheng. 2004. *Enterprise Business Guide for Zhongguancun Entrepreneurs Back from the Overseas*. Beijing: Beijing University Press.

Yatsko, Pamela. 2001. *New Shanghai: The Rocky Rebirth of China's Legendary City*. Singapore: John Wiley and Sons.

Yeoh, Brenda S. A. 2005. "The Global Cultural City? Spatial Imagineering and Politics in the (Multi)Cultural Marketplaces of South-East Asia." *Urban Studies* 42 (5–6): 945–58.

Yeung, Henry Wai-chung. 2004. *Chinese Capitalism in a Global Era: Towards Hybrid Capitalism*. New York: Routledge.

Yeung, Yue-man. 2005. "The Pan-PRD and ASEAN: China FTA as Agents of Regional Integration in Pacific Area." Hong Kong (China): Chinese University of Hong Kong.

"You Must Expand!" 2005. *Ports and Harbors*, July.

"Young Consumers to Set the Pace for China Boom." 2005. *Financial Times*, October 13.

"Young Spielbergs by the Thousands." 2005. *BusinessWeek*, December 26.

"Your Own World." 2005. *Newsweek*, September 16.

Yusuf, Shahid. 2001. "The East Asian Miracle at the Millennium." In *Rethinking the East Asian Miracle*, ed. Joseph E. Stiglitz and Shahid Yusuf, 1–53. New York: Oxford University Press.

————. 2005. "Two Tales of Regional Development in China: The Pearl River Delta vs. the Northeast." Background paper, World Bank, Washington, DC.

Yusuf, Shahid, M. Anjum Altaf, and Kaoru Nabeshima, eds. 2004. *Global Production Networking and Technological Change in East Asia*. New York: Oxford University Press.

Yusuf, Shahid, and Kaoru Nabeshima. 2005. "Creative Industries in East Asia." *Cities* 22 (2): 109–22.

————. 2006a. *China's Development Priorities*. Washington, DC: World Bank.

————. 2006b. "Two Decades of Reform: The Changing Organization Dynamics of Chinese Industrial Firms." Policy Research Working Paper 3806, World Bank, Washington, DC.

Yusuf, Wang, and Nabeshima. 2006. "Fiscal Policies for Innovation." Washington, DC: World Bank.

Yusuf, Shahid, and Weiping Wu. 2002. "Pathways to a World City: Shanghai Rising in an Era of Globalisation." *Urban Studies* 39 (7): 1213–40.

Zerkin, Allen J. 2006. "Mainstreaming High Performance Building in New York City: A Comprehensive Roadmap for Removing the Barriers." *Technology in Society* 28 (1–2): 137–55.

Zhang, Junfu. 2003. *High-Tech Start-Ups and Industry Dynamics in Silicon Valley*. San Francisco: Public Policy Institute of California.

Zhang, Junfu, and Nikesh Patel. 2005. *The Dynamics of California's Biotechnology Industry*. San Francisco: Public Policy Institute of California.

Zhao, Simon X. B., Roger C. K. Chan, and Kelvin T. O. Sit. 2003. "Globalization and the Dominance of Large Cities in Contemporary China." *Cities* 20 (4): 265–78.

Zhao, Xiaohui. 2006. "Total Number of Mobile Phone Users Reached 416 Million in China." http://news.xinhuanet.com/newscenter/2006-05/21/content_4578819.htm.

Zhu, Jieming. 2002. "Urban Development under Ambiguous Property Rights: A Case of China's Transition Economy." *International Journal of Urban and Regional Research* 26 (1): 41–57.

Zhu, Jieming, Loo-Lee Sim, and Xing-Quan Zhang. 2006. "Global Real Estate Investments and Local Cultural Capital in the Making of Shanghai's New Office Locations." *Habitat International* 30 (3): 462–81.

INDEX

C

D

S

T

W

Y

Z

ABOUT THE AUTHORS

Shahid Yusuf is economic adviser in the Development Economics Research Group at the World Bank. He holds a Ph.D. in economics from Harvard University in Cambridge, Massachusetts. Dr. Yusuf is the team leader for the World Bank–Japan project on East Asia's Future Economy and was director of the *World Development Report 1999/2000: Entering the 21st Century*. Prior to that, he served the World Bank in several other capacities.

Dr. Yusuf has written extensively on development issues, with a special focus on East Asia. His publications include *The Dynamics of Urban Growth in Three Chinese Cities*, with Weiping Wu (Oxford University Press 1997); *Rethinking the East Asian Miracle*, edited with Joseph Stiglitz (Oxford University Press 2001); *Can East Asia Compete? Innovation for Global Markets*, with Simon Evenett (Oxford University Press 2002); *Innovative East Asia: The Future of Growth*, with others (Oxford University Press 2003); *Global Production Networking and Technological Change in East Asia* and *Global Change and East Asian Policy Initiatives*, both edited with M. Anjum Altaf and Kaoru Nabeshima (Oxford University Press 2004); *Under New Ownership: Privatizing China's State-Owned Enterprises* with Kaoru Nabeshima (Stanford University Press 2005) and *China's Development Priorities* with Kaoru Nabeshima (World Bank 2006). He has also published widely in various academic journals.

Kaoru Nabeshima is an economist in the Development Economics Research Group at the World Bank. He holds a Ph.D. in economics from the University of California, Davis. Dr. Nabeshima is a team member for the World Bank–Japan project on East Asia's Future Economy and was a coauthor of *Innovative East Asia: The Future of Growth* (Oxford University

Press 2003), *Under New Ownership: Privatizing China's State-Owned Enterprises* with Shahid Yusuf (Stanford University Press 2005), and *China's Development Priorities* with Shahid Yusuf (World Bank 2006), and he was coeditor for *Global Production Networking and Technological Change in East Asia* and *Global Change and East Asian Policy Initiatives* (Oxford University Press 2004). His research interests lie in the economic development of East Asia and the innovation capabilities of firms.